The Politics of Welfare State Reform in Continental Europe

This book challenges existing theories of welfare state change by analyzing pension reforms in France, Germany, and Switzerland between 1970 and 2004. It explains why all three countries were able to adopt far-reaching reforms, adapting their pension regimes to both financial austerity and new social risks. In a radical departure from the neo-institutionalist emphasis on policy stability, the book argues that socio-structural change has led to a multidimensional pension-reform agenda. A variety of crosscutting lines of political conflict, emerging from the transition to a post-industrial economy, allowed governments to engage in strategies of political exchange and coalition building, thus fostering broad cross-class coalitions in support of major reform packages. Methodologically, the book proposes a novel strategy to analyze lines of conflict, configurations of political actors, and coalitional dynamics over time. This strategy combines quantitative analyses of actor configurations based on coded policy positions with in-depth case studies.

Silja Häusermann is Assistant Professor at the University of Zurich in Switzerland. She has been Visiting Fellow at Harvard University and a Max Weber Fellow at the European University Institute in Florence, Italy. She was awarded the Ernst B. Haas Best Dissertation Prize of the European Politics and Society section of the American Political Science Association, the Jean Blondel Ph.D. Prize of the European Consortium for Political Research, the Junior Scientist Award by the Swiss Political Science Association, and the Young Researcher Prize by the *Journal of European Social Policy* and the European Social Policy Analysis Network. She has published articles on comparative welfare state analysis, public opinion and welfare states, and the Europeanization of national politics in journals such as *European Journal of Political Research*, *Socio-Economic Review*, *European Societies*, *Journal of European Social Policy*, and *Journal of European Public Policy*.

Cambridge Studies in Comparative Politics

General Editor
Margaret Levi   *University of Washington, Seattle*

Assistant General Editors
Kathleen Thelen   *Massachusetts Institute of Technology*
Erik Wibbels   *Duke University*

Associate Editors
Robert H. Bates   *Harvard University*
Stephen Hanson   *University of Washington, Seattle*
Torben Iversen   *Harvard University*
Stathis Kalyvas   *Yale University*
Peter Lange   *Duke University*
Helen Milner   *Princeton University*
Frances Rosenbluth   *Yale University*
Susan Stokes   *Yale University*

Other Books in the Series
David Austen-Smith, Jeffry A. Frieden, Miriam A. Golden, Karl Ove Moene,
   and Adam Przeworski, eds.,   *Selected Works of Michael Wallerstein: The
   Political Economy of Inequality, Unions, and Social Democracy*
Andy Baker,   *The Market and the Masses in Latin America: Policy Reform and
   Consumption in Liberalizing Economies*
Lisa Baldez,   *Why Women Protest: Women's Movements in Chile*
Stefano Bartolini,   *The Political Mobilization of the European Left, 1860–1980:
   The Class Cleavage*
Robert Bates,   *When Things Fell Apart: State Failure in Late-Century Africa*
Mark Beissinger,   *Nationalist Mobilization and the Collapse of the Soviet State*
Nancy Bermeo, ed.,   *Unemployment in the New Europe*
Carles Boix,   *Democracy and Redistribution*
Carles Boix,   *Political Parties, Growth, and Equality: Conservative and Social
   Democratic Economic Strategies in the World Economy*
Catherine Boone,   *Merchant Capital and the Roots of State Power in
   Senegal, 1930–1985*
Catherine Boone,   *Political Topographies of the African State: Territorial Authority
   and Institutional Change*

Continued after the index

The Politics of Welfare State Reform in Continental Europe

MODERNIZATION IN HARD TIMES

SILJA HÄUSERMANN

University of Zurich

CAMBRIDGE
UNIVERSITY PRESS

CAMBRIDGE UNIVERSITY PRESS
Cambridge, New York, Melbourne, Madrid, Cape Town, Singapore,
São Paulo, Delhi, Dubai, Tokyo

Cambridge University Press
32 Avenue of the Americas, New York, NY 10013-2473, USA

www.cambridge.org
Information on this title: www.cambridge.org/9780521183680

First published 2010

Printed in the United States of America

A catalog record for this publication is available from the British Library.

Library of Congress Cataloging in Publication data

Häusermann, Silja.
The politics of welfare state reform in continental Europe : modernization in hard times / Silja
Häusermann.
   p.   cm. – (Cambridge studies in comparative politics)
Includes bibliographical references and index.
ISBN 978-0-521-19272-9 (hardback)
1. Pensions – Government policy – France.   2. Pensions – Government policy – Germany.
3. Pensions – Government policy – Switzerland.   I. Title.   II. Series.
HD7175.H38   2010
331.25'22094–dc22   2009046106

ISBN 978-0-521-19272-9 Hardback
ISBN 978-0-521-18368-0 Paperback

This thesis was accepted as a doctoral dissertation by the Faculty of Arts of the University of
Zürich in the summer semester 2007 on the recommendation of Prof. Dr. Hanspeter Kriesi and
Prof. Dr. Herbert Kitschelt.

Contents

List of Figures

List of Tables

Preface

Who gets what and why? is not only a defining question of political science; it is also the question that drives the personal interest and intellectual commitment of many political scientists. I am no exception. Analyzing and explaining the distribution of resources and opportunities in our societies becomes even more important in hard times of fiscal austerity and increasing social needs. What happens when the pie gets smaller while the hunger – or at least the appetite – of the parties around the table grows? This is exactly the situation that has emerged in continental European welfare states since the late 1970s: new and old social needs grow in a context of fiscal austerity. Many political scientists view this distributional struggle as fought by essentially two sides: those who want to cut back on welfare and those who defend existing social rights. But this is wrong. Just as political actors – in Esping-Andersen's famous terms – do not fight for spending per se, they do not attack or defend the welfare state per se. Different actors, generally far more than two, want different things from the welfare state. Once we become aware of this complexity of actors and preferences, it is clear that the possibilities for changing alliances and various distributional reforms are manifold. Consequently, the question is not about whether we end up with more or less welfare but about who ends up with what. This is what this book is about: who gets what and why in the reform of continental pension regimes in hard times.

The idea for this book originated in the early 2000s, when I was a student assistant performing research on the internationalization of Swiss decision-making processes at the University of Lausanne. The project focused on strongly internationalized policy reforms, such as the liberalization of telecommunications, public procurement, and competition policy, but the project also directed my attention to a few pension and unemployment policy reforms, which had been selected as weakly internationalized control cases. As was the case with the other policy fields, I traced the institutions and procedures of decision making in the reforms. While doing so, I became more and more intrigued by the plurality of policy goals the different actors had set their sights on. Some actors fought for poverty relief, some for gender equality, others against gender equality, some for financial stability, some for privatization, and others for the status quo (i.e., for the preservation of the postwar achievements of the welfare state). There was much more to welfare politics, I saw, than a distributional class struggle.

These ideas remained in the back of my mind for some time, until I enrolled at the University of Zurich in 2003 and was given the opportunity to pick a topic of my choice for my Ph.D. research. That was when I decided to look more closely at the dynamics of post-industrial welfare reform politics. I came to Zurich to write a Ph.D., and I found so much more: fantastic advisers, plenty of opportunities to pursue and present my research in Zurich and abroad, the most wonderful colleagues, and a very special someone who supported this project from the dissertation proposal to the published book. I would like to express my gratitude to all of them and to name some in particular.

My deep gratitude goes first and foremost to Hanspeter Kriesi for his perspicacious advice, his generous support, and his constant encouragement. Thanks to him, I was able to develop both my theoretical thinking and my empirical work further than I would have on my own. His burning interest in understanding how politics affects people's lives has been a most impressive and motivating inspiration to me ever since I was his undergraduate student. I am also very grateful to Herbert Kitschelt for providing me so generously with many highly pertinent and stimulating comments. Many of the ideas in this dissertation stem from his work, and I feel truly honored that he invested so much time and intellectual effort in this project.

Furthermore, I wish to express my gratitude to Giuliano Bonoli, whose work was probably the single greatest inspiration for my own ideas, and to Bruno Palier for receiving my research with an equally supportive and critical eye. Both have been incredibly generous with their time and intellectual support; they have provided me with numerous opportunities to present and discuss my work with them and with other scholars in the field. I also feel deeply indebted to Yannis Papadopoulos and André Mach, under whose guidance I had the chance to enter the world of empirical research and who are very present in many of the ideas developed in this book.

My colleagues and friends at the University of Zurich have made my Ph.D. years both enjoyable and stimulating. My warm thanks to all of them; I wish to mention by name a few people to whom I am particularly indebted: Simon Bornschier for his patience and support, for countless discussions of my arguments both at home and in the office, and for having his critical eye on my fascination with cross-class alliances. Tim Frey for teaching me so many things about File-Maker and Illustrator, the design of a usable and useful database, and many lessons about work, computers, social skills, and (almost) everything else in life. Daniel Oesch, Romain Lachat, Philip Rehm, and Thomas Sattler provided extremely valuable and useful input at several stages of the research process. Furthermore, I warmly thank Sarah Nicolet and Isabelle Engeli for their consistently pertinent comments and their constant support.

During the work on this project, I also had the chance to spend half a year as a visiting Fellow at the Department of Government of Harvard University and to travel to numerous international conferences to develop and present my research. It would be impossible to name all the people whose comments have contributed to the development of my ideas; I am grateful for all of them. My special thanks go to Peter A. Hall, Peter A. Gourevitch, Torben Iversen, Karen M. Anderson, Klaus Armingeon, Philip Manow, Julia Lynch, Christoffer Green-Pedersen, Kees van Kersbergen, Anton Hemerijck, Fabrizio Gilardi, Fiona Barker, Kyoko Sato, and Mathieu Leimgruber.

Spending a year as a postdoctoral researcher at the European University Institute in Florence in 2008–9 allowed me to finalize the manuscript in an intellectually, socially, and culturally heavenly context (not to speak of the culinary delights that come with living in Tuscany). I would like to thank Ramon Marimon and the Max Weber Program for this invaluable opportunity that was crucial for my work on this book. Extremely precious advice and support at the European University Institute came from Adrienne Héritier, Peter Mair, Ben Ansell, David Art, Jane Gingrich, Martin Kohli, Eleonora Pasotti, Roger Schoenman, Furio Stamati, and Sven Steinmo. They and many other colleagues at the European University Institute made this year a wonderful and unforgettable experience.

At Cambridge University Press, I am particularly indebted to Kathleen Thelen and Margaret Levi. As editors of the Cambridge Studies in Comparative Politics series, they were incredibly generous with helpful comments that allowed me to improve this manuscript. Their intellectual commitment and support were extremely encouraging and a true lesson in how academia can and should work. My special thanks also go to Eric Crahan, who has been the most efficient and agreeable editor imaginable. Emily Spangler, Jason Przybylski, Manish Sharma, and Katherine Faydash were also part of this impressive team that did a great job throughout all the stages of the production of this book. I am also grateful to Colin Shepherd and to Alyson Price for copyediting different versions of the manuscript. Some of the ideas in this book have been previously published in the *European Journal of Political Research*. I thank the European Consortium for Political Research and Wiley Blackwell for permission to reproduce these contents.

Finally, my deep gratitude goes to my parents, Gerold and Elisabeth, and my brother, Lukas. Very early on – and more so than they probably know – they sparked my interest in politics around the kitchen table at dinner; remaining ever supportive of my decision to turn this interest into a profession, my parents also taught me that political science research must never be an end in itself but focus on real-life problems and on the distribution of resources and opportunities in the society it is part of.

Silja Häusermann
Cortona, August 2009

The Politics of Welfare State Reform in Continental Europe

"Eppur si muove"

Welfare State Change Despite Institutional Inertia

Welfare states count among the major achievements of Western industrialized democracies in the twentieth century. Today, however, they face a number of challenges: declining economic growth, unemployment, and demographic aging threaten their financial viability, and the post-industrialization of labor markets and family structures has created new social risks, which are insufficiently covered by the existing social protection schemes. There is a double risk of policy deficiency: welfare states may spend too many scarce resources on old risks while not addressing the most pressing problems of post-industrial society. Given that only effective welfare states can be legitimate, the future of modern welfare states depends not least on their ability to adapt to changing social and economic needs and demands. This book argues that welfare states *can* be reformed, and it demonstrates the conditions for successful policy change: multidimensional reform politics, coalitional engineering by policy entrepreneurs, and an institutional context that favors negotiation and compromise.

Against both conventional wisdom and recent scholarly research, this book argues that the main question is not just whether welfare states can be preserved or whether they have to be radically dismantled. Rather, the challenge that social policy makers face today is the genuine adaptation of social protection to a profoundly altered economic and social context: modernization in hard times. *Modernization* refers to the adaptation of existing institutional arrangements to the economic and social structures of post-industrialism: the transition to a (high-skill) service economy, high rates of temporary or long-term unemployment, flexible labor markets, the spread of atypical and female employment, family instability, and mounting demands for individualization and gender equality. The *hard times* result from the gap between declining resources and the growing (financial) needs that these modernization processes entail. Indeed, lagging growth and massive unemployment undermine the financial basis of welfare states. Similarly, declining birthrates and demographic aging alter the balance between the actively employed and the nonworking population, adding to what Pierson (2001: 410) famously called a context of "permanent austerity." In addition to undermining the revenues of welfare states, unemployment and demographic changes also create enormous increases in expenditures: demographic aging causes skyrocketing health and pension costs, and the economic crisis increases unemployment- and disability-related insurance expenditures. Moreover, post-industrial labor markets, a changing family structure, and female labor market participation have given rise to a whole range of new social needs, many of which modern welfare states are poorly prepared to meet. Such post-industrial social needs and demands typically include claims for the welfare coverage of the atypically employed, for gender equality in social insurance schemes, for external child-care facilities, for poverty relief for single parents and – more generally – for minimum income security for people with discontinuous employment biographies. Hence, there is both a strong pressure for retrenchment *and* a pressure for welfare state expansion. These are the two sides of post-industrial modernization.

Although the foregoing structural changes affect the viability and effectiveness of all modern welfare states, the challenge is clearly paramount in the countries of continental Europe. Continental welfare states combine the strongest challenges in terms of new social risks and economic downturn with social protection schemes, which are ill suited to meet these challenges in at least three respects. First, contrary to Anglo-Saxon and Scandinavian welfare states, in which substantial parts of social expenditure are tax-financed, continental social insurance schemes rely almost exclusively on contribution financing by means of non-wage-labor costs. In times of slower economic growth and increasing unemployment, this not only means that fewer people have to finance growing expenditure but it also raises the costs of labor. In addition, the male-breadwinner institutions of continental Europe have led to both low female labor market participation and low birthrates, two structural characteristics that put additional strain on the financial viability of these welfare states. And finally, continental insurance schemes distribute benefits on the basis of and proportional to contribution payments, which means that people with insufficient contribution records – such as atypically employed or part-time workers, unemployed people, homemakers or single mothers – face specific poverty risks. These new social risks are less salient in Scandinavian welfare states, where social protection schemes are more universalistic and benefits and labor market participation rates are more egalitarian. In summary, continental European welfare states are hard cases for successful welfare state reform: they face both the most urgent need for modernization and the most adverse conditions for that very modernization. This is why the present book focuses specifically on welfare reform dynamics in continental Europe, even though many of the theoretical arguments regarding the dynamics of policy reform travel to other countries, too.

Let us start with a look at the record of welfare state adaptation in the recent past. Over the past twenty years, there have been many modernizing reforms in the continental labor market, in pension schemes, and in family policies. Some of these have dealt with retrenchment and financial consolidation, whereas others have addressed new social needs and demands. A few examples may give a more concrete idea of what I mean by modernizing reforms: several countries have profoundly reformed their labor market and unemployment insurance policies.

For instance, the Dutch labor market was transformed into a part-time economy during the 1990s and has strongly improved the social coverage of atypical workers. At the same time, activation policies have been expanded, and Dutch sickness and disability programs have been cut back significantly (Hemerijck, Unger, and Brisser 2000). Similarly, labor markets have been significantly liberalized in Spain from the mid-1980s onward, a process that allowed the country's rates of atypical employment – notably fixed-term contracts – to rise to the highest rates in Europe (Guillén 2010). In Germany, several waves of the so-called Hartz reforms – enacted at the beginning of the 2000s against massive public protests – radically lowered long-term unemployment benefits (Clegg 2007). At the same time (and this is far less widely known), the last wave of the Hartz reforms required that the projected long-term savings resulting from this retrenchment be invested in the development of external child-care infrastructure to improve the work-care balance for female workers.

The pension schemes of continental Europe have undergone equally dramatic changes: in several social pacts throughout the 1990s, the legal age of retirement in Italy was raised, benefits were cut, supplementary occupational funds were established, and the rules for public and private sector pensions were harmonized (Ferrera and Gualmini 2000). The Austrian government enacted massive cutbacks of benefits and early retirement options in 2003, balancing them with means-tested benefits for poor pensioners and an increase of educational pension credits (Busemeyer 2005). Similarly, the German pension system was transformed over the course of several reforms from 1992 to 2004, evolving from a typical continental pay-as-you-go scheme to a highly diversified system of old-age income security. Today, this system relies on a combination of minimum pensions, regular insurance benefits, and capitalized funding (Schludi 2005; Schulze and Jochem 2007). During the 1990s and early 2000s, capitalized pension funds have also made their way into the French pension system, alongside a massive reduction of regular pension levels (Palier 2002). Equally important, Switzerland transformed the very structure of its basic pension scheme in 1995 when it increased the retirement age for women and switched from a male-breadwinner regime to a completely individualized insurance system (Bonoli and Mach 2000; Häusermann, Mach, and Papadopoulos 2004).

Finally, family policy has also undergone major transformation in a wide range of continental welfare states. Belgian family policy has become increasingly focused on female labor market participation, with the introduction of parental-leave schemes and massive tax deductions for external-care costs in the 1980s. These reforms were followed by an expansion of external child-care options and part-time work opportunities in the 1990s (Marques-Pereira and Paye 2001). Similarly, France extended its already highly developed family policy regime by adding new subsidies in the 1990s: one of them makes it possible for families to hire child-care helpers, and the other supports low-income families with a generous child-rearing allowance (Jenson and Sineau 2001). In 2004, Swiss women became entitled to maternity insurance, and the parliament decided to support external-care infrastructure in 2003 (Ballestri and Bonoli 2003). In Germany, reforms centered on the work-care balance have gone even further (Leitner, Ostner, and Schratzenstaller 2004): in 2001, the German government instated a right to part-time employment for both parents and raised the level of educational benefits.

All of these reforms – some restrictive, some expansive – dealt with the modernization of continental welfare states (i.e., with their adaptation to demographic, economic, and social structural change). The very occurrence of these reforms, however, leaves us with at least three unresolved puzzles, which lie at the heart of this book.

The first puzzle deals with the *reform capacity* of continental welfare states. It has been argued, most prominently by authors like Esping-Andersen (1996: 2), that continental welfare states are sclerotic, "frozen" institutional regimes. From a theoretical perspective, this diagnosis is perfectly sensible: the very design of such welfare states – based on insurance and contribution financing – creates liabilities and vested interests in the existing institutional arrangements, which makes major change risky and highly unlikely from both an electoral and an institutionalist perspective (Pierson 1996, 2001). The focus on policy stability in the welfare literature of the 1990s was also very much in line with the classical approaches in policy analysis, which consider institutional change rare and driven by exogenous shocks (see the idea of punctuated equilibria by Baumgartner and Jones [2002] and the concept of dominant advocacy coalitions in Sabatier and Jenkins-Smith [1993]). Very much in contrast with these expectations, however, the foregoing examples show that there *has* been ample institutional change in the past two decades. The previously mentioned reforms represent instances of major, if not paradigmatic, policy change not only because many of the cutbacks were very sharp[1] but also because they have, in many respects, transformed the very logic and structure of social insurance schemes. The introduction of means-tested pension minima and capitalized pension funds in France and Germany represents a systemic shift away from the collective insurance principle, which has been at the heart of the continental postwar welfare state. Similarly, the introduction of gender equality in pension insurance, the expansion of external child-care infrastructure, and the support of part-time employment change policies in a direction that is diametrically opposed to the male-breadwinner logic, which traditionally has been a key characteristic of these regimes. These changes are systemic and therefore paradigmatic. How can we explain these surprising reforms? The recent literature has started to acknowledge and describe that institutions are less stable than expected (e.g., Streeck and Thelen 2005; Palier, 2010). However, we still lack an explanation of the *politics* of change: How are political majorities built? Under what conditions is change possible or even likely?

---

[1] For instance, the reference period for pension calculation was extended from ten to twenty-five years in France, from five years to the whole duration of the career in Italy, and from fifteen to forty years in Austria. The Organisation for Economic Co-operation and Development (2007) estimates that, after taking their full effect, pension reforms in countries such as France and Germany will lower benefit levels by 10–25 percent.

The mere occurrence of reforms is not the only puzzling aspect about the observed institutional changes, however. The second surprising feature of the reforms is that so many of them seem to go *against* the interests of the main stakeholders of industrial welfare states. Indeed, the continental welfare regimes are largely the outcome of a class compromise between the organizations of labor and capital from the main industries. Therefore, the standard male employees in the industrial sector (i.e., the insiders) are the early winners of institutional creation and the main beneficiaries of existing insurance plans. People outside this core workforce, by contrast – namely labor market outsiders, the atypically employed, or the non employed – have always remained at the margins of continental welfare states. Neo-institutionalist theory would predict that the institutions have consolidated the power of the insiders over time at the expense of the outsiders. But quite to the contrary, many of the recent reforms have *lowered* the social rights of insiders to a considerable extent, even in core insurance schemes such as unemployment (e.g., in France, Germany, Switzerland, and Belgium) and pensions (e.g., in Switzerland, Germany, France, Italy, and Austria). To sum it up quite simply, the recent reforms have enacted the very kind of policies we would not expect to occur.

The third puzzle deals with the winners rather than the losers of recent reforms. To a great extent, recent welfare state expansion has been directed toward social groups that are particularly *weak* in terms of political representation and power. Gender equality in social insurance and educational pension credits, for example, respond to the specific interests of women. Child- and elderly-care infrastructure (and more generally policies on work-care balance) support young families. Social insurance coverage of atypical work and the creation of means-tested benefit minima are reform strategies that benefit mainly labor market outsiders. All these risk groups – notably the low skilled, young, female, and atypically employed – tend to be underrepresented, both in political parties and in trade unions. How did their needs take on such acute political relevance in a context of austerity, which seemingly forecloses any expansion whatsoever?

These three puzzles make it clear that both the scope and the direction of recent continental welfare state modernization are unexpected and need to be explained. This book proposes an analytical model that allows for the understanding of these seemingly contradictory reform trends. The need for such an explanatory model is obvious, as much of the existing literature has just started to acknowledge the actual scope of the recent changes and is still far from explaining it systematically. Furthermore, the most common explanatory approaches found in the existing welfare state literature – functionalism, power resources, and institutionalism – fail to explain the dynamics of post-industrial modernization. Functionalism, the explanation of policy outputs by structural requirements, may be able to account for some cross-regime variation. For instance, gender and family patterns changed earlier in Scandinavia, and deindustrialization started sooner there than in continental Europe. But although this reasoning can shed some light on the more gender egalitarian and universalistic welfare schemes in the Nordic welfare states (Bonoli 2006), it certainly fails to explain the scope of cross-country differences in reform outputs among the continental countries. Power resources theory, which focuses on the balance of power between labor and capital, falls short particularly when it comes to the expansive reforms mentioned herein. Indeed, the beneficiaries of recent social policy expansion are not the traditional clientele of the labor movement. Rather, they are the politically disenfranchised – the weak. In terms of power resources theory, it is thus difficult to understand why, in a context of financial austerity, countries would *expand* their benefits for atypically employed, working women, or the poor. It may be more promising to explain recent *retrenchment* with power resources, interpreting restrictive reforms as the result of a context of austerity that changes the balance of bargaining power in favor of capital (see, e.g., Korpi and Palme 2003). With this argument, however, power resources advocates run aground on the cogent institutionalist claim of path-dependency: over time, the very existence of continental welfare states has extended the ranks of stakeholders in the existing insurance schemes far beyond those of the traditional constituencies of the left, to an extent that makes retrenchment at the expense of insiders politically unlikely (Pierson 1996). Moreover, neo-institutionalism is as unable to explain the recent expansive reforms as is power resources theory. So, if functionalism, power resources, and institutionalism fail, how can we go beyond these approaches?

Outline of the Argument

The failure of the existing literature to provide a conclusive explanation for post-industrial reforms results from the fact that most authors tend to adopt too narrow a focus – directing their attention either to a single dimension of the reforms (e.g., retrenchment or new social risk policies or privatization), or to a single explanatory factor (e.g., power resources or institutions or electoral risk or structure). Although each of these theoretical perspectives may explain a part of the ongoing dynamics in continental welfare states, their interrelations are key in accounting for the whole picture. In this book, I propose an explanatory model of institutional change that integrates several theoretical perspectives and conceptualizes different reform dimensions as elements of the same, multidimensional policy space.

   The argument goes as follows: the translation of social and economic structural change into actual policy output depends on the *interplay* of structure, institutions, and actors' preferences and strategies, and it consists of three steps. The first step is the translation of structural change into policy-specific *conflict dimensions*. I argue that structural developments, such as deindustrialization, demographic aging, and family instability, create potentials for political conflict if and only if they challenge the preexisting institutions. Hence, increasing divorce rates, for instance, may not challenge a universalistic and gender egalitarian social-democratic welfare state regime, but they do put a male-breadwinner system into question. Similarly, high levels of unemployment have more dramatic consequences for the financial viability of welfare states that are financed by means of payroll taxes than for those regimes that rely on general taxation. Hence, if such a clash between evolving structures and stable institutions generates institutional friction (i.e., an institutional misfit), there arises a potential need for the adaptation and reform of institutions. Those who suffer from this misfit are supposed to have a keen interest in institutional adaptation, and those unaffected by it do not or may hold a stronger interest in the status quo. Continental welfare states – built on contribution financing, work-related eligibility for coverage, earnings-related benefits, and decentralized management (Bonoli and Palier 1998) – are particularly at odds with the structural developments of growing austerity and post-industrialization. Therefore, a variety of different institutional misfits emerge, with an ensuing variety of potential reform dimensions.

This variety of potential reform dimensions – and this is the second step – engenders different crosscutting conflict lines, each one splitting social interests in a distinct way. For instance, some conflict lines may oppose the preferences of labor and capital, whereas others are likely to divide social groups according to skill levels or labor market status (insiders versus outsiders). These different risk and preference profiles define a range of potential class and cross-class conflicts at the socio-structural level, and these various socio-structural potentials are spread differently across the constituencies of political parties, trade unions, and employer organizations. Therefore, I expect a plurality of crosscutting conflict lines in the political decision-making processes, giving rise to a *multidimensional space* in which reform politics unfold.

The third step of the explanatory model deals with the translation of these diverse alliance potentials into *actual reforms* (i.e., with the determinants of the reform capacity and the actual policy output). To begin with, the multidimensionality of the policy space creates possibilities for political exchange. Rational policy makers can and will strategically exploit such possibilities. In times of austerity and in a context of mature welfare states, the success of welfare reforms depends on the formation of large coalitions supporting them. By combining several conflict dimensions in a single reform package, policy makers may be able to foster such broad cross-class agreements. More specifically, policy makers may try to blur the opposition against retrenchment by compensating cuts with policies aimed to foster cross-class conflict. But the story does not end here, because two (institutional) factors influence the chances of success of such coalitional engineering strategies. First, the more that labor, business, and political parties are fragmented, the more flexible is the reform-specific coalition formation – and the greater the chances for coalitional engineering. By contrast, where economic interests and political parties are concentrated, coalitions are more stable and actors cannot opt in and out of specific and variable reform coalitions as flexibly. In a regime with a high number of veto points – and this is the second factor – such an inability to foster broad cross-class agreements lowers the capacity for reform.

In summary, successful welfare state modernization in continental Europe depends on the capacity of policy makers to build encompassing reform coalitions in a multidimensional policy reform space. And this capacity, in turn, depends on their strategies of coalitional engineering and on the institutional framework within which they deploy these strategies.

The main claim of this book – that multidimensional politics create reform opportunities in hard times – may very well apply to welfare reforms in all regimes and even to policy change more generally (Engeli and Häusermann 2009). In that sense, continental pension reform is just one example of a larger class of phenomena to which this theoretical argument could be applied. But there are reasons why, in this book, I choose to develop and test the argument with regard to pension policy reforms in Germany, France, and Switzerland – three continental pension regimes that share most of the structural and political reform challenges but differ strongly with regard to the institutional framework of decision making that conditions the success of coalitional engineering. Continental pension policy reform is a case of hard testing, because endogenous stabilizers and mechanisms of path dependency are strongest in this prime example of a supposedly inert, frozen policy. Hence, if multidimensional politics and cross-class coalitions allow for adaptation even in pension politics, this is strong evidence for the relevance of these dynamics in the modernization of welfare states more generally.

Contributions of the Book

There is a huge, highly informed, and sophisticated literature dealing with the development of (continental) welfare states and pension policy over the past thirty years. One may ask whether there is a need for another book on the recent pension policy development. If this study focused merely on retracing major reforms, one might well doubt its usefulness, even though the pace of change in today's welfare states certainly fosters a need for ongoing empirical examination. But that is beside the point. This book deals more generally with the dynamics and determinants of institutional change and policy reform. It makes four theoretical contributions to some of the most vibrant current strands of theorizing and research, and it presents a new empirical and methodological approach to studying policy change over a long time and across multiple countries.

The first contribution is a conceptualization of the coalitional dynamics underlying institutional change. One of the most promising current theoretical attempts to explain recent policy reforms in institutionalist terms is the concept of gradual transformative change, developed by several authors in a volume edited by Streeck and Thelen (2005). Reconsidering the early institutionalist focus on stability and inertia, these authors posit that major change may occur in a series of seemingly minor institutional adaptations, whereby institutional arrangements are gradually undermined, complemented, and/or replaced by new ones. The existing institutions themselves may condition such change by shaping actors' interests and – given their "inherent openness and under-definition" – by providing "rule takers" with more or less leeway in the implementation (Streeck and Thelen 2005: 15). Hence, although the focus of this new approach has so far been on the conceptualization of the mechanisms of change, it is clear that an actual explanation of gradual transformative change must be based on actors, their preferences, and their behavior and strategies. Thereby, this second-generation institutionalism must integrate a good deal of agency and power resources variables to gain convincing explanatory power (Mahoney and Thelen [2010] actually go in this direction). Indeed, the authors of this approach insist on the importance of the underlying actor configurations and on the "shifting coalitional basis" of institutions (Thelen 2004: 33). In that sense, the insight that the key to understanding institutional change lies in the plurality of conflict lines and alliance potentials is not new. However, we still lack a conclusive theoretical account of the politics and the coalitional dynamics of institutional change. This is precisely what this book delivers: an explicit theoretical and empirical focus on the multidimensionality of policy reform spaces to explain institutional change.

The second theoretical contribution speaks to the literature on cross-class alliances. So far, this literature has demonstrated the relevance of numerous political cleavages other than class (e.g., Mares 2003; Hiscox 2001; Rueda 2005), and in this sense, it can be read as research on the multidimensionality of politics. To some extent, this book simply provides further theoretical and empirical evidence for the claims that labor and capital are not homogeneous categories and that political coalitions in welfare state reforms are oftentimes built on determinants other than class, such as skill levels, insider-outsider labor market status, or values. But the major contribution I want to make here is with regard to the socio-structural explanation of such cross-class alliances in a post-industrial context. In this book, I argue that conflict lines, which crosscut labor and capital, are inherent in the post-industrial class structure itself. Given the growing share of service sector jobs in the employment structure, female labor market participation, and the spread of higher education, post-industrial labor markets have become so diversified that we must think in terms of a new class schema that divides the workforce into a highly differentiated set of classes. Labor has become an increasingly heterogeneous category that encompasses stark differences in terms of income, chances for mobility, and political preferences. Hence, different categories of labor vary strongly with regard to their risk profiles, interests, values, and – consequently – political preferences. For these reasons, the cross-class alliances that we observe in post-industrial policy making are neither surprising nor accidental nor fortuitous; they are genuinely rooted in the post-industrial class structure. This book shows that the literature on cross-class alliances may benefit greatly from drawing explicit theoretical and empirical links between the socio-structural micro-level of class and the positions of collective political actors in the reform processes.

The third theoretical contribution of this book is to highlight the importance of cultural value divides in post-industrial welfare state reform dynamics. Social policy making is often viewed as a mere distributional struggle between conflicting material interests, and given the fact that welfare states depend on the taxation, distribution, and redistribution of income, this is doubtless a sound focus of the analysis. But there is more to welfare states than preventing poverty and insuring the risk of income loss. Social policy is and has always been a means of regulating social stratification, family patterns, and gender roles by positive and negative incentives, particularly in continental welfare states (see, e.g.,

Van Kersbergen 1995; Orloff 1993; Esping-Andersen 1999). The institutions of the welfare state entail a moral definition of the aspired societal order. Thus, political struggles regarding the design of welfare state institutions are almost always both distributional conflicts *and* value conflicts. The value aspect of welfare politics is, of course, particularly salient in reforms that deal explicitly with the issues of individualization, familialism, and gender equality. Given the growing misfit between male-breadwinner institutions on the one hand, and the realities of post-industrial family instability, increased female labor market participation, and the spread of discontinuous, atypical employment biographies on the other hand, these value issues have become key topics in welfare state modernization. Therefore, actors' social policy preferences cannot be understood through their material interests alone. Their positioning on a cultural value divide, in regard to libertarian-progressive versus traditionalist values (Kitschelt 1994), must also be considered. Although the relevance of this value divide may seem straightforward in policy fields such as environmental policy or arts and culture, this book stresses its relevance even to the field of welfare state research. Values are, to be sure, not completely independent of socio-structural characteristics such as skill or income levels. But they can reinforce or hamper the cohesion of interest-based alliances, and they can be a basis for coalition formation in their own right.

The fourth and final theoretical contribution of this book is that it challenges a trend in the current institutionalist literature that consists in downplaying the importance of macro-institutions – such as electoral regimes and consensus democracy – in the explanation of policy reform outputs. Rather, it is argued that welfare regimes' micro-institutions (i.e., institutional policy arrangements) (Bonoli and Palier 1998) endogenously structure the political decision-making processes (see, e.g., Streeck and Thelen 2005; Palier and Martin 2007). I would agree with this claim when it comes to the substance of the reforms we witness in a particular regime type. Indeed, recent reforms in continental welfare states display striking similarities, despite the very different macro-institutional regimes of these countries. However, one must be careful not to overshoot the mark in criticizing the traditional focus on macro-institutions: electoral systems and state structure may not account for the content of reforms, but this book shows that these institutions remain important in explaining the *scope* of welfare state reforms. Macro institutions influence the extent to which political parties and interest organizations are willing and able to engage in processes of variable and selective coalition formation. Therefore, these institutions remain relevant to the explanation of intra-regime variation in reform capacities and reform outputs.

Finally, this book proposes a new empirical and methodological strategy for the analysis of policy change, which strikes a balance between large-N regression studies and historical case studies. When analyzing the coalitional dynamics of welfare state change, both of these traditional approaches present specific advantages but also difficulties. Case study research allows for investigating the very mechanisms of political exchange and for tracing actor configurations in detail, but it is difficult to apply this strategy to a large number of reform processes over time. Purely quantitative studies, in contrast, tend to lack precise information on the empirical motivations and policy positions of actors. As a result, preferences of parties, unions, and business organizations are often more assumed than empirically observed. In this book, I try to find a viable and fruitful middle ground between the two approaches by proposing an alternative strategy: I coded actor positions on policy reforms and analyzed this data both quantitatively and qualitatively.

The empirical analysis comprises all thirty-six pension reforms that took place in Germany, France, and Switzerland between 1970 and 2005. The temporal and geographical scope of the analysis is important, as I want to analyze the impact of structural changes and the impact of institutions on coalitional dynamics.[2] For the purpose of tracing actor configurations and coalitional dynamics, I coded the detailed policy positions of the involved actors both at the beginning of the reform processes (with regard to the different elements of the reform debate) and at the end (with regard to the whole reform package). The idea of collecting the early statements is that these positions reflect preferences before negotiation and package building (similar to what Mares [2003: 2, 48] calls "pre-strategic preferences"). At this early stage, actors present their own ideas and goals for the upcoming reform process. At the end of the decision-making process, by contrast, negotiations are over and actors can only agree or reject the package, not shape its content any further. My theoretical argument implies that this final position should depend more on institutional constraints, strategies, and bargaining than on the initially articulated, issue-specific reform preferences. The coded actor positions on all reforms could then be analyzed empirically by means of descriptive statistics, multidimensional scaling, and factor analysis to identify the dimensionality of the policy reform spaces and the precise actor configurations.

Contrary to other fields – such as party system research – the coding of actor positions is used rather rarely in welfare state analysis, which is surprising, given that much of the current literature on welfare reforms deals with coalitional dynamics over time. Indeed, many major studies in this field consider the key to understanding institutional change and policy change in actor configurations and coalitions (e.g., Gourevitch 1986; Swenson 1991, 2001; Pierson 2001, 2004; Kitschelt 2001; Thelen 2004; Streeck and Thelen 2005; Palier 2005; Rueda 2005; Iversen and Soskice 2006; van Kersbergen and Manow 2009). And an important literature also stresses the importance of time (i.e., the need to analyze institutional and policy development in sequences over a long time span.[3]) However, when the development of actors and coalitions over time is the focus of research, we need adequate tools to collect systematic information on actor preferences

---

[2] Between 1970 and 2005, postindustrialization has transformed the societies and economies of all countries in continental Europe. Institutions, by contrast, vary across countries, and France, Germany, and Switzerland differ significantly with regard to their institutional frameworks of decision making.

[3] On welfare state change and time more generally, see, e.g., Pierson 2001; Thelen 2004; Bonoli 2005; Palier and Martin 2007; on policy change, see, e.g., Sabatier and Jenkins-Smith 1993.

over many reforms. This is precisely what this book proposes: a simple coding technique as a means for systematizing large amounts of data and analyzing them in a systematic and readily traceable way. At the same time, the coding remains very close to, and must be embedded in, a detailed, qualitative understanding of reform dynamics and actor motivations, which is crucial for explaining the interactions of actors, strategies, and institutions. Therefore, the methodological approach (presented in more detail in Appendix 1) of this book proposes a balance of qualitative and quantitative methods to add to the existing toolbox of welfare state analysis and policy analysis more generally.

Plan of the Book

Chapter 2 situates this book in the context of the existing welfare state literature and outlines the analytical framework for a coalitional approach to the analysis of post-industrial reform dynamics. Because both the current challenges and the current actor configurations depend heavily on the welfare state architecture of the industrial era, the chapter provides an overview of the key institutional characteristics of continental welfare regimes before demonstrating how austerity and post-industrialism challenge the efficiency and effectiveness of these institutions. Finally, this chapter provides a new explanatory model of policy reform in multidimensional policy spaces.

Chapter 2 provides a general model of institutional change in modern (continental) welfare states. However, each policy field faces its own range of challenges and entails specific reform dimensions. This is why the subsequent chapters – Part I of the analysis – then break the general theoretical argument on reform dynamics down to pension politics. In Chapters 3–5, the book develops a specific analytical framework for the analysis of post-industrial pension policy making in France, Germany, and Switzerland. Chapter 3 shows how the institutional misfit between structural change and continental pension schemes leads to four post-industrial conflict potentials (insurance, capitalization, targeting and recalibration) that divide social interests according to class, skill levels, labor market status, and values. Chapter 4 explains the extent to which these diverse conflict lines become manifest in the policy-making processes of the three countries. More specifically, it establishes the link between sociostructural risk and value profiles; their mobilization by political parties, trade unions, and employer organizations; and the manifestation of different class and cross-class alliances in pension-reform processes. Finally, Chapter 5 explains how these actor alliances translate into policy outputs that depend on strategies of coalitional engineering and the institutional framework in different countries. Throughout these three chapters, the book develops four hypotheses on the dynamics of institutional change and discusses them in terms of their specific observable implications for pension reform in France, Germany, and Switzerland. Part II of the book consists of three detailed country chapters (Chapters 6–8) that provide an empirical analysis of the determinants and the contents of pension policy reforms in France, Germany, and Switzerland between 1970 and 2005.

Chapter 9 presents the results in a comparative perspective and discusses their generalizability. It is argued that the theoretical framework may also be applied to other countries and other policy fields, and the chapter briefly illustrates this wider applicability of the model with regard to selected pension reforms in other continental countries and with examples of French, German, and Swiss family policy changes. The book then concludes with a discussion of the political implications of its results.

2

Modernization in Hard Times

The Post-Industrial Politics of Continental
Welfare State Reform

This chapter develops a coalition-centered theoretical framework for the analysis of continental welfare state change in a post-industrial context. The question is whether, why, and how structural challenges lead to policy reform. In other words, if the structural context changes and existing institutions become problematic or dysfunctional, what are the mechanisms that lead to policy adaptations? And what are the chances of these adaptations occurring?

The literature agrees that all western welfare states have been facing tremendous structural challenges in recent decades, in terms of both financial austerity and new social needs (see, e.g., Pierson 1996, 2001; Esping-Andersen 1999; Scharpf and Schmidt 2000; Bonoli, George, and Taylor-Gooby 2000; Huber and Stephens 2001). But there is no agreement as to how welfare states change in response to such challenges. Are they dismantled, preserved, or even restructured? In part, the inconclusive evidence with regard to the magnitude and direction of change is a result of the inherent difficulties of researching a moving target (i.e., the challenge of observing a trend still very much in progress). It is also a result of the fact that different welfare regimes develop in different directions. Structural challenges are filtered through the lenses of national politics and institutions. Hence, the same challenges produce different results in different countries (Pierson 2001, 2004; Scharpf and Schmidt 2000). But the literature on welfare state change also remains somewhat inconclusive, because different studies focus on different explanations and drivers of change. A focus on institutional and ideational rigidities (e.g., Pierson 1996; Castles 2004) tends to underestimate the possibility for reform that arises from changing actor preferences, whereas a pronounced focus on interests and power relations (e.g., Scharpf and Schmidt 2000; Korpi and Palme 2003) carries the risk of overestimating the effects of changes in the balance of power while neglecting the institutional constraints. Therefore, a theoretical framework for the analysis of welfare state change must build on both actors and institutions. Institutions not only affect the substantial policy preferences of actors but also define an incentive structure for those actors' strategic behavior in terms of coalition building. In turn, coalition building is crucial for actual policy change, especially in the coordinated market economies of continental Europe that are characterized by multiple power-sharing institutions, such as proportional representation, coalition governments, multiparty systems, and corporatism.

In addition to a joint focus on actors and institutions, timing and sequencing are particularly relevant for the analysis of welfare state change. Post-industrial welfare politics may differ sharply from the politics of the industrial age (as Pierson [1996, 2001] famously claimed), but they are certainly not independent of the politics of this industrial age. Time matters, because preexisting institutions set the stage for subsequent reforms (Pierson 2000b, 2004; Streeck and Thelen 2005; Bonoli 2007; Palier and Martin 2007). More specifically, institutions may not only influence actors' preferences but they may even create actors and actor interests. Because of their differential distributive effects, institutions produce winners and losers, who then become new actors in subsequent reforms (see also Mahoney and Thelen 2010). From this, it follows that political actors, their preferences, and reform agendas are largely endogenous. An explanation of post-industrial politics thus needs to build on what we know about industrial politics. When developing an analytical framework for the study of post-industrial welfare change, we must therefore start by identifying the actors, power relations, and institutions that characterized the development of these welfare states in the postwar period. This reasoning also implies that analytical frameworks need to be welfare regime specific, as the preexisting power relations and institutions are precisely the things that define a regime. Therefore, I develop the theoretical model of this book with reference to the specific context of continental Europe, though the reader will find that many of the key variables and mechanisms can certainly and easily be adapted and transferred to other welfare regimes.

This theoretical chapter thus starts by discussing actors – the builders of the continental welfare regime, its main stakeholders, and its clients, as opposed to those of other regimes. It shows that the standard male industrial workers, their unions, and their employers are the early winners (Thelen 2004) of continental institution building. Consequently, the institutional setup of the continental social protection regimes was tailored to their needs. The second section of this chapter presents the institutional characteristics of continental welfare regimes and the reasons they became so sharply dysfunctional with the transition to austerity and post-industrialism. On the basis of this discussion of preexisting actors and institutions, and building on the recent literature on new social risks (Bonoli 2005) and multidimensional reform politics (Pierson 2001; Levy 1999), the chapter then develops a new coalitional model of welfare state change. This model integrates timing by stressing the importance of the conjuncture of different reform dimensions that create a multidimensional space for political exchange and coalition formation.

Mind the Origins: The Builders of Continental Welfare States

The institutionalist thesis of sequencing implies that we need to take into account the driving mechanisms for the development of the continental welfare state until the 1970s to understand contemporary reform dynamics. Past politics explain the stakes of different actors in existing institutions and their subsequent preferences with regard to reforms. Hence, we need to know who the actors were at the origin of the continental welfare state. By whom and for whose needs and interests was the regime created? Over time, several different theories have singled out the major contributions of different actors to the growth of continental welfare states, and here I review briefly the main insights of those theories.

In the wake of functionalist and statist approaches to the explanation of social policy development,[1] the power resources approach – developed during the late 1970s and 1980s by authors such as Stephens (1979) and Korpi (1983) – was the first theory that focused explicitly on actors and politics as the main determinants of welfare states. Power resources theory assumes a basic antagonism between the welfare state and the market, and it interprets social policy as a triumph of the working class over capitalist interests. Ideology becomes an important factor in this view, as it is hypothesized that different political actors – and their constituencies – want genuinely different things. Therefore, taking into consideration just who holds power in the government is crucial. Welfare states differ because of different power relations among actors and coalitions with specific political goals. Esping-Andersen (1990), in his seminal work on the three worlds of welfare capitalism, labeled welfare regimes according to their defining power relations and key actors. In his account, a strong social democracy in Scandinavia established an egalitarian and decommodifying social-democratic regime, thus freeing workers from many constraints of capitalist exploitation. Liberal regimes, by contrast, provide only subsidiary poverty relief, so workers need to rely almost exclusively on their own earning capacity in the market. Finally, the corporatist welfare states of continental Europe reflect the ideologies of a strong Catholic movement and corporatist guilds. Even though social spending is high, these welfares states are not egalitarian: they are stratifying and build on the family rather than the individual as the unit of society.

---

[1] From the late 1950s to the 1980s, the dominant understanding of social policy development was mainly *functionalist* and, to a large extent, devoid of actors. That understanding implied that the postwar expansion of industrialization generated economic well-being, a demand for social citizenship rights, and the need for and supply of social policies (see, e.g., Titmuss 1958; Peacock and Wiseman 1961; Wilensky 1975; Flora and Alber 1981). In reaction to industrialization theory, a more *statist* or institutionalist approach was developed mainly in the comparative historical work of authors such as Heclo (1974), Orloff and Skocpol (1984), Skocpol (1992), and Immerguth (1992). They argued that similar structural developments trigger different responses, depending on the state structure in a specific country. More recent studies have pursued this line of theorizing by focusing on the independent effects that electoral institutions and institutional veto points have on the extent and structure of welfare state policies (Immergut 1992; Bonoli 2000; Huber, Ragin, and Stephens 1993), and on the relationship between institutions and the power of particular actors (Birchfield and Crepaz 1998; Iversen and Soskice 2006).

Esping-Andersen's work (1990) – and the power resources approach more generally – has created a widely used and accepted base for further research because the distinction among the three regimes elucidates striking real-world policy differences in the generosity and structure of different welfare states. However, there are still divergent explanations for the differences (i.e., divergent accounts of the underlying actors and the coalitions that drive their emergence). As outlined previously, the original power resources theory argued that the type of welfare state mainly depends on the role and on the power of the left – trade unions and social-democratic parties (Stephens 1979; Korpi 1983). Consequently, continental welfare states could not become as egalitarian and universalistic as the Scandinavian regimes because the Christian democratic parties mobilized a large part of the working class, thereby undermining the mobilization potential of the left. A number of subsequent studies have shifted the focus away from this concentration on the left by analyzing the contributions of other political actors to the building of (continental) welfare states.

A first strand of critical studies showed that the left was not the only pro-welfare force and tended to promote welfare state expansion in alliance with other classes and ideological movements. With regard to the Nordic model, these analyses pointed out the crucial alliance between workers and the middle class (Baldwin 1990), and between workers and farmers (Esping-Andersen 1990; Bartolini 2000), in the design of universal, egalitarian benefit schemes. They showed that, while the left advocated the expansion of social protection, the interests of the farmers and the middle class explain why these countries developed universalistic protection schemes with high and egalitarian benefit levels. Similarly, van Kersbergen (1995) and – more recently – van Kersbergen and Manow (2009) showed that the continental welfare states are not just an incomplete version of the Nordic model but a genuinely different product of a social-conservative alliance of the left and Christian democracy. On the basis of the Catholic social ethic, Christian democrats advocated social policies with a double aim. In their view, social protection should strive to relieve poverty for all members of society and to insure the material well-being of male breadwinners and their families, but it should also act as an engineering device to protect a natural order. Therefore, continental insurance-based social protection has preserved the existing social stratification and strengthened the importance of the male breadwinner in the society. Because social democrats in continental Europe on the whole defended the interests of (male) workers in industrial society, they could agree with the Christian democrats on this structure for the welfare state, even though it was not egalitarian and certainly not universalistic. These analyses convincingly demonstrated that the continental welfare regimes, as they had developed until the 1970s, were most clearly in the material interest of male industrial workers – so-called labor market insiders – and enshrined a normative ideal and a social reality of conservative, patriarchal social structures. In summary, a cross-class coalition of Christian democrats and social democrats was the driving force of continental welfare regimes in the realm of party politics.

In addition to political parties, trade union and employer interests need to be considered as well. Here, too, the power resources literature basically assumed that welfare state generosity was a direct function of the power of organized labor. However, as in the parliamentary arena, cross-class coalitions played an important role in the shaping of continental welfare regimes. The literature on varieties of capitalism has been the most prominent recent answer to power resources theory in this regard, exploring employer interests in social policy. On the basis of the groundbreaking historical work of Swenson (2002), the French *école de regulation* (Boyer 1990), and Streeck's concept of different modes of production (1991), Hall and Soskice (2001) proposed a production regime theory, which clearly contradicts Esping-Andersen's (1990: 22) claim that "employers have always opposed de-commodification." In a coordinated market economy (Hall and Soskice 2001), capitalists depend on a highly skilled workforce with industry-specific training and low labor market mobility to preserve their comparative advantages. Because workers have no incentive to invest time and money in specific skills training unless they can expect a certain stability of employment and status, business supports a rather high level of earnings insurance and employment protection regulation. This is readily apparent in the policies from the Nordic and the continental welfare regimes (Mares 2003). From this perspective, existing social policies reflect an equilibrium rather than a conflict between the interests of employees and employers (Estevez-Abe, Iversen, and Soskice 2001).[2] Labor and capital are not necessarily opponents, and their interests may be structured by conflict lines such as economic sectors or firm size rather than class (Mares 2001b). Continental social protection regimes respond to the needs and preferences of the employers and trade unions of the main industrial sectors. They insure the core workforce against wage loss and, at the same time, create an incentive structure that provides employers with the kind of workforce they need. Apart from its focus on cross-class coalitions, this research on employer's social policy interests also bears two additional, important insights for my analysis of continental welfare state change: first, the interests of employers and employees

---

[2] The jury is still out on the empirical evidence of power resources versus varieties of capitalism. Both schools have assembled large amounts of evidence, but most of it is less contradictory than it at first seems to be. For example, power resource research has relied heavily on large-N regression analysis, demonstrating a significant relationship between the mobilization of the labor movement and the size of the welfare state (Esping-Andersen 1990; Korpi 1983; Huber and Stephens 2001; Korpi and Palme 2003; for a more qualitative historical approach, see also Huber and Stephens 2001). This result, however, is not necessarily incompatible with the cross-class coalition hypothesis of the production regime theory. A strong centralized labor movement should not necessarily be interpreted as a clear opponent to capital; it can also be viewed as a reliable partner for stable cross-class alliances. Indeed, much empirical evidence has been compiled in recent years to suggest a reinterpretation of this quantitative evidence of the power resources literature. Most of this critique is based on comparative historical analysis, retracing the positions of labor and capital. By these means, it is shown that some employers have advocated the creation and maintenance of welfare schemes in fields as different as pensions, accident, and unemployment insurance (Mares 2003), health insurance (Martin 1995, 1997), wage bargaining (Thelen 2001; Swenson 1991a, 1991b), and early retirement policies (Manow 2001).

must be observed empirically rather than assumed (Pierson 2000: 794). And second, labor and capital need to be disaggregated into meaningful categories such as sectors or firm size for the purpose of analysis, as their interests are far from being homogeneous across the economy.

From the cumulative evidence of these different strands of theorizing and research, it follows that, in the industrial era, a large cross-class coalition of industrial capitalists, unions, social democrats, and Christian democrats built the continental European welfare states. The social insurance protection schemes that have become typical for these regimes answered the needs of the constituencies of the actors: industrial workers and their families. However, while being highly successful in the industrial era, the features of the continental welfare model turned out to be worst suited to the multiple challenges of a post-industrial era.

Why Continental Welfare States Have Become Dysfunctional in a Post-Industrial Context

In Esping-Andersen's (1990) typology, the corporatist regime is defined by a medium level of decommodification and a high level of stratification. Despite rather high overall levels of spending, decommodification remains modest in such a regime because benefits are granted not as a matter of social citizenship rights (universalism) but on a contribution-related basis (insurance). This means that benefits are proportional to contributions, and therefore proportional to previous earnings, and labor market participation is a precondition for entitlement to benefits. This generates a strong need for citizens to commodify their workforce, and it fosters a pronounced rift between insiders and outsiders (Esping-Andersen 1999a). Insiders are people in unionized sectors with stable, full-time, and permanent work contracts, whose income is fully insured against the main life risks. Outsiders, by contrast, are in atypical employment, are unemployed, or are outside paid employment, and their discontinuous employment biographies lower entitlement to social benefits. During the golden age of economic growth in continental Europe, there was generally full male employment, and outsiders were mostly women whose participation in the labor market was discouraged. During this period, women enjoyed social rights as wives or widows of their male breadwinners. Hence, it was both a normative ideal and an empirical reality that most outsiders were indirectly covered by the social insurance programs through marriage and family.[3] The typical family policy of conservative welfare states reinforced this patriarchal organization of gender roles and work-life organization. Financial transfers to families tended to be generous, which contributed to allowing families to live on a single wage only. In addition, the lack of child-care infrastructure discouraged female labor market participation, as did tax laws that

---

[3] This structure of benefit entitlements had the explicit (and most certainly deliberate) effect of rewarding the traditional family and of making divorce not only a normatively condemned practice but also a financial risk for women (Orloff 1993; Lewis 1993; van Kersbergen 1995).

penalized families with two wage earners. In that sense, the typical institutions of the continental welfare state, inherited from the time of welfare state growth, encourage and reward the labor market participation of the male breadwinner.

The corporatist regime type also generates a high amount of stratification because benefit levels tend to be earnings related. The underlying principle is that, in the event of a life risk (e.g., old age, accident, invalidity, sickness, unemployment), the beneficiary should be able to maintain his or her living standards (i.e., place in the social stratification) for a given time. Stratification is the result of the alignment of the working-class social democrats with middle-class voters: in order to achieve the support of the middle class for welfare state expansion, the members of the middle class had to become beneficiaries of financial transfers, too. However, the continental European left was not strong enough to push through a universalistic scheme as in Scandinavia, and thus the best possible option for the left was to support earnings-related insurance.[4]

Insurance-based social policy is the main feature of stratification, and familialism explains why continental welfare states focus so much on the decommodification of labor market insiders. In that sense, *income insurance* and *familialism* are the two key principles of continental welfare states. Beyond these key principles, however, the specific design of continental welfare state policies needs to be conceptualized with regard to more readily observable institutional characteristics. Bonoli and Palier (1998, based on Ferrera 1996) have defined four sets of welfare institutions, which allow us to characterize a welfare regime as more or less continental, or Bismarckian. First, in an ideal-typical continental welfare state, eligibility for benefits depends on labor market participation and employment status rather than citizenship rights. Hence, the more strongly eligibility is tied to employment, the more clearly a welfare regime is continental. Second, the structure of benefits is earnings related rather than flat and egalitarian. The level of the replacement rate (i.e., the percentage of previous earnings paid in the case of a risk) is therefore the key measure for the generosity of welfare policies. The higher this rate, the more the welfare regime focuses on income replacement as a typical feature of continental social policy. Third, in accordance with the insurance principle, benefits tend to be financed by contributions on wages rather than by general taxes. This strengthens the direct link between labor market participation and welfare coverage. Accordingly, the degree of contribution financing of the welfare regime can be regarded as an indicator of continental social policy. Last, the administration and management of social security programs typically involves the social partners – labor and capital – who co-decide on social policy regulations, thereby becoming de jure or de facto veto players with regard to welfare reforms. The degree of co-management is thus a last indicator of continental welfare policies.

---

4 It should be noted that – in a production regime theory perspective – earnings-related benefits could also be interpreted as a straightforward answer to investment in specific skills, which is highly important in the coordinated market economies of Western Europe (Estevez-Abe et al. 2001).

These four institutional characteristics help us understand why the continental welfare states have become so dramatically dysfunctional over the past thirty years. Given their financing and eligibility structure, the success of continental welfare states in covering the social needs of the population largely depends on full male employment and economic growth. In the decades of economic growth after 1945, these conditions were met, for the most part. Employers were able to pay generous and increasingly equal wages, which allowed the state to encourage organization of the labor market based on single-earner families, ever earlier exit from the labor market, and increasingly generous pension transfers. The heavy dependence on full employment, however, started to become a serious liability from the 1970s onward, when several structural developments converged toward the beginning of what Pierson (2001: 410) called a context of "permanent austerity."

The most important developments were the transition to a service-based economy and fading economic growth. Iversen and Wren (1998) have argued that the simultaneous combination of full employment, wage equality, and budgetary restraint would hardly be tenable in this movement from an industrial to a service economy: employment in the service sector is generally less productive than industrial employment. Hence, an increase in service-sector employment should lead to increasing wage inequality, unless the sectors reequilibrate wages (which the highly productive industrial sectors are unlikely to accept). An increase in public service-sector employment, however, is largely prohibited by the budgetary restraints that stem from fading growth. Moreover, the high payroll taxes and the developed employment protection regulations in continental labor markets discourage job growth in the private service sector. This is why high rates of (long-term) unemployment have become a sad constant in most continental European economies. In the 1970s and early 1980s, the welfare states tried to remedy this problem by reducing the size of the workforce – promoting early retirement and conservative family policies – and by raising social contributions on the wages of the employed to finance rising unemployment insurance costs (Palier 2002; Palier and Martin 2007). This reaction reflected the hopes that the employment crisis would be only cyclical, not structural. Unfortunately, this was rather shortsighted: the transformation of the employment structure proved long term and lasting. In the end, the strategy of reducing the size of the workforce generated increasing old-age (early retirement) and disability pensioners and family policy benefit recipients, thereby increasing the cost of labor even more and worsening the problem of lagging job growth. It goes without saying that long-term low employment rates are calamitous for a welfare state in which eligibility, the level of benefits, and the financing of social protection all rely on employment. Indeed, ever fewer people must bear the burden of financing benefits for ever more beneficiaries. Esping-Andersen (1996b: 66) termed this configuration the problem of "welfare without work," that is, an unbalanced proportion of contributors and beneficiaries.

Demographic changes (e.g., a declining fertility rate) only added to the structural disequilibrium caused by the realities of the welfare-without-work phenomenon. As outlined previously, female labor market participation tends to be low in continental welfare states. Because of the growing uncertainty of male breadwinners' income and the frustration of an increasingly highly trained female workforce unable to reconcile work and child care, fertility rates declined dramatically, especially in Western and Southern Europe, adding to the problem of having fewer labor market participants finance the pension benefits of more pensioners who were living longer, thereby raising both pension and health-care costs.

With declining numbers of people paying contributions to support more beneficiaries, states can increase contribution levels for the employed, increase the public debt to cofinance the growing social expenditures, or lower benefit levels and social rights. The first two solutions are more attractive from an electoral standpoint, but these options have been largely avoided for two reasons. First, higher contribution levels have become less tolerable because of the constraints of international economic competition (here, economic globalization finally appears on the scene of the continental welfare regime drama as the last "usual suspect" [Schwartz 2001: 17]). Second, the stability pact of the European Economic and Monetary Union precludes exorbitant public household deficits. Therefore, permanent austerity and the pressure for retrenchment have become fixtures on the political agendas in these countries. What seemed to be at stake at the beginning of the 1990s was nothing less than the "survival of the European welfare state" (Kuhnle 2000).

A New Model of Post-Industrial Welfare State Change

Since the beginning of the 1990s, an important literature has emerged on the lack of adaptation of the European welfare states to the pressure for retrenchment. While an early power resources literature expected dismantling of the welfare state, the subsequent neo-institutionalist literature explained and predicted the ongoing stability of welfare institutions. By now, however, both of these have turned out to be wrong. Continental welfare states have been neither dismantled nor frozen, but they do undergo complex processes of reconfiguration along a number of reform dimensions. This section briefly shows the sense in which previous theories of welfare state transformation have failed to explain the current restructuring of welfare states, and it then provides a new explanatory model.

Retrenchment theories based on power resource assumptions predicted a dismantling of continental welfare states and envisioned a scenario comparable to the cutbacks of social benefits in the UK in the 1980s (Myles and Pierson 1997). Because power resources theory views the extent of social protection as the momentary reflection of the power balance between labor and capital, it hypothesized that large-scale unemployment would quasi-automatically shift bargaining power in favor of capital and consequently lead to fewer social rights for workers (Scharpf and Schmidt 2000; Korpi and Palme 2003). However, until the late 1990s, there was no massive retrenchment of the existing benefit structures (Huber and Stephens 2001; Stephens, Huber and Ray 1999; Pierson 2001). Quite the contrary, expenditure levels continued to rise, and the size of the welfare state was not significantly reduced in any of the Nordic and continental countries.

The observation of stability instead of retrenchment brought institutionalist approaches to the forefront, which focused on mechanisms of path dependency, inertia, and institutional equilibria. Advocates of varieties of capitalism have suggested that welfare policies are complementary to existing institutions in other realms of production regimes (Hall and Soskice 2001; Estevez-Abe et al. 2001), which stabilizes existing institutional arrangements. Moreover, in the production regime perspective, existing welfare state policies are interpreted as in the common interest of organized labor and capital. Hence, even if it were true that increasing budgetary restraint and unemployment strengthen the power of capital, this would not necessarily require the dismantling of the welfare state; capitalists might as well support existing social policies (Mares 2003).[5]

Paul Pierson (1996, 2001) launched an equally institutionalist theory of the new politics of the welfare state. His reasoning rested on the idea that the mature welfare state is inherently averse to any change, as it creates constituencies of beneficiaries powerful enough to make retrenchment too risky a strategy for any government in a democratic electoral context. Indeed, he argued that, by developing generous programs, policy makers have triggered unintended consequences: these benefit programs transform the set of actors and interests involved in social policy making, making it too politically costly to cut them back. The empirical evidence seemed to support institutionalist claims of stability throughout the 1990s. However, it took only a few years to reveal that this story of inertia did not account for the complex reform dynamics at play in European welfare states, either. There was growing empirical evidence that even the continental welfare states were changing considerably, and not just in the direction of retrenchment. As illustrated in Chapter 1, many reforms actually *extended* existing coverage schemes to new groups of beneficiaries (Bonoli 2005a, 2006b), such as labor market outsiders, women, and long-term-care patients. Others enacted changes that transformed the very structure of welfare state design, moving, for example, from contribution financing to more tax financing and capitalization.

There is a growing literature documenting and categorizing these institutional changes (see, e.g., Palier and Martin 2007; Streeck and Thelen 2005; Armingeon and Bonoli 2006; Palier forthcoming). This literature is important because it challenges the idea of institutional inertia and sclerosis. However, a conclusive new theoretical framework explaining the current reform dynamics is still lacking. This is what I develop in the remainder of this chapter, building on three strands of recent theorizing: (1) new social risks, (2) timing, and (3) the multidimensionality of welfare state reform.

The literature on new social risks, mainly based on the works of Bonoli (2005a, 2006b), contains a crucial insight for my theoretical framework: pressure for

---

[5] In a similar vein, Katzenstein (1984) and Gourevitch (1986) had already demonstrated much earlier how social partners often reach important agreements in times of serious crisis, eschewing dissolution in favor of cooperation.

retrenchment is *not the only* structural challenge facing European welfare states. The transition to post-industrial labor markets and the changing family structure (what Esping-Andersen [1999] calls the failure of labor markets and families) have generated a specific set of new risks, which tend to be covered only poorly by existing welfare states, especially in continental welfare regimes.[6] Old risks are those accidents of life that endanger the income of the male breadwinner in industrial society (e.g., old age, short-term unemployment, sickness, disability, accidents). These risks are still as important as they were in industrial society, and the social insurance programs of the continental welfare state strive to protect individuals from exactly this set of threats. Alongside these old risks, however, three changes in the labor market have brought a new set of poverty risks to the forefront (see also Taylor-Gooby 2005). First, women are taking on paid work in increasing numbers and many of them (mostly low-skilled women and single mothers) struggle for a decent wage and for the ability to combine work and care. Second, the increasing need to give care to elderly relatives imposes additional stress on people (mostly women) who need to earn a living in the labor market. Third, changes in labor market structures have increased poverty and long-term unemployment risks for less skilled workers, workers with obsolete skills, and employees with atypical work contracts. It appears clear that these risks harm people who, for various reasons, are not in stable employment. Therefore, they are particularly salient in continental welfare regimes, where social rights depend precisely on stable, standard employment.[7] However, new social risks go well beyond new poverty risks. The demand for child care and care of the elderly or social benefits for divorced spouses are examples of social needs that have arisen from the transition to post-industrial social and economic structures. The development of these policies may be motivated not necessarily, or exclusively, by efforts to curb poverty but by value considerations: indeed, the lack of those policies is at odds with the social structures and values of a post-industrial society, in which individualization and gender equality are highly valued by a proportion of the society that has grown considerably since the 1950s (Kitschelt 1994).[8] Hence, new social risk policies are likely to be not only interest driven but also value driven.

The new social risk literature has made it clear that post-industrial welfare state reform is not only about retrenchment but also about a plurality of constraints, needs, and demands. This is of crucial importance for the understanding of reform

---

[6] The country chapters in two edited volumes by Armingeon and Bonoli (2006) and Taylor-Gooby (2005) provide descriptions of the lack of new social risk coverage in most continental European countries.

[7] The new risk groups may become larger in the Nordic and liberal welfare states, too, but because of their more egalitarian structure of benefits – especially in the universalistic Nordic scheme, where social rights are based on citizenship – these welfare states also cover the post-industrial risk groups (Bonoli 2006; Huber and Stephens 2006).

[8] Kitschelt (1994) has best conceptualized this new divide of libertarian and authoritarian values. Libertarians stress the importance of universalism, individualism, free lifestyle choices, and gender equality, whereas authoritarians prioritize traditional power and family structures.

politics in a multidimensional policy space, which I develop in this book. However, to explain recent social policy reforms, we need to spell out more explicitly the (temporal) links between new and old social risk politics. Timing is of crucial importance, as policy makers deal with a whole research agenda, not with single reform issues. Therefore, we cannot understand new social risk policies unless we analyze them in the context of retrenchment pressure and cost containment policies, and vice versa.

Timing matters (Pierson 2000b, 2004) because the politics of reform depend on when and in which context an issue emerges on the agenda. The structural changes leading to new social risks had already occurred in the Nordic countries in the 1960s, a time of economic growth and prosperity. Providing universalistic benefits and services, such as generous child care in Scandinavia, was, of course, much less contentious in times of abundance (Bonoli 2006b). The same development is difficult to imagine in the continental world, where the new demands for welfare state modernization emerged twenty years later (i.e., in hard times). In continental Europe, new social risks and a change in values arose precisely at a time when resources became scarce, not only with regard to new social risks but also with regard to the maintenance of existing levels of social protection. When the pie becomes smaller, distributional conflicts become sharper. Welfare politics in an era of austerity are, to some extent, a zero-sum game and put in opposition the needs of different constituencies. Consequently, only the *conjuncture* of the pressures of austerity and post-industrialization, and their simultaneous clash with preexisting welfare institutions, can account for the particular opportunity structure for policy reforms that emerged from the 1970s in continental Europe. This conjuncture generates particular constraints and opportunities for reforms: the different challenges produce a multidimensional reform agenda, meaning that the demands for welfare reform go in very different directions. In addition, actors are likely to defend their narrow interests because the context of austerity makes solidarity among different constituencies more costly and more difficult. This idea of multidimensionality and narrow actor preferences immediately carries the need for a coalitional approach to the understanding of institutional change. Post-industrial reform politics in continental Europe become politics of exchange in policy spaces structured by multiple conflict lines.[9]

Having pointed out the relevance of new social risks and timing, I would like to refer to the recent literature on multiple, concurrent reform dimensions as a third and final key element in the construction of my theoretical framework. This literature is particularly useful for identifying the specific conflict lines that structure the modernization of continental welfare states. Levy (1999), in his compelling actor-centered analysis of French reform politics, argues that continental welfare regimes often display highly unequal, segmented benefit structures and frequently provide privileges to particular groups of beneficiaries. In a post-industrial society

---

[9] Bonoli (2001), Natali and Rhodes (2004), and Clasen and Clegg (2006) mention political exchange as an important mechanism of reform early on. However, this early literature is rather inductive and does not fully theorize the dynamics of the political exchange behind these policy packages.

and in times of austerity, these inequalities tend to lose legitimacy in the eyes of the public. Simultaneously, new risks appear on the agenda. In his analysis, he shows how this configuration of diverse challenges provided France's socialist government with an opportunity to "turn vices into virtues" (Levy 1999) – cutting back existing privileges and reallocating expenditures to new risk groups. More theoretically driven, Pierson (2001) argues that a close look at recent reform challenges evidences at least three different goals of post-industrial continental policy reforms: (1) cost containment, which encompasses all attempts to make the generous industrial welfare state more fiscally viable, (2) recommodification, which means that many policies aim to bring women, early retirees and the unemployed back into paid work by means of activation policies, and (c) recalibration, or the adaptation of the welfare state to new organizational technologies (i.e., rationalizing) and new social needs and demands (i.e., updating, which comes close covering new social risks). Pointing to selective evidence from Bonoli (2001b) and Manow (2001), Pierson then suggests that this combination of reforms might open up opportunities for political exchange and unexpected coalitions of actors. Pierson thus hints that an explanation of recent reform outputs needs to focus on coalitional dynamics in a multidimensional policy space.

Unfortunately, the distinction among cost containment, recommodification, and recalibration is problematic because it is not exclusive. Many cost-containing reforms are simultaneously commodifying, as they force workers to rely more strongly on the labor market to make a living. Similarly, the merging of insurance plans for the public and private sectors is both recalibrating and cost containing. In summary, many reforms pursue several such goals simultaneously. However, both Levy's and Pierson's conceptualizations of possible reform goals are useful for identifying four overarching reform trends that dominate the agenda of continental welfare state modernizations: (1) retrenchment of benefit levels, (2) reform of financing mechanisms, (3) targeted reforms of the welfare privileges of specific occupational groups, and (4) an adaptation of welfare states to new social needs and demands. These are the four reform dimensions on which my theoretical framework relies.

Calls for the lowering of benefit levels have become loud and powerful in all continental welfare states. The argument that low labor market participation rates cannot generate enough contribution payments to finance ever-growing social insurance expenditures puts the levels and the very structure of the existing social policies into question. In this context, *retrenchment* has become a predominant focus of reform proposals. Such proposals all pursue the same goal of cost containment, even though they come in very different forms: lowered replacement rates, tightened eligibility criteria, longer required contribution periods, shorter benefit periods, and so on.

However, austerity also motivates reform proposals that target not just the level but also the very design and financing structure of the continental welfare state. Although the reforms tend to have cost-containing effects as well, they simultaneously focus on what Pierson termed recommodification (2001: 421). A far-reaching recommodification trend comes in the form of privatized and individualized pay-as-you-go social insurance. Pay-as-you-go financing implies that the risks of all the insured are pooled, and that the benefits paid at time o are financed by means of the contributions of all insured at time o. This financing structure can become problematic when the ratio of contributors and beneficiaries becomes unbalanced. *Capitalization* and privatization strengthen the link between contributions and rights, as every risk group finances only its own benefits. This implies a stronger differentiation (or desolidarization) of risk structures and insurance premiums. In the most extreme case of desolidarization, individuals formally finance their own insurance in an individualized insurance market.

Furthermore, austerity contributes to the questioning of social protection privileges for certain groups of insured. This is another characteristic of the highly stratifying and segmented continental welfare states, which often include differentiated insurance schemes for groups such as public-sector employees, executives, or workers in particular industries (Esping-Andersen 1990). The continental social insurance programs often grant particularly generous conditions and benefits to these occupational groups, and they are often even cofinanced by general tax revenue (i.e., by all taxpayers). Although these differences may have been tolerable in times of abundance, many of them have become anachronistic and now lack legitimacy (Levy 1999). Hence, the *targeting* of particular occupational privileges is a third dimension of continental welfare state reform, and it is both cost containing and recalibrating.

Finally, the agenda of continental welfare state modernization contains a large set of new social needs and demands. These reform issues relate to what Pierson calls *recalibration* (2001: 421). The entry of women into the labor market and the proliferation of atypical work contracts have increased the number of insufficiently insured people, making more salient the issues of new social risks or labor market precariousness. In addition, the traditional organization of work and family, based on stable families organized around a single male breadwinner in stable full-time employment, is being increasingly questioned. This blueprint not only has become obsolete in light of contemporary social realities (e.g., rising divorce rates, more skilled female workers, declining fertility rates, rampant unemployment in industrial sectors) but also contradicts the normative values and lifestyle aspirations of large social groups in a post-industrial society. The existing institutions of the continental welfare state are entirely at odds with post-industrial values such as gender equality, individualization, and the pluralism of individual lifestyles. For these reasons, the clash of post-industrial social needs with existing continental welfare state institutions brings forth political claims for improved coverage for outsiders and even questions the whole underlying principle of the stratified, insurance-based welfare regime. The increased presence of women in the labor force also amplifies demands for the protection of nonstandard employment and raises claims for a child-care and elderly-care infrastructure to allow for the conciliation of work and care. In Pierson's terms (2001), this strand of post-industrial reform policy is recalibrating, but it is also important not to overlook its commodifying character. Because many women are no longer able or willing to rely on a male breadwinner, the (commodifying) solution is to allow more women to earn their individual social insurance rights themselves. This reform strategy does not question the insurance-based principles of the continental welfare

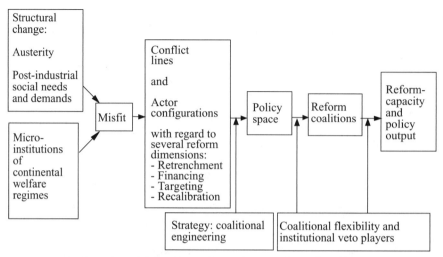

FIGURE 2.1. Analytical model for the analysis of post-industrial welfare state reform in continental Europe

state but aims to enlarge the scope of coverage. The inclusion of atypical work in insurance goes in this direction, as does the strengthening of the child-care infrastructure, maternity insurance, and parental leave schemes. Such policies are both value driven and commodifying. They can be seen in the perspective of an ideological trend toward a social investment state, whose underlying principle is to enable all citizens to participate in the labor market (Lister 2004).

Over the past twenty years, reforms along these four dimensions – retrenchment, capitalization or privatization, targeting, and recalibration – have dominated the continental welfare reform agendas. Each of the four dimensions involves a specific set of winners and losers, which is why all of them generate their own distinctive conflict lines and actor configurations. This plurality of actor configurations provides the basis and potential for multidimensional politics: policy entrepreneurs can try to link and combine different conflict lines to form specific majorities for their reform projects. Their chances of succeeding in this attempt of coalitional engineering depend on the institutional framework, and power-fragmenting institutions are more favorable than power-concentrating institutions for flexible coalition building. If policy makers are strategic enough to propose large reform packages, and if the institutional framework allows for some flexibility, then the multidimensionality of the policy space becomes the key factor allowing for policy change and welfare state modernization.

With this discussion of the literature, we are now ready to put the pieces together: I propose an integrated model for the analysis of post-industrial welfare state reforms in continental Europe in Figure 2.1.[10] The model leads from the

---

[10] The reader will easily see that the model can be adapted to other regimes by a respective specification of the relevant micro-institutions and reform dimensions.

emergence of structural change over the reconfiguration of policy spaces and actor configurations to the formation of reform coalitions and actual policy outputs.

Let me go briefly through the main steps of the model. The structural challenges of austerity and post-industrial social needs clash with the old micro-institutions of the continental welfare regimes. These inherited institutions are unable to deal successfully with the new post-industrial environment, both in terms of financial sustainability and in terms of their effectiveness in providing welfare to the relevant risk groups. The misfit that results from this inadequacy translates into a plurality of potential reform dimensions and conflict lines, which can be mobilized by policy makers in the reform processes. Through processes of coalition building in multidimensional policy spaces, policy makers can enhance the reform capacity of a country, provided that they act in a favorable macro-institutional environment. In a way, and quite paradoxically, the fact that continental welfare regimes are challenged so massively and in so many respects simultaneously may contribute to the very modernization of the regimes.

To assess the empirical value of this multidimensional explanation of recent welfare state modernization, one needs to analyze each policy field separately, as each constitutes a distinct realm of reform politics with specific issues, actors, and institutions. A meaningful analysis of post-industrial welfare state reforms therefore requires two analytical steps. First, one must draw an inventory of the conflict dimensions that define the reform space of a specific policy field. Second, within this policy space, one must model the constantly evolving positions of actors along the major lines of conflict to identify opportunities and constraints for alliances and the building of majorities. This book provides a detailed theoretical and empirical account of the post-industrial reform agenda for pension policy in Germany, France, and Switzerland. Pension policy is the prototype of a supposedly sclerotic social policy scheme, with entrenched institutions and actors unlikely and unwilling to change. At the same time, it is a policy field facing the toughest challenges in terms of financial sustainability and societal modernization. Therefore, the crucial relevance of multidimensionality for pension modernization also speaks to the dynamics of continental welfare reforms more generally.

PART I

PENSION REFORM IN CONTINENTAL EUROPE

A Framework of Analysis

3

A New Reform Agenda

Old-Age Security in the Post-Industrial Era

Both austerity and post-industrialization challenge all the major social policy schemes of the continental welfare states. Whether it is in labor market and unemployment policy, health-care provision, family policy, child and elderly care, poverty alleviation, or old-age security, there are serious threats to the long-term financial viability, and – simultaneously – challenges stemming from newly emerging social needs. However, each social policy scheme is affected by the same structural developments in a very specific way, and policy makers must thus react in an equally specific way. In labor market policy, for instance, the challenge consists in easing the structural adjustment of job markets under the constraint of financial austerity (on recent labor market and unemployment policy developments, see, e.g., Esping-Andersen and Regini 2000; Rueda 2005; Clasen and Clegg 2006; Clegg 2007), whereas health policy makers struggle to find a middle ground between the technologically feasible and the economically rational in a context of demographic aging (on recent health policy developments, see, e.g., Wendt and Thompson 2004; Hassenteufel and Palier 2007). In a similar vein, family and care policy is caught amid contradictory developments: there has been an explosion of care needs for both the elderly and children; an increase in women seeking paid work outside the home; and increasing poverty rates, especially among single mothers (on recent family policy developments, see, e.g., Jenson and Sineau 2001; Dienel 2002; Leitner, Ostner, and Schratzenstaller 2004). Not least, social assistance reform is supposed to combine answers to growing needs – which often result from retrenchment in other fields – with an increased accent on activation, social investment, and recommodification (on recent social assistance policy developments, see, e.g., Cattacin et al. 2002; Lister 2004). Finally, the concurrence of different reform pressures is no less acute in pension policy, which is by far the largest social policy program in mature welfare states. Financial stability is threatened by low economic growth rates, enduring unemployment, and demographic aging. At the same time, new needs arise from changing labor markets, declining family stability, and calls for gender equality. In summary, each policy field deals with its very own, specific post-industrial reform agenda.

These differences are important because the policy-specific sets of challenges determine the politics and reform dynamics in each respective policy subsystem. This is why the theoretical and empirical analysis of reform politics must be broken down separately for each policy. This is precisely what I do in this first part of the book, by focusing on continental pension policies.

The decision to use pension policy to test my theoretical model of post-industrial social policy making may seem somewhat awkward at first glance. Indeed, the most obvious new social needs have emerged in the fields of family policy, child care, elderly care, and long-term unemployment and/or activation (Bonoli 2005). Old-age income security, by contrast, is a typical "old" risk, which has been a centerpiece of the welfare state from its very beginnings in the postwar era. Since workers' pension rights have been at the heart of the industrial class compromise between labor and capital, pension policy has been regarded as one of the main battlefields of the industrial class conflict. In addition, pension policy deals with long-term commitments and is therefore unlikely to vary strongly over time in terms of actors, interests, and coalitions. As Bonoli and Palier (2007: 556) put it, continental pension systems "represent the quintessence of difficulties to be associated with Bismarckian welfare institutions," because they are so sensitive to demographic changes and lacking (job) growth. At the same time, these systems are particularly difficult to reform because of their visibility and legitimacy with the electorate. All of these features would lead us to expect stable, if not inert, conflict dynamics (i.e., the contrary of multidimensionality and changing conflict lines).

Nevertheless, I argue for precisely the foregoing reasons that pension policy is a particularly promising case for the hard testing of my modernization thesis, according to which new post-industrial conflict lines, namely value divides and cross-class antagonisms, become decisive in the explanation of contemporary reform outputs. Indeed, few analysts of the welfare state would be surprised by the emergence of cross-class conflicts and value-driven reform dynamics in fields such as family or long-term-care policy. By contrast, it is much less intuitive that these new dimensions of policy making are considered key even in pension policy. Yet this is precisely what I want to demonstrate in the following chapters. By doing so, I contradict a range of recent analyses, which – though not necessarily questioning the existence of new social needs in other social policy fields – analyze pension politics only as a conflict of retrenchment versus stability (e.g., Schludi 2005; Schulze 2007; to a large extent also Myles and Pierson 2001 and Kitschelt 2001). I argue that this focus on the single (albeit highly important) reform dimension of retrenchment is precisely what accounts for the failure of these analyses to make sense of recent reform capacity and reform outputs.

Conflict Dimensions in Continental Pension Policy

Old-age security schemes are under pressure from two major sources – financial austerity on the one hand and demands for expanded outsider coverage, gender equality, and individualization on the other hand. Both pressures result from the fact that continental pension policy is particularly at odds with post-industrialism.

The following discussion thus starts with a brief characterization of the ideal-typical institutions of continental old-age security schemes and then proceeds to demonstrate the specific challenges that the new context implies for those schemes.

The institutions of continental pension policy reflect what Esping-Andersen (1990, 1999) identified more generally as the characteristics of continental regimes: the decommodification of labor market insiders, social stratification, and the enactment of a male-breadwinner society. Insider decommodification results from the principle of equivalence, which holds that insurance rights are proportional to contribution payments. Labor market insiders – workers in standard employment – contribute to public insurance schemes over the forty years or so of a standard employment biography and thereby earn rights to income replacement upon their retirement. Because these pension regimes are the outcome of class compromise between labor and capital (Huber and Stephens 2001; Palier 2002), almost all workers are insured in the basic public pension scheme, whereas private (occupational) pensions tend to be marginal (Schludi 2005). The continental insurance schemes generally work on a pay-as-you-go (PAYG) basis, which means that the contribution payments of the current working population are directly used to pay the pension entitlements of the current retired generation. Coverage for workers in standard employment is rather generous, with income replacement rates at around 60 percent of the former gross income (i.e., on average, about 80 percent of the former net income) (Organisation of Economic Co-operation and Development [OECD] 2005). High replacement rates for standard employees are intended to guarantee status preservation (i.e., the maintenance of the living standard an insured person enjoyed during his or her working life) (Schludi 2005). In addition, the status of labor market insiders and male breadwinners in their families is strengthened through a range of direct and derived insurance rights in case of disability or death (e.g., widows' pensions). Typically, these derived rights are also tied to the level of the former income (Abramovici 2002).

The equivalence principle is also the primary reason for the strong stratification effect of these regimes. Because benefits depend greatly on the former income, the levels of inequality tend to be much the same for the retired population as they are for the active population (OECD 2005). This means that continental pension policy has few redistributive effects. In addition, continental pension schemes are highly unegalitarian because of the corporatist fragmentation of insurance schemes: there usually exist several special pension insurance schemes for particular occupational groups, notably for civil servants, executives, and farmers.[1] The fragmentation of insurance schemes coincides with the sectoral fragmentation of the economy and of trade unions in coordinated market economies (Hall and Soskice 2001). Therefore, insurance conditions may differ

---

[1] Esping-Andersen (1990) even used pension insurance fragmentation as a proxy for the degree of corporatism in a country. He counted no fewer than ten major occupational pension schemes in France, six in Germany, twelve in Italy, seven in Austria, and five in Belgium, against much fewer, more centralized schemes in the Anglo-Saxon and Scandinavian world.

strongly among the various insurance schemes, being on average decidedly more generous for high-skilled employees and civil servants.[2] Finally, the equivalence principle and corporatist insurance fragmentation aside, the third source of strat- ification comes in the form of exclusive eligibility rules. On the one hand, workers generally need a minimum amount of labor market participation to have access to a regular public pension scheme, which tends to exclude or penalize temporary or part-time employment. On the other hand, entitlement to a full pension typi- cally requires a contribution record of thirty-seven to forty-five years. This only amplifies the inequalities inherent in the system, and it exacerbates the divide between labor market insiders and outsiders: whereas insiders work in standard employment, outsiders typically have discontinuous and incomplete employment biographies (Häusermann and Schwander 2009).

This brief characterization of the ideal-typical micro-institutions of continen- tal pension policy shows clearly that these "pension schemes ... have been devel- oped by men with men in mind" (Finlayson 1988, qtd. in Myles 1984: 135). They provide highly developed, secure, and rather generous old-age income protection for male breadwinners and, indirectly, for their families. This gender differential effect is the result of three factors: first, the culture of subsidiarity and familialism in continental Europe in the 1950s and 1960s provided a normative blueprint for the society, which the state was supposed to support and further; second, in the industrial era, the male-breadwinner society was not only a normative goal but also the social reality – characterized by full male standard employment, low female employment, and low divorce rates. Hence, the continental pension schemes were a highly apt and widely effective (i.e., a functional response to the social needs of that time). The third reason is, of course, actor related: as a mat- ter of fact, continental welfare regimes were indeed designed by men: by trade unions, employer organizations, and governments, all of them strongholds of industrial patriarchy in the 1950s and 1960s. They shaped insurance conditions according to the interests of their male-breadwinner constituency.

From the 1950s onward, the continental pension schemes grew sharply, in line with these principles of insider decommodification, stratification, and male- breadwinner security. The remarkable growth of pension regimes reflects the corporatist class compromise (Myles and Pierson 2001; Huber and Stephens 2001). However, while still in the phase of expansion, the institutions of continen- tal pension policy started to become dysfunctional. From the 1970s onward, the institutions increasingly clashed with growing austerity pressures, post-industrial social structures, and emerging libertarian values. This clash produced a variety of *misfits* with regard to benefit structures, the mode of financing, and the cri- teria of eligibility. My first hypothesis in this study deals with the implications of these contradictions for the politics of pension reform: the misfit between the structural pressures of austerity and post-industrialism on the one hand and

---

[2] Striking examples of such privileges can be found in the public-sector pension regimes of Austria, France, and Germany; these systems are financed by means of general taxation instead of contri- butions. This means that private-sector workers assume the costs of both their own pensions and the considerably higher pensions of civil servants.

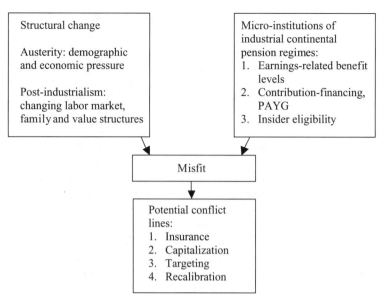

FIGURE 3.1. Structural potentials for a post-industrial pension-reform agenda

the micro-institutions of the continental pension regimes on the other hand leads to potentials for new conflict lines in the continental pension policy space (see Figure 3.1). It is important to note that, even if a misfit between structure and institutions is blatant, the ensuing political conflict lines are only potential; although such conflict potentials may be structurally available, they must be mobilized by actors to become salient and relevant in politics. Hence, a simple functionalist view on institutional change would be inherently misleading. However, I assume that the potentials for post-industrial conflict lines are largely similar across the different continental welfare states.

The post-industrial continental pension agenda can be grouped into four broad dimensions of reform: (1) generous insurance conditions stir debates on the retrenchment of benefit levels; (2) demographic threats raise the issue of complementing PAYG schemes with capitalized pension plans; (3) post-industrial labor markets create specific needs for targeting policies, which improve the coverage of occupational groups in precarious employment relations; and (4) family instability and libertarian values lead to claims for recalibrating policies to cover people (mostly women) with discontinuous employment biographies. Each of these potential reform dimensions entails a distinct pattern of conflict among and between beneficiaries, contributors, firms, and so on. In the following, I develop the content of each conflict potential more precisely and identify the likely winners and losers for each of them.

Insurance: The Distributional Politics of Cost Containment
Continental pension policies provide rather generous pensions for retirees with a complete contribution record. Benefit levels were raised consistently until the

1970s; this was done by altering the general insurance parameters, such as the level of replacement rates, the pension calculation formula, the age of retirement, or the indexation of pensions to inflation. However, all these improvements have come at a high cost. By the mid-1990s, the pension systems of all the continental welfare regimes experienced growing annual deficits of 2 percent to 7 percent of the national gross domestic product (GDP) (Schludi 2005). Declining economic growth and rising unemployment rates prevented the revenues from keeping pace with the expenditures for a growing population of retirees. The prospects of waning financial stability were already emerging toward the end of the 1970s; over time, the conditions transformed into a context of "permanent austerity" by the 1990s (Pierson 2001: 410), when economic problems were increasingly accentuated by demographic aging. Advocates of cost containment and retrenchment argue that the existing level of benefits is no longer viable in the post-industrial context of austerity, and their opponents stress the need for stable income security, particularly in times of failing labor markets. For these reasons, conflicts over cost controls have become increasingly frequent in pension policy making in continental welfare regimes. The more vulnerable the institutional design of pension schemes is to economic and demographic threats, the more prominent these debates become. I label this conflict line "insurance," because it deals with the extent of insurance rights and with the restructuring of general insurance conditions. Insurance conflicts come in very different forms: because it is electorally risky for governments to promote retrenchment with highly visible measures (Pierson 1996), they may pursue the same goal in some more hidden way. Examples of such obfuscated cost-containing strategies include cutting back on early retirement possibilities; lengthening the required contribution period for a full pension; extending the reference period for the calculation of pension rights (e.g., 60 percent of the best twenty instead of ten years of the career); lowering the value of pension credit points; changing the indexation mechanism from gross to net wages or to prices; and switching from defined-benefit to defined-contribution schemes, thereby tightening the link between contributions and benefits.

Insurance reforms may include both expansion and retrenchment, but debates concerning retrenchment have become more salient in the post-industrial era. Either way, insurance reforms affect all insured in the same way, and they affect all employers similarly, as they influence the cost of labor through pay-roll taxes. For this reason, I hypothesize that debates on insurance divide capital and labor (i.e., they tend to produce a *class conflict*). Employees defend pension rights, whereas capitalists are interested in containing pension costs. All other post-industrial pension-reform dimensions, however, are more likely to foster cross-class conflicts.

Capitalization: Redefining Solidarity in Pension Financing
Insurance, and especially retrenchment, are key issues on the continental pension-reform agenda. However, an exclusive focus on the level of benefits tends to overlook reform proposals that go even deeper, tackling the fundamental logic of the continental pension regimes as such. One of these more structural reform

dimensions concerns the financing mechanisms of pension schemes. As outlined earlier, most continental pension schemes are contribution financed and operate on a PAYG basis. Contribution financing implies solidarity among all members of the risk pool. The legitimacy of this financing mode depends on the link between the amount of contributions every insured pays and the level of benefits that he or she can expect on retirement. This link may become distorted, however, if the two groups of beneficiaries and contributors become increasingly distinct. Demographic aging induces precisely this kind of drift: the contributing generation becomes smaller, and the number of beneficiaries increases. In continental welfare states, the old-age dependency ratio is expected to rise from about 1:4 in the late 1990s to almost 1:2 in no more than thirty or forty years (Schludi 2005). Hence, demographic aging may shatter the confidence of contributors in the stability of the scheme. If the intertemporal equivalence between contributions and benefits fails, the pension scheme actually turns from insurance to redistribution, shifting wealth from the active population toward the nonactive population. For this reason, I hypothesize that, in a context of demographic aging, conflicts concerning the extent of solidarity in pension financing will become increasingly frequent. Such conflicts may particularly arise with regard to reform proposals that promote the supplementing of PAYG schemes with capitalized pension funds. Advocates of capitalization argue that the insurance character of pension regimes needs to be preserved. Therefore, they suggest the introduction of funded pension layers, through which each generation of contributors will finance its own pensions. Funded pension schemes are generally not universal but imply a more limited risk pool, ranging from the workforce of a sector or a firm (in the case of occupational pensions) to each individual contributing for his or her very own and private pension plan. Hence, capitalization may imply some solidarity in a generation, but it certainly reduces intergenerational solidarity, which the advocates of PAYG see as the very core of pension policy. Therefore, capitalization puts the advocates of individual capitalized pension funds into conflict with the proponents of intergenerational solidarity.

Advocates of capitalization propose to add funded pension pillars to the existing public pension schemes (Bonoli and Palier 2007), so that employees would both contribute to the general public scheme and to their own, capitalized savings scheme. As a result, capitalization should result in a conflict structured by *skills*, because it is more attractive for high-skilled and/or high-income earners to invest part of their salary in pension savings than it is for the low skilled, whose incomes leave little room for savings that go beyond the regular pension contributions to the public schemes. Furthermore, pension funds provide employers with the opportunity to create highly attractive pension savings plans for their most valuable employees. In Switzerland, many employers pay two-thirds or even the whole amount of executives' contributions to the occupational pension pillar (Suter and Mathey 2000). Thereby, they ensure and reward the loyalty of highly skilled employees. Hence, capitalization is likely to foster intra-labor heterogeneity based on *skills*, as for highly skilled employees, funded pension savings plans can be an attractive (and often fiscally encouraged) investment option. On the side of employees, preferences are likely to be equally heterogeneous: capitalized (occupational) pensions may be a suitable means for large firms to reward their most valuable employees. But small firms, especially in small trade and manufacturing, often lack the critical size to provide adequate funding opportunities for their employees. To such small firms, the introduction of funded occupational pension layers may be more of a hindrance than an opportunity. Following this line of logic, I expect a cross-class conflict based on *firm size* and *skill levels* when it comes to capitalization.

Targeting: Tailoring Old-Age Coverage for Vulnerable Occupational Groups

The third post-industrial conflict dimension deals with benefit eligibility. Eligibility for full pension benefits in continental welfare regimes depends on a full contribution record. Post-industrial economies, however, produce an increasing number of labor market outsiders in precarious and atypical employment (Esping-Andersen 1999; Häusermann and Schwander 2009). Outsiders often lack a complete contribution record because of part-time work, temporary work contracts, or periods of unemployment, and thus they run the risk of old-age poverty, despite having been active on the labor market. The proliferation of precarious and atypical work engenders debates over the need for targeting reforms, which are focused on the needs of particular occupational groups. Hence, I suggest that conflicts concerning the eligibility to pension benefits will also become increasingly important in post-industrial continental pension politics.

Targeting policies loosen the tight link between contributions and benefits by distributing selective benefits according to specific needs. One example of this can be found in particular means-tested pension benefits for people in precarious employment relations, such as older workers with very long employment careers in physically demanding jobs. Another example is specific insurance conditions for part-time workers, whose income is too low to qualify for sufficient pension rights. The underlying logic of targeting reforms is to channel scarce resources to the most needy risk groups. Therefore, there is a flip side to expanding benefits for underprivileged workers, namely lowering benefits for overprivileged groups. As described earlier, continental pension regimes tend to provide particular privileges to high-skilled or public-sector employees. Such privileges are purely based on status – not on needs – and they may seem unjustified in a context of austerity. Levy (1999) calls such status privileges the vices of continental welfare states – aspects that can be turned into virtues, if such resources are reallocated to recipients who are actually in need of them.

In terms of conflict patterns, targeting reforms benefit labor market outsiders, whereas insiders (typically male workers with standard employment contracts) do not depend on needs-tested schemes. Quite the contrary, standard workers may prefer to safeguard the equivalence principle. Moreover, contribution financing of benefits enjoys high legitimacy with insiders (Palier 2002), as it gives them the impression that they have earned their social rights. For this reason, insiders have no interest in replacing contributions as the basis of social rights by need.

This stands in marked contrast to the situation of labor market outsiders; increasing labor market participation is often not a viable option for this group, which means that it depends on specific means-tested old-age income security. Therefore, I expect targeting to foster a divide within labor according to *insider* and *outsider status*.

However, labor market status is not the only factor that shapes preferences on targeting; targeting reforms are also strongly tied to *values* – an aspect that tends to blur class-conflict lines even further. Indeed, post-industrial labor markets also reflect post-industrial patterns of family and work organization. Most atypical workers are women and, more generally, young parents struggling to balance work and care obligations because of the lack of child-care facilities in continental welfare regimes. Part-time work, for instance, is the typical rather than atypical form of female employment in all of the continental welfare states (except France). The typical female employment biography is the three-stages model (Anderson and Meyer 2006): after working full-time for a few years, women exit the labor market to care for children and reenter the workforce on a part-time basis a few years later. This model implies interrupted female work biographies and low average-income levels, which penalizes them in terms of career prospects and social (pension) rights (Bridgen and Meyer 2008). Pension insurance discrimination stemming from atypical employment is also a problem for couples who choose to share work and care obligations more equally. If both partners work part-time, they incur substantial losses in social security rights. This example illustrates the normative and normalizing side of continental pension policy: it creates strong incentives for traditional family organization and gendered labor market segmentation. For precisely this reason, conflicts on targeting are not merely struggles over the distribution of material resources. By normalizing atypical and gendered work patterns, targeted reforms also contribute to gender equality, individualization, and free lifestyle choices. Consequently, they are also a matter of values. Hence, I expect them to split not only insiders and outsiders but also *libertarians* and *traditionalists*.

Finally, I hypothesize that employers' interests are divided over targeting. Firms in predominantly male sectors of employment have little reason to support any increase in pension rights that predominantly aid women, and – more generally – labor market outsiders. However, employers in sectors with a strong female workforce may be more open to this kind of claim, as increased social protection for atypical work may provide positive incentives for female labor market participation. Hence, cross-class conflict is likely to occur not only within labor but also within capital – between firms with a predominantly female workforce and those that predominantly employ men.

Recalibration: Gender Equality in a Male-Breadwinner Pension Regime
Recalibration, similar to targeting, deals with the adaptation of eligibility criteria to post-industrialism. However, whereas targeting policies cover particularly precarious occupational groups, recalibration reforms focus on the pension rights of people who are not active on the labor market. This is a significant share of the

population in continental welfare states, due in no small part to low female labor market participation rates (less than 50 percent until the 1980s).[3] Still, female labor market participation is less than 60 percent in most of continental Europe. Hence, a substantial part of the working-age population is not in employment at all.

Under the aegis of the male-breadwinner model, women were traditionally covered through derived rights. But this pattern of insurance has become increasingly dysfunctional, both in terms of the rising rates of divorce, single parenthood, and nontraditional family structures and with regard to the normative beliefs and values of the post-industrial society. In a continental context, a gender-egalitarian pension regime would need to be universalistic (i.e., independent of labor market participation). I call reforms that go in this direction recalibration.[4] The difference between recalibration and targeting not only is one of degree but also is systemic: recalibrating policies grant pension rights independently of labor market participation, cutting the link between contributions and benefits. Examples of recalibrating reforms are pension credits for carers or the splitting of pension contributions and rights between spouses during marriage or in the case of divorce.

Recalibration related conflict patterns should be similar to the ones related to targeting when it comes to labor but different when it comes to capital. In terms of labor, recalibration should set *outsiders* and *insiders* in opposition to each other, as a trend toward universalism in social insurance benefits labor market outsiders. In contrast to targeting, however, there is no reason employers would support recalibrating reforms, because recalibration reduces (rather than increases) incentives for labor market participation. Indeed, although targeting preserves the imperative of commodification – by making even atypical work more remunerative – recalibration breaks with this imperative and creates actual decommodification (Esping-Andersen 1990). So, although recalibration may split labor with regard to employment status, I expect homogeneous preferences among capital. Finally, libertarians should support recalibration more strongly than traditionalists because recalibration contributes to gender equality. Similar to targeting, recalibration implies the idea that the state should intervene in society to provide all individuals, men and women, insiders and outsiders, with equal opportunities for choice. Libertarians share these goals, and hence tend to support recalibration. Traditionalists, by contrast, put a stronger emphasis on traditional household patterns and gender roles. For this reason, I also expect recalibration to give rise to a value conflict between *libertarians* and *traditionalists*.

---

[3] Numbers are from the OECD labor force statistics, 1985–2006 (www.oecd.org).
[4] Through recalibrating reforms, the individual rather than the household becomes the central venue of social policy. In this fashion, recalibration adapts the pension regime to changing social structures and values, which is why I choose to borrow the concept from Pierson (2001: 425), who defines it more generally as "reforms [that] seek to make contemporary welfare states more consistent with contemporary goals and demands for social provision."

TABLE 3.1. *Expected Patterns of Support and Opposition in Post-Industrial Pension Politics*

Institution	Conflict Line	Expected Preferences and Conflict	
		Pro	Contra
Level of benefits	Insurance	Labor (mainly low skilled)	Capital
Financing	Capitalization	High-skilled labor and capital	Low-skilled labor and capital
Eligibility	Targeting	Outsiders Libertarians Employers with a mainly female workforce	Insiders Traditionalists Employers with a mainly male workforce
	Recalibration	Outsiders Libertarians	Insiders Traditionalists Capital

In summary, I argue that the post-industrial pension-reform agenda consists of four dimensions of pension policy modernization: insurance, capitalization, targeting, and recalibration. All four dimensions have the potential to become conflict lines, as they produce specific patterns of winners and losers. Although debates about insurance are likely to be fought along class lines, capitalization, targeting, and recalibration are supposed to foster heterogeneity within labor on the basis of skill levels, labor market status, or values. Table 3.1 summarizes these hypotheses.

I expect that the same four structural conflict potentials develop in all continental welfare states challenged by austerity and post-industrialism. However, although the continental pension regime discussed here is an ideal type, all welfare states are hybrids. Each country demonstrates different degrees of continentalism and Bismarckianism. This variation results in cross-national differences in the design of the specific pension policy regimes. The differences determine the extent to which austerity and post-industrialism actually challenge the specific pension system. In other words, cross-national institutional differences influence the size of the misfit that results from the clash between structural development and institutional inertia. Hence, although I suppose that the structural pattern of conflict potentials is similar throughout all continental welfare regimes, I also suspect that the *importance* of each conflict potential in a given country depends on the size of this misfit. In this sense, the reform agenda in a specific country is largely endogenous to the institutional heritage itself.

I use the reminder of this chapter to briefly elaborate on the specific pension-reform agendas in France, Germany, and Switzerland – the three cases selected for this study. Each of these countries represents an instance of the continental pension regime: Germany is the prototype, France exemplifies a Bismarckian regime combined with several Beveridgian elements, and Switzerland represents a continental latecomer with a multitiered pension scheme. Their institutional specificities explain diverging accents of the national pension agendas.

France: Social Security Deficit and Income Inequality in Failing Labor Markets

Insurance and capitalization have become the most pressing reform issues on the French pension-reform agenda since the late 1980s. The level of pension expenditure and the deficit of the *sécurité sociale* – the French welfare state household – have grown considerably above the OECD average. In addition, the spread of atypical employment and the alarming rates of unemployment accentuate the strong income inequalities that have always characterized the French economy. Hence, despite the early enactment of a first minimum pension scheme in 1956, targeting has become a highly prominent issue. In turn, France has somewhat less pressing reform needs in the field of recalibration, as high female employment rates help to alleviate the need for recalibrating policies that would support nonworking women. The following paragraphs explain this agenda in some more detail.

The main pillar of the French old-age income-security scheme is the *régime général*, the basic public pension scheme, which was founded in the interwar period and strongly expanded steadily up until the 1970s (for a historical overview, see Palier 2003). In the decades following World War II, benefit levels rose massively as a result of both the prospering economy of the *trente glorieuses* and the high poverty levels among the elderly in the aftermath of the war. Concurrently, the *régime général* became more and more universal, covering all private-sector employees (about 60 percent of the insured population; Schludi 2005) at the end of the 1970s. All other employees were (and are) covered by particular occupational schemes, notably for the self-employed (12 percent of the insured) and public-sector employees (*régimes spéciaux*, about 20 percent of the insured). These special pension schemes always provided far more generous benefits than the *régime général*. In addition, trade unions and employers founded a complementary pension scheme of their own in 1947 for high-skilled executives (*cadres*), thereby reinforcing the stratifying effect of the fragmented French pension insurance landscape.

In spite of the inherent inequality of the emerging system, benefit levels improved for all those insured until the 1970s. The state pension endorsed a replacement rate of 50 percent of the reference income (i.e., the average income level of the ten best years of earnings). By the 1980s, a full pension (i.e., the pension entitlement requiring 37.5 years of contribution payments) had even reached a replacement rate of 70 percent of the average former (lifetime) income. In addition to the rising benefit levels, expansive reforms during the 1950s and 1960s introduced a range of additional benefits for education, unemployment, and sickness and/or accidents. These developments all account for the comparatively high levels of French pension expenditure: from around 10 percent of the GDP in the 1970s, the share of pensions in the national income increased to 12.5 percent in 1990 and to more than 13.5 percent in the early 2000s, or about one percentage point higher than the European Union average. The average yearly growth rate of pension expenditure throughout the 1980s was more than 10 percent (Palier 2002). Pensions amount to almost half of the total public expenditure, a level exceeded only by the southern European countries (Abramovici 2002). These particularly high pension costs account for a large part of the growing deficit in the overall social security household. A social security leakage ("trou de la Sécu," Palier 2002: 172) began to creep up as early as the 1970s, when the average annual growth in public social expenditure rose at a speed of more than 4 percentage points faster than economic growth. Thus, revenues could not keep pace with rising social security expenditures. From 1974 onward, the deficit of the social security household has become a constant, bearing straightforward implications for the agenda of welfare state reforms.

Growing financial austerity stems from demographic aging (the old-age dependency ratio is supposed to rise from twenty-three in 1995 to forty-eight pensioners per hundred persons of working age in 2050), and from the sluggish economic growth and severe unemployment crises that have been plaguing France since the late 1970s. This economic downturn has undermined the pension system's financial basis, which is entirely based on contribution – and PAYG financing. Declining employment in such a system means declining revenues while needs and expenditure rise. In addition, the government reacted to growing unemployment with labor-shedding strategies, promoting early retirement for vast categories of the workforce (Levy 2000). The actual average exit age from the labor market was no more than fifty-eight years at the end of the 1990s. In addition to increasing unemployment levels, this strategy has further shaken the financial health of the pension system. Therefore, cost control rather than expansion has become the leitmotif in French pension-reform debates from the 1980s onward. Debates on insurance (more specifically retrenchment) have become increasingly salient in France for these very reasons.

Along with increasing retrenchment pressure, however, capitalization has emerged on the agenda as an alternative way of financing pension rights. Still, in the late 1990s, less than 5 percent of French pensions were capitalized or "funded" (Schludi 2005: 26), even though government reports had endorsed a shift toward funding and a multi-pillar strategy from the 1980s onward (Palier 2003). These reports considered funded pensions to be beneficial in several respects: lowering the demographic threat to pension finances, bolstering France's low savings rates, and providing alternative income sources to the elderly in case of declining state pensions.

While the misfit among austerity pressure, contribution financing, and high levels of expenditure has become blatant in France, the imperative for targeting policies is somewhat less obvious. This is mostly because the French pension regime has always combined the equivalence principle of Bismarckian insurance with some elements of Beveridgian poverty alleviation. In marked contrast to Germany, for example, a minimum pension (*minimum vieillesse*) for the workforce was introduced already in 1956. Moreover, there is no minimum employment requirement (set in terms of weekly hours or the duration of the employment relationship) to qualify for pension insurance eligibility: paid labor is always insured, whether standard or atypical, permanent or temporary. Furthermore,

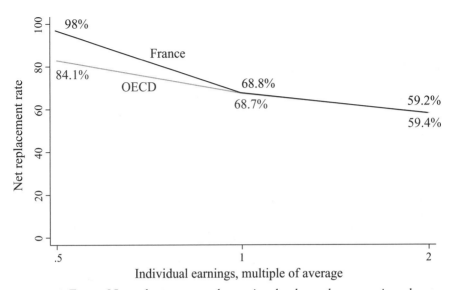

FIGURE 3.2. France: Net replacement rates by earnings level, mandatory pension schemes, men
Notes: Numbers rely on OECD pension models, calculating the replacement rate for a worker with a full employment biography, under the legal conditions of 2002.
Source: OECD 2005

given the existence of both a minimum pension (about 30 percent of average earnings) and a maximum pension (corresponding to 50 percent of the social security contribution ceiling level), French public pension insurance is also rather redistributive, as shown in Figure 3.2. For France and the OECD average, the figure compares the net income replacement rate of a male worker who earned the average income, half of the average income, or double the average income during his entire working life. The figure is based on all mandatory pension schemes. The redistributive effect of the French pension regime appears clearly, as replacement rates decline with growing income levels and lie above the OECD average for the least privileged strata.

At first glance, one might thus think that targeting is not an issue in France, as low-wage earners are taken care of in the public scheme. However, the redistributive effect of the French pension scheme must be considered more carefully, as the egalitarian appearance of Figure 3.2 is somewhat misleading. First, France's degree of income inequality is among the highest in the OECD, approaching the level observed in the United States (Levy 2000). Therefore, many people earn considerably less than half the average income; even high replacement rates cannot wholly make up for such low wages. Second, the minimum pension is very low (i.e., about 30 percent of average earnings). Finally, and most important, the numbers in Figure 3.2 apply only to individuals with a full contribution record of 37.5 years – a requirement that most outsiders cannot feasibly meet. Pension rights, including the minimum pension, however, decline dramatically for workers, as soon as they lack contribution years. Therefore, the French pension institutions are indeed highly stratified, particularly with regard to outsiders. Given the equivalence principle, old-age income security is highly precarious for the atypically employed and for people with discontinuous employment biographies.[5] Because atypical employment is on the rise in France and in most other OECD countries (Jaumotte 2003), targeting is increasingly important as a post-industrial pension policy issue in France.

Recalibration, by contrast, plays a more marginal role, as almost 80 percent of women are employed.[6] France supports female labor market participation with extensive family policy and child-care arrangements, and with a tax system that does not harshly penalize second earners (Jaumotte 2003). For these reasons, policies focusing on particularly underprivileged occupational groups (i.e., targeting reforms) also improve the pension rights of women. This is why recalibration has remained less salient in France. In summary, insurance, capitalization, and targeting are the main conflict lines that structure the debates in post-industrial French pension politics.

Germany: The Prototype of a Challenged Continental Pension Regime

The German pension system of the 1970s came fairly close to typifying the continental social insurance model. Old-age income security was based on the equivalence principle, organized almost exclusively in a basic public PAYG insurance scheme, and administered by strong trade unions and employer organizations. Equally exemplary are the challenges that have arisen from the 1970s onward. Austerity and demographic change have torn holes in pension households, atypical employment has spread, and nontraditional family patterns have emerged, undermining the traditional German male-breadwinner institutions. For these reasons, German pension politics have become marked by the entire range of continental reform dimensions: insurance reforms focus on retrenchment; debates on the introduction of a multitiered pension system stress capitalization as a key issue; and finally, labor market changes and family instability create new poverty traps that may need to be addressed with specific targeting and recalibrating policies.

German old-age income protection relies mainly on the basic pension insurance (*Grundrentenversicherung*), which covers more than 80 percent of the insured workforce and is managed by the social partners, under the supervision of the government. As in France, German public pension insurance is a single-pillar, PAYG-financed system. It relies strongly on the equivalence principle, as there is neither a minimum nor a maximum pension; pension rights depend directly

---

[5] Income inequalities between men and women are higher after the age of sixty-five than during working life. In 1997, the average monthly pension of a man was 1,342 euros, as opposed to 767 euros for the average women's pension. This difference of 43 percent contrasts with an average income difference during the working age of 11 percent (Palier 2003). Hence, the inequalities after retirement clearly stem from the equivalence principle favoring insider decommodification.

[6] Value for 2001. The rate has risen from a bit more than 60 percent in 1981 to 80 percent in the early 2000s. Of female workers, 20 percent to 25 percent (tendency on the rise) are in part-time employment (Jaumotte 2003).

on the contribution record. The target replacement rate is set at 70 percent of lifetime earnings, assuming a full insurance career of forty years. In addition, some firms and sectors have developed capitalized occupational pensions, although these have never become a generalized practice and remained relatively marginal (Schmähl 1997). This quasi absence of capitalization is a consequence of early critical junctures, as the German system dates back to the political choices of the early Bismarckian social security laws at the end of the nineteenth century (Jacobs 2004). Privileged insurance status for civil servants is a second result of this Bismarckian legacy: civil servants are covered by a special scheme (*Beamtenversorgung*), which is tax financed and delivers much higher benefits than the basic public scheme, namely 75 percent of the final pay packet (i.e., the last six months of employment) after thirty-five years of service. But overall (i.e., even in private-sector insurance), pension rights improved massively until the 1970s. In addition, rights for widows became increasingly generous, and provisions for non-contributory benefits for times of education and unemployment were markedly enhanced. Contributions were (and still are) paid in terms of pay-roll taxes. These have risen continuously, in line with the improving benefit levels, increasing to more than 19 percent of wages in the 1990s. With expenditure levels of about 12 percent of the GDP at the end of the 1980s, Germany was situated in the middle field of the EU countries and slightly below the average of the other continental welfare states (Abramovici 2002).

Germany has also experienced similar financial troubles as the other continental regimes since the 1970s. A first deficit resulted from the economic downturn in the 1970s. With slight cuts and the economic recovery in the 1980s, however, the household was carefully rebalanced. More serious financial problems started only in the 1990s, when a combination of job market failure, demographic aging prospects, and – most obviously – reunification pushed the German pension scheme deep into the red (Manow and Seils 2000). As in France, contribution-financed social insurance became a vicious circle: rampant unemployment withdrew revenues from the pension household – pushing contribution levels up. This, in turn, hampered job growth. Labor shedding is difficult in Germany, but early retirement was favored for particular groups of employees – once again undermining the revenue sources for pension insurance (the exit age from the labor force was at about sixty by the end of the 1990s, whereas the legal age of retirement is sixty-five). In addition, demographic threats were (and are) particularly salient in Germany, where an underdeveloped child-care infrastructure and changing family structures have contributed to depressed fertility rates, to an average of about 1.3 in the mid-1990s. This could raise the old-age dependency ratio to more than fifty-five retirees per hundred people of working age by 2050 and increase the pension expenditure level to more than 30 percent of the GDP (Schludi 2005: 48). Finally, reunification came as a shock for the German social insurance system, as people in the new Länder were immediately granted similar social rights to people in the West, without having contributed during their working life. Hence, pension expenditures on average grew by more than 8 percent per year from 1990 to 1993, and by about 3 percent subsequently (Manow and Seils 2000).

For all these reasons – both structural and conjunctural – insurance (notably cost containment) became a huge issue in the 1980s and even more so from the 1990s onward. More and more experts considered the exorbitant level of payroll taxes, and thus labor costs, to be a major reason for the so-called German disease (e.g., Manow and Seils 2000; Kitschelt and Streeck 2003). The retrenchment of benefit levels was increasingly considered a *conditio sine qua non* for the improvement of the long-term viability of the social insurance schemes and of the German economy as a whole.

The emergence of capitalization as a salient reform strategy also has its roots in the difficult economic context of the 1990s. It must, however, also be linked to the demographic threat overshadowing the German pension system. As outlined earlier, very low birth rates undermine the basis for intergenerational solidarity. Moreover, only about 9 percent of the pensions in the 1990s were funded (Schludi 2005). Therefore, there appeared to be a broad scope for expanding different forms of individual or collective pension savings, complementing or even replacing parts of the public PAYG-financed benefits.

Although dramatic, financial austerity is still only one of the problems the German pension system has faced in recent years. More so than France's pension scheme, German basic pension insurance in the 1970s was built to promote status preservation for labor market insiders. Eligibility for any kind of pension insurance rights depended, and still depends, on a minimum contribution period of five years. A full pension presupposes a contribution record of forty years and marginal (*geringfügig*) employment (fewer than fifteen work hours per month, two months per year, or a minimum income of 325 euros per month) does not qualify for insurance coverage at all. The self-employed are not insured by any mandatory means but may apply for voluntary inclusion. Hence, in the German system, atypically employed outsiders either have no chance of qualifying for insurance or accumulate only meager contribution records. The German pension system is also particularly stratifying, rather than redistributive, which can be clearly seen in Figure 3.3.

The income replacement rate of underprivileged income strata is not only more than twenty percentage points less than the OECD average – it even lies below the replacement rate of the average earner. This means that the generosity of the pension scheme increases with rising income levels. Moreover, this graph applies only to individuals with a full contribution record of forty years; people with interrupted employment biographies earn even lower pension rights. Such poor coverage of the atypically and precariously employed has become a growing problem since the 1970s, with the spread of more flexible forms of employment. Part-time employment still accounts for only about 10 percent of the workforce, but among women, the part-time level is more than 35 percent. In addition, despite a lack of precise statistics, experts assume that the proportion of marginal employment has risen sharply since the early 1980s: in 2003, more than 4 million individuals were exclusively employed in such marginal jobs. An almost equal number of employees was counted in temporary employment (Neuhold 1999). These developments have put targeting on the German pension-reform agenda.

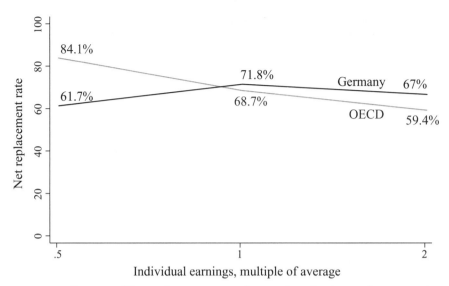

FIGURE 3.3. Germany: Net replacement rates by earnings level, mandatory pension schemes, men
Notes: Numbers rely on OECD pension models, calculating the replacement rate for a worker with a full employment biography, under the legal conditions of 2002.
Source: OECD 2005

For German women, however, the story does not end here. In addition to the perils of unstable labor markets, their employment biographies are shaped by the incentive structure of a male-breadwinner society. In the 1970s and 1980s, hardly any child-care facilities existed in Germany, except for the left-alternative *Kinderläden* in major cities (Naumann 2005). Care work was and still is concentrated in the core family, discouraging female labor market participation at least for the first five years of child rearing. Moreover, the income of the second earner is taxed at a rate one and a half times as high as the breadwinner income (Jaumotte 2003). Gendered employment patterns directly relate to the gender differences in pension rights: men's average basic pension in the old Länder is more than double that of the average individual female pension (Allmendinger 2000).[7] Given these institutional arrangements, which keep women away from paid employment, women's pension rights cannot be improved by means of targeting reforms; indeed, most women are completely absent from the labor market for long periods of their employable years. The German constitutional court (in a decision that has subsequently been overturned by the European Court of Justice in 1995; Neuhold 1999) even sentenced the German pension institutions for gender discrimination, because they penalize normal female biographies. This sentence shows that the dour state of female old-age protection had come into

[7] In addition, even employed women concentrate in jobs and sectors that do not benefit from additional, voluntary occupational pension schemes. Only 12 percent of employed women, compared with 36 percent of employed men, receive additional old-age income from these schemes (Allmendinger 2000).

deep conflict with the social realities of divorce and individualization, and with post-industrial values (Schmähl 2000). Hence the appearance of recalibration as a fourth conflict dimension on the post-industrial German pension-reform agenda.

Switzerland: Challenges for Modernization in a Continental Laggard

Of the three countries in this study, Switzerland is certainly the least typical case of a continental welfare state. Esping-Andersen (1990) even classified it with the liberal regimes. In line with the more recent literature on this subject (Obinger 1998; Armingeon 2001; Bonoli and Mach 2000; Bonoli 2006b; Häusermann forthcoming b) I argue, however, that Switzerland – through no less a hybrid than any other welfare state – is a predominantly continental regime. Because the notion of the continental welfare states is key to this study, it is important to discuss briefly the motive behind this classification.

The characterization of Switzerland as a liberal regime was to some extent based on modest levels of aggregate expenditure. However, apart from reflecting a somewhat unfinished welfare state that was still growing in the early 1970s, the data indicating modest expenditure were based on an incomplete account of the Swiss welfare state. Many observers focused exclusively on purely state controlled social insurance schemes. The Swiss welfare state, however, consists of a variety of public and semiprivate schemes that provide social security, especially in the field of pensions. Although the first tier of the Swiss pension system is a public scheme, the second tier (i.e., occupational pensions) is privately organized, yet still part of Swiss old-age income protection (as it is mandatory and most insurance conditions are legally enacted). The size of the welfare state is a bad indicator for classification, anyway; what matters most is the institutional design. If social schemes are designed in such a way as to produce insider decommodification, stratification, and a male-breadwinner society, the regime is indeed continental. And as I show herein, this is definitely the case for Swiss pension policy.

The early regime literature also classified Switzerland with the liberal regimes because of the slow growth of the Swiss welfare state. Direct democracy and federalism were the main institutional hurdles for the creation of encompassing social policies (Armingeon 2001; Gilliand 1993). This slow development of the Swiss welfare state bears crucial implications for this study, as it affected the resulting post-industrial pension policy reform agenda in several ways. First, austerity pressure never became as massive as in the other countries, meaning that insurance – while certainly an issue – has remained a somewhat less salient conflict in Switzerland than in Germany and France. Second, capitalization became widespread, mandatory, and thus a normal means of pension financing at a very early stage. Therefore, debates on the introduction of funded pension schemes disappeared from the reform agenda and debates on the reform of the capitalized schemes dealt with insurance elements rather than the introduction of funding as such. Finally, the slow development and patchy pension coverage accentuated new social risks for women and the atypically employed since the 1970s – enhancing the salience of targeting and recalibration on the reform agenda.

The Swiss public pension system was still unfinished when the country entered the era of austerity in the mid-1970s. Up to that moment, it had consisted of only a basic pension scheme – the first-tier AHV (Alters- und Hinterlassenenversicherung) – that was financed on a PAYG basis and provided universal coverage. A full AHV pension ranges from about 1,000 to 2,000 Swiss francs (i.e., between 15 percent and 30 percent of the average income), depending on contributions. The right to a full pension presupposes a full contribution record of forty-five years. However, though it is highly redistributive, the first-tier benefits are too low to ensure the "decent living standard" for the elderly that the constitution prescribes. Hence, at the beginning of the 1970s, it was obvious to all political actors that the Swiss pension insurance system had to be complemented. While the left advocated the expansion of the first-pillar, right-wing parties and employers wanted to develop the preexisting private and capitalized occupational pension schemes into a fully grown second tier. Advocates of capitalization prevailed in a popular referendum, and the second tier became mandatory in 1982 (Bonoli 2001a; Leimgruber 2008). Mandatory occupational pension insurance covers all employees with an income above a threshold of about a third of average earnings (Bonoli and Mach 2000). This second tier is a purely individual, capitalized, and mostly defined contribution pension scheme; it entails very little solidarity among the insured (except for disability and sickness pensions). Moreover, the second tier has remained semiprivate, because it is administered by several hundred private and semiprivate companies. In addition, the second tier's legal framework prescribes only minimum rights (a minimum and ceiling threshold for eligibility, and a minimum interest rate that must be granted on the capitalized savings). However, employers are fiscally encouraged to provide more generous insurance conditions to their employees, and they tend to do so – especially for highly skilled and executive-level employees (CONSOC Recherche 2003; Bundesamt für Sozialversicherungen 1995). Both the first and the second tiers are financed by means of pay-roll taxes on wages of about 20 percent, split equally between employees and employers.[8] Together, the benefits of both tiers are intended to provide a 60 percent replacement rate to the average income earner.

With the economic crisis of the 1970s, the first-pillar pension scheme ran into a deficit for the first time (Kriesi 1980). After a recovery in the 1980s, the financial situation of the AHV worsened dramatically in the mid-1990s, when growth virtually stopped, unemployment soared, and the AHV was in the red between 1995 and 1999. This austerity pressure was reinforced by the prospects of an upcoming demographic problem: in the light of an alarmingly low birth rate (1.4 children per woman), Switzerland may face an old age dependency ratio of almost fifty retirees per hundred active people in 2050. Increased longevity also puts pressure on benefit levels in the second pillar, as the savings that individuals accumulate need to last for an increasingly long period after retirement. In addition,

---

[8] Contribution levels are about 8 percent in the first pillar (employers and employees paying 4 percent each). In the second pillar, notional contributions depend on the age of the employee, ranging from 7 percent to 18 percent of income.

failing stock markets in the early 2000s threatened the financial stability of the pension funds.

In international comparison, of course, Switzerland's economy suffered less than it's neighboring countries (Bonoli and Mach 2000). But for the Swiss, the sudden (and previously unknown) household imbalances, unemployment, and declining growth came as a shock. Cost containment became a very important issue on the post-industrial reform agenda. What made the pressure for retrenchment somewhat less dramatic in Switzerland, as compared to France and Germany, was the fact that the Swiss pension system was still in the making on entering the era of austerity (Häusermann 2010b). Because of this lag, benefit levels in the public PAYG pension scheme never even reached the levels extant in neighboring countries. Hence, for Switzerland, the misfit between structural challenges and existing institutions was somewhat less blatant. Therefore, while it certainly was (and is) an important conflict, insurance has not become as dominant in Switzerland as in other countries.

By contrast, targeting and recalibration have appeared quite prominently on the agenda, as one of the most distinct features of Swiss pension insurance is the highly stratifying effect of the multi-pillar system. Although the first pillar provides low but egalitarian benefits, the second pillar covers only the standard workforce (i.e., employees in dependent, stable work relations lasting more than three months and providing an income of more than 30 percent of average earnings). This excludes a broad range of atypical workers and the self-employed (for a detailed discussion of this problem, see Nova and Häusermann 2005). At the end of the 1990s, almost 25 percent of all employees were not eligible for second-pillar coverage (SGK-N 2002). These inequalities are, of course, highly gendered. In 2001, 35 percent of employed women lacked occupational pension coverage, and their average second-pillar pension amounted to no more than 58 percent of the average male pension (Bundesamt für Statistik 2004). Overall, most pensioners still rely primarily on the public AHV pension after retirement.[9] Because these benefits are too low to ensure a decent living standard, a means-tested pension supplement was added to the first pillar in 1965, which raised the lowest pensions to a level just above social assistance (Bonoli and Mach 2000).

A complete picture of the highly stratifying effect of the Swiss pension schemes also requires integrating the occupational and private pension pillars. As outlined earlier, most employers grant particular second-pillar pension rights to their high-skilled workforce. Moreover, the third pillar of the Swiss pension scheme consists of tax concessions for voluntary personal pension plans, and these represent a substantial part of old-age revenues only for the very privileged income strata (Bundesamt für Sozialversicherungen 1995). All of these additional privileges for the middle- and high-income strata result in a highly unegalitarian pension system. Therefore, one must distinguish between two important lines in Figure 3.4: the bold line is exclusively based on mandatory insurance schemes and

[9] Up to a monthly individual income of 4,000 Swiss francs (about 2,700 euros), more than 80 percent of this pension revenue stems from the first tier (Balthasar et al. 2003).

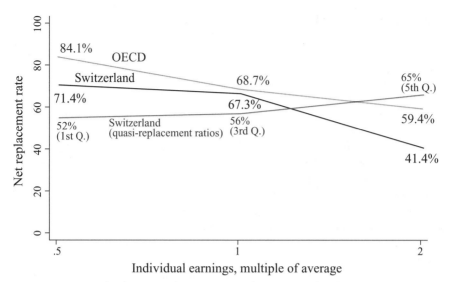

FIGURE 3.4. Switzerland: Net replacement rates by earnings level, mandatory pension schemes, men

Notes: Numbers rely on OECD pension models, calculating the replacement rate for a worker with a full employment biography, under the legal conditions of 2002.

Quasi-replacement ratios: Average income of the 1st, 3rd and 5th quintile of pensioner households as a proportion of the average income of these quintiles among the working population households.

Source: OECD 2005, Bundesamt für Statistik 2003

full contribution careers. According to these numbers, Swiss replacement rates remain below the OECD average, but because they decline with rising income levels, the Swiss pension system looks rather redistributive. If one looks at the quasi-replacement ratios, however, the picture changes completely.

The quasi-replacement ratios compare the *actual* revenues of income quintiles among pensioners with the revenues of the same income quintiles among the active generation. Thus, the quasi-replacement ratios also take into account the voluntary but state-subsidized pension plans (and the precariousness of people with incomplete contribution careers). This second line shows that Swiss pension policy is actually regressive rather than redistributive, as replacement rates rise with rising income levels. In summary, the Swiss pension system is particularly stratifying, as it grants tax privileges to high incomes while providing only patchy coverage to low-wage earners. This institutional arrangement becomes increasingly ill suited with regard to the rise in atypical employment since the 1980s: rates of part-time employment have risen to more than 30 percent of the total workforce. Among employed women, almost 60 percent work part-time only. Similarly, self-employment grew to almost 20 percent (Rechsteiner 2002). The atypically employed are particularly at risk in the second tier: almost 20 percent of the employed men and almost 40 percent of the active women were not entitled to occupational pension coverage at the end of the 1990s (Häusermann 2002). Therefore, it appears clearly that targeting has become a salient reform dimension in post-industrial Swiss pension politics.

Given the Swiss pension system's focus on high income, continuous employment biographies, it is also evident that those outside the labor market tend to incur considerably lower pension rights. Throughout their work biographies, most Swiss women incur periods of labor market absence, and they combine periods of both part-time and full-time work. The missing contribution years – spent outside the labor market or in part-time work – reduce women's pension rights dramatically, especially in the second tier. Furthermore, the patchy state of female old-age protection also stems from institutionalized conservatism. In the pension system as it had developed until the 1980s, women lost their entitlement to their own pension on getting married; typically, their occupational pension – if they had any – was also dissolved on marriage. The idea was, of course, that these women would henceforth be covered through their spouse's pension rights and through derived rights. For these reasons, divorce became a substantial poverty risk (for a detailed discussion of the feminization of old-age poverty in Switzerland until the 1990s, see Leitner and Obinger, 1996). For all these reasons, the misfit between rising family instability and claims for gender equality, on the one hand, and the male-breadwinner institutions, on the other hand, was particularly blatant in Switzerland – a circumstance that accounts for the presence of recalibration on the Swiss pension-reform agenda.

In this chapter, I have argued that continental pension regimes are particularly at odds with austerity pressure; demographic aging; and post-industrial labor markets, family structures, and values. The misfit between these structural developments and the micro-institutions of continental pension regimes – strict eligibility criteria, high benefit levels for insiders, PAYG financing – leads to four conflict dimensions in post-industrial continental pension modernization: (1) insurance, (2) capitalization, (3) targeting, and (4) recalibration. Given the country-specific institutional frameworks and socioeconomic charcteristics, all four of these dimensions figure prominently in Germany; France is somewhat less concerned with recalibration; and the Swiss multi-pillar pension scheme largely eschews debates on capitalization. Insurance reforms generate winners and losers in terms of the old class-conflict, opposing labor and capital. Capitalization, targeting, and recalibration, by contrast, divide winners and losers in ways that differ from the old class-conflict patterns (i.e., according to skill levels, labor market status, values, and firm size). To observe how these conflict lines are articulated in the national decision-making processes, the next step is to analyze how skill levels, labor market status, values, and firm size are organized collectively. This is the subject of the next chapter.

4

Changing Alliances

Conflict Lines and Actor Configurations

So far, this book has introduced the four conflict dimensions in post-industrial pension policy making. Each of these dimensions entails a specific configuration of winners and losers with particular risk profiles: the divide between employees and employers points out winners and losers in conflicts over insurance; skill level and firm size delineate the winners and losers in matters of capitalization; and labor market status and values bear strongly on the interest profile of individuals with regard to targeting and recalibration. Hence, while actors' positions on insurance are class related, the three other reform dimensions divide winners and losers along conflict lines that cut across labor and capital. We can thus expect post-industrial pension politics to give rise to multiple crosscutting conflict lines, thereby generating a variety of class and cross-class alliances in the pension policy process. This is the second hypothesis of the analytical framework of this book, and it is developed in detail in this chapter.

The analytic step from sociostructural risk profiles to political divides in the policy-making processes of France, Germany, and Switzerland must be theorized. To become an actual conflict in pension politics, each of the potential antagonisms needs to be mobilized by collective political actors interested in change and powerful enough to be heard. Hence, the key question in this chapter is, Who speaks on behalf of these different risk profiles? That is, Who articulates these potential conflict lines in the actual policy making arenas of the different countries? More precisely, I ask which collective actors are likely to represent the sociostructural potentials defined by skills, labor market status, values, and firm size in the policy-making processes. Thereby, this chapter makes a very structuralist argument: conflict lines in decision-making processes change because the constituencies of political parties and interest organizations change. In the following pages, I show that a closer look at the sociostructural class basis of the relevant pension risk groups allows us to make sense of the conflict patterns and coalitional dynamics to be expected in the political decision-making arenas.

The Class Basis of the New Pension Politics

Many recent studies on the politics of the welfare state have made a strong claim for the importance of cross-class alliances, relying on a range of different criteria, such as firm size and industries (e.g., Mares 2000, 2003a, 2003b), sectors exposed and sheltered from international competition (e.g., Manow 2001), production factor mobility (e.g., Hiscox 2001), skill specificity as a measure of risk exposure (e.g., Iversen and Soskice 2001, Iversen, Cusack, and Rehm 2006), and insider-outsider labor market status (e.g., Rueda 2005, 2006). However, although it presents a necessary and compelling emendation to the class-centered power resources approach, the terminology used in this cross-class literature often reveals a too-simple conceptualization of the class structure: labeling any form of intra-labor or intra-capital heterogeneity a cross-class conflict implies that labor and capital are the two single classes relevant in a discussion of distributional conflicts. However, tertiarization, the feminization of the workforce, and the expansion of higher education have deeply transformed the class structure in post-industrial economies (Kriesi 1998b; Oesch 2006). Old class categories such as "labor," or distinctions such as "blue collar workers versus white collar workers" and "manual workers versus non-manual workers" (Erikson and Goldthorpe 1993) no longer denote homogeneous risk categories. Therefore, the meaning of *classes* (defined as social groups whose members share a similar position in the occupational system [Oesch 2006], and therefore espouse similar policy preferences and values) must be reconceptualized. When taking the literature on the transformation of classes in post-industrial economies seriously, one realizes that intra-labor heterogeneity is far less surprising than the notion cross-class alliance may suggest. By "redrawing the class map" (Oesch 2006), this literature provides much-needed analytical tools for the analysis and interpretation of contemporary social policy making. In the following, I establish the relationship between the risk profiles in pension policy and sociostructural classes in a post-industrial economy, arguing that classes provide the missing link between social risk groups and the articulation of their needs and demands by political parties and trade unions.

How, then, are post-industrial classes linked to skill levels, insider-outsider status, and values? On the basis of Kriesi's (1998b) horizontal differentiation of the new middle class, Oesch (2006) has developed a class schema that accounts for contemporary labor market stratification. While old class schemata mostly posit an exclusively vertical stratification, this post-industrial class schema relies on two different dimensions: the extent of marketable skills and the type of work being done. Oesch's vertical axis relies on skills: the higher the level of marketable skills, the more advantages an occupation presents in terms of income and work autonomy.[1] In addition, Oesch and Kriesi introduce a horizontal differentiation

---

[1] The criterion of skills replaces the difference between blue-collar and white-collar workers, or between manual and nonmanual work. Industrial class schemata, such as the one by Eriksson and Goldthorpe (1993) assumed that white-collar, nonmanual workers are necessarily more privileged than blue-collar, manual workers. In a post-industrial economy, however, low-skilled service occupations are by no means more advantageous than low-skilled jobs in production (Oesch 2006).

Independent work logic	Technical work logic	Organizational work logic	Interpersonal work logic	
Large employers and self-employed professionals (CA)	Technical experts (CA)	Higher-grade managers (CA)	Sociocultural professionals (SCP)	Professional/ managerial
Petty bourgeoisie with employees (CA)	Technicians (MSF)	Associate managers (CA)	Sociocultural semi-professionals (SCP)	Associate professonal / managerial
Petty bourgeoisie without employees (MSF)	Skilled crafts (BC)	Skilled office workers (MSF)	Skilled service (LSF)	Generally / vocationally skilled
	Routine operatives and routine agriculture (BC)	Routine office workers (MSF)	Routine service (LSF)	Low/ un-skilled

Based on Oesch (2006) and Kitschelt and Rehm (2005). For the classification of occupations (ISCO-2d codes), see appendix 2

FIGURE 4.1. The post-industrial class schema

based on people's work logic. This distinction accounts for whether a job relies mainly on technical competence (technical work logic), managerial power (organizational work logic), face-to-face interaction with clients (interpersonal work logic), or self-employment (independent work logic). The central focus of people's occupations differs, and these differences in work logic affect people's preferences and values.

Figure 4.1 represents this new class schema graphically. It contains fifteen classes, which, following Kitschelt and Rehm (2005), can be summarized into five larger post-industrial classes or class groups: capital accumulators, mixed service functionaries, low service functionaries, blue-collar workers, and sociocultural professionals.

Capital accumulators (about 14 percent of the workforce according to data from the ISSP Role of Government III Survey [International Social Survey Program 1996]) are higher level managers, employers, self-employed in liberal professions (e.g., physicians, lawyers), and technical experts. This group is highly skilled and tends to work in private industries or services. High-skilled sociocultural professionals and semiprofessionals, by contrast (about 25 percent of the workforce), tend to work in nonprofit or public organizations, or in the service sector. They are typically employed in client-interactive jobs (e.g., teachers, therapists) and have a significant amount of autonomy at work. On the low-skilled side of the vertical stratification, we need to distinguish between blue-collar workers (about 25 percent of the workforce) and low service functionaries (about 14 percent of the workforce). This distinction coincides to some extent with a sectoral public-private divide; the low-skilled service functionaries' services are frequently employed in the public sector (personal services), whereas blue-collar workers concentrate in private industry (e.g., metal industry, chemistry, mining, construction). It should be noted, however, that low-skilled service employment is also strongly represented in retail commerce, hotels and restaurants, and other

TABLE 4.1. *Post-Industrial Class Groups and Pension Policy Risk Profiles*

	Insiders	Outsiders
High skilled	Capital accumulators	Sociocultural professionals
Low skilled	Blue-collar workers	Low service functionaries

private services. Finally, mixed service functionaries (about 20 percent of the workforce) are a residual category. Their very heterogeneous profile in terms of skills and work logic makes it difficult to formulate clear-cut hypotheses concerning their preferences on pension policy reforms. Thus, my analytical focus lies on the poles of the new class structure (i.e., capital accumulators, blue-collar workers, low service functionaries, and sociocultural professionals).

Rethinking post-industrial pension politics in terms of this post-industrial class schema, it is clear that the new pension risk groups – as identified in Chapter 3 (Table 3.1) – are spread over diverse classes: low-skilled employees should oppose capitalization against the highly skilled, independent of their work logic. By contrast, outsiders should support targeting and recalibration against insiders, regardless of skill levels and the employment sector. Similarly, libertarians are supposed to advocate recalibration, irrespective of either work logic or skill level. There is no single new class conflict that might replace the old class conflict. However, despite not forming a single class of their own, the victims of post-industrial risks – such as women, low-skilled workers, or the atypically employed – are not spread randomly across the different classes either. Rather, they concentrate in several different but clearly identifiable class groups. Indeed, I argue that the post-industrial class schema (as shown in Figure 4.1) reflects precisely the conflict potentials (in terms of skills and insider-outsider status) that become relevant in post-industrial pension politics: the vertical axis distinguishes sociostructural mobilization potentials in terms of skills, and the horizontal work-logic dimension coincides with insider-outsider job profiles (see Table 4.1).

The vertical axis, which connotes employees' skill levels, is fairly straightforward. The posited relation between work logic and employment status, however, requires some further explanation. Work logic and labor market status coincide, because both depend on the same underlying variables, namely sector and gender. Interpersonal work-logic jobs tend to cluster in services, both private and public. The employees in these interpersonal classes run a very high risk of being outsiders for two reasons. First, most of them are female: women in continental welfare states typically have interrupted and atypical work biographies because of traditional family structures and the lack of child-care facilities. Second, the workforce in the relatively new (private) service sector is organized only weakly in the labor movement (Ebbinghaus 2006b). Post-industrialization, in a sense, added the service-sector pillar to the industrial class schema. Because of this, there is weak trade union organization in these occupations, which adds to the likelihood of sociocultural professionals and low service functionaries being outsiders.

To show the close match of risk profiles and classes empirically, I rely on micro-level data from the ISSP 1996 Role of Government III survey for the countries discussed in this book (International Social Survey Program 1996).[2] For the analysis, active individuals (aged eighteen to sixty-four) are categorized into the four aforementioned risk groups according to occupation (for ISCO88 2-digit codes, see Appendix 2).[3] Skill level is operationalized by the percentage of people with tertiary education and average net monthly income. Insider-outsider status is indicated by the ratio of part-time employment and by gender. Particularly high values of each indicator in Table 4.2 are highlighted.

Table 4.2 confirms the match-up of risk profiles and post-industrial classes. Capital accumulators and sociocultural professionals are highly skilled. As hypothesized, both groups are materially privileged. However, the income levels of sociocultural professionals are considerably lower than those of capital accumulators. This difference is related to the high proportion of part-timers among sociocultural professionals. As expected, part-time employment clearly clusters in occupations with interpersonal work logic. It is the only form of atypical work for which the ISSP provides information, but it can be regarded as a proxy for atypical employment conditions in general (including time-limited contracts, and other precarious labor conditions), as different forms of atypical employment tend to accumulate in particular occupations (Talos 1999). The spread of atypical work contracts varies from country to country, but what matters when looking at national conflict patterns is the comparison of the risk profiles within each country. In this respect, the picture is similar across the three cases: atypical employment is marginal among blue-collar workers and capital accumulators as compared to sociocultural professionals and low service functionaries. Equally similar across all countries is the strong concentration of women in the latter two groups. The highly feminized profile of these occupations is further evidence for my argument that sociocultural professionals and low service functionaries tend to be labor market outsiders. Indeed, many empirical studies demonstrate the deficient integration of female workers in social insurance schemes (Oesch 2006; Mühlberger 2000; Talos 1999; Bridgen and Meyer 2008) and trade unions (Oesch 2006; Ebbinghaus 2006; Häusermann and Schwander 2009).

Referring to the material interests of these classes, it already appears that each post-industrial conflict line is likely to foster its distinct cross-class alliance: sociocultural professionals are supposed to support both capitalization and targeting and/or recalibration, the former on the basis of their privileged skill level and the latter because of their outsider status. However, they are likely to find themselves in different patterns of alliance: low service functionaries are the most likely ally in the struggle for targeting and recalibration, whereas capital accumulators are supposed to join them in the support of capitalization. Finally, all post-industrial classes have an interest in supporting generous insurance

---

[2] The national surveys were conducted in the context of other regular national surveys. Because of the differences in the methodology of data gathering, the data presented must be read as showing general tendencies rather than precise profiles. However, my focus lies on the within-country rather than between-country differences for the risk groups, which eases the problems of comparability.

[3] I am grateful to Philip Rehm for this data. The classification is based on individual respondents (rather than households). If the information for a respondent is lacking, the spouse's value is used.

TABLE 4.2. *Skill Levels and Insider-Outsider Status of Post-Industrial Class Groups*

	Indicators of Skill Levels					
	Percentage with Tertiary Education[a]			Average Monthly Income[b]		
	France	Germany	Switzerland	France	Germany	Switzerland
Capital accumulators	72.9	47.2	67.7	19,560	4,042	6,800
Blue-collar workers	8.9	0.8	10.1	7,450	2,413	4,110
Sociocultural professionals	68.0	40.4	38.0	11,587	3,182	4,880
Low service functionaries	30.6	1.9	8.3	6,531	1,837	3,240
Number of observations	1,132	1,584	1,646	936	1,308	1,524

	Indicators of Insider-Outsider Status					
	Percentage Part-Time Employed[c]			Percentage Female		
	France	Germany	Switzerland	France	Germany	Switzerland
Capital accumulators	4.4	4.7	16.7	16.0	26.7	17.4
Blue-collar workers	3.7	3.9	9.8	13.2	11.6	16.6
Sociocultural professionals	9.4	15.8	39.8	56.7	59.2	59.0
Low service functionaries	17.4	25.0	46.2	66.9	68.2	70.3
Number of observations	1,132	1,587	1,647	1,132	1,587	1,647

[a] Tertiary education includes any higher education (university, tertiary training, tertiary technical universities). Numbers for Germany include only completed education, whereas numbers for France and Switzerland also include incompleted studies.
[b] Income in French francs (France), Deutsche mark (Germany), and Swiss francs (Switzerland).
[c] Part-time employment includes employment below 35 hours per week.
Notes: Values for Germany are a weighted average of values for West and East Germany, according to population size.
Source: ISSP 1996 role of Government III (V205, V217, V206, V200, V208).

conditions, with the exception of capital accumulators, many of whom are employers (i.e., self-employed or members of management).

The potential for cross-class alliances becomes even more evident when we add values to the picture. Attitudes toward targeting and recalibration depend as much on libertarianism and traditionalism as on material interests. Values can be an equally strong basis for alliances as common interests, and the two need not coincide. While it remains debatable whether libertarian values originate in education, class, or other (antecedent) processes of socialization, it is undisputed that they correlate strongly with both high skill levels and occupations with interpersonal work logic (Kitschelt 1994). Consequently, given the link between work

TABLE 4.3. *Value Profile of Post-Industrial Class Groups*

	Insiders	Outsiders
High skilled	Capital accumulators, *ambiguous value profile*	Sociocultural professionals, *libertarian*
Low skilled	Blue-collar workers, *traditionalist*	Low service functionaries, *ambiguous value profile*

logic and labor market status I established earlier, in the following paragraph I present the expected value profiles of the post-industrial class groups.

Sociocultural professionals should be strongly libertarian, given their inter-personal work logic and high skills. Blue-collar workers, by contrast, have the opposite profile, which should make them strongly traditionalist. Capital accu-mulators and low service functionaries are exposed to contradictory influences. Table 4.4 provides empirical evidence for these value profiles. It displays aver-age value profiles for the classes relative to the mean in the population. On the left side of the table, one can see the degree of libertarianism versus traditional-ism, and high numbers indicate strongly libertarian values. On the right side, I have added the average attitudes toward state interventionism versus economic liberalism to emphasize the blatant contrasts between these two dimensions of political values and preferences.[4] Light-gray shades highlight significantly lib-ertarian and state-interventionist attitudes, and dark-gray shades point to tradi-tionalist or market-liberal positions.

As expected, the libertarianism-traditionalism dimension clearly pits blue-collar workers against sociocultural professionals. The profiles of the other classes are less clear cut and vary considerably across the three countries. Swiss capital accumulators, for example, display a libertarian profile, while French capital accu-mulators are more traditionalist. The strongly contrasting results between the two preference axes (libertarianism versus traditionalism and state interventionism versus market liberalism) makes it very clear that values cannot be reduced to mere material interests. While blue-collar workers and sociocultural professionals are the two antipodes on the cultural value axis, the interventionism-liberalism axis produces other extremes, namely capital accumulators versus the low skilled (see also Häusermann 2008). Regarding the impact of interests and values on actors'

[4] Both dimensions have been constructed by means of a factor analysis, relying conceptually on Kitschelt and Rehm (2005). All data from the ISSP 1996 Role of the Government III. The libertarianism-traditionalism dimension displays the results of factor analyses (one analysis per country, all unidimensional, Eigenvalue between 1.66 and 1.73) based on variables measuring atti-tudes on spending for the environment, education, culture and the arts (V25, V28, V32). The interventionism-liberalism dimension displays the results of factor analyses (one analysis per coun-try, all unidimensional, Eigenvalue between 3.1–4.1) based on variables measuring attitudes on government responsibility with regard to income inequality, job creation, support for declining industries, working time regulation, job market regulation, health care, old-age income security, unemployment insurance, redistribution, and housing (V16, V20, V23, V24, V36, V38, V39, V41, V42, V44).

TABLE 4.4. *Attitudes on Libertarianism and State Interventionism by Post-Industrial Class Groups*

	Libertarianism			State Interventionism		
	France	Germany	Switzerland	France	Germany	Switzerland
Capital accumulators	−.12*	.03	.17**	−.78***	−.45***	−.27***
Blue-collar workers	−.21***	−.11***	−.18***	.24**	.26***	.23***
Sociocultural professionals	.19***	.23***	.20***	.07	−.04	−.01
Low service functionaries	.10	.01	−.12**	.34***	.31***	.26***
Mean	−.07	−.02	.16	.05	−.11	.63
Number of observations	1,043	1,494	1,540	952	1,324	1,255

*$p < .05$; **$p < .01$; ***$p < .001$ (t-test).
Notes: Values are the deviation of the average position of a group relative to the country mean.
Source: ISSP 1996 Role of Government III. Values are factor scores. For the composition of the factors, see the relative footnote.

positions in pension politics, I argue that values reinforce or mitigate the effect of interests. Let me illustrate this claim with an example: both sociocultural professionals and low service functionaries are likely to favor targeting and recalibration because these policies are in their best outsider interests. But sociocultural professionals might have an even stronger preference for these reforms because their material interests are underpinned by a libertarian value profile. Blue-collar workers, in turn, should be particularly hostile to targeting and recalibration, because these reforms not only focus on beneficiaries other than themselves but also contradict the traditionalist values of these low-skilled male insiders. Table 4.5 summarizes the structural class basis of the expected conflict lines, as I have just derived them.

The final step involves translating these sociostructural class potentials to the political arenas of each country, as we are interested in the actual policy-making processes. A conflict potential remains not only invisible but also politically irrelevant, unless collective actors mobilize it. Therefore, I shall focus the empirical part of this study (Chapters 6–8) on the positions and alliances of *collective* actors in the reform processes rather than on the policy preferences of individuals. The sociostructural micro-level analysis of interests and values presented in this chapter, however, is necessary for the meaningful interpretation of actor configurations at the level of collective decision-making processes. Indeed, it is only by knowing about constituencies and their preferences that one can understand the motivations that drive the alliances of collective actors. In the remainder of this chapter, I thus analyze the class and risk constituencies of political parties, trade unions, and employers in France, Germany, and Switzerland and discuss their likely positions regarding pension reform. Hence, I rely on the (class)

TABLE 4.5. *The Structural Class Basis of Post-Industrial Pension Politics*

Conflict Line	Risk Profiles		Structural Class Basis	
	Pro	Contra	Pro	Contra
Insurance	Labor (mainly low skilled)	Capital	Blue-collar workers Low service functionaries (Sociocultural professionals)	Capital accumulators
Capitalization	High-skilled labor and capital	Low-skilled labor and capital	Capital accumulators Sociocultural professionals Large firms	Blue-collar workers Low service functionaries Small firms
Targeting and recalibration	Outsiders and libertarians	Insiders and traditionalists	Sociocultural professionals (Low service functionaries) Employers with female workforce	Blue-collar workers (Capital accumulators) Employers with male workforce

composition of their core constituencies to identify the parties expected to be particularly sensitive to specific interest and value profiles. This development of hypotheses on policy positions and alliance potentials relies on the strong and possibly problematic assumption that collective actors mainly aggregate the preferences of their members. This assumption neglects the complexity of interest aggregation, even though the positions taken by collective actors undeniably depend not only on whom they represent but also on how this representation is institutionalized procedurally (Anderson and Lynch 2007) and on the selection and socialization of the elites (Campbell and Lynch 2000). In this book, I nevertheless make this strong structuralist argument for the sake of theoretical clarity. In addition, although I expect the positions of collective actors to reflect the preferences of their members, I do not assume that there is a direct and perfect link. For example, I do not expect that the proportion of service-sector members of a trade union precisely predicts the position of that actor in a specific reform. Rather, I expect that a trade union with a large share of service-sector members is more receptive to reforms that affect this section of the workforce than is a trade union whose members are almost exclusively employed in the industrial sector. In that sense, what counts for the analytical model of this book are trends and comparisons, for which a structuralist approach holds important insights.

Expected Positions of Political Parties in Post-Industrial Pension Politics

In contrast to the socialist and social democratic parties that organized labor almost a century ago, hardly any post-industrial political party was founded explicitly in the name of gender, skill levels, or labor market status. Rather, the

TABLE 4.6. *Party Preferences of Post-Industrial Risk Groups: France*

	Support for the Left		Support for the Right			
	New Left	Old Left/Labor	Center Right	Moderate Right	Radical Right	None
Capital accumulators	−7.6**	−9.0**	+3.4	+4.9*	+0.9	+1.2
Blue-collar workers	−3.6	+1.2	−4.3**	−4.6*	+7.3**	+1.9
Sociocultural professionals	+4.7**	+4.6*	+1.6	−0.4	−3.5***	−3.1
Low service functionaries	+2.1	−0.2	−2.5	−2.0	+0.4	+2.3
Mean in workforce	39.0%	40.4%	9.9%	17.0%	6.2%	18.3%
Number of observations	1,054	1,054	1,054	1,054	1,054	1,054

$^*p < .05;$ $^{**}p < .01;$ $^{***}p < .001$ (t-test).

Notes: Values are percentage points of over- or underrepresentation of each group's party support relative to the country mean. New left: green and social democratic parties (les Verts, Parti socialiste [PSF]; old left: communist, and social democratic parties (PSF, Parti communiste [PCF], radical left parties); center right: Union pour la Démocratie Française (UDF); moderate right: Rassemblement pour la République (RPR); radical right: National Front; none: no party preference, no vote.
Source: ISSP 1996 Role of Government III. Question wording: "Which political party or movement do you feel close to?"

post-industrial labor markets have transformed preexisting parties from the inside. To a great extent, post-industrial interests and constituencies were absorbed in the existing party system (Kitschelt 1994; Kriesi et al. 2006), except for the rise of the libertarian green parties and the traditionalist new right-wing populists.

Tables 4.6 to 4.8. display the over- or underrepresentation of post-industrial classes within party electorates, relative to the mean share of that party in the workforce. I assume that parties are particularly responsive to the preferences and values of their distinctive core constituencies (i.e., the groups that appear to have an overproportional preference for the party), even though core constituencies might not be their largest support group from a strictly numeric standpoint.[5] Significant underrepresentation is highlighted with dark-gray shades, whereas significant overrepresentation is marked in lighter gray. Table 4.6 displays the patterns of class representation in France.

French capital accumulators (high-skilled insiders) have a strong preference for the moderate-right parties – the centrist Union pour la Démocratie française (UDF) and particularly the Gaullist Rassemblement pour la République (RPR) – and they clearly reject both the old and the new leftist parties. This pattern reflects their strong rejection of state interventionism. Hence, we can expect the parties

---

5 In absolute terms, for example, German sociocultural professionals are more supportive of the SPD than of the Green Party (Table 4.7). Nevertheless, their share among Green Party voters is massively higher than among any other party electorate. Therefore, sociocultural professionals are just one constituency among others for the SPD, but they are the core constituency of the Green Party. For this reason, I assume that, in my example, the Green Party will be particularly responsive to the concerns of sociocultural professionals (i.e. libertarian, high-skilled outsiders).

of the moderate right to advocate the preferences of market-liberal high-skilled insiders in favor of retrenchment and capitalization. In addition, the decidedly traditionalist profile of capital accumulators should make the UDF and RPR more reluctant to support targeting and recalibration. The traditionalist value profile is the common denominator of capital accumulators and blue-collar workers. The latter have become the distinctive core constituency of the French National Front, which combines traditionalist values with a more favorable stance on state interventionism (Bornschier 2010). Again for reasons of state interventionism, blue-collar workers also remain overrepresented among the old left, and clearly underrepresented among the moderate right. However, the expected positions of the old left parties are difficult to predict, because they also represent the interests and values of sociocultural professionals, whose values and risk profiles are quite the opposite from those of blue-collar workers. Indeed, France's sociocultural professionals are highly skilled and libertarian. They are a clear stronghold of the new left (i.e., the Green Party and the Socialist Party). The Green Party should thus espouse a clear preference for targeting and/or recalibration and capitalization, with a somewhat less strict preference for generous insurance conditions. The Socialist Party, by contrast, is rooted in both the old- and the new-left electorate. Therefore, the French old-left parties face a dilemma: they must negotiate a deep-seated loyalty to their industrial core constituency, the blue-collar workers, while appeasing their new membership, the sociocultural professionals. One might expect the Socialist Party to be hesitant and split on capitalization and targeting and recalibration, with regard to which the positions of these two groups diverge decidedly. Finally, low service functionaries show no distinctive and discernable party preference.

The picture is similar, for the most part, in Germany (Table 4.7). As in France, market-liberal capital accumulators are the core voters of the moderate right (Freie Demokratische Partei FDP) and – more clearly so – of the German Christian Democratic Party (Christlich Demokratische Union CDU and Christlich Soziale Union CSU): capital accumulators clearly reject the old left associated with state interventionism. However, they also tend to be somewhat overrepresented among the electorate of the Green Party (i.e., the libertarian new left). This is particularly interesting, as it coincides with the strong preference of the sociocultural professionals for this new-left party. This convergence of capital accumulators and sociocultural professionals in the new left stems from two separate circumstances: (1) capital accumulators in Germany are far less traditionalist than their French counterparts, and (2) German sociocultural professionals have a strong state-interventionist profile.

In terms of party positions, this implies that the Green Party should be rather strongly in favor of capitalization, targeting, and recalibration, and that its opposition to retrenchment might be somewhat less pronounced. The FDP and the CDU/CSU can be expected to advocate cost containment and capitalization quite strongly, though they might reject targeting and/or recalibration, which do not benefit their high-skilled insider constituency. Nevertheless, two qualifications may temper right-wing opposition against outsider coverage and gender equality. First, capital accumulators in Germany have an ambiguous value profile; second,

TABLE 4.7. *Party Preferences of Post-Industrial Risk Groups: Germany*

	Support for the Left		Support for the Right			
	New Left	Old Left/Labor	Christian Democracy	Moderate Right	Radical Right	None
Capital accumulators	+3.7	−6.1**	+8.4**	+2.9	−1.4*	−7.5***
Blue-collar workers	−5.6***	+1.8	−3.6*	−3.5***	+3.0**	+8.1***
Sociocultural professionals	+10.2***	+1.2	−7.2**	+2.1	−1.8**	−6.4***
Low service functionaries	−6.3**	+0.8	+0.8	−2.29	−1.3*	+9.8***
Mean in workforce	15%	28.1%	27.5%	8.1%	1.8%	18.0%
N observations	1,301	1,301	1,301	1,301	1,301	1,301

$^*p < .05$; $^{**}p < .01$; $^{***}p < .001$ (t-test).

Notes: Values are percentage points of over- or underrepresentation of each group's party support relative to the country mean. New left: green party (Bündnis 90/Grüne); old left: communist and social democratic parties (Sozialdemokratische Partei Deutschlands [SPD], Partei des Demokratischen Sozialismus [PDS]); Christian democracy: Christlich Demokratische Union (CDU)/Christlich Soziale Union (CSU); moderate right: Freie Demokratische Partei (FDP); radical right: Nationaldemokratische Partei Deutschlands (NPD), Deutsche Volksunion (DVU), Republikaner; none: would not vote (the categorization follows Oesch 2005). *Source:* ISSP 1996 Role of Government III. Question wording: "If there is a general election next Sunday, which party would you elect with your second vote?"

the Christian democrats were generally the "natural choice" (Kolinsky 1993: 123) for women until the late 1970s (Rusciano 1992), because of religious beliefs and traditional gender roles. Women turned politically to the left throughout the Western democracies not least as a result of their changed status in labor markets and households (Inglehart and Norris 2000; Iversen and Rosenbluth 2006). Since then, Christian democracy has lacked an actual core constituency and struggles to find a way between the preservation of their male-breadwinner past and a strategic modernization of its policy positions (van Kersbergen and Manow 2009; Frey 2009). The position of the old left – notably the German Social Democrats (Sozialdemokratische Partei Deutschlands SPD) – is also complex to predict, because their core constituencies have become more diverse; both sociocultural professionals and blue-collar workers continue to be overrepresented in the electorate of this party. This cross-class appeal of the German old left makes the SPD face the same kind of dilemma the French socialists confront: the old left must choose whether to support capitalization, targeting, and recalibration in the interest of their libertarian, high-skilled outsider electorate (sociocultural professionals) or to reject it on the behalf of the traditionalist low-skilled insiders (blue-collar workers). Finally, the most distinctive trait of low service functionaries is again their tendency not to identify with any party at all. However, it should be noted that their profile also indicates a general distrust of extremes: they are underrepresented both among the voters of the radical right and among green voters.

Finally, Switzerland displays a peculiar characteristic with regard to capital accumulators who are rather clearly libertarian, despite the fact that they also favor strong market liberalism (see Table 4.4). This leads to a rather heterogeneous pattern of party preferences (Table 4.8).

TABLE 4.8. *Party Preferences of Post-Industrial Risk Groups: Switzerland*

	Support for the Left		Support for the Right			
	New Left	Old Left/Labor	Christian Democracy	Moderate Right	Radical Right	None
Capital accumulators	+1.5	+0.1	−1.7	+5.5*	+1.8	−7.0*
Blue-collar workers	−4.3**	−2.8	+2.1	−4.0***	+1.4	+4.3
Sociocultural professionals	+6.8***	+6.5***	+0.8	−0.4	−2.4**	−4.6*
Low service functionaries	−2.5	−3.3	−2.2*	−0.5	−2.9**	+7.4**
Mean in workforce	19.2%	16.6%	5.6%	8.0%	6.6%	58.6%
N observations	1,636	1,636	1,636	1,636	1,636	1,636

$^*p < .05$; $^{**}p < .01$; $^{***}p < .001$ (t-test).

Notes: Values are percentage points of over- or underrepresentation of each group's party support relative to the country mean. New left: green and social democratic parties (Grüne Partei Schweiz [GPS], Grünes Bündnis [GB], Sozialdemokratische Partei Schweiz [SPS]); old left: social democratic and communist parties (SPS, Partei der Arbeit [PdA], Progressive Organisationen der Schweiz [POCH]); Christian democracy: catholic and protestant parties (Christlichdemokratische Volkspartei [CVP], Evangelische Volkspartei [EVP], Christlichsoziale Partei der Schweiz [CSP]); moderate right: market liberal parties (Freisinnig-Demokratische Partei der Schweiz [FDP], Landesring der Unabhängingen [LdU], Liberale Partei der Schweiz [LPS]; radical right: conservative and radical right-wing parties (Schweizerische Volkspartei [SVP], Freiheits-Partei der Schweiz [FPS], Schweizer Demokraten [SD] Lega); none: no party preference (the classification follows Oesch 2005).

Source: ISSP 1996 Role of Government III. Question wording: "Generally, do you feel affiliated or sympathize with a specific political party (without necessarily being a member)?"

Although the moderate right, notably the market-liberal Radical Party (Freisinnig-Demokratische Partei FDP), is the main representative of capital accumulators, the new left – i.e. the Green Party (Grüne Partei Schweiz GPS) and the Social Democrats (Sozialdemokratische Partei Schweiz SPS) – and the populist right – i.e. the Swiss People's Party (Schweizerische Volkspartei SVP) – also gather a slightly overproportional share of their votes. Capital accumulators' preference for the new left is probably the result of education and values, whereas their support of the populist right is more likely the result of right-wing market liberalism and of their insider status. Hence, capital accumulators in Switzerland have a mixed and interesting profile; as libertarians, they share an affinity with the new left, and as insiders they gravitate toward the right together with the traditionalist blue-collar workers. The core constituency of Switzerland's old left is similar to that of the Green Party. However, the old left scores somewhat weaker among capital accumulators than does the Green Party and stronger among blue-collar workers. This indicates that libertarian values are probably less important in explaining the party support for the old left than for the Green Party. Even more so than in the German case, the Swiss Christian Democrats (Christlichdemokratische Volkspartei CVP) lack a clear-cut core constituency. Until the late 1980s, they had widespread and firm support in the Catholic cantons, mostly among low-skilled men and religious women. With secularization and modernization, however, they lost a clearly identifiable sociostructural basis and their programmatic policy positions have become negotiable and blurred (Gees 2004; Frey 2009). Finally, Switzerland is in line with France and Germany in terms of low-skilled outsiders (low service functionaries) who have no discernable party-political representation.

This rather mixed and complex pattern of support – with some parties drawing on several classes and others lacking a clear core constituency – produces a complex picture of the expected configuration of the Swiss political parties in pension politics. The moderate right-wing parties, notably the FDP, should clearly support retrenchment. Their position on targeting and recalibration, by contrast, is difficult to predict, as they might reject it on the behalf of their insider constituency or support it on the basis of the libertarian value profile of their core electorate. The new and old lefts, in turn, should be decidedly in favor of targeting and recalibration and have a somewhat less pronounced stance on insurance (especially among the Green Party, the spearhead of the new left). The right-wing populist party SVP mobilizes both blue-collar workers and capital accumulators. Therefore, it probably has no clear profile with regard to retrenchment. By contrast, the SVP is likely to reject targeting and recalibration, given the very low representation of outsider interests in its electorate.

Overall, the pattern of expected party conflicts that emerges from this analysis is rather similar across the three countries: generally, the new left advocates the interests and values of sociocultural professionals, and the old left builds on a mixed constituency of blue-collar workers and sociocultural professionals. Moderate right-wing parties tend to be the voice of market-liberal capital accumulators, and the radical right largely draws on blue-collar workers. Low service functionaries, by contrast, are politically alienated; their most significant party preference is the nonvote, which is a reason for serious concern, as they belong to the most precarious risk groups of all and because their number is growing in post-industrial economies.

This analysis of the core constituencies of today's parties is also perfectly in line with the findings of recent (electoral) research on changing patterns of party support. Three developments are key. First, the electoral constituencies of left parties have diversified under post-industrial conditions (see Kitschelt and Rehm 2005; in a similar vein, see Oesch 2005; Häusermann 2008). This development has been particularly strong in countries such as Germany, France, and Switzerland, where polarization on economic issues has become weaker and has been partly replaced by polarization on cultural issues since the 1970s. In these countries, the left-wing parties build on a very heterogeneous coalition of classes, which presents them with particular dilemmas in social and economic policy reforms. Second, in the wake of societal transformation of family structures and labor markets, the Christian democratic parties have lost much of their traditional (female) constituencies. Today, their electorate is very heterogeneous both culturally and economically, and these parties are stuck in both a structural and strategic dilemma regarding the choice of the constituencies in whose interest they advocate social and economic policies (van Kersbergen and Manow 2009; Frey 2009). Third and last, low-skilled blue-collar workers increasingly tend to cast a conservative vote

(Oesch 2005; Bornschier 2010; Kriesi et al. 2008). Although Kitschelt (1997) claimed that the magic formula for the success of the new radical right in the late 1980s and early 1990s was its combination of market liberalism with cultural con-servatism, Bornschier (2010) shows that these parties indeed have been and still are decidedly traditionalist. Economically, by contrast, they have a very diffuse and negotiable profile, which most certainly results from the favorable attitudes of blue-collar workers toward state intervention.

Expected Positions of Trade Unions in Post-Industrial Pension Politics

As with political parties, post-industrial risk profiles increase the heterogeneity of interests among workers and lead to growing intra-labor conflict (see, e.g., Ebbinghaus and Manow 2001; Ebbinghaus 2001; Mares 2000, 2001a; Trampusch 2005). Consequently, social policy analysis can no longer conceptualize labor and capital as unitary actors but must unpack different trade union interests.[6]

Labor organization rates in France are extremely low, comparatively, dropping from slightly more than 20 percent of the workforce in the 1970s to less than 8 percent at the end of the 1990s. These low numbers, however, do not reflect the power resources of the unions. In times of crisis, the French *syndicats* have repeatedly proved able to mobilize large mass demonstrations, movements that gathered far more participants than their formal members, and thus they managed to successfully veto ongoing reforms. Moreover, they are closely involved in the management of most social protection schemes (Palier 2003) – something that confers a de facto veto power on them. Thus, in spite of their weak organizational strength, French unions are crucial actors in the reform processes.

High-skilled employees and managers in France are mostly organized within the Confédération Générale des Cadres (CGC).[7] The CGC's share of the orga-nized workforce is rather small (between 5 percent and 7 percent since 1970), but because it has a skill-specific profile, it has a clear role in the labor movement. It is also the only large union that organizes a majority of its members – about 64 percent in 1993 – in the private sector, both in industry (mainly metal and chemicals) and in services (banks and insurance). This quota is inverted for the

---

[6] Identifying the core constituencies of trade unions is more difficult than for political parties because of a scarcity of data. Ebbinghaus and Visser (2000) provide statistics and qualitative and historical information on trade union membership in Western Europe by sectors, gender, and skill levels, but when information on the organization of gender and insiders or outsiders is lacking, the analysis of trade union constituencies must rely on proxies, such as service-sector employment as a proximate measure of female membership.

The link between the preferences of the members and the position of the trade union may, of course, be rather tenuous, depending on the country-specific historical and political context. Trade unions in France base their power on mobilization rather than membership. They are thus more independent from their members than German unions (Ebbinghaus and Visser 2000). Nevertheless, as with parties, I assume that the membership profile indeed holds insight on the expected positions a union will defend.

[7] The numbers in this section are – unless otherwise indicated – taken from the tables in Ebbinghaus and Visser (2000: 269–77, CD-ROM).

TABLE 4.9. *Representation of Post-Industrial Risk Constituencies in the Main (Peak) Labor Unions After the 1970s: France*

	Insiders/Men	Outsiders/Women
High-skilled workforce	Confédération Générale des Cadres (CGC)	Confédération Française Démocratique du Travail (CFDT) / Confédération Générale des Cadres (CGC)
Low-skilled workforce	Confédération Générale du Travail (CGT)	Confédération Française Démocratique du Travail (CFDT)

four main competitors of the CGC: the communist Confédération Générale du Travail (CGT), the moderate socialist Confédération Française Démocratique du Travail (CFDT), the socialist-syndicalist Force Ouvrière (FO), and the Christian democratic Confédération Française des Travailleurs Chrétiens (CFTC), all of which recruit more than two-thirds of their members from the public sector. Although the CGT was clearly the biggest and most powerful union in the 1970s, counting almost half of the organized workforce among its members, the CGT's dropped to less than 25 percent in the mid-1990s. The CFDT, by contrast, has emerged as an equally powerful rival of the CGT. Both the CGT and the CFDT organize primarily the lower-skilled employees. Aside from their ideological differences (the CGT being communist and the CFDT reformist), the two unions differ markedly in terms of the gender composition of their membership, because they recruit in different sectors. The CGT is the most important labor union in male-dominated industries (e.g., utilities, railways, the chemical and metal industries). In these sectors, the CGT still represents between a third and half of the organized workforce, but its share of organized labor in commerce dropped from 30–50 percent in the early 1970s to only 12–18 percent by the 1990s. In the service sectors – banks, insurance, and commerce – the CFDT has become the main advocate of labor interests, representing between 30 percent and 40 percent of the organized employees. Moreover, the CFDT is also the strongest union in public health, education, and textiles, three sectors with high female labor representation.

In summary (see Table 4.9), high-skilled workers (capital accumulators and some of the sociocultural professionals) rely on the CGC, whereas low-skilled male insiders (blue-collar workers) are strongly represented by the CGT. Finally, the CFDT counts a higher proportion of women – both high- and low-skilled – among its members and therefore is also expected to be more open to outsider interests.

In terms of policy preferences, Table 4.9 implies that the CGC and – to a lesser extent – the CFDT should be more favorable toward capitalization than the CGT, which is exclusively a low-skilled union. By contrast, the CFDT is likely to support targeting in favor of outsiders, working against the insider-driven interests of the CGT (and less so those of the CGC). All unions, however, are supposed to fight retrenchment and defend generous insurance conditions for all employees.

The German structure of trade unions is more vertically concentrated than the French one; one highly powerful peak union (the Deutscher Gewerkschaftsbund [DGB]) represents more than 80 percent of the organized workforce (about 30–40 percent of all workers). The DGB's main rivals are the public sector union Deutscher Beamtenbund (DBB) (about 10 percent of the organized workforce) and the high-skilled union Deutscher Angestelltenverband (DAG) (5–6 percent of the organized workforce).[8] Other peak associations, such as the Christian democratic Christliche Gewerkschaft Deutschland (CGD) and the union of managers Union Leitender Angestellter (ULA) are of only marginal importance compared to the former three. This strong vertical concentration and the traditionally strong ties of the DGB to the SPD (Trampusch 2004) and the neo-corporatist arrangement of decision making (Katzenstein 1987) are the main reasons trade unions have been a powerful actors in German decision making since the 1950s.

Even though the DGB's share of high-skilled, white-collar workers has been increasing steadily (from 14 percent in 1970 to 30 percent at the end of the 1990s), it remains the stronghold of the low-skilled, blue-collar unions such as IG Metall (metal industry) and IG Bau (construction and mining industries). German high-skilled employees in the private sector are organized in the DAG, whereas white-collar civil servants are represented by the DBB. However, although the DBB represents insiders with highly privileged work contracts, the DAG recruits in diverse sectors such as industry, commerce, banking and financing, public administration, and welfare services. Therefore, the DAG is by far the most "feminized" trade union. Between 1970 and 1998, its share of female members grew from an already sizable 32 percent to 55 percent. In this fashion, the DAG has become the single largest and most powerful trade union with a majority of women members. In comparison, female representation in the DGB and the DBB has always remained low (rising from about 15 percent in the 1970s to no more than 30 percent at the end of the century). Given the DAG's strong roots in feminized service sectors, I expect the DAG to be particularly responsive to the needs and demands of high-skilled outsiders. Furthermore, sectoral differentiation is apparent in the organization of low-skilled workers. While industrial unions like IG Metall and IG Bau are the powerful strongholds of low-skilled male insiders (less than 20 percent female members), low-skilled women have traditionally been a core constituency of the Gewerkschaft Öffentliche Dienste, Transport und Verkehr (ÖTV), the union for public services and transport (about 45 percent female members) and Gewerkschaft Handel, Banken, Versicherungen (HBV), the union for commerce, banking, and insurance (about 67 percent female members). In the DGB, however, these feminized sectoral unions have always remained a minority. It is therefore crucial to note that in 2001, ÖTV, HBV, and DAG – together with the unions for postal services and the media – merged into Vereinte Dienstleistungsgewerkschaft "ver.di", a new service union that has become the second-largest union in the DGB. Ver.di was conceived explicitly

---

[8] The numbers in this section are – unless otherwise indicated – taken from the tables in Ebbinghaus and Visser (2000: 305–37, CD-ROM), as well as Armingeon (1988).

TABLE 4.10. *Representation of Post-Industrial Risk Constituencies in the Main (Peak) Labor Unions After the 1970s: Germany*

	Insiders/Men	Outsiders/Women
High-skilled workforce	Deutsche Angestellten-Gewerkschaft (DAG) / Deutscher Beamtenbund (DBB)	Deutsche Angestellten-Gewerkschaft (DAG) (member of ver.di since 2000)
Low-skilled workforce	Deutscher Gewerkschaftsbund (DGB) (IG Metall, IG Bau)	Gew. öffentlicher Dienst (ÖTV) / Handel Banken Versicherungen (HBV) (both members of ver.di since 2001)

as an institutional reform adapting the German trade union movement to the challenges of the service economy. Thus, ver.di is the foremost trade union in sectors with a high proportion of women and outsiders, both high and low skilled. Table 4.10 summarizes these profiles.

Again, all unions are expected to defend similar policy positions against retrenchment. By contrast, DAG and DBB should be more open to the introduction of capitalized pensions than the low-skilled unions DGB and ver.di. Finally, DAG may advocate targeting and recalibration together with ver.di, against the male bastions DGB and DBB.

In Switzerland, about a third of the workforce was organized until the 1990s, but this rate declined to slightly more than 25 percent by end of the twentieth century.[9] The weakness of organized labor is both the fruit of Switzerland's liberal hegemony (Mach 2006) and the result of labors' ideological fragmentation (i.e., its split into socialist, Christian democrat, or secular unions; [Kriesi 1998]). Despite this fragmentation, trade unions are important political actors in Switzerland for institutional reasons. Given the direct democratic (Neidhart 1970) and neo-corporatist decision-making context (Katzenstein 1985), labor and capital negotiate reforms early in the policy-making processes in powerful committees; they traditionally have strong ties to parliamentarians, and they can mobilize support against reforms in popular referenda.[10]

Given the fragmentation of the unions, there is a highly differentiated landscape of labor interests in Switzerland. High-skilled employees are organized within the Verein der Schweizerischen Angestelltenverbände (VSA), a white-collar peak union, which has been representing between 13 percent and 16 percent of the organized workforce since the 1970s. This union is rather small but important because of its clear membership profile and strong organizational basis among the employees in commerce, in the banking and insurance sector, and in

[9] The numbers in this section are – unless otherwise indicated – taken from the tables in Ebbinghaus and Visser (2000: 673–703, CD-ROM), as well as Fluder et al. (1991) and Fluder (1996).
[10] In Switzerland, each law can be contested in an optional popular referendum, if an actor is able to collect fifty thousand signatures against it within ninety days after the approval of the bill in parliament.

TABLE 4.11. *Representation of Post-Industrial Risk Constituencies in the Main (Peak) Labor Unions After the 1970s: Switzerland*

	Insiders/Men	Outsiders/Women
High-skilled workforce	Vereinigung Schweizerischer Angestelltenverbände (VSA)	Vereinigung Schweizerischer Angestelltenverbände (VSA)
Low-skilled workforce	Schweizerischer Gewerkschaftsbund (SGB) / Christlichnationaler Gewerkschaftsbund (CNG)	Gewerkschaft Verkauf Handel Transport Lebensmittel (VHTL) / Verband des Personals öffentlicher Dienste (VPOD)

industry. However, the VSA still operates in the shadow of the nation's largest union, the Schweizerischer Gewerkschaftsbund (SGB), the socialist peak trade union, whose share of the organized workforce has been almost 50 percent during the past thirty years. The SGB is the political representative of powerful industrial unions in the construction (Gewerkschaft Bau und Industrie [GBI]) and metal industries (Schweizerischer Metall- und Uhrenindustrieverband [SMUV]). The SGB has a smaller Christian democratic rival sibling, the Christlichnationaler Gewerkschaftsbund (CNG, named Travail.Suisse since 2003) with a similar constituency, yet a smaller share of the organized workforce (only about 10 percent). Women are markedly underrepresented in the Swiss labor movement, accounting for no more than 15–20 percent of the organized workforce. This is not terribly surprising, as most women in Switzerland work part-time (outsiders) and in the weakly unionized service sector. The SGB, for instance, counted not more than 10–20 percent of women among its members between 1970 and 2000. Hence, women and outsiders are concentrated mainly in three unions: the high-skilled VSA (almost 30 percent of female members since the end of the 1980s), the Gewerkschaft Verkauf Handel Transport Lebensmittel (VHTL), a sectoral union in food industry and retail commerce (25–30 percent female members) and the Verband des Personals Öffentlicher Dienste (VPOD), the public-sector union in utilities, public administration, education, health and welfare services (whose female membership has continuously risen from 13 increased in the mid-1970s to 37 percent in the late 1990s). Both VHTL and VPOD are members of the SGB, within which they are, however, very minor players: the VHTL represents about 5 percent of the SGB members and the VPOD about 10 percent. Hence, as in Germany, Swiss women and outsiders remain marginal in all of the important peak unions (Armingeon and Beyeler 2000). The labor movement has remained the stronghold of male insiders, both low and high skilled. Table 4.11 summarizes the main advocates of post-industrial risk constituencies in Switzerland.

In terms of policy preferences, I expect the more feminized service sector unions (VHTL, VPOD) and the VSA to be more favorable to targeting and recalibration than the predominantly male SGB and CNG. By contrast, all unions, including VSA, should argue against retrenchment, as in the other countries.

Expected Positions of Employers' Organizations in Post-Industrial Pension Politics

The recent literature has become increasingly ambiguous regarding the expected preferences of business on welfare policies. In contrast to the conventional assumption that capital will always and by definition opt for the lowest possible benefit levels, recent research has shown that large firms in high-skilled sectors may actually support generous income replacement as an incentive for employees to specialize in specific skills (Mares 2003; Estevez-Abe et al. 2001). However, employers – even in high-skilled sectors of coordinated market economies – will most certainly not support high replacement rates as such. Their interests lie in strongly stratified and segmented benefits, which enable them to differentiate the incentives for various groups of employees. Even though they may favor generous benefits for the most skilled and valuable part of their workforce, employers have little reason to claim more than minimum coverage for the low skilled. Hence, it is capitalization rather than insurance that is most likely to gather the (partial) support of business in post-industrial pension politics. Not all firms are of the critical size, however, to be able to provide funded pension schemes to their workforce. Hence, I expect employers in high-skilled sectors and large firms to support capitalized pensions, whereas small and low-skilled firms have a stronger interest in pooling risks across the whole economy. Therefore, although I expect a unified front of employers in favor of cost containment, intra-capital conflict should emerge most strongly with regard to capitalization, on the basis of firm size. Targeting is the second reform dimension that is likely to split capital. Demographic prospects forecast a shortage of skilled labor within the next fifteen to twenty years. Hence, employers in sectors relying on a female, highly skilled workforce are increasingly interested in the participation of skilled women workers in the labor market. Targeting reforms can be an incentive for such women to participate in the labor market, because they make typically female work patterns more remunerative in terms of social rights. By contrast, employers of low-skilled and/or male-dominated sectors (e.g., construction, small trade) are unlikely to support any such claims for targeting in favor of outsiders; these employers have no interest whatsoever in contributing financially to risk pools that their employees will hardly ever benefit from. Therefore, I expect a conflict between employers in feminized and high-skilled (service) sectors, and employers in male-dominated and/or low-skilled sectors. Finally, there is little reason to expect any firm to support the granting of social rights to people absent from the labor market, as recalibration does. Therefore, I assume a unified front of employers against these reforms.

To identify the business organizations most likely to mobilize these conflicts, one would ideally focus on sectoral employer organizations with a clear profile in terms of skill, gender, and size (e.g. construction, retail trade, banking, the machine industry). However, business is generally more strongly coordinated than labor. Sectoral business organizations do not intervene in political reform processes on their own, unless there is a blatant conflict among different sectors.

Therefore, the focus in this book is on peak organizations. The distinction between the peak organizations of large and small firms comprises much of the variation in terms of the relevant risk profiles. Indeed, large companies in all countries are organized separately from small trade; these sectoral differences correlate strongly with skill levels and gender. Large firms tend to employ a higher proportion of highly skilled employees, whereas small firms cluster in the lower skilled sectors. Similarly, small-business employer organizations primarily represent sectors like construction, bastions of the male workforce. Large firms in highly productive service sectors – such as banking and insurance – tend to be more dependent on the female workforce, and thus I expect them to be somewhat more open to the claims of outsiders.

In France, large firms in the industrial sector are represented by the Conseil National du Patronat Français (CNPF) (named today Mouvement des Entreprises de France [MEDEF]), and small entrepreneurs are represented by the Confédération Générale des Petites et Moyennes Entreprises (CGPME). The increasing importance of suborganizations such as the organization of female employers (Association de Femmes Chefs d'Entreprise) within the MEDEF indicates an increasing willingness to meet post-industrial demands (Bunel 1995). The CGPME, by contrast, is rooted in small business – mostly crafts and construction. The difference between the two organizations is not only structural but also ideological: representatives of the CGPME insist on the existence of "deux patronats...: le patronat réel et le patronat de gestion" (i.e., employers who own their business and invest their own fortune and reputation in the business as opposed to managers who work for a firm and are not personally involved in it) (Bunel 1995: 50). This ideological distinction becomes manifest in the more patriarchal and value-conservative profile of the CGPME. In Germany, the Bundesvereinigung der Deutschen Arbeitgeberverbände (BDA) represents the interests of the large capital owners and managers, and its smaller rival, the Zentralverband des deutschen Handwerks (ZdH), is the primary lobby of small businesses and construction firms. The BDA is clearly the most powerful employer's organization in Germany (Schroeder and Silvia 2003). The distinction between the BDA and ZdH is based on the economic sector (crafts versus industry and/or services) rather than on ideology or firm size, as in France. But the structural differences in terms of skill levels, gender and – particularly – firm size, are largely analogous to the differences between the MEDEF and CGPME in France. Finally, a similar pattern can be found in Switzerland, where the association of small businesses and crafts Schweizerischer Gewerbeverband (SGV) confronts the peak organization of business interests Schweizerischer Arbeitgeberverband (SAV). The powerful SAV represents the export-oriented firms of the Swiss economy, such as pharmaceuticals and machines, whereas the power of the SGV is rooted in the sheltered sectors, such as construction (Kriesi 1998; Mach 2006). These differences led to an increasingly difficult relationship between the two during the 1990s, when the representatives of large capital put market liberalization on the agenda and ended their traditional solidarity with the sheltered sectors (Mach 2006). These conflicts led to a generalized deepening of the split

TABLE 4.12. *Representation of Business Interests in Peak Employer Organizations*

	Crafts and Small Trade/ Small Firms	Industry and Services/ Large Firms
France	Confédération Générale des Petites et Moyennes Entreprises (CGPME)	Mouvement des Entreprises de France (MEDEF) (formerly CNPF)
Germany	Zentralverband des deutschen Handwerks (ZdH)	Bundesvereinigung der deutschen Arbeitgeberverbände (BDA)
Switzerland	Schweizerischer Gewerbeverband (SGV)	Schweizerischer Arbeitgeberverband (SAV)

between SGV and SAV. This split is also likely to become manifest in pension policy making, as SGV and SAV differ with regard to firm size, sector, and skill levels: the SAV is more strongly represented in large firms with a more skilled workforce, whereas the SGV is mostly rooted in low-skilled, domestic sectors such as construction. Table 4.12 shows the two main employer organizations in all three countries.

The implications of the distinction between crafts and small firms and industry and services and/or large firms with regard to pension policy preferences are straightforward: I expect the MEDEF, BDA, and SAV to be more favorable to capitalization and somewhat more open to claims for targeting than the craft organizations CGPME, ZdH, and SGV. All employer organizations, in turn, are likely to support retrenchment and to reject recalibration.

To systematize expectations of the preferences of collective actors in France, Germany, and Switzerland developed in the preceding paragraphs, Table 4.13 contains the expected conflicts among the major political parties, trade unions, and business associations in the three countries. It can be read as a fleshed-out version of hypothesis 2, which posits that post-industrial pension politics in continental welfare states will involve multiple crosscutting conflict lines, because of the underlying sociostructural changes that drive and define this post-industrial era. In addition, Table 4.13 translates the hypotheses on post-industrial risk profiles from the sociostructural level to the macro level of decision-making processes in France, Germany, and Switzerland.

Until this point in the development of the analytical model of this book, we have seen that post-industrial pension reform gives rise to a plurality of conflict lines and to a variety of potential alliances for or against reforms. The ranks of likely supporters (or winners) are cross-class and heterogeneous in each of these dimensions. Thus, they all have the potential to combine the interests of very different groups, and in so doing, to create opportunities for "ambiguous agreements" (2005: 137) and "unexpected coalitions" (Pierson 2001: 427). To an extent, this very cross-class appeal of reforms like targeting and capitalization explains successful pension policy reforms that have taken place since the 1980s: employers may join with the high-skilled workforce to support capitalization.

TABLE 4.13. *Expected Conflict Lines in Post-Industrial Pension Politics*

Conflict Line	Risk Antagonism	France Pro	France Contra	Germany Pro	Germany Contra	Switzerland Pro	Switzerland Contra
Insurance	Labor vs. capital	Social Democrats PSF, Communist party PCF, National Front, (Green party), CFDT, CGT, (CGC)	Centrist party UDF, Conservative party RPR, MEDEF, CGPME	Social Democrats SPD, Socialist party PDS, (Green party), DGB, Ver.di, DAG, (DBB)	Liberal party FDP, Christian Democrats CDU/CSU, BDA, ZdH	Social Democrats SPS, Christian Democrats CVP, Communist party PdA, (Green party), SGB, CNG, (VSA)	Liberal party FDP, (Conservative party SVP, SVA, SGV
Capitalization	High-skilled labor and capital vs. low-skilled labor and capital	Centrist party UDF, Conservative party RPR, Green party, (Social Democrats PSF), MEDEF, CGC, (CFDT)	National Front, Communist party PCF, CGPME, CGT, (CFDT)	Liberal party FDP, Christian Democrats CDU/CSU, Green party, (Social Democrats SPD), BDA, DAG, DBB	Socialist party PDS, ZdH, DGB, Ver.di		
Targeting and recalibration	Outsiders and libertarians vs. insiders and traditionalists	Green party, (Social Democrats PSF), CFDT	Centrist party UDF, Conservative party RPR, National Front, (MEDEF), CGT, (CGC)	Green party (Social Democrats SPD), DAG, Ver.di	Christian Democrats CDU/CSU, (Liberal party FDP), DGB, ZdH, (BDA)	Green party, Social Democrats SPS, VSA	Conservative party SVP, (Christian Democrats CVP), (Liberal party FDP), SGV, (SAV), (SGB), (CNG)

Notes: This table focuses on the major actors only. Actors in parentheses are those for which the hypotheses are ambiguous; capitalization is not a distinctive conflict dimension in Switzerland (see Chapter 3); for abbreviations, see Tables 4.6.–4.12. in this chapter.

Market-liberal right-wing parties with a libertarian electorate may open to the claims of women for recalibration. And outsiders may find allies among the employers of a highly skilled female workforce to further labor market participation incentives through policies targeting the coverage of atypical employment.

However, the alignment of actors along the four conflict lines in Table 4.13 makes it clear that most conflicts foster an equally heterogeneous alliance of opponents: major trade unions, old-left parties, radical right-wing parties, and small firms, for instance, may mobilize against capitalization. The opposition may be even stronger when it comes to targeting and recalibration, because there is a broad front of insider-actors who have no interest whatsoever in supporting them, including radical right-wing parties, most of the moderate right-wing parties, and employer organizations, and even the majority of trade unions (along with some old-left parties). The constituencies of all these actors have hardly any reason to mobilize in favor of (low-skilled) outsiders, and this broad alliance potential for opponents to this kind of change is the reason why the new social risk literature is generally very skeptical with regard to the chances for targeting and recalibrating reforms (Bonoli 2006; Kitschelt and Rehm 2005; Ballestri and Bonoli 2003).

However, the fiercest opposition that post-industrial pension reformers are likely to face comes from actors rallying against cost containing – and even retrenching – reforms. Indeed, retrenchment reduces the existing social rights of all insured. Left-wing parties and all trade unions, and even some of the right-wing parties, are likely to mobilize in favor of preserving existing pension levels. Hence, as the literature has rightfully argued time and time again, cost-containing reforms in times of austerity will be most difficult to implement. This is true not only because the benefits of long-term financial stability are more dispersed than its immediate costs (Pierson 1996, 2001), but also because the conflict over insurance conditions is so polarized and so vital that it will have the strongest mobilizing potential and carry the biggest electoral risks (Kitschelt 2001).

This is where the dynamics of political exchange come into play. In a policy space that combines different dimensions of reform, the ranks of supporters and opponents of specific policies may be split. If different actors prioritize different reform dimensions, the mechanisms of political exchange create potentials for strategic package deals. The chances for such package deals to work out politically, however, depends on the coalitional flexibility and the number of veto players in a country. This is the final step in the theoretical framework this book develops, and it is the subject of Chapter 5.

5

Reform Outputs

Strategies of Coalitional Engineering

This last step in the development of the theoretical model of this book links the structural variables to policy outputs, that is, to the actual reform capacity of different countries. It deals with the mechanisms translating patterns of socio-structural conflict into policy change. Socio-structural reform potentials do not translate directly into policy outputs. Rather, they are mediated by politics. Politics in democratic contexts consist in the construction of viable majorities – or coalitions working for or against change. When and how such majorities are forged depends on two factors, which are not inherent in the configuration of preferences discussed in the previous chapter. First, the building of majorities depends on the strategies of policy entrepreneurs, mostly governments. Strategy involves setting the reform agenda in a way that guides the relevant actors in a particular direction – a practice I refer to as *coalitional engineering*. Most typically, this maneuvering involves actors' attempts to mobilize certain issues while keeping other topics away from the debates. Second, the effectiveness of these strategies depends on the behavioral and institutional opportunity structure the government is confronted with. In other words, the success of coalitional engineering depends on the willingness of political parties, trade unions, and employers' associations to join reform coalitions (i.e., it depends on their coalitional flexibility) and on the ability of governments to impose reforms against those opponents who are unwilling to join this coalition (i.e., on the presence or absence of veto players. The effects of these two variables – coalitional flexibility and institutional veto players – interact. The coalitional flexibility of political parties and economic interest organizations results from fragmentation: where power and the interests of actors are fragmented, coalitions are more variable than when parties and unions are strongly coordinated and speak with one voice. When governments confront opponents with low coalitional flexibility, the only way to enact successful policy change is to impose it against their will. This is only possible, however, if the opponents lack institutional veto power. Consequently, coalitional flexibility is a necessary condition for policy change in systems with institutional veto players, whereas change may be reached without the consent of large coalitions in their absence. Hence, the *reform capacity* in a particular country depends on strategies of coalitional engineering on the one hand and on the interaction between coalitional flexibility and the number of veto players on the other hand. In the following sections, I develop these two final hypotheses in more detail.

Coalitional Engineering in a Multidimensional Reform Space

The third hypothesis in the theoretical framework of this book argues that in the post-industrial era, governmental bill proposals are increasingly and strategically formulated in such a way as to include different reform dimensions, thereby allowing for political exchange in a multidimensional policy space. Why should this political mechanism become more important in the hard times of austerity? The answer is twofold. First, when resources become scarce, politics take on the character of a zero-sum-game, which sharpens distributional conflicts. Actors not only defend their interests; they also defend them against one another, which increases the probability of division and exchange. Second, and this is less obvious, political exchange may become increasingly important for successful reforms, because the defenders of the status quo have become more numerous and more powerful. The theoretical explanation of the power of these status quo stakeholders lies, of course, in Pierson's (1996: 147) brilliant analysis of "policy feedbacks." Policies tend to institutionalize and strengthen the power of the actors who created them in the first place, because institution building is a "contest among actors to establish rules, which structure outcomes to those equilibria most favorable to them" (Knight 1999: 20, qtd. in Thelen 2004: 32). By means of mechanisms of sequencing and increasing returns, institutions perpetuate and even accentuate power asymmetries between the early winners and early losers of this contest (Pierson 2000a, 2004). The early winners not only capture the immediate gains from newly created institutions; they also tend to adopt a key role in the control and management of these policy schemes. In this fashion, they consolidate their power over the early losers further down the road. This is one of the most prominent mechanisms of institutional path dependency, and it explains why institutional change becomes less and less likely over time.

There is another aspect in which Pierson's argument on policy feedback is highly relevant for understanding why political exchange has become crucial to post-industrial welfare reforms. Indeed, institutions not only privilege the needs of the "early winners" but also tend to produce their own constituencies of beneficiaries, thus adding an additional break on subsequent change. Pension policy is the most blatant example in this respect. Continental pension schemes are the outcome of a compromise between the unions and the employers of the industrial economy. Because of this, the members of the industrial sectors' core workforce are the early winners of pension institution building: they achieved increasingly generous pension rights during the three decades of steady postwar economic growth (Myles 1984; Schludi 2005). With the maturation of the pension regimes over time, however, the number of stakeholders in the existing schemes has also

grown: because continental pension insurance is based on the equivalence principle, time is the key factor producing growing numbers of contributors and beneficiaries, who have earned their own rights. Hence, in mature pension systems, all
employees – not to mention pensioners themselves – have an interest in generous
pension insurance and would be hurt in one way or another by retrenchment.
On the basis of this endogenous stabilizing mechanism, Pierson (1996, 2001) has
made his famous claim that, for electoral reasons, radical retrenchment in a fully
grown welfare state is highly unlikely, irrespective of the formal leeway of governments; a contention that is perfectly in line with the institutionalist literature
that views inertia as the normal status of institutions (Pierson 2000a; for a review
of the literature on institutional change, see Engeli and Häusermann 2009).

Pierson's analysis seems highly convincing at first glance. It explains why governments that want to modernize pension systems (i.e., to adapt them to the
challenges of austerity and post-industrialism) face a tremendously difficult task.
Nevertheless, retrenchment and comprehensive pension system restructuring
have taken place since the late 1970s. How can we make sense of these reforms
in the light of Pierson's insights? I argue that the key to this puzzle lies in a
distributional approach to institutional change and in a careful examination of
the role of actors' strategies. Pierson's argument on power asymmetries wrongly
assumes some sort of "institutionalist hegemony" of the early winners (Thelen
2004: 32), preempting subsequent contention. However, the more recent literature on institutional change – to which Thelen (2004), Hacker (2002, 2005),
Streeck and Thelen (2005), and Mahoney and Thelen (2010) are probably the
most important contributors – shows that institutions never eliminate the underlying political struggles for two main reasons: first, institutions rely on a "coalitional basis" of interests, which may shift gradually when the social, political, or
economic context changes (Thelen 2004: 33).[1] The preferences of early winners
are not frozen but may change if the costs and benefits that these actors derive
from existing institutions change in the wake of exogenous structural developments. Second, institutions also remain contested because they contain their
very own, endogenous sources of change: indeed, institutions produce not only
early winners and supporters of the status quo, but given their complex distributional consequences, they also produce different sets of institutional losers who
hold specific preferences with regard to institutional reform (see also Mahoney
and Thelen forthcoming). In that sense, institutions endogenously create their
own enemies. The implications for continental pension regimes are straightforward: these regimes have different distributional consequences for the high and

---

[1] A clear example of this can be seen in the preferences of employers with regard to male-breadwinner
institutions. In the industrial era, capitalists benefited from male-breadwinner institutions, as they
provided them with a sufficient amount of qualified male workers while regulating the work supply
by keeping women away from the labor market. Given the female educational revolution of the
past thirty years, however, as well as the demographic developments that are supposed to lead
to a shortage of skilled labor within the next twenty to thirty years (Jaumotte 2003; Reinberg
and Hummel 2003; Fuchs 2003), the same male-breadwinner welfare institutions have become
uneconomical for employers.

low skilled, for insiders and outsiders, and for women and men. Thereby, these institutions endogenously create new social risks among those social groups that are disadvantaged or neglected by the initial institutional setup. The victims of these new social risks, in turn, are potential contestants of the status quo. Outsiders, the low skilled, and women are interested in structural institutional change rather than in the mere expanding or scaling back of existing industrial pension schemes. Thus, even though Pierson was correct in emphasizing the pension system's growing constituency of beneficiaries, I would argue that he underestimated the importance of actors interested in a genuine reform of these schemes along dimensions other than insurance (namely targeting, recalibration, and capitalization). This is where we may find the answer to the previous question: how could policy makers achieve change in the face of an overwhelming front of defenders of the status quo? The answer this book proposes is that the policy makers built on the plurality of reform dimensions, thereby dividing the opposition against retrenchment.

Riker (1986) has formulated this strategy most powerfully in his conceptualization of heresthetics. Heresthetics, as an "art of political manipulation," denotes an attempt to "structure the world so you can win" (Riker 1986: ix). It consists of a strategy to overcome political opposition by framing the debate in a way that confronts opponents with a dilemma and forces them to take sides with one part of their constituency, thereby inevitably alienating the other part.[2] In policy making, this relates directly to the ability of governments to formulate policy proposals, which include several reform dimensions, thereby creating strong opportunities for political exchange in a multidimensional reform space. I hypothesize that this strategy of coalitional engineering is particularly effective in the context of austerity, because politics has turned from a positive to a zero-sum game. Indeed, during the industrial era of economic growth, pension politics was a positive-sum game; the issue at stake was how best to share the fruits of economic growth among different groups of beneficiaries while no constituency really lost anything. Even when the needs of particular risk groups appeared on the reform agenda, they could be accommodated without threatening the benefits of other risk groups. The introduction of educational pension credits for mothers in France in the early 1970s is a good case in point. Even trade unions, which represent the labor force

---

[2] A telling example that Riker (1986: 1) provides in his book *The Art of Political Manipulation* goes back to a debate between Lincoln and his Democrat rival Douglas in the town of Freeport, Illinois, in 1858. Douglas was running for senator of Illinois in 1858 and preparing the ground for his presidential campaign of 1860. In the debate, Lincoln raised the issue of slavery, on which the Democrats were internally divided. He forced Douglas to take a clear stance on whether federal states should be given the competence to ban slavery autonomously from their territory. This question put Douglas in a dilemma. If he answered yes, he would please his Illinois constituency and enhance his chance to become senator in 1858, yet he might lose the support of the Southern territories, necessary to win the presidential elections in 1860. By answering no, however, he would alienate his Northern voters. The whole strategy was to put Douglas in a position in which he had to answer the same question for both election campaigns at the same time (i.e., to confront him with a package deal).

rather than nonworking mothers, supported this expansion because it implied no negative cost whatsoever for their own clientele. Thereby, the context of welfare state growth facilitated solidarity within the left (i.e., among the trade union movement and social-democratic parties) and within the right.

Austerity, however, has profoundly changed the rules of the game. In today's context, pension politics is more like a zero-sum game (Riker 1987), in which one group's benefit comes at the expense of another group. The stakes become higher for each risk group, and solidarity among different constituencies is more difficult to uphold. Hence, when resources become scarcer, risk groups will not only struggle for their own interests but may even begin to oppose reforms that benefit other risk groups. To build on the foregoing example, if an improved coverage of nonworking mothers comes at the cost of retrenchment for standard workers, economic austerity may cause low-skilled insider unions to view recalibration with increasing skepticism. More generally, I expect collective actors to defend the narrow interests and values of their core constituency more clearly and more selectively in the context of austerity than in the context of expansion. As a result, policy packages threaten the solidarity between formerly allied risk groups and collective actors. In other words, such packages may not give rise to a single left-right conflict dimension anymore, but they may create a truly multidimensional policy space. In this way, they are likely to provide a more open structure of alliance opportunities.

Governments may, of course, combine the four pension-reform dimensions (i.e., insurance, targeting, recalibration, capitalization) in any way, yet some combinations and strategies are more plausible than others. Cross-class conflict lines (capitalization, targeting, recalibration) may blur the polarization that is supposed to prevail with regard to insurance. Indeed, insurance in the age of austerity means retrenchment, which – as outlined earlier – faces opposition far beyond the organized labor movement. All trade unions, the old left, the new left, the radical right, and even part of the moderate right are likely to oppose retrenchment on behalf of their constituencies (see Table 4.13). Therefore, multidimensionality and political exchange may become particularly important in reforms that involve retrenchment, for any government in any political system. For this reason, let me illustrate my discussion of coalitional engineering with two examples of packages that involve retrenchment. The following figures draw on the expected policy preferences of political constituencies that I have developed in Chapter 4. They illustrate the dilemmas that coalitional engineering may create for particular constituencies and for the collective actors who represent them.

The first hypothetical example, illustrated in Figure 5.1, is a reform bill that combines retrenchment on overall insurance conditions (insurance is the horizontal dimension) with expansive recalibrating measures (recalibration is the vertical dimension). The positions of different constituencies in this pension-reform space are derived from their risk profiles (see Table 4.2) and from their values concerning libertarianism and state intervention (see Table 4.4). As discussed in Chapter 3, blue-collar workers and insider unions have both a material interest in generous insurance conditions and a traditionalist value profile. Their

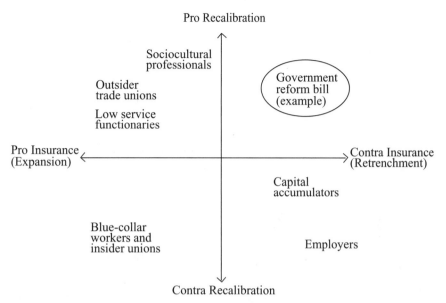

FIGURE 5.1. Expected positioning of political constituencies with regard to insurance and recalibration

positioning in the lower-left corner in Figure 5.1 is as straightforward as the position of sociocultural professionals in the upper-left quadrant. I positioned them somewhat more to the right, however, because of the ambivalence of their attitudes on state interventionism. Low service functionaries, being outsiders, should support recalibration, but given their more skeptical stance on libertarianism, their preference for recalibration is somewhat less pronounced. Finally, capital accumulators are clearly located toward the retrenchment pole of the retrenchment dimension; as insiders, they do not depend on recalibration. However, their value profile with regard to libertarianism is vague – a condition that shifts them to a more moderate position on the vertical axis as compared to employers. It is clear that no actor will be fully happy with a reform proposal that includes both retrenchment on insurance (e.g., a lengthening of the required contribution period) and expansive reforms on recalibration (e.g., a universal minimum pension). The advocates of blue-collar workers (low-skilled industry unions, the radical right-wing parties, the old left parties) may even oppose it ferociously. However, depending on how the advocates of capital accumulators and sociocultural professionals perceive the relevance of the issues at stake, the government may succeed in getting parties of the new left, some moderate right-wing parties, and even some outsider unions on board. The moderate right-wing parties face a dilemma, as they must decide whether to accept recalibration to achieve retrenchment, thereby alienating their more socially conservative basis, or to reject recalibration, thereby losing out on retrenchment. An even more complex dilemma arises for the new left: green parties and libertarian social democrats

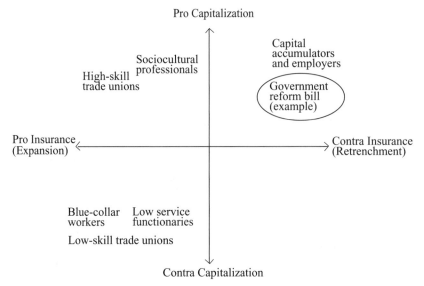

FIGURE 5.2. Expected positioning of political constituencies with regard to insurance and capitalization

must betray their traditional solidarity with blue-collar workers, if they want to do justice to their primarily libertarian constituencies. The problem is most acute for the social-democratic parties, which often count both old- and new-left constituencies among their core electorate (see Tables 4.6–4.8). Hence, in this example, coalitional engineering by the government may produce a social-liberal-libertarian coalition.

Figure 5.2 illustrates the second hypothetical example: a reform bill that combines retrenchment with the introduction of capitalized pension. Here, the positioning of constituencies on the vertical dimension is structured by actors' skill levels rather than labor market status or values. This means that capital accumulators and low service functionaries' positions change drastically, as compared to Figure 5.1. Capital accumulators are highly skilled and rely least on insurance, whereas low service functionaries are low skilled and depend on the public insurance scheme.[3] A package deal of retrenchment and capitalization again presents a challenge to the new left. The green parties and the social democrats can either align with their old-left constituency and low-skilled unions (by defending existing pension levels) or tolerate retrenchment, hoping to secure compensation for their highly skilled voters via capitalization. If they privilege insurance over capitalization, the high-skilled coalition for capitalization fails. But if they prioritize capitalization, a rather far-reaching transformation of the pension scheme may come into reach for the government.

---

[3] If I place this latter constituency somewhat to the right of blue-collar workers, it is because low-skilled outsiders are less privileged in the existing pension schemes, so they have less to lose from retrenchment than their male insider equivalents.

Both examples suggest that that the success of coalitional engineering depends largely on the relative importance that the collective political actors attribute to the different reform dimensions. If priorities differ among actors, the exchange rate for concessions differs among them, too, opening ways for political exchange. Thereby, the formation of policy-specific "legislative coalitions" in multidi- mensional policy spaces becomes "unstable... and susceptible to manipulation" (Laver and Schofield 1990: 119); in other words: policy outputs that otherwise seem highly unlikely become possible. I argue that this is precisely what has hap- pened in post-industrial continental pension politics since the late 1970s. Some studies have already provided selective evidence for such compromises in French and Swiss welfare reforms (Bonoli 2000, 2005; Levy 1999). The foregoing figures and arguments provide the theoretical underpinnings for the claim that political exchange becomes particularly important in the era of austerity.

Riker's idea of heresthetics and the corresponding analysis of policy-making dynamics and strategies are highly insightful. However, Riker (1986) makes implicit assumptions with regard to the behavior of actors that are problematic. First, actors are not entirely free to take any stance in the political reform space at any moment. Such a pure rational-choice model neglects the constraints on the coalitional flexibility of political actors. Trade unions, employers' associations, and political parties may have to coordinate their positions with other actors for historical, institutional, or electoral reasons.[4] If such constraints make them unwilling to join a carefully crafted compromise proposed by the government, the strategy of coalitional engineering may fail, if the opponents hold institutional veto power. Hence, my last hypothesis deals with the expected cross-country differences in coalition formation and policy outputs in France, Germany, and Switzerland – three countries that differ significantly with regard to coalitional flexibility and the number of veto players.

The Combined Impact of Coalitional Flexibility and Veto Players on Reform Capacity

The three hypotheses I have developed so far posit similarities across the pension regimes of France, Germany, and Switzerland on a range of variables, including a) the structural developments toward austerity and post-industrial social needs; b) the resulting conflict and alliance potentials among risk groups defined in terms of skill levels, labor market status, class, and values; and c) governmental strategies for the creation of multidimensional policy reform spaces that allow for political exchange. The fourth and final hypothesis of the theoretical model guiding the analyses in this book deals with cross-national differences in the determinants of successful coalitional engineering. Thereby, its goal is to account for differences with regard to the opportunities for modernizing reforms and the overall reform capacity of the three countries.

---

[4] In a similar vein, Shepsle (1979) and Laver and Schofield (1990: 126) have argued that institutions create incentives for particular coalitional "equilibria," thereby limiting the "unpredictability" of policy outputs in legislative processes that involve multiple reform dimensions.

The newly emerging conflict dimensions do not automatically restructure the configuration of actors according to skill levels, labor market status, or values. Whether the new conflict dimensions actually become salient dividing lines in the national pension reform processes depends on the coalitional flexibility of trade unions, employers' organizations, and political parties. Coalitional (in)flexibility results first and foremost from the fragmentation or concentration of actors both in the party political and in the corporatist arenas. If the power and interests of trade unions, employers' associations, and political parties are fragmented, the probability that new reform dimensions become manifest in the decision-making processes increases and so do the chances for new cross-class and value related reform coalitions. By contrast, the stronger the concentration of power and interests among the actors, the higher the probability that even post-industrial pension politics will eventually result in a one-dimensional conflict, opposing labor to capital and the governing to the opposition parties.

What do we mean by fragmentation versus concentration of power and interests? In the realm of labor and capital, concentration depends largely on the degree of vertical and horizontal integration of trade unions and employers' organizations (i.e., on the degree of corporatism). In the strongly corporatist systems of continental Europe, strong sectoral trade unions and business organizations are vertically integrated in peak associations (Schmitter 1979; Schmitter and Streeck 1981), which reinforces intra-labor and intra-capital cohesion. These systems allow for, but also require, each side to speak with one voice in the policy-making arena, thereby avoiding the formation of selective cross-class coalitions. In fragmented systems, by contrast, heterogeneity based on different sectors, firm size, or contrasting ideological stances is more frequent, because the institutionalized concentration of power and interests is weak. Hence, I expect that coalitional engineering is much more likely to divide the interests of different unions or employer organizations if they are fragmented, because their coalitional flexibility is higher.

A similar reasoning can be applied to political parties. The coalitional flexibility of political parties depends not only on the number of parties but also, and probably more so, on electoral constraints. In a majoritarian electoral context, where governmental power tends to alternate, opposition parties have almost no means whatsoever to influence the policy making process in parliament. As a result, their positions and interests are concentrated, and they speak with one voice against the government. The impact on coalition formation in (pension) policy-making processes is straightforward: in a concentrated context with weak coalitional flexibility, no opposition party has an interest in supporting any governmental proposal (what Schludi [2008] calls positional distance). There is hardly any chance that a left-wing opposition party, for example, will ever find itself aligning with a governing right-wing party on a specific reform, irrespective of the actual content of the reform bill. By contrast, in a fragmented system with a variable composition of political parties in government, policy-making coalitions form more pragmatically and political parties remain more flexible with regard to policy alliances. Even if the electoral polarization between government and opposition may be stark at a specific point in time, the chance of variable coalitions remains higher,

TABLE 5.1. *Coalitional Flexibility in France, Germany, and Switzerland*

		Political Parties	
		Fragmented	Concentrated
Trade unions **and employer** **organizations**	**Fragmented**	High coalitional flexibility *Switzerland (labor)*	Medium coalitional flexibility *France*
	Concentrated	Medium coalitional flexibility *Switzerland (capital)*	Low coalitional flexibility *Germany*

because the conflict line between government and opposition is redrawn after each election. An oversized or minority coalition is the extreme case of this kind of power fragmentation among political parties; it most clearly decouples policy specific coalition formation from immediate electoral constraints. Consequently, I expect governments in systems characterized by power fragmentation in the party-political realm to be more successful in fostering encompassing reform coalitions.

Table 5.1 shows the determinants of coalitional flexibility for the three countries: the weaker the concentration of unions and employers, and the more power fragmentation in the realm of political parties, the greater are the chances for varying, policy-specific coalition formation, and reform capacity. In such a system, the prospects of success for coalitional engineering are, a fortiori, higher than in the reverse case. The three countries included in this study differ precisely on their levels of coalitional flexibility, as can be seen in Table 5.1.

Overall, coalitional flexibility is highest in Switzerland, lowest in Germany and in between the two in France. Let me explain this characterization briefly for each country. In Switzerland, coalitional flexibility is high, in both the corporatist and the parliamentary arenas. Trade unions are well developed, but for historical reasons, they remain ideologically and sectorally fragmented (Mach and Oesch 2003; Fluder 1996; Fluder et al. 1991; Ebbinghaus and Visser 2000). According to Visser (1987), the Swiss labor movement is characterized by a medium degree of horizontal and vertical integration. Business interests, by contrast, have traditionally been more concentrated (Kriesi 1986).[5] In the party-political realm, fragmentation is even stronger. Switzerland has a multiparty system, proportional representation, and coalition governments at all state levels. Coalitional flexibility is particularly strong, as the country has been governed by a grand coalition including all major parties since 1959. These four parties – the Social Democratic Party, the Christian Democrats, the Liberal Party, and the Swiss People's Party – represent more than 80 percent of the seats in parliament. Hence, there is

---

[5] However, their cohesion has been declining since the 1990s, following the liberalization of the domestic markets, an issue that has dramatically split the sectors producing primarily for the domestic market (small businesses in crafts) and the export oriented sectors (large firms in industry and services) (see Mach 2006).

no actual concentration in the party system. The implication for coalitional engineering is that policy-making majorities in parliament change from one policy reform to another and on a basis that is both variable and pragmatic.

Somewhat surprisingly, Germany is quite different from Switzerland when it comes to coalitional flexibility. At first glance, describing its political parties as concentrated may be unexpected, as the country has a multiparty, proportional election system with some rights for the opposition in parliament (Powell 2000). However – in stark contrast to the consensus-requiring institutions of federalism and bicameralism (Lehmbruch 2000) – the electoral competition between the two major parties (the SPD and the CDU/CSU) became intensely polarized between the 1970s and the early 2000s (Wessels 2004). Indeed, while until the 1970s, the small Liberal Party's (FDP) moderate stance between the SPD and the CDU/CSU ensured some coalition flexibility, the electoral polarization of the party system has increased since then with the emergence of the Green Party. Between the late 1970s and the early 2000s (the period under scrutiny in this book), electoral concentration provoked a stark divide between government and opposition parties. In policy-making terms, such a configuration means that it is hard for an incumbent party to form a policy-specific coalition with a political party in the opposition – regardless of the actual similarities or differences in their respective policy preferences (Schludi 2008). Furthermore, trade unions and employers' organizations are rather strongly concentrated in Germany (Ebbinghaus and Visser 2000). Wages are negotiated at the industry level, which lends sectoral trade unions a strong position vis-à-vis the peak association, the Deutscher Gewerkschaftsbund (DGB). Traditionally, however, the unions of the key sectors (e.g., metal, chemistry) have been so dominant in the trade union movement that they have contributed to concentration rather than undermining it. Visser (1987) describes the German system as having a high degree of horizontal integration and a medium degree of vertical integration.[6] As a consequence, intra-labor and intra-capital heterogeneity is rather unlikely to manifest in the policy process.

Turning finally to France, we find the example of a hybrid case, combining an exceedingly fragmented system of corporatist interests with a strongly concentrated structure of party politics in parliament. French trade unions have a weak organizational density and are politically and sectorally strongly fragmented (Ebbinghaus and Visser 2000). Each of the five major unions (Confédération Générale du Travail [CGT], Confédération Française Démocratique du Travail [CFDT], Confédération Générale des Cadres [CGC], Force Ouvrière [FO], and Confédération Française des Travailleurs Chrétiens [CFTC]) is a peak union of its own, and there is no formal institutional structure to coordinate

---

[6] More recently, however, cohesion in the trade union movement may have weakened, given the merger of several smaller service unions (HBV, ÖTV, DAG) into ver.di in 2001 (Schroeder and Wessels 2003; Müller and Wilke 2003). With this restructuring, the (highly feminized) service sectors explicitly counterbalance the traditional predominance of the industrial unions, which may increase fragmentation.

them. Therefore, the trade unions almost never speak with one voice in the policy-making processes. The organization of business interests, as opposed to trade unions, is more coordinated, but ideological fragmentation matters here, too. The CGPME and the MEDEF define their differences not only with regard to firm size and sectors but also in terms of their political orientation – the former being more conservative, and the latter emphasizing a radically market-liberal position (Bunel 1995). Hence, fragmentation is strong both within capital and even more so within labor, which provides for strong coalitional flexibility. The reverse, however, is true with regard to political parties; here, the institutions of majority or plurality elections lead to strong concentration. Although the preferences related to heterogeneity may be quite high within government and opposition, they nevertheless speak with one voice on policy reforms, because the political parties in opposition have virtually no say whatsoever in policy making. This contrast between concentration with regard to political parties and fragmentation with regard to associations implies that governments face only weak chances for coalitional engineering in the parliamentary realm but have more leeway when dealing with trade unions and employers.

The implications of these institutional differences for pension policy modernization in hard times are straightforward: given the different patterns of coalitional flexibility, the potential for coalitional engineering is greatest in Switzerland, lower in France, and lowest in Germany. Hence, one can expect new reform dimensions – namely capitalization, targeting, and recalibration – to become more relevant in Switzerland and France than in Germany. In Germany, it should be difficult for policy entrepreneurs to mobilize coalitions along conflict lines other than the labor-capital divide in the corporatist arena and the government-opposition divide in the parliamentary arena. Let me point out briefly the counterintuitive implications of this argument. In the mainstream comparative politics literature, a large degree of power sharing (i.e., a high number of veto points) is supposed to block and impede reforms (Lijphart 1999). My argument here is precisely the opposite: power fragmentation in the corporatist and partisan arenas enhances the chances for reform, because this fragmentation allows for more variable coalition formation, which is crucial in the context of hard times and multidimensional reform politics.

Does this mean that modernizing reforms are impossible where coalitional flexibility is low? Not necessarily. The chances of coalitional engineering depend not only on coalitional flexibility but also on the power of the government with regard to reform opponents. Indeed, a lack of coalitional flexibility is only problematic for a country's reform capacity if the opponents have actual institutional veto power (Tsebelis 2002[7]). By contrast, if no compromise is needed, reforms may be pushed through unilaterally. My argument in this fourth and last

---

[7] Tsebelis (2002) distinguishes between institutional and partisan veto players, the former being generated by the constitution, whereas the latter are a result of the political game. My focus here is on institutional veto players (i.e., institutions), which provide particular actors with a constitutionally enshrined power to obstruct reforms.

hypothesis is precisely that reform capacity depends on the interaction between the number of institutional veto players and coalitional flexibility. In other words, if governments confront veto players that have only low incentives for coalitional flexibility, then reform capacity may be considerably hampered. In a purely majoritarian system, for instance, the government does not need the consent of any further actor – other than the coalition parties – to successfully implement a policy change. In principle, such a majoritarian government may not even need to tie package deals. The more veto players and veto power a government faces, however, the more important coalitional flexibility becomes for the reform capacity of a country. The reform capacity of a particular country will be weak if that country's government faces both low coalitional flexibility and a high number of institutional veto players. In this case, the decision-making process is likely to be highly conflictual and may even result in reform deadlock. Where coalitional flexibility is high, by contrast, veto power can be overcome by political exchange.

On this veto player variable, the three countries also differ considerably. French governments do not need the approval of the opposition parties to implement a reform, as the French parliamentary system operates on a very clear majoritarian logic. By contrast, French governments do face veto players in pension policy, as the power of trade unions and employer organizations is firmly based in the semiautonomous management of the major pension schemes (Palier 2002). In addition, French trade unions, despite their organizational weakness, have a strong and more informal capacity for mobilizing the French public and may overthrow governmental reforms in the streets. Therefore, French governments indeed depend on the formation of broad coalitions to ensure at least tacit support of parts of the unions and capital. The fragmentation of economic interests, however, provides the government with the necessary leeway for coalitional engineering, which should enable modernizing reforms. In the German case, by contrast, there is a marked contrast between low coalitional flexibility on the one hand and relatively strong institutional veto players on the other hand – conditions that may create serious obstacles for German reform capacity (Lehmbruch 2000). Trade unions are important actors, but their agreement to a reform is not formally required. However, a very serious threat to reform capacity stems from the powerful upper chamber (Bundesrat), representing the governments of the German Länder.[8] Under divided majorities in both chambers, it becomes very difficult for the government to ensure the necessary reform compromises and to avoid policy deadlock. Hence, if German governments confront a majority of the opposition parties in the Bundesrat, they lack the leeway for coalitional engineering. Finally, Switzerland is the least problematic of the three cases in terms of the expected reform capacity, as we expect a high degree of coalitional flexibility that allows the government to deal with the (equally) high number of veto players. Therefore, the new reform dimensions are supposed to become manifest in the decision-making arena and should enable modernizing compromises.

---

[8] The Bundesrat has become a very powerful institutional veto player even in welfare state policies, as the Länder are involved in decisions on taxation and implementation.

In a nutshell, hypothesis 4 predicts a rather strong capacity for pension policy modernization in hard times in France and Switzerland, the two countries in which new reform dimensions are likely to become highly relevant. The situation in Germany is more complex: in a context of divided government, the lack of coalitional flexibility may hamper reform capacity. When the government holds a firm majority in parliament, by contrast, the only consensus it must achieve is within the ranks of the coalition parties, which may allow for pension modernization.

Recapitulation of the Analytical Model and Hypotheses

The hypotheses developed in Chapters 3–5 are not alternative or competing explanations of the same political phenomenon. Rather, they form an integrated analytical model for explaining post-industrial pension reform dynamics in continental welfare states. This model links socio-structural change and policy change – spelling out successively the determinants of reform agendas, actor configurations, policy reform spaces, coalition formation, and policy outputs. Given this design of the theoretical model, the result of each analytical step becomes a determinant (i.e., an independent variable) in the subsequent stage of the analysis. Hence, only the interplay of the different determinants allows us to make sense of pension modernization in each country. Together, the four hypotheses provide a conclusive account of when, why, and how continental pension policies are modernized (i.e., adapted to structural developments). Table 5.2 reviews the implications of the four hypotheses for each country, providing a synthetic overview of the expected national reform trajectories.

With regard to France, class, skill levels, and insider-outsider interests should become the major structuring determinants of post-industrial pension politics, whereas sociocultural value divides on recalibration are supposed to remain less relevant. This implies that in a context of austerity, the government may attempt to create multidimensional policy spaces by launching reforms with regard to cost containment, the introduction of capitalized pension funds, and targeted coverage for particular occupational groups. Nevertheless, broad cross-class coalitions remain highly unlikely in the parliamentary arena, whereas the fragmentation of the trade union movement allows for greater coalitional flexibility. In theory, this institutional configuration should allow the government to implement modernization along the lines of insurance, capitalization, and targeting, with the consent of (parts of) the trade union movement, and against the opposition parties.

Because Germany is the prototype of a continental pension regime challenged by both austerity and post-industrial needs, the full range of conflict potentials is expected to appear in post-industrial pension politics. Strategic governments are supposed to draw on this variety of potential actor alliances to create opportunities for political exchange in the policy reform processes. The German pension reform capacity and reform output, however, depends on more than just the government's strategic skills. Political exchange may fail if the opposition parties act as veto players in parliament. Still, as long as the government holds a firm majority

TABLE 5.2. *Hypotheses: Expected Patterns of Pension Politics in France, Germany, and Switzerland*

Hypothesis	France	Germany	Switzerland
H$_1$: The misfit between structure and institutions fosters new conflict potentials with regard to the level of benefits, financing and eligibility.	*Expected reform agenda* Insurance Capitalization Targeting	*Expected reform agenda* Insurance Capitalization Targeting Recalibration	*Expected reform agenda* Insurance Targeting Recalibration
H$_2$: The actor configurations on these conflict lines are structured by class (insurance), skill levels (capitalization), labor market status (targeting/ recalibration), and values (recalibration).	*Expected conflict lines* Class conflict Skill-level conflict Insider-outsider conflict	*Expected conflict lines* Class conflict Skill level conflict Insider-outsider conflict Cultural value conflict	*Expected conflict lines* Class conflict Insider-outsider conflict Cultural value conflict
H$_3$: Policy makers tie reform packages to create multidimensional policy spaces, particularly in times of austerity (strategies of coalitional engineering).	*Expected packages* Insurance/ capitalization Insurance/ targeting	*Expected packages* Insurance/ capitalization Insurance/ targeting Insurance/ recalibration	*Expected packages* Insurance/ targeting Insurance/ recalibration
H$_4$: The success of coalitional engineering depends on the interaction between coalitional flexibility and the number of veto players	Low coalitional flexibility among political parties, who *are not* veto players; high coalitional flexibility among trade unions and capital High coalitional flexibility among trade unions and capital	Low coalitional flexibility among political parties, who *are* veto players in case of divided government; low coalitional flexibility among trade unions and capital, who *are not* veto players	High coalitional flexibility among political parties, trade unions, and capital
	Expected outcome Opportunities for modernizing reforms	*Expected outcome* Opportunities for modernizing reforms in case of *nondivided* government; danger of gridlock in case of *divided* government	*Expected outcome* Opportunities for modernizing reforms

in parliament, it should be powerful enough to implement encompassing, though mostly unilateral, reforms along all dimensions of modernization.

Finally, capitalization should not appear on the post-industrial reform agenda in Switzerland, because funded pensions have existed in Switzerland for several decades already. Rather, cost containment, targeted coverage for specific occupational groups, and recalibrating reforms for labor market outsiders are expected to prevail in the debates and to give rise to different crosscutting actor configurations. Given both the high number of veto players and the high coalitional flexibility among parties and social partners, there is a strong incentive for governments to tie encompassing reform packages. Hence, the odds for pension policy modernization are rather good, as long as policy makers manage to exploit the opportunities of a multidimensional policy space.

PART II

DETERMINANTS OF SUCCESSFUL PENSION REFORM IN CONTINENTAL EUROPE

6

France

Trade Union Fragmentation as an Opportunity for Reform

This chapter analyzes French pension politics since 1970. It starts by providing empirical evidence that targeting and capitalization have become new conflict lines in French pension politics, dividing trade unions (and to a lesser extent employers) according to skill levels and the insider-outsider status of their members. A second section shows how conservative governments repeatedly succeeded in exploiting these intra-labor divides by designing reform packages, which confronted the left with the dilemma of having to choose between either old class loyalties or modernizing cross-class compromises. The choices the actors made and the consequences therefrom are then explained with reference to trade union fragmentation and the institutional framework of decision making: reformist trade unions approved the reforms, against the industrial trade unions and left-wing parties. Hence, if – and only if – the governments are willing and able to exploit the multidimensionality of the pension policy-making space, pension reform in France becomes possible.

From the 1970s onward, the French pension system underwent far-reaching reforms, as did many other fields of social security in France (see, e.g., Levy 2000; Palier 2002; Vail 2004). The following section provides an overview of these pension reforms. The debate in the 1970s was based on a certain consensus that pension levels had to be raised and that the pension system was, in general, underdeveloped. However, the left and the right claimed different levels of expansion, and the generous reforms of the right-wing Union pour la Démocratie Française (UDF) and Rassemblement pour la République (RPR) governments in the 1970s were, to some extent, a strategy to counter the more radical demands of the trade unions and the socialist and communist parties. The latter also claimed the lowering of the retirement age to sixty.[1] The conservative governments argued that such radical reforms would be too costly, but they nevertheless increased the

---

[1] There was, however, strong disagreement within labor about the retirement age for women. The CGT and the Communist Party were in favor of the age of fifty-seven, whereas the CFDT and the Socialist Party rejected the idea of a different retirement age for men and women.

overall level of pension benefits. In addition, they also introduced systemic changes by extending complementary pensions to all workers (creating the mandatory Association pour le régime de retraite complémentaire des salaries [ARRCO], as an equivalent to the preexisting Association générale des institutions de retraite des cadres [AGIRC] for managers only) and by introducing generous derived benefits for widows and educational pension credits for mothers. In 1975, the age of retirement was lowered to sixty for workers with particularly difficult work conditions. This reform was strongly criticized by members of the left, who interpreted it as an insufficient response to their demand for a lower retirement age for *all* insured.

The age of retirement became an extremely polarizing issue in the 1981 election campaign, which brought the left to power. The new socialist government lowered the general retirement age to sixty right after the elections and introduced a minimum pension for low-income earners in 1983. However, these remained the only pension reforms in the 1980s, because the left-wing government then remained somewhat paralyzed in light of the financial and demographic pressures that began to develop, and it preferred to raise contribution rates rather than tackle benefits (Palier 2006). In addition, it published a number of administrative reports pointing to the need for cutbacks and financial consolidation. Nevertheless, the left-wing governments postponed all the recommended reforms during the 1980s (Palier 2003). It was only the new right-wing RPR government under Édouard Balladur that cut back benefit levels in the *régime général* in 1993: the required contribution period for a full pension was lengthened from 150 to 160 trimesters and full pensions were newly calculated as a percentage of the average income over twenty-five years instead of ten years. Simultaneously, however, the Balladur reform increased tax revenues for the *régime général* (with 1 percent of the Contribution the Solidarité Généralisée [CSG]) and introduced a special fund (Fonds de Solidarité Vieillesse [FSV]) that would finance noncontributory benefits, such as educational credits or pension rights for the unemployed. When the conservative prime minister Alain Juppé tried to emulate the 1993 cutbacks in the civil servants' pension regimes two years later, he faced massive protests led by public-sector unions and eventually had to withdraw his reform proposal.

After this reform failure, which had received a lot of attention in the media, French pension policy debates deviated on a new issue, namely capitalization and individualized pension savings plans. Capitalization had previously been nonexistent in French pension policy. The intergenerational solidarity that the pay-as-you-go (PAYG) system implies was an integral part of the Keynesian class compromise (Palier 2002). However, with the structural demographic changes and a generally low savings rate in France, the purely PAYG-financed pension system became a liability. Various pension savings instruments were created by the conservative government in 1997 and by the socialist Jospin government in 2001. In addition, Lionel Jospin also created a capitalized fund within the FSV to alleviate the financial burden of the public pension scheme. However, pension reform remained a particularly urgent but polarized and delicate topic.

Therefore, Jospin did not dare to tackle the reform of civil servants' pensions after the massive protest in 1995; instead, he concentrated on the development of expertise by publishing several heavily debated reports (Charpin, Zaidman and Aubert 1999; Taddei, Charpin and Davanne 1999; Teulade 1999) on financial and demographic perspectives (Palier 2002; Schludi 2005). In addition, he learned from Juppé's failure against the unions when he created the Conseil d'Orientation Retraites (COR), a permanent commission for expertise and negotiation, which should have allowed the government, employers, and trade unions to reach consensus on reform priorities. The COR certainly contributed to a more pragmatic approach to pension reforms by some unions, but despite all the reports and talks, no actual reform was adopted under the socialist government. It was only after the right (RPR and UDF) had regained power that the new prime minister, Jean-Pierre Raffarin, managed to cut back civil servants' pension rights and to lengthen the contribution period required for a full pension in the public sector. In this 2003 reform, he also introduced early retirement and higher minimum pensions for workers with more than forty years of contribution.

This brief reform overview of the past three decades shows two main trends. On the one hand, reforms along the insurance dimension have become exclusively focused on financial consolidation and retrenchment from the 1990s onward. On the other hand, new issues and new conflict lines appeared prominently on the agenda. Table 6.1 details the reform issues that have been at stake over time in France.[2] The issues of each reform are categorized according to the four conflict lines that I have identified theoretically in the first part of this book.

Development of Conflict Lines

In light of the structural challenges to the French pension regime, the theoretical model of this book suggests that – in addition to distributional conflicts over benefit levels – alternative conflict lines (capitalization, targeting, recalibration) become increasingly important. Their relevance is supposed to depend on the misfit between national pension institutions and post-industrial risk profiles.

The evidence in Table 6.1 confirms this expectation. Conflicts about *capitalization* (i.e., the individual versus solidaristic financing of pensions) indeed became prominent in France in the 1990s, when both conservative and socialist governments introduced new, highly controversial capitalized pension savings plans. These were adopted in reaction to several governmental reports since the 1980s (Tabah 1986; Teulade 1989; Commissariat général du Plan 1991; Bruhnes 1992), which had highlighted the fact that the French contribution-financed PAYG system was particularly at odds with demographic and economic developments (Palier 2002). In addition, the turn from the Keynesian paradigm of

---

[2] The selected reforms include all reforms adopted by law (i.e., in a standard policy-making procedure in parliament). For an account of the reform of AGIRC and ARRCO through collective agreements in 1995, see Schludi (2005).

TABLE 6.1. *Development of Conflict Lines in French Pension Reforms*

Reform	Insurance	Capitalization	Targeting	Recalibration
Pension law (Loi Boulin), 1971	1. Pension increase		1. Early retirement for disabled workers	1. One-year educational pension credit
Law on complementary pensions, 1972	1. Mandatory character of the schemes		1. Pension coverage for unemployed 2. Harmonizing complementary pensions	
Law on pension increase, 1975a	1. Higher widows' pensions 2. Labor market support for widows 3. Wider access to insurance			1. Three-year educational pension credit 2. Wider access to insurance
Law on pension eligibility, 1975b			1. Early retirement for long careers 2. Early retirement for mothers	
Pension law, 1983	1. Retirement age 60		1. Minimum pension	

Pension law, 1993 (Balladur reform)	1. Higher retirement age 2. Lower benefit levels 3. Indexation on prices 4. Increase of CSG		1. Fund (FSV) for noncontributory benefits	1. Fund (FSV) for noncontributory benefits
Law on pension savings, 1997 (Loi Thomas)		1. Capitalized pension savings plans		
Law on financing social security, 1999	1. Reserve fund within FSV 2. Indexation on prices			
Law on income savings, 2001		1. Individual long-term savings plans 2. Small-business savings plans		
Pension law, 2003 (Raffarin)	1. Lower benefit levels 2. Lower widows' pensions	1. Individual pension savings plans	1. Harmonization of public/private pensions 2. Higher minimum pension 3. Early retirement for long careers	1. Educational credits for civil servants

economic policy to monetarism shifted the attention from demand-side management to supply-side factors (Hall 1986) and thus highlighted the low savings
rates in France. Therefore, capitalization not only became an issue on the reform
agenda but also fostered considerable conflict. Indeed, the introduction of capitalization became a highly symbolic issue, representing the inefficiency of the
inherited institutions.

Similarly, the strongly employment-related French *régime général* tends to
exclude the unemployed, the atypically employed, and – in particular – labor
market outsiders from sufficient pension coverage. This was not very problematic in the industrial era, as unemployment was low and most outsiders were covered indirectly, through the pension rights of their spouses. With post-industrial
labor markets and unstable families, however, the insufficient coverage of these
particular risk groups became more obvious (Palier and Mandin 2004). Hence,
conflicts about *targeting* (i.e., reforms dealing with these protection loopholes)
have become important on the agenda from the 1970s onward. Advocates of targeting claim that specific advantages should be granted to particular occupational
risk groups on the basis of needs rather than earned rights. Targeting therefore
promotes a more egalitarian structure of the pension scheme, defying the strong
Bismarckian stratification principle. Opponents of targeting reject these selective measures and plead for reforms within the *régime général*. According to them,
reforms should increase pension levels for all workers rather than just introducing
targeted minimum pensions to address the most blatant poverty risks.

Conflicts on *recalibration*, by contrast (i.e., the granting of pension rights
independently of labor market participation) have remained less important in
France. This can be meaningfully explained with reference to the interaction
of structural developments and path-dependent institutions. French pro-natalist
family policies created favorable conditions for female labor market participation much earlier than was the case in other Western European countries. Most
mothers in France are active on the labor market, though often in services, atypical
employment, or as outsiders (Jenson and Sineau 1994). Hence, pension policies
for specific occupational groups benefit them directly, and gender equality can
be achieved through targeting and insurance, whereas in countries with lower
female labor market participation, such reforms may not reach many women at
all. Hence, the few recalibrating reforms of the right-wing governments in the
1970s applied mostly to women who were mothers of three children or more, and
the reforms remained rather isolated.[3] The absence of recalibration also confirms
the expectations of our theoretical model, because it argues that the preexisting
institutions influence the precise kind of conflicts that become relevant in subsequent phases of change.

---

[3] However, these reforms (1971 and 1975) strikingly resemble the recalibrating reforms in Germany
and Switzerland in the 1980s and 1990s. They probably occurred earlier in France because of the
pro-natalist heritage on the one hand and because the feminist movement of 1968 was strong and
argued for state intervention on the other hand (Jenson and Sineau 1994). The German feminists,
to quote a contrasting example, refused state intervention during the 1970s (Naumann 2005).

Development of Actor Configurations

What are the alliances that form with regard to the different conflict lines? As the following analyses will show and explain, French pension policy actors indeed align differently on targeting and capitalization than on insurance, which is in line with the second hypothesis of this book.

Insurance-related reforms affect all insured, as they change pension rights proportionally to each worker's contribution record. Therefore, class conflict – separating unions from employers' organizations and left-wing from right-wing parties – had prevailed on these issues over the previous three decades. Figure 6.1 shows the positions and movements of the actors with regard to insurance reforms.[4,5] The values reflect the average position of the actors on all insurance-related reform issues in each period (as presented in Table 6.1). Zero indicates high benefit levels within the *régime général*, i.e., a lower age of retirement, gross wage indexation, generous derived benefits such as widow's pensions, a refusal of any attempt at retrenchment. To the contrary, an actor positioned more toward the value of 2 claims more modest pension benefit increases or – in the 1990s – even retrenchment.[6]

The Confédération Générale du Travail (CGT) and the Confédération Française Démocratique du Travail (CFDT) clearly advocated generous pension policies throughout the whole period, and a similar observation is true for the Parti Communiste (PCF) and the Parti Socialiste (PSF), even though the latter moved somewhat to the right over the three decades, as in other fields of economic and social policy (Hall 2006). Positions are more varied on the right of the political spectrum. In the 1970s, there seemed to be a large consensus on the expansion of pension policies. Indeed, the right-wing government of UDF and RPR implemented no less than three reforms between 1971 and 1975, increasing pension levels and widows' pensions and extending access to the *régime général* and to the newly compulsory complementary pension schemes. Even the business organizations largely backed the reforms, not least to delegitimize the left's claims for more radical benefit expansion. This low level of class conflict, however, came to a sudden end when the newly elected socialist-communist government

---

[4] In France, the landscape of political parties has evolved massively since the 1970s. For reasons of comparability, I have summarized the main parties and parliamentary factions into four categories: (1) Gaullistes: Groupe de l'Union des Démocrates pour la République (UDR), Groupe du Rassemblement pour la République (RPR), Groupe de l'Union pour la Majorité Présidentielle; (2) Centristes: Groupe des Républicains Indépendants (GRI), Groupe Progrès et Démocratie Moderne, Groupe Union pour la Démocratie Française, Groupe Union du Centre, Groupe Union pour la Démocratie Française et du Centre, Groupe des Réformateurs Démocrates Sociaux, Groupe de l'Union Centriste; (3) Socialistes (PSF): Groupe Socialiste, Groupe du Parti Socialiste et des Radicaux de Gauche, Groupe de la Fédération de la Gauche Démocrate et Socialiste; (4) Communistes (PCF): Groupe des Représentants Communistes et Républicains, Groupe Communiste.

[5] See Appendix 1 for a description of the data. The CNPF changed its name to MEDEF (Mouvement des Entreprises de France) in 1998.

[6] Coding is presented in detail in Appendix 1.

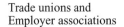

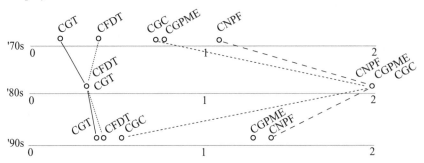

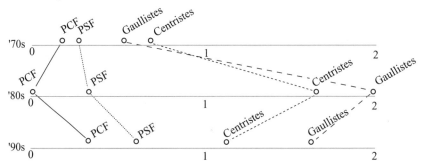

FIGURE 6.1. France: Average positions of actors on insurance over three time periods, 1971–80, 1981–90, 1991–2003

lowered the retirement age to sixty in 1983, thereby implementing a long-standing demand of the left. Right-wing parties, business, and the trade union of managers (Confédération Générale des Cadres [CGC]), were radically opposed to this expansive measure. Therefore, the 1983 reform created a sharp left-right antagonism in pension policy in the 1980s.

During the 1990s and early 2000s, retrenchment became the new credo of the conservative governments in the 1993 and 2003 reforms (by the Balladur and Raffarin governments, respectively). And even the socialist government under Jospin advocated a slight shift to net wage indexation in 1999. Hence, the left-right polarization became somewhat less stark, but the class conflict remained the dominant actor configuration in the era of austerity: all trade unions, as well as the communist and the socialist parties, claimed less restrictive reforms, whereas business and the right-wing parties – mostly the conservative Gaullists – wanted to go further down the road of retrenchment. Hence, one can say that, since the 1970s, the left-right conflict has increased and today dominates the alignment of the actors in the retrenchment debates.

The picture looks rather different, however, with regard to capitalization. Capitalized pension schemes, even though theoretically available to any individual, are more favorable for high-income, high-skilled employees in large firms than for less qualified workers and for employees in small firms. A shift of pension provision from the general PAYG scheme to capitalized savings therefore redistributes income from the lower- to the higher-skilled workers. Consequently, we would expect that high-skilled unions (mostly the CGC in France, and to some extent the CFDT, the main trade union in high-skilled sectors such as finance, insurance, and commerce; see Chapter 4) would be more favorable to capitalization than low-skilled unions (CGT, which organizes mostly low-skilled labor market insiders). Similarly, large firms (Conseil National du Patronat Français [CNPF]), which have the capacity to develop occupational pension plans, are supposed to be more favorable than small firms (Confédération Générale des Petites et Moyennes Entreprises [CGPME]). With regard to political parties, the communists should oppose capitalization and the right-wing parties should support it, because they tend to represent lower- and higher-income electorates, respectively. The socialist party still represents voters with, on average, a lower income than the right-wing party voters (see Chapter 4) and should therefore be more skeptical toward capitalization. Education and skill levels, however, are increasing among the socialist voters, so the party could theoretically join either side, advocating either the interests of blue-collar workers or of sociocultural professionals.

Capitalized savings plans have been at stake in three reforms between 1997 and 2003. With the Loi Thomas in 1997 (abolished a few years later by the socialist government), the conservative Juppé government first introduced the *plans d'épargne retraite*. In 2001, however, the socialist government under Jospin pursued the same policy development with savings plans for individuals and small businesses. Finally, the conservative Raffarin government further extended the possibility of capitalized savings in 2003. Figure 6.2 shows that the steps toward capitalized pensions have increasingly divided the left, mainly between high- and low-skilled trade unions. Contrary to the three data points (1970s, 1980s, 1990s) that were displayed in Figure 6.1 on insurance, positions here are shown separately for each of the three reforms. Zero represents a rejection of capitalization and very tight controls of access and management, whereas actors closer to the value of 2 want to encourage private savings on a more widespread but voluntary and less controlled basis.

While all the unions remained skeptical about the introduction of private capitalized savings in 1997 (position values of less than 1), the CFDT and CGC, contrary to the CGT, defended a more moderate stance on this issue later on, when the socialist government introduced capitalization in 2001. The CGC approved both governmental proposals for an extension of individual saving plans in 2001 and 2003 and the CFDT went even further, asking for a stronger development of these plans than the government proposed. While the position of the CGC results straightforwardly from the privileged labor market position of its highly skilled members, the approval of capitalization by the CFDT is somewhat more puzzling. It can, however, be explained, on the one hand, by the fact that the CFDT indeed organizes more high-skilled sector employees than the CGT and, on the other hand, the CFDT counts more outsiders among its members, who are not the

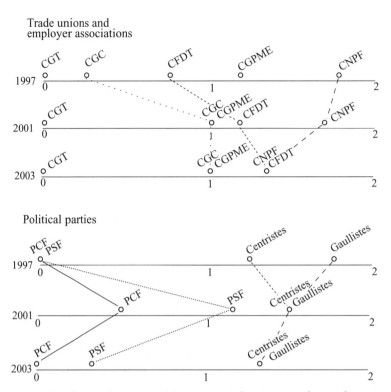

FIGURE 6.2. France: Average positions on capitalization over three reforms in 1997, 2001, and 2003

main beneficiaries of the *régime général*. Even though capitalization may not be the best option for them, they are less attached to defending the *régime général*. The CFDT aims at a French pension system that is highly redistributive and egalitarian for low-income earners but leaves more room for individual pension savings and choice for the middle- and upper-income classes,[7] thereby catering both to its high-skilled service clientele and to the labor market outsiders among its members. The CGT, by contrast, represents mainly low-skilled labor market insiders, who have a clear interest in protecting the generous but contribution- and earnings-related *régime général*. Among the employers, the CGPME (small businesses) approves of capitalization as a "necessary measure,"[8] but it advocates a strongly state-controlled version of occupational savings, because small firms are not able to provide firm-specific savings plans to their employees, whereas the large firms (Conseil National du Patronal Français/Mouvement des Entreprises de France) would want to leave the greatest possible freedom to the individ- uals and firms.[9] This result, again, is in line with hypothesis 2, according to

[7] Interview, CFDT, Paris, July 13, 2005.
[8] Interview, CGPME, Paris, July 19, 2005.
[9] Interview, MEDEF, Paris, July 13, 2005.

which we should see a divide between small and large firms on the issue of capitalization.

Party positions, finally, show a straightforward divide between the communist and the right-wing parties, among whom the UDF (Centristes) advocates a more tightly controlled development of capitalization than the Gaullist parties RPR/Union pour un Mouvement Populaire (UMP). Unsurprisingly, the position of the Socialist Party seems very unstable, and it depends heavily on whether the party is in power or in opposition. Already in 1997, the PSF was deeply divided between the opponents of capitalization, who succeeded in defining the official party position, and some socialist exponents such as Dominique Strauss-Kahn, François Hollande, and Michel Rocard, who had highlighted the need for some capitalization in various government reports since the mid-1980s.[10] When in government, the advocates of capitalization gained power and the socialist government itself introduced pension funds in 2001. The "workerist" stance against capitalization gained again in importance in the party as soon as the PSF was back on the opposition benches. Hence, the class conflict has become increasingly blurred with regard to capitalization. A cross-class alliance between CGC, CFDT, the employers, and right-wing parties (as well as parts of the PSF) advocates the promotion of private savings plans.

Cross-class conflict is also expected with regard to targeting, because targeting reduces the status-related stratification of Bismarckian pension systems, from which insiders benefit, and strengthens a more flat-rate, egalitarian pension scheme in favor of outsiders. Targeted reforms have become very important on the reform agenda. On the one hand, they improve pension coverage for particular risk groups (lowering the age or retirement for workers with long careers or in precarious work, creating means-tested minimum pensions for workers with insufficient contribution records, or introducing tax-financed, noncontributory benefits for specific periods of work interruption), and on the other hand, they reduce particular status-related privileges (aligning civil service pension provision on private-sector pensions or harmonizing the complementary pension schemes of low-skilled workers and managers). Opponents of targeting insist on granting pension improvements not only to particular risk groups but also – via insurance reforms – to all the insured. They also defend existing privileges against retrenchment. Trade unions representing a large proportion of outsiders (women and service-sector employees can be used as a rough proxy; see Chapter 4), such as the CFDT, and to a lesser extent the CGC, are therefore supposed to be more supportive of targeting than insider unions such as CGT, who organize mainly the industry and the public sector. Business should be rather supportive of a purely contribution-related pension scheme, but employers in more feminized sectors may advocate targeting as a relatively inexpensive reform strategy (Bonoli 2005) to keep women in the labor market.

The main result in Figure 6.3 is that the CGC and, increasingly, the CFDT indeed tend to support targeting as a reform strategy. The old left (i.e., the CGT and the Communist Party [PCF]), by contrast, continue to insist on universally

[10] Minutes of the parliamentary debates on the Loi Thomas (97–277), AN January 22, 1996, p. 3705.

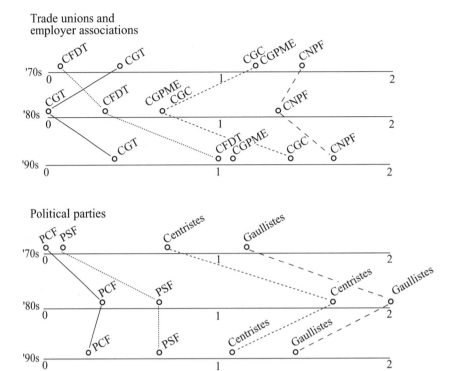

FIGURE 6.3. France: Average positions of actors on targeting over three time periods, 1971–80, 1981–90, 1991–2003

granted pension improvements. The expected insider-outsider conflict within labor, however, appeared only recently, in the 1990s, whereas the pattern is closer to class conflict in the 1970s and to some extent in the 1980s (except for the CGC, which always preferred targeted reforms to widespread pension improvements for all insured). On the conflict line in Figure 6.3, the value of 0 represents a position that advocates the granting of benefit increases to a very large share of beneficiaries, whereas the value of 2 represents a position that targets benefits only to the neediest on a means-tested basis. Hence, an actor who shifts to the right increasingly advocates the targeting of benefit expansion rather than uniform improvement within the insurance scheme. The data points reflect the reforms by conservative governments in the 1970s, by the leftist government in the 1980s, and again by conservative governments from the 1990s onward, respectively (see Table 6.1).[11]

Until the 1990s, both the CFDT and the CGT claimed not only improvements for particular risk categories but also more generous policies for all beneficiaries, insiders and outsiders. The CGC, by contrast, already privileged a more limited

---

[11] The Jospin government (1998–2002) had not introduced any targeting reform.

expansion of pension insurance, except for the 1980s, when they backed the introduction of a generous minimum pension by the socialist government. With regard to parties, there is again a remarkable similarity in the positions of the CGT and the PCF, both defending insiders, whereas the PSF has become more favorable to targeted intervention. In summary, the right-wing parties and employers, who prefer targeted reforms and the cutback of public-sector privileges were joined from the 1990s onward by the CGC and the CFDT to form a cross-class coalition in favor of a more means-tested, flat-rate pension scheme. The split between the CFDT and the CGT appears most clearly in the recent Raffarin reform of 2003, which cut back public-sector pensions to align them with private-sector benefit levels. While CFDT and CGC supported this harmonization, the CGT defended existing benefit levels. The CGT's strong membership in the low-skilled insider public sector provides a plausible explanation for this conflict. The question remains, however, as to why the insider-outsider conflict between CFDT and CGT appeared only in the 1990s, given that the differences in the membership profiles of both unions have not changed drastically since the 1970s. Part of the answer lies in the fact that French unions, unlike, for example, their German counterparts, are less membership driven (not least because of their overall very weak organizational density) but rather political actors (Visser et al. 2000). This gives the union elites considerable leeway to decide on the policy direction they support. Deliberate changes in strategy are therefore more frequent and abrupt than in other countries. The CFDT made such a shift most clearly in the late 1980s, moving from an old leftist and insurance-preserving stance to a more reformist and egalitarian position. In the 1990s, the CFDT described itself as "neither left, nor right" and "resolutely reformist" (Visser et al. 2000: 241) and advocated a "responsible and cooperative" approach to social policy issues (Palier 2006: 125). However, I argue that this reversal of positions can be understood only by taking into account that, from the 1990s onward, the underlying thrust of all reforms was directed toward cost containment or retrenchment. The context of austerity began to have a clear impact on the reform agenda, transforming pension policy making from a positive-sum to a zero-sum game. In this new context, all actors had to reevaluate their main interests and priorities, because the distributional conflicts became sharper. This new context weakened the class solidarities that had prevailed in the 1970s and 1980s, when all trade unions advocated more generous benefits for insiders and outsiders. From the 1990s onward, the unions started to defend more narrow interests and class solidarity waned. According to the head of the social policy section of the CFDT, his trade union today recognizes the need even for a certain retrenchment and prioritizes changes that prevent old-age poverty among those who cannot build sufficient pension rights during their employment career, such as low-income workers or atypical workers and women with shorter employment biographies. Those categories are more strongly represented in the CFDT than in the industrial CGT.[12]

---

[12] Interview, CFDT, Paris, July 13, 2005.

Finally, the position of the CGC in favor of targeting is somewhat surprising, as the union represents high-skilled employees in rather privileged employment conditions who generally rely less on targeted benefits. However, the CGC organizes the workforce in both industry and services. Therefore, the CGC is more strongly rooted in the feminized sectors of the economy, and because women are outsiders more frequently than men are, this difference in the membership structure may explain part of the openness of the CGC for targeting reforms (see Chapter 3). But the strong preference of the CGC for targeting indicates that there must be more to this position than pure membership logic. Indeed, the position of the CGC must be understood with regard to the whole architecture of the pension regime: highly skilled employees increasingly have the possibility of complementing their pensions by means of capitalized savings plans. Therefore, they become less dependent on generous pension levels in the *régime général* and may opt for a pension scheme that combines means-tested basic redistribution with a high degree of inequality in individual (i.e., less solidaristic) complementary pensions (what Palier [2006: 118] calls the progressive dualization of the French welfare state).[13] This reasoning also explains why the right-wing parties and part of the employers support some of the targeting measures, even though they have no direct interest in them.

Reforms involving recalibration (in particular pension credits for mothers) have been scarce in France (see Table 6.1), and the alliances on this conflict line have remained rather stable (not shown). Centrist parties (RPR and UDF) advocated and pushed familialist reform elements in the 1970s, when the context of pension politics was still clearly oriented toward expansion. The left-wing parties and trade unions have been favorable to noncontributory pension credits throughout the whole period, even though this was clearly never their main concern. Hence, these issues benefited from a cross-class coalition of the right-wing parties and the left against rather clear opposition from employers. Recalibration therefore split the right, opposing conservative parties and employers. However, this conflict line has largely disappeared from the reform agenda, which can be explained by the very high female labor market participation in France, because of which women build their own pension rights.

Hence, over time, capitalization and targeting have become increasingly important conflict lines, as has insurance. In the context of financial austerity, they divide labor according to different logics. While the class conflict persists on insurance issues, capitalization splits the labor movement mostly according

---

[13] However, whereas the egalitarian position of the CFDT today seems rather stable, the CGC is for egalitarianism only when the privileges of its own members remain untouched. One of the next reform debates in France will indeed tackle the harmonization of the complementary pension regimes for managers and workers. On this issue, however, CGC rejects any harmonization and thus has formed a coalition with CGT to preserve status differences. As a representative of the CGC put it: "la CGT a le respect de la hiérarchie" (Interview, CGC, Paris July 21, 2005).

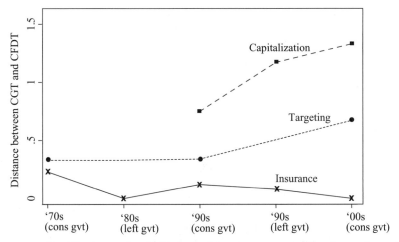

FIGURE 6.4. The increasing divide in the labor movement in French pension politics: distance between the average positions of CGT and CFDT over time

to skill levels, and targeting generates insider-outsider cleavages.[14] These developments create an increasingly divided trade union movement, with CFDT and CGT as the main adversaries. This result appears most clearly in Figure 6.4, which displays the average distance between CFDT and CGT over time on the three main conflict lines. The five time points correspond to the different governments since the 1970s.

After having analyzed the development of conflict lines in French pension policy, I now turn to the analysis of the dimensionality of the policy space and the dynamics of political exchange.

Development of Reform Dimensionality Depending on Time and Austerity

I have identified four different conflict lines in contemporary pension policy making. The actors align differently on these conflicts, and they have stronger preferences with regard to some of them than with regard to others. Governments can exploit these differences when designing reform bills. More specifically, they can combine multiple issues in a single reform package to divide actors according to different conflict lines. This strategy may create opportunities for negotiation and

[14] The theoretical model developed in the first part of this book also suggested that policies affecting gender equality in the welfare state would divide actors not only according to their members' or electorate's interests but also according to their preferences for libertarian versus traditionalist values. Libertarians should favor recalibration and targeting more than traditionalists. The actors with the most libertarian constituencies in the French system of parties and unions are probably the CFDT (rooted in highly feminized service sectors) and the new left (i.e., the Socialist Party) (Andersen and Evans 2003). Both increasingly favored targeting and have always promoted recalibration. However, recalibration has remained a minor issue in France, and targeting reforms were never constructed in terms of gender equality but in terms of general poverty relief.

TABLE 6.2. *Dimensionality of Reforms in France: results of Factor Analysis*

	The Reform Includes Elements That Belong to...	
	One Conflict Line	**More Than One Conflict Line**
Purely expansive reforms	1975b, 1997, 1999, 2001 (all 1-dimensional)	1971, 1972, 1975a, 1983 (all 1-dimensional)
Reforms that included retrenchment		1993 (2-dimensional), 2003 (3-dimensional)

Notes: Factor analysis run on the coded positions of the actors; all results displayed in Tables 6.3 and 6.4 and Appendix 3; Eigenvalue of factors ≥ 1, Varimax rotation; for more details on data, see Appendix 1.

coalition formation, which may enhance the chances of success of the reforms. The third hypothesis, developed in Chapter 5 of this book, suggests exactly that. If governments succeed in combining a variety of reform issues that answer particular expectations of different actors, they may foster ambiguous agreements (Palier 2005; see also Schickler 2001) in favor of these reforms (i.e., a large consensus, in which a wide range of actors agree to the same reform for different reasons). The multidimensionality of the reform space may also help overcome opposition to reforms by enabling negotiation: actors make concessions on one conflict line to secure their particularly valued preferences on another line of conflict. Negotiation is, of course, most important in times of austerity. To overcome resistance to retrenchment, governments may have to compensate at least some of the losers. Hence, I expect reforms to be packages of different conflict lines, particularly when retrenchment is at stake. Furthermore, I expect those packages to divide actors along a plurality of independent conflict dimensions.

To test this hypothesis, I ran a factor analysis of each pension reform to determine the dimensionality of the reform space (see Appendix 1 for a detailed account of the methodological approach). A one-dimensional solution means that across all the reform elements, the actors positioned themselves in a similar way (see Table 6.1 for the issues). In other words, a one-dimensional result means that the position of an actor on a reform issue allows for the making of predictions about his or her position on all other issues in this reform. Consequently, a two-dimensional solution means that the preferences of the actors on one set of reform elements are largely independent of their preferences on the other issues of the same reform.[15]

Table 6.2 summarizes the evidence on package building and the dimensionality of reforms. Each reform is denoted by the year in which it took place. Six of the ten reforms combined elements belonging to different reform dimensions. Only two of them, however, actually gave rise to multiple, empirically independent dimensions of conflict. The tying of reform packages does not seem to be a necessary condition for successful reforms in France. The evidence,

[15] A trade union, for instance, may agree with the social democrats on pension increase but disagree with the same social democrats on the introduction of occupational pensions. That means that knowing the position of each actor on pension increase bears no information on that actor's position on occupational pensions.

however, is strong for retrenchment as a determinant of multidimensionality. Indeed, both reforms that included cuts in existing benefits (retrenchment on insurance) combined those with expansive reforms elements related to targeting and/or recalibration. And those reforms divided the actors along multiple dimensions of conflict, forming a two-dimensional reform space in 1993 and even a three-dimensional space in 2003.

The purely one-dimensional reforms require further explanations. Most reforms of the conservative governments in the 1970s, as well as the left government's pension reform of 1983 indeed combined different conflict lines in a single reform package. Nevertheless, all actors aligned empirically along a single class-conflict dimension (upper-right quadrant in Table 6.2). How can this be explained, knowing that targeting and recalibration do generate within-labor conflict? The answer lies in the fact that all reform elements were *expansive*. Insurance-related issues expanded the overall benefit level within the *régime général*, answering partly, though not completely, the demands of the left. To address particular risks that would remain insufficiently covered even after the expansion of insurance, governments also included targeting and recalibrating reform elements, which secured the approval of the conservative parties and the employers. As shown earlier (Figure 6.3), the intra-class conflict on targeting appeared only in the 1990s, when reform packages began to involve trade-offs improving the benefits of a particular risk group at the expense of another. Reforms in the 1970s did not have that aspect of a zero-sum game but basically left nobody worse off. This, of course, allowed and facilitated class solidarity and led to ambiguous agreements, which most actors supported in the name of their particular constituency. Hence the one-dimensional policy space.

The second somewhat puzzling result in Table 6.2 is the four "pure" reforms, involving only a single conflict line (upper-left quadrant). The 1975 and the 1999 reforms were rather minor in scope, the former lowering retirement age for workers with long careers and for mothers, and the latter confirming indexation on prices and creating a special fund to improve the financial stability of the *régime général*. More surprising, however, is that the two reforms aimed at – highly controversial – capitalization were not designed according to the "divide et impera" principle. In light of the strong polarization that capitalization has always provoked in France, one might have expected that the government would counterbalance the reforms with other, more consensual elements. A plausible explanation of this not happening is that governments precisely wanted to avoid capitalization being viewed as a substitute for public pensions. Their discourse was always that individual pension savings should not replace public pensions but merely complement them. The socialist government in particular even discursively tried to construct the savings plans as an economic rather than a social policy reform.[16] Increased savings should accumulate French investment capital and prevent the foreign control of French firms, their impact on pensions being a mere side effect (for a detailed account of the debates on private pensions

---

[16] Parliamentary Report Balligand, Commission des Finances, No 2594; minutes of the parliamentary debates in the Assemblée Nationale, October 10, 2000; January 16, 2001; February 7, 2001.

in France, see Palier 2003a). Hence, combining the introduction of these plans with other pension-reform elements would have (further) undermined the credibility of this discourse. In addition, the reforms were expansive, because they increased public subsidies for individual savings. For these reasons, and because of the strong technicality that tends to obscure the distributional consequences of capitalization (Pierson 2001), the reforms could be adopted without provoking ferocious opposition.

In summary, the most striking finding in Table 6.2 is that the coalitional dynamics of pension politics are indeed changing in the context of austerity and because of austerity. As long as all reforms aimed at expansion, the actors were divided along a single line of conflict, arguing about the precise level of benefit increase. When retrenchment was at stake, however, the preferences of the actors split along different, independent (i.e., crosscutting) conflict lines. Hence, it appears that, in the context of austerity, the political space of pension reform has indeed become increasingly multidimensional.

We can now take a more detailed look at this new pension-reform space by means of the factor analysis results for the two reform packages of 1993 and 2003. I selected these two reforms because they involve retrenchment and illustrate the trade-offs that the actors confronted. Table 6.3 and Figure 6.5 show the results of

TABLE 6.3. *France: Results of the Factor Analysis on the "Balladur" Pension Reform, 1993*

Issues of the Reform Debate	Insurance (F1)	Targeting (F2)
Indexation of pensions on prices	0.95	0.05
Increase of contributions (CSG)	0.88	−0.09
Lengthening of the required contribution period	0.97	0.17
Increase in the age of retirement	0.87	0.39
Separate financing (FSV) of non contributory benefits	0.07	0.99
Eigenvalue	3.49	1.04
Explained variance	70%	21%

Actors	Factor Scores	Factor Scores
Trade union CFDT	−1.09	0.82
Trade union CGT	−1.07	−0.61
Managers' Union CGC	−0.79	1.70
Large-Firm Employer Association CNPF	1.38	−0.84
Small-Business Employers' Association CGPME	0.49	0.78
Gaullist Conservative Party RPR	0.90	0.55
Centrist Conservative Party UDF	0.77	0.42
Socialist Party PSF	−0.58	−0.74
Communist Party PCF	−1.05	−1.57

Notes: Factor analysis run on the coded positions of the actors; all factors with Eigenvalue ≥ 1, Varimax rotation; data and methodological approach presented in Appendix 1. Bold numbers (factor loadings) indicate the dimension to which the reform-issue belongs.

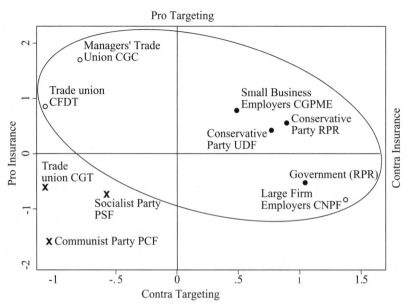

FIGURE 6.5. France: Scatterplot of the factor scores of actors in the Balladur reform of the pension system, 1993

the factor analysis and the positioning of the main actors in the two-dimensional policy space of the 1993 pension reform.[17]

The horizontal axis represents actors' preferences on issues related mainly to insurance, such as cutbacks in the *régime général* (F1; increase in the age of retirement, lengthening of the contribution period, increase of contributions). On this dimension, one can see a classical distributional class conflict, opposing trade unions and left-wing parties against the right-wing parties and employers. On the vertical axis, however, which represents targeting (F2), the left was deeply split. This axis reflects the introduction of the Fonds de solidarité vieillesse (FSV), a separate scheme for the financing of noncontributory benefits such as contributions for unemployed or educational credits. While the CGC and CFDT – despite initial criticisms (Schludi 2005) – welcomed the FSV as a means to tax-finance these solidaristic, redistributive measures and to unburden the *régime général*, the CGT and the parties of the left saw the measure quite differently. According to them, the FSV would endanger noncontributory benefits, because these are not part of regular pension rights anymore. According to the opponents, any risk should be covered within the *régime général* instead of creating separate (meaning rival) schemes. The right was more cohesive on the issue, even though the CNPF (large employers) advocated very restrictive use of the FSV.

---

[17] The labeling of the resulting factors in terms of insurance, targeting, capitalization, and recalibration is, of course, not a direct result of the data analysis but an interpretation based on the reform issues that load highly on the respective dimensions.

The actors whose position is marked by a cross eventually rejected the whole reform package, whereas a dark point indicates the actors who agreed to it. The positions of CFDT, CGC, and CNPF are symbolized by a circle, which means that they criticized the reform but did not mobilize against it, and hence somewhat implicitly put up with it (the ellipse includes all actors of the final reform coalition). It seems that the CFDT and CGC had a stronger preference for targeting than for insurance (accepting the reform *despite* retrenchment), and, conversely, CNPF prioritized insurance (accepting the reform *despite* targeting). I do not have an independent measure of the salience of a conflict line for each actor, but research on directional voting has shown that the direction and intensity of positions tend to be correlated (Rabinowitz and Macdonald 1989; Laver and Hunt 1992), which means that an actor positioned at the extreme of an axis also tends to weight this conflict strongly.[18] This seems to provide a plausible explanation for the approval of the reform by CGC and CNPF – though the evidence is weaker for CFDT – because both are positioned at the extremes of the targeting axis (the CGC) and the insurance axis (the CNPF) and have less pronounced preferences on the other conflict. Therefore, they could more easily make concessions on the issue that is secondary to them to secure an output that met their preferences on their most valued axis. In summary, the 1993 reform shows that targeting as a second conflict dimension crosscut the class divide on insurance and allowed the Balladur government to tie a package of reform issues that divided the left-wing opposition.

The 2003 Raffarin reform gives a very similar picture with some nuances. The policy space of this reform was three-dimensional (Table 6.4), and the first two dimensions are displayed in Figure 6.6. The third dimension is composed mainly of pension credits to mothers (i.e., by recalibration). The horizontal axis represents the factor on which issues related to insurance load high (F2; indexation of pensions, lowering of widows' pensions). Again, a rather clear distributional class conflict can be observed, even though the socialist party PSF has moved considerably to the right on this distributional axis. On the vertical axis, formed by issues related to targeting (F1; minimum pensions and early retirement for workers with long careers, aligning public sector pensions on the *régime général*) and capitalization (introducing capitalized private saving plans for civil servants), however, the left and the right were deeply split internally. The CFDT and CGC rejected the cuts on insurance but accepted a reorientation of the French pension system toward a more redistributive and targeted coverage of particular risk groups, such as low-income workers, and a more egalitarian benefit structure between public and private sectors. The MEDEF, the UMP (Gaullist), and the UDF (centrist) agreed to this reorientation, too. However, the

---

[18] The Laver-Hunt evidence is based on expert surveys on party positions. However, it must be noted that it is mostly the extremist parties (notably communist parties and the radical right), who differ strongly with regard to the saliency they attribute to different conflict lines. The other, more moderate parties, by contrast, weight the different conflict lines more similarly (Laver and Hunt 1992: 133).

TABLE 6.4. *France: Results of the Factor Analysis on the "Raffarin" Pension Reform, 2003*

Issues of the Reform Debate	Targeting and Capitalization (F1)	Insurance (F2)	Recalibration (F3)
Harmonization of the required contribution periods in public and private sectors	**0.91**	0.25	0.04
Lowering of retirement age for long career workers	**0.84**	0.23	0.39
Individual pension savings plans	**0.83**	0.37	−0.17
Increase of minimum pension	**0.79**	0.18	0.52
Lowering of widows' pensions	0.49	**0.82**	0.22
Indexation of pensions on prices	0.20	**0.95**	0.19
Increase of educational pension credits for civil servants	0.07	0.22	**0.93**
Eigenvalue	3.11	1.89	1.4
Explained variance	44%	27%	20%
Actors	Factor Scores	Factor Scores	Factor Scores
Trade union CFDT	0.70	−1.32	−0.81
Trade union CGT	−1.35	−0.97	0.37
Managers' Trade Union CGC	1.18	−1.23	−0.38
Large-Firm Employer Association MEDEF	1.19	0.52	1.73
Small-Business Employers' Association CGPME	−0.40	0.86	1.45
Gaullist Conservative Party UMP	0.67	0.62	0.12
Centrist Conservative Party UDF	0.36	1.15	−1.62
Socialist Party PSF	−1.04	0.35	−0.48
Communist Party PCF	−1.44	−0.88	−0.07
Government (UDF)	0.13	0.99	−0.31

Notes: Factor analysis run on the coded positions of the actors; all factors with Eigenvalue ≥ 1, Varimax rotation; data and methodological approach are presented in Appendix 1. Bold numbers (factor loadings) indicate the dimension to which the reform-issue belongs.

CGT, the PCF, the PSF, and – to a somewhat lesser extent – the small-business employers, opposed this reorientation and defended the status quo. The position of the CGPME (small business employers) compared to the MEDEF is plausible and particularly interesting: the CGPME remains much more attached to the preservation of income-related public pensions, not least because the introduction of occupational pension plans is more difficult in small businesses than in large firms.[19]

[19] Interview, CGPME, Paris, July 19, 2005.

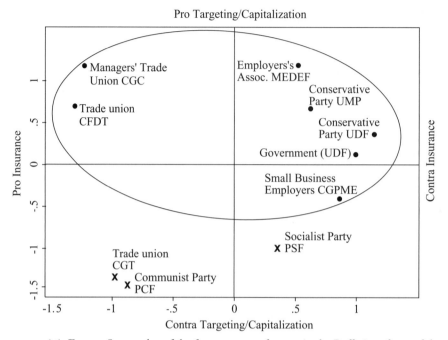

FIGURE 6.6. France: Scatterplot of the factor scores of actors in the Raffarin reform of the pension system, 2003

Again, the symbols indicate the final stance of the actors on the whole reform package, and the ellipse highlights the reform coalition. It appears very clearly that the targeting-capitalization axis became the decisive conflict line in this reform. The CGPME conceded the systemic changes in targeting and capitalization to secure its strong preferences on benefit cuts in general pensions. The CGC, conversely, accepted the cuts to favor targeting and capitalization. The PSF rejected the whole reform package because of its skepticism about targeting and capitalization, more so than because of the benefit cuts.[20] The position of the CFDT is again somewhat puzzling. Even though this trade union seems to have clear and strong preferences against cutbacks in the *régime général*, it finally agreed to them in favor of expansive reforms with regard to targeting and capitalization. How can this be explained? The politicized nature of the labor movement in France may provide part of the explanation, as the unions more freely take on strategic positions that may deviate from the narrower immediate interests of their members. In that sense, the approval of the reform by the CFDT was part of its reformist program and preference for a reorientation of the French pension architecture.

[20] In addition, in the majoritarian French system, the opposition parties must speak with one voice and must reject government reforms, independently of their actual policy preferences. Hence, the position of the PSF is as much institutionally determined as reflecting a real policy preference.

Development of Reform Coalitions, Reform Capacity, and Output

So far, this chapter demonstrated that new conflict lines became important for French reform capacity in the era of retrenchment. The multidimensionality of the policy space facilitated the adoption of modernizing reform packages. Hence, unexpected cross-class alliances among labor and capital and among right-wing and left-wing parties formed in favor of the reforms. The chances for the success of such new coalitions, however, depends on coalitional flexibility and on the institutional decision-making framework: as I argued in Chapter 4 of this book, a concentrated structure of unions and employers' associations and of government and/or opposition parties may impede the formation of cross-class coalitions. The more fragmented these actors are, the more room there is for the formation of new and varying reform coalitions along new conflict lines.

To test the importance of the cross-class conflict lines, I coded actors' positions on the final reform packages.[21] Table 6.5 shows the correlations between the positions of the actors on the individual conflict dimensions (factor scores) and their final positions on the whole reform packages.

TABLE 6.5. *Relative Importance of Conflict Dimensions: correlations between Factor Scores and Final Actor Positions on the French Pension Reforms in 1993 and 2003*

Final Position on 1993 Reform		Final Position on 2003 Reform	
Insurance (F1)	0.62	Insurance (F2)	0.25
Targeting (F2)	0.68	Targeting and capitalization (F1)	0.88
		Recalibration (F3)	0.04

Notes: For the factor analysis results, see Tables 6.3 and 6.4; data presented in Appendix 1.

In both reforms, the new conflict lines (targeting and capitalization) explain the final positioning of the actors at least as well as insurance, or even better. As shown earlier, insurance is the one conflict line that most consistently fostered a class conflict throughout the whole period. Consequently, in the 1993 reform, the new conflict line had become roughly as important as the class conflict, and cross-class conflict had become clearly dominant in explaining the outcome of the 2003 reform.

Targeting and capitalization have become so important mostly because of the split within the trade union movement. While all unions share similar positions against retrenchment, their preferences differ strongly when it comes to targeting and capitalization. This within-class divide remained relevant even in the formation of the final reform coalitions, because the fragmentation in labor and in capital are strong in France. The French party system, however, is majoritarian

[21] Coding is as follows: 0 = approval, 1 = refusal without mobilizing against the reform, 2 = refusal with mobilization against the reform (strikes, referenda, votes against the reform in parliament); see Appendix 1.

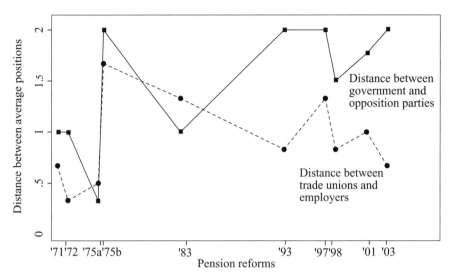

FIGURE 6.7. The effect of coalitional flexibility on class conflict: Development of the average distance between actor positions on French pension reforms over time

and highly concentrated in two major blocks on the left and the right (party discipline in parliament, the Assemblée Nationale, is high; Grunberg 2006). This
means that modernizing coalitions between left- and right-wing parties (i.e.,
government and the opposition) are rare, even in cases where their preferences
are actually close. Therefore, class conflict among parties remained stronger
than among unions and employer organizations. Figure 6.7 provides further evidence in favor of this interpretation of the evidence for the fourth hypothesis of
the model. Class conflict is operationalized by the distance between the average
position of labor (trade unions and left-wing parties) and capital (employers associations and right-wing parties). A value of 2 indicates maximum class conflict
and a value of o indicates identical positions.

   Class conflict was low in the 1970s, both among interest associations and
among parties, as most actors agreed on the expansion of the *régime général*. By
the end of the 1970s and during the 1983 reform of the left-wing government,
polarization increased starkly. From the 1990s onward, when retrenchment and
capitalization appeared on the reform agendas, the level of class conflict in pension reforms fell between labor and capital but remained constantly high among
political parties. Government and opposition parties have been diametrically split
in their final votes on reforms, even if their initial preferences in the policy space
were rather similar. For example, the right-wing parties rejected the introduction
of private savings instruments by the socialist government in 2001, even though
they had introduced very similar measures only a few years earlier and continued
to promote capitalization after their return to power. This illustrates that polarization between parties is high for institutional electoral reasons, not because of
genuinely different policy preferences.

Hence, the preconditions for the formation of cross-class coalitions and for recalibrating compromises in France are bad in terms of coalitional flexibility with regard to political parties but good with regard to unions and employers. Moreover, dividing the unions' opposition has turned out to be a necessary condition for reforms: because of their strong position in the management of the insurance schemes and their high capacity for mobilization, the social partners are de facto veto players whose agreement is needed for a reform to succeed.[22] Juppé, who in 1995 did not try to negotiate reform or to tie any recalibrating package, but proposed only elements aimed at retrenchment, failed precisely because he neglected the heterogeneity in the unions, arousing massive protest from the unified union movement (on the comparison of the Balladur 1993 and the Juppé 1995 reforms, see also Bonoli 1997; Vail 1999; Schludi 2005; Da Conceiçao-Heldt 2006). Hence, coalitional flexibility and the number of veto players in France allow for the necessary coalitional engineering, as hypothesis 4 suggested (see Chapter 5). If governments exploit the potential multidimensionality of the policy-making space, they can foster sufficient cross-class support for pension reforms. This means that substantially, French pension policy is most likely to evolve further along the lines of targeting and capitalization, combined with retrenchment, as these are the issues that are likely to gain the support of a reformist coalition.

Conclusion

The upshot of this analysis of French pension reforms since the 1970s is clear: we find ample evidence for the expected dynamics of post-industrial pension politics. The French scenario also makes it clear that country-specific dynamics must be taken into account and that conflict lines cannot be analyzed independently of one another. When looking at the issues that have dominated the post-industrial reform agenda, the pattern predicted by the first hypothesis of the theoretical model of this book is fully confirmed: benefit levels in the basic insurance scheme have always been an important issue on the agenda, but the focus of the reforms turned sharply from expansion to cost containment and retrenchment after the 1980s. Along with this goal reversal, capitalization emerged as a highly polarizing issue in the French pension debate over insurance reforms. Proposals to shift part of the pension financing from PAYG to capitalized and individualized pension funds were initiated by both left- and right-wing parties, and they implied head-on questioning of the (intergenerational) solidarity in pension financing. The third dimension of French pension policy making is targeting. As early as the 1970s, governments introduced particular pension privileges for women, low-skilled workers, and the disabled. From the 1990s onward, such noncontributory benefits (i.e., pension rights that are not earned with regular contribution payments but granted on the basis of special needs) once again became an important issue,

[22] Opposition parties, by contrast, are not veto players. They can be outvoted in parliament by the majority and have few further means of opposition.

with the creation of a special fund for their financing and targeted measures for workers in precarious employment. Gender equality and particular benefits for women, by contrast, were never a very controversial topic. This is largely because France has a high female labor market participation rate and a highly developed family policy.

The results concerning actor configurations and alliance potentials are even more striking. As expected, insurance reforms gave rise to a strong class conflict, setting left-wing and right-wing parties in opposition and setting labor against capital from the 1980s onward (Figure 6.1). This class conflict, however, has become considerably blurred with regard to capitalization and targeting reforms. Capitalization (Figure 6.2) has increasingly divided trade unions. The CGC and the CFDT came to support the introduction of capitalized pension schemes in 2001 and 2003, whereas the CGT has rejected any capitalization from the very outset and still rejects it. This divide is mostly based on skill-level differences, as the CGC and the CFDT mobilize more strongly in high-skilled service sectors such as banking and insurance. Similarly, the intra-capital heterogeneity predicted by hypothesis 2 is confirmed; small firms are more skeptical of capitalization than are large firms. The French socialists' ambivalent position on capitalization adds to the evidence that skill levels are the decisive criterion structuring this conflict: the PSF represents both low-skilled (blue-collar workers) and high-skilled voters (sociocultural professionals). Consequently, capitalization has always been highly controversial in this party, and its position has varied, depending on whether the party was in opposition or in government. Finally, targeting strongly reinforced intra-labor heterogeneity from the 1990s onward (Figure 6.3). The CFDT, the CGC, and to some extent the PSF, started to advocate the granting of needs-tested benefits to specific risk constituencies, whereas both the CGT and the PCF rejected this as a weakening of the insurance principle and the *régime général*. This controversy – which pitted advocates of the traditional insurance scheme against advocates of a more egalitarian, means-tested benefit structure – reflects the different sensibilities to the needs of outsiders. The CFDT and CGC became willing to accept these targeted expansive measures, whereas the CGT defends insider privileges in the general public insurance scheme. The rift between the CFDT and the CGC (Figure 6.4) is truly the most striking change in the actor configuration of the French pension policy subsystem.

However, the evidence for these new conflict patterns must be qualified in two ways. First, the differentiation of class interests became clearly observable only in the 1990s (i.e., in the context of austerity), when pension politics became a zero-sum game. Before this, trade unions and left-wing parties advocated similar positions on both targeting and recalibration in the 1970s. Hence, together with the transformation of the post-industrial class structure, the context of austerity has led to a differentiation of interests among labor and among capital. Second, the French case reveals the limits of analyzing conflict lines separately from one another. Both the favorable stance of the CFDT on capitalization and the support of targeting by the CGC and right-wing parties can be explained only with reference to the overall reorientation of the French pension architecture. A new coalition – consisting of reformist trade unions, the right and sections of the left-wing parties – advocates the overhaul of the continental insurance scheme in a dualized (Palier 2002) regime, consisting of egalitarian minimum basic protection and a highly stratified and individualized regime for the better off. This overall redesign of the French pension regime appears clearly in the policy packages that the right-wing governments put together in 1993 and 2003. The packages combined retrenchment in the *régime général* with expansive reforms on targeting. In both reforms, the policy space has indeed become multidimensional. In addition, coalitional engineering by the right-wing conservative governments succeeded, as the French trade union movement is so highly fragmented. Hence, in both reforms, new cross-class conflict lines became decisive for the final policy package (Table 6.5). However, quite unexpectedly, the French governments did not tie packages of retrenchment and capitalization. Rather, they framed capitalized pension schemes as a macroeconomic policy supposed to increase savings rates in the French economy, thereby endeavoring to keep the issue separate from pension-reform debates. This can be explained by the fact that capitalized funding has always been highly controversial in France; the issue was unsuitable for credit claiming with the broader public. The political parties, trade unions, and employers' organizations, however, have always understood capitalization as a full part of the overall pension reform strategy. This strategy is in line with Palier's (2002) thesis of a dualized welfare state that provides flat-rate, egalitarian minimum coverage for outsiders and inegalitarian insurance (capitalization) for the high skilled and insiders. The main losers in this change are the formerly privileged low- and medium-skilled insiders. They are hit hard by retrenchment but benefit from neither expanded minimum protection nor the new capitalized savings schemes.

7

Germany

Institutional Obstacles to Multidimensional Reform Politics

The brief overview of the development of German pension policy institutions over the past three decades at the beginning of this chapter will show that the pace of change and systemic reform has been accelerating with the entry of Germany into an era of permanent austerity during the 1990s. While most of the literature in this decade was still highly skeptical with regard to the reform capacity of the German welfare state (see, e.g., Manow and Seils 2000; Esping-Andersen 1996b; Schmidt 2000; Kitschelt 2001), the important reforms that have been implemented since the coming to power of the red-green coalition government in 1998 prove the thesis of inertia wrong. The analysis of conflict lines in this chapter show that insurance reforms cut benefits severely and that, simultaneously, capitalization, targeting, and recalibration became important topics of reform, creating insider-outsider and skill level conflicts within the left. This increasing heterogeneity within the German left is the main result of the analysis of conflict lines and policy spaces in this chapter. The second stage of the analysis demonstrates that German governments tied reform packages combining different conflict lines for two main reasons. On the one hand, they tried to gather the partial approval for these highly controversial reforms from trade unions and/or opposition parties, but on the other hand, these packages were very important to enable agreement among the different coalition partners within the government. However, electoral competition and the concentration of trade unions and business organizations are fairly strong in Germany, so the distributional class divide over insurance has remained the dominant conflict line even in times of austerity, despite elements of targeting, recalibration, and capitalization in the reforms. Both trade unions and employers usually spoke with one voice, and the opposition parties hardly ever explicitly supported a reform proposal by the government, irrespective of its content. Hence, even when the policy space actually provided the potential for cross-class alliances, the new alliances ran a high risk of breaking apart at the end of the decision-making process. The government's strategy, therefore, to push reforms through against fairly strong opposition by trade unions and opposition parties worked only as long as the government had the upper hand in the power balance with the opposition. When the opposition acquired clear veto power in the second chamber (the Bundesrat), this development severely hampered reform capacity in Germany, a fact that eventually contributed to the formation of a grand coalition in fall 2005.

As it had developed until the 1970s, the German pension system clearly reflected – and to a large extent still reflects today – the characteristics of a conservative, Bismarckian social-insurance welfare state (Bonoli and Palier 1998): eligibility for coverage in the public pension scheme depends on labor market participation; benefits are income related, stratifying, and contribution financed; and the social partners are directly involved in the management of the basic pension insurance scheme (Gesetzliche Rentenversicherung [GRV]) under the supervision of the government (see Chapter 3 for more details).[1] In addition to the public pension schemes, some firms and sectors developed capitalized occupational pensions, but these never became a generalized practice. Being highly earnings related, the German pension system also tended to exclude growing groups of labor market outsiders, notably the atypically employed and women (Mühlberger 2000; Schmähl und Michaelis 2000; Riedmüller 2000; Lepperhoff, Meyer and Riedmüller 2001). Hence, pension benefits in Germany were rather generous for standard beneficiaries and their families, allowing them to maintain their living standard after retirement (Schludi 2005), but they were also highly unequal and ill suited for the challenges of post-industrial family and labor market structures.

Let us start with a brief overview of the main policy developments over the period of analysis. In the 1970s, the coalition government of the Social Democratic Party (Sozialdemokratische Partei Deutschlands [SPD]) and the market-liberal Free Democratic Party (Freie Demokratische Partei [FDP]) raised pension levels and introduced some systemic changes to respond to societal transformations. With regard to the overall benefit level, the three reforms of 1972, 1974, and 1976 successively lowered the retirement age to sixty-three instead of sixty-five, and improved pension rights for low-income earners with long careers. In addition, the coalition government opened (voluntary) access to the basic pension scheme for the nonemployed (women) and the self-employed. Moreover, it introduced the splitting of pension rights after divorce, a long-standing claim of the women's movement, and created a separate pension insurance scheme for artists in 1981. These systemic reforms show that the social-liberal government had always considered welfare policies as a means not only of poverty reduction but also of social modernization (Nullmeier and Rüb 1993). Moreover, in the context of growth and financial prosperity in the early 1970s, the reforms were

---

[1] All dependent workers and recipients of unemployment benefits are compulsorily covered by the basic pension scheme GRV. Entitlement presupposes an insurance record of at least five years at the age of sixty-five. A full pension in the 1970s replaced about 70 percent of the recent former income. It required a contribution record of forty years and average lifetime earnings. Benefits in the civil servants pension scheme (*Beamtenversorgung*) are much higher, at 75 percent of the final pay (Schludi 2005; Busemeyer 2005; Hering 2004).

supported by all major parties, as they responded to the very diverse needs of a wide variety of beneficiaries and constituencies (Alber 1987).

The economic crisis in the mid-1970s, however, stopped benefit expansion. The social-liberal government in 1977, as well as the right-wing coalition of the Christian Democratic Party (Christlich Demokratische Union [CDU] and Christlich Soziale Union [CSU]) and the FDP in 1983 enacted cutbacks, without, however, implementing any structural change in the pension system (what Schludi [2005: 130] calls "short-term stabilization"). Nevertheless, these early cost-containment measures made Germany one of the very few countries in which pension spending actually decreased throughout the 1980s (Schludi 2005). From this period onward, all reforms remained purely restrictive on the insurance dimension. The financial leeway gained by retrenchment allowed the CDU/CSU-FDP government to implement the last purely expansive reform in 1985, introducing child-care benefits for mothers and a minimum pension for employees with incomplete employment careers or low pension rights.

In the 1990s, Germany entered the era of permanent austerity, not only because of the general economic downturn in jobs and growth but also as a result of the enormous costs of unification, which were financed to a large extent by means of social insurance (Manow and Seils 2000).[2] In this new context, cost containment became the dominant theme of reforms on the insurance dimension. The 1989 reform raised the age of retirement and changed the rule of indexation from gross to net wages. It became the last reform that received the support of both the government and the opposition. Afterward, the German pension consensus (Nullmeier and Rüb 1993; Hinrichs 2000) became unviable; the context of austerity transformed pension politics from a positive-sum game to, at best, a zero-sum game. Hence, the right-wing CDU/CSU-FDP government clearly put the accent of its reforms during the 1990s on retrenchment, with measures such as lower crediting of periods of vocational training in 1996 and benefit cuts in 1997. Simultaneously, though, the reforms included some expansive elements, such as the coverage of marginally employed workers in 1996 and increased pension rights for mothers in 1989 and 1997.

The 1997 reform, however, never came into effect because the newly elected SPD–Green Party government invalidated it right after coming to power in 1998. The new government parties immediately started more fundamental reforms: in 1998 and 1999, insurance conditions for part-time employees and the marginally employed were improved. After these first, expansive reforms, however, the new left-wing government faced financial consolidation in light of dramatically worsening demographic and economic prospects. In 2000, the SPD-Green government cut pension expenditures in the basic public pension scheme by lowering disability pensions and reducing special pension rights for handicapped workers. In the very important Riester reform of 2001, pension rights were cut from a

---

[2] After 1991, social security benefit levels in former East Germany were immediately raised to the level of that in West Germany, even though the beneficiaries in East Germany did not have comparable contribution records.

replacement rate of about 70 percent to 64 percent, and widows' pensions were lowered as well. Simultaneously, however, the government introduced and expanded private and occupational capitalized savings opportunities and considerably raised pension rights for women, parents, and low-income workers by strengthening the means-tested minimum pension (Grundsicherung) and improving pension credits for mothers raising children (Anderson and Meyer 2006; Meyer 1998).[3] In the same year, the 2001 reform was also emulated in the civil servants' pension regime, cutting back on their particular pension privileges. Finally, the 2004 reform further reduced pension benefit levels and early retirement possibilities. These measures were again accompanied, though, by the introduction of a minimum replacement rate for low-income workers. Moreover, in the most recent reform, the CDU/CSU claimed improved benefits for families, but these were rejected by the SPD-Green government.

Table 7.1 points out that all four orientations of pension policy reform – insurance, targeting, recalibration, and capitalization – appeared on the German reform agenda.

Development of Conflict Lines

Of the three countries included in this analysis, Germany is the most typical Bismarckian system, because it combines a single-pillar, pay-as-you-go (PAYG) and contribution-financed scheme with a typical male-breadwinner system. Switzerland differs from this scheme because capitalization developed sooner, and France is different insofar as female labor market participation was encouraged much earlier than it was in the other two countries. Hence, Germany has become most challenged by post-industrialization; therefore, all three alternative reform strategies became highly relevant after the 1970s. While the SPD-FDP government and the right-wing CDU/CSU-FDP government implemented a range of recalibrating reforms, capitalization and targeting became particularly prominent on the reform agenda with the SPD-Green government from 1998 onward.

Table 7.1 shows that *insurance* was a high priority on the reform agenda throughout the whole period of analysis. Pension rights for the standard insured had grown steadily and become very generous by the beginning of the 1970s. This not only was the result of consensual politics between the major parties and the social partners but also reflects the typical pattern of a coordinated market economy (Hall and Soskice 2001; Estevez-Abe, Iversen, and Soskice 2001), in which investment in skills and continuous employment biographies are strongly rewarded by generous insurance schemes. Therefore, this basic pension insurance was highly functional in the industrial era, as it created positive incentives for standard employment and effectively insured the salary of the male breadwinner. With the appearance of permanently high unemployment levels

---

[3] The new rules on educational pension credits created incentives for mothers of one to return to the labor market after a year at the latest, whereas mothers of two or more children were encouraged be full-time carers during the first three years of their children's lives.

TABLE 7.1. *Development of Conflict Lines in German Pension Reforms*

Reform	Insurance	Capitalization	Targeting	Recalibration
Pension-reform law, 1972	1. Lowering of the retirement age (flexible retirement at 63) 2. Acceleration of pension indexation		1. Introduction of a minimum pension for low-income earners with long careers 2. Voluntary access to the basic public pension scheme for self-employed	1. Voluntary access to the basic public pension scheme for nonemployed 2. One-year educational pension credit
Law on the improvement of occupational pensions, 1974	1. Increase of occupational pension levels		1. Guarantee of individual pension savings in case of labor market mobility	
First reform of the marital law, 1976				1. Splitting of pension rights after divorce
Law on the pension adaptation, 1977	1. Postponing of pension indexation 2. Increase of pension contribution levels 3. Increase of contributions to the basic pension scheme by insurance and sickness insurance schemes 4. Lowering of reserve funds for the basic pension scheme			
Law on social insurance for artists, 1981			1. Introduction of pension insurance for artists	

Law on the public budget, 1983	1. Postponing of pension indexation 2. Increase of contribution rates to basic pension scheme 3. Increase of sickness insurance contributions to be paid by pensioners		
Reform of widow's pensions and educational benefits, 1985		1. Expansion of minimum pension regulations	1. Harmonization of widows' and widowers' pensions 2. One year educational pension credit
Pension reform law, 1989	1. Increase of the retirement age 2. Indexation of pensions on net instead of gross wages	1. Consolidation of minimum pension regulations	1. Expansion of educational credits 2. Summation of educational credits for early retirement 3. Consolidation of minimum pension regulations 4. Debate on the splitting of pension rights between spouses
Pension-reform law, 1996	1. Increase of the retirement age 2. Lowering of coverage in case of career interruptions for training 3. Cuts in disability payments by the basic pension scheme	1. Coverage of marginally employed workers by the pension insurance	

(continued)

TABLE 7.1 (*continued*)

Reform	Insurance	Capitalization	Targeting	Recalibration
Pension-reform law, 1997	1. Lowering of pension levels (demographic factor) 2. Cuts in early retirement options 3. Lowering of disability pensions 4. Increase of financial stability of the basic public pension scheme (through 1% of value-added tax)		1. Debate on the introduction of means-tested universal pension coverage	1. Increase of educational pension credits 2. Debate on the introduction of means-tested universal pension coverage 3. Debate on an individualized pension insurance for women
Bill on corrections in social insurance law, 1998	1. Abolition of the 1997 demographic factor 2. Abolition of the 1997 cuts in disability pensions		1. Improved coverage of part-time employees in the basic pension scheme	
Law on marginal employment, 1999			1. Coverage of marginally employed workers in pension insurance	
Reform of disability pensions, 2000	1. Cuts in disability pension levels 2. Introduction of a new disability pension scheme with lower benefits 3. Direct payments of the unemployment insurance to the basic pension scheme for coverage of unemployed			

Pension reform law, 2001	1. Lowering of widows' pension benefits 2. Lowering of general pension benefit levels	1. Introduction of individual and occupational pension savings plans	1. Introduction of a universal, means-tested minimum pension scheme	1. Improved pension coverage for carers 2. Splitting of contributions and benefits between spouses 3. Individualization of poverty relief (children do not have to pay for parents) 4. Introduction of a universal, means-tested minimum pension scheme
Reform of civil servants' pensions, 2001		1. Introduction of individual pension savings plans for civil servants	1. Lowering of benefit levels for civil servants 2. Lowering of the level of widows' pensions for civil servants	1. Increase of educational pension credits for civil servants
Law on pension sustainability, 2004	1. Lowering of general pension benefit levels (*Nachhaltigkeitsfaktor*) 2. Cuts in early retirement options 3. Lowering of pension coverage in case of employment interruption for training		1. Introduction of a target minimum replacement rate (46%) and a maximum contribution rate (22%)	1. Debate on improved pension coverage for families

and demographic aging, however, this generous scheme turned into an Achilles' heel, because it became highly unsustainable in an economy characterized by "welfare without work" (Esping-Andersen 1996b: 66). As in other countries, governments from the late 1970s to the early 1990s reacted to these structural problems with conjunctural rather than systemic reforms, raising contribution levels and changing indexation rules. It was only in the 1990s that the perception of a need for deeper retrenchment spread more widely, although the trade unions, the left-wing parties, and even the labor wing of the CDU continued to claim that the basic pension scheme was stable and safe (Busemeyer 2005). From 1997 onward, however, retrenchment became a leitmotif of all pension reforms. The right-wing CDU/CSU-FDP government reduced pension rights massively in 1996 and 1997, but what the SPD and the Green Party implemented in cutbacks between 2000 and 2004, was – paradoxically – even more drastic than anything the right-wing government had ever proposed in the 1990s (Schludi 2005; Hering 2004). By 2004, the general replacement rate in the basic pension system had fallen to a level of 46 percent (with, however, a transition period of about twenty-five years), and in 2005, the SPD government announced that the age of retirement would be raised from sixty-five to sixty-seven, a retrenchment that would have been unthinkable a few years earlier.[4] By this time, the SPD government even explicitly affirmed that basic pensions were not supposed to cover the whole cost of living in old age anymore.

This drastic about-face on insurance, however, is only one side of the German pension politics story. Table 7.1 shows that *targeting* had become a second axis of reform, especially for the social-liberal government in the 1970s and even more so for the SPD-Green government in recent years. The former extended the basic public pension insurance for the self-employed and nonemployed on a voluntary basis and created the special scheme for artists (who experience, almost by definition, unstable employment), whereas the latter improved the coverage of the part-time and marginally employed at the end of the 1990s, lowered the privileges of civil servants in 2001, and initiated the creation of a universal means-tested basic pension scheme in the same year. In addition, even the right-wing CDU/CSU-FDP government extended coverage for the atypically employed in 1998 and 1999. With these reforms, pension coverage for labor market outsiders was considerably improved, which compensated partly for the cutbacks on insurance. These expansive elements never went as far as outsider representatives – such as women's organizations or the Green Party (see Chapter 4; Schulze and Jochem 2007) – demanded, but they reflect the lively, ongoing debate over preferable strategies for adapting the ill-suited German pension institutions to post-industrial structural change.

Furthermore, the right-wing government implemented some *recalibration* in 1985 and 1997. As in other Bismarckian welfare states, women's old-age pensions were particularly low in Germany, as most of them depended exclusively on derived rights. The social-liberal government had already responded to the most

---

[4] Meanwhile, the age of retirement was indeed raised to sixty-seven in March 2007.

pressing problems in 1976 by introducing the splitting of pensions in the case of divorce. However, the conservative government also found ways to raise women's pension rights – without necessarily changing the traditional family structure – by granting educational pension credits to mothers in 1985. In the beginning, these educational credits applied only to women who were not active in the labor market.[5] This can be considered a strategy of conservative recalibration, as it creates no incentives for female labor market participation or changing gender roles. Nevertheless, the 1985 reform strengthened the individual pension rights of women. Women's old-age poverty and the individualization of pension rights (*Eigenständige Alterssicherung der Frau*) remained a constant topic on the agenda throughout the 1990s, notably in the debates on the introduction of a universal minimum pension (which would primarily benefit women).

Finally, *capitalization* first appeared in 2001 on the reform agenda. As in France, the introduction of private pension savings was highly controversial and occurred only rather late. This can be explained by the highly path-dependent nature of pension policy. It is extremely costly to switch from a PAYG, single-pillar scheme to a capitalized pension scheme because the returns on the first pillar increase over time and there would necessarily be at least one generation paying both their current pensions and their own capitalized savings. In France, the government managed to introduce private savings by separating them rhetorically from pensions and presenting them as an economic policy designed to raise savings rates (see Chapter 6). In Germany, by contrast, the left-wing government stressed the complementary nature of the private pension pillar and presented it explicitly as an alternative to the basic public pension scheme. How can we understand this difference between France and Germany? As the analysis of coalitional dynamics herein shows, the German government could succeed only by framing pension reforms as a genuine system change (i.e., the development of a multi-pillar system) consisting of a universal means-tested minimum pension and complemented by a considerably retrenched earnings-related public pension and private pension savings schemes. This reorientation started only in 2001 and remains incomplete, but the reforms made by the SPD-Green government all point in this direction.[6]

Development of Actor Configurations

The systemic transformation of the German pension system was the result of underlying coalitional realignments. Three main trends are crucial: first, on insurance, class-conflict prevailed and even intensified during the 1980s and 1990, until

---

[5] From 1999 onward, however, they were added to earned pension rights, following a ruling of the constitutional court.

[6] Schludi (2005) shows that the initial government proposals actually promoted the system change far more clearly and coherently than it was finally enacted. These government proposals show that the reorientation was actually a coherent intention of the government rather than a fortuitous combination of separate reform efforts.

the SPD and the Green Party made a sharp turn toward retrenchment at the end of the 1990s. Second, the class conflict was already blurred much earlier with regard to recalibration and – less so – with regard to targeting: while the political parties found some common ground regarding certain policies for outsiders, large parts of both labor and capital wanted to preserve a purely earnings-related insurance scheme for insiders. Finally, capitalization gave rise to a skill-level divide in the labor movement. The time periods I have chosen to analyze the reforms in this section are somewhat different from the ones chosen in France for substantial reasons. As in France (but unlike in Switzerland), the color of the government has an important impact on the reform output. Therefore, it is important to look separately at the conservative government in Germany before 1998 and the left-wing government after 1998. The right was in power from 1982 until 1998. This period is divided to show the turning point of unification and permanent austerity around 1990.

I expect the class conflict, as developed in Chapter 4, to prevail with regard to insurance, putting left-wing parties and trade unions in opposition to employers and conservative parties. This pattern indeed emerges with regard to trade unions and employer organizations throughout the analyzed period and with regard to the political parties in the 1980s and 1990s. In the earliest and most recent period, however, the alignment of political parties on insurance upset the logic of class conflict.

As in France, the early periods of German pension reform – the years of prosperity and benefit expansion in the 1970s – were characterized by a relative consensus among the political parties. The social-liberal government implemented expansive reforms and the CDU/CSU largely agreed on them. Even among trade unions and political parties, the level of conflict was relatively low. In this period, pension policy making was still a positive-sum game, with reforms satisfying the needs and demands of very different constituencies, and Germany experiencing what was later characterized as a pension consensus. Some observers even affirmed that German pension politics were somewhat de-politicized (Nullmeier and Rüb 1993) in this period. Figure 7.1 shows, however, that the class conflict became more acute during the 1980s and 1990s, when distributional conflicts about the level of pension rights in the public insurance scheme sharpened and cost containment became the single dominant reform strategy in insurance reforms. A value close to zero means that the actor advocated generous benefits (e.g., a low age of retirement, indexation on gross wages, generous earnings-related benefits), whereas an actor positioned toward the other end of the axis would privilege more restrictive insurance conditions. I have linked the positions of the actors with dotted lines to highlight their shifts.

In the 1970s, the political parties more or less agreed on a wide range of expansions. The economic prospects were good, which led to logrolling and a stark increase in pension expenditure levels (Alber 1987). Even the first cutbacks in 1977 did not generate massive conflict, because the reduction in benefits was compensated by increased revenues through contributions and other social insurance schemes, notably unemployment and sickness insurance. This strategy was

Trade unions and
employers associations

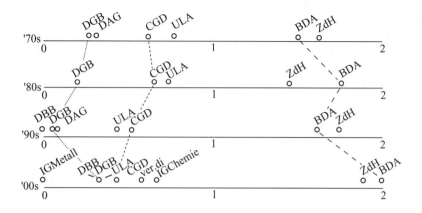

Political parties

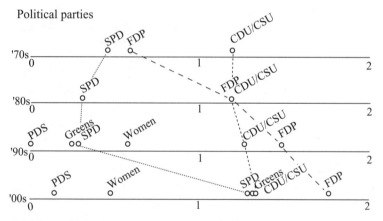

FIGURE 7.1. Germany: Average positions of actors on insurance over four time periods, 1971–80, 1981–90, 1991–7, 1998–2004

effective in reducing political conflict especially among the political parties, but it soon came at the high cost of rising deficits.

With austerity came class polarization. By the 1990s, the positions of the main peak trade unions and employers' associations had become clearly antagonistic, and a sharpened conflict can be observed between the left- and the right-wing parties. The increasing class polarization in the 1980s and 1990s was the result of several developments: on the one hand, the peak trade unions Deutscher Gewerkschaftsbund (DGB) and Deutsche Angestellten-Gewerkschaft (DAG) shifted more clearly to the left, which is also true for the SPD and other left-wing parties, the Green Party and the communist Partei des Demokratischen Sozialismus (PDS). On the other hand, the FDP transformed into a clearly right-wing, market-liberal party after the 1970s. In 1989, the issue of cutbacks became highly controversial because most trade unions considered this reform a turning point toward the lowering of benefits.[7] The polarization had only just begun, however, and it was mostly in 1996 and 1997 that the Green Party and the SPD, as well as the trade unions, ferociously rejected the heavy retrenchment that the right-wing government was implementing (e.g., lowered benefits, demographic factor, higher retirement age). A unified left then organized the first mass protests in Bonn against conservative pension reforms, and the left-wing parties decided to focus on these cutbacks as a major topic in the pre-1998 election campaign. It is not least because of this massive mobilization for the defense of existing benefit levels in the 1990s that the radical shift to the right of the Green Party and the SPD after their coming to power in 1998 is so striking. The red-green government did indeed annul the conservative cutbacks, but it implemented even heavier cuts only a few years later, not only reducing the possibilities for early retirement but also drastically lowering the general level of benefits. The 2000s, therefore, brought about a real split within the left, as the SPD and the Green Party clearly parted company with the trade unions, the Communist Party, and the women's movement (see the shift to the right in Figure 7.1). In the 2004 reform, for instance, experts warned in a parliamentary hearing that with the cutbacks, only very few pensioners would still be able to earn enough pension rights for a full pension.[8] The trade unions, by contrast, preserved rather homogeneous positions on insurance. As a representative of the main metalworker union IG Metall said, it was always easier to formulate a unified position of the labor movement to protect existing benefits than to claim for specific new benefits.[9] Therefore, the general turn of insurance politics in the direction of cost containment facilitated unity in the trade union movement.

How can one explain the sharp turn of the left-wing parties after 1998? Part of the answer surely lies in problem pressure: the parties were newly in government and had to deal more pragmatically with the financial difficulties of the pension regime than they did during their time in the opposition. A second reason, however, is because of their membership. The SPD and – to an even greater degree – the Green Party represent increasingly high-skilled voters and outsiders, notably socio-cultural professionals. By cutting back on insurance benefits, the parties certainly hurt the material interests of these constituencies, but they simultaneously created alternative means for the high skilled, allowing them to accumulate pension savings (see also the somewhat more moderate positions of the high-skilled unions IG Chemie and DAG on insurance). For the outsiders (e.g., women, the atypically employed), the red-green government also further developed a basic minimum pension scheme. The main losers of the cutbacks were low-skilled labor market insiders (i.e., the main constituencies of the industrial trade unions). This shows that actor positions on insurance in Germany must

---

[7] Interview, ver.di, Berlin, September 20, 2004.

[8] Alber (2001) estimates that the recent pension reforms add up to cuts of about 20 percent of the regular pension levels.

[9] Interview, IG Metall, Berlin, September 16, 2004.

Trade unions and
employers associations

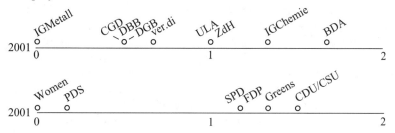

Political parties

FIGURE 7.2. Germany: Average positions of actors on capitalization, 2001

be analyzed while simultaneously keeping an eye on the alternative directions of reform, as cutbacks were only one part of an overall restructuring of the pension system.

The most controversial systemic change that the red-green government introduced after 1998 was the introduction of capitalization in the German pension system. In 2001, the government not only created new private pension savings schemes (*private Vorsorge*) but also expanded occupational pension schemes (*betriebliche Vorsorge*). It is important to note that the new schemes were massively subsidized,[10] particularly for low-income earners, to facilitate their generalization. I suggested in the first part of this book that capitalization should give rise to skill-level conflicts because pension savings are more accessible for high-income earners and employees in large firms. Capitalization has indeed created considerable intra-labor heterogeneity, as shown in Figure 7.2.

Actors on the left reject capitalization and claim tight public control of savings schemes, whereas actors on the right favor individual capitalized pension schemes and more flexible solutions. Because I expected intra-labor conflict on this issue, I display the positions not only of peak unions but also of two important sectoral unions, IG Metall (low skilled, blue collar) and IG Chemie (high skilled, blue collar). All major parties supported the introduction of private pensions as a means to shift the financing of German old-age protection toward more demographic sustainability. The striking finding in Figure 7.2, however, is the strong divide within the trade unions. IG Metall, as the main blue-collar union, ferociously rejected capitalization, whereas the peak unions (i.e., the public-sector union Deutscher Beamtenbund [DBB], the Christian trade union Christliche Gewerkschaft Deutschlands [CGD] the service-sector union Vereinte Dienstleistungsgewerkschaft [ver.di], and the German peak union DGB) took more moderate positions (though they strongly expressed their preference for unique

---

[10] The government decided on 20 billion euros per year to subsidize private pension savings. With regard to occupational pensions, employers could save social security contributions if they agreed to contribute to employees' occupational pension savings.

first-pillar pension insurance). However, IG Chemie rather quickly accepted the overall orientation of the reform and adopted a much more pragmatic stance, negotiating public subsidies for occupational pensions.[11] Therefore, IG Chemie was able to reach a cross-class agreement with the employers in the chemical industry, who agreed to contribute financially to the savings of their employees. Today, this sector provides rather favorable pension savings opportunities to its employees, none of which could be implemented in the metal industry (IG Metall) or the service sector (ver.di), the latter organizing many women with discontinuous employment biographies.[12] This development clearly reflects the skill-level divide that capitalization created. High-skilled sectors deal more easily with capitalized and individualized pension savings than do low-skilled sectors and small firms. It is therefore understandable that IG Chemie and the Bundesvereinigung der deutschen Arbeitgeberverbände (BDA, employers in large firms) were more favorable to capitalization than were the blue-collar and service-sector unions and the small firm employers Zentralverband des deutschen Handwerks (ZdH). Overall, the introduction of capitalization has clearly exacerbated sectoral divides in the labor movement and created a potential for alliances structured along skill levels rather than class.[13]

The class conflict in German pension politics, however, was blurred not only by the introduction of capitalization but also by targeting. Advocates of targeting (close to zero on the conflict line in Figure 7.3.) were inclined toward a more egalitarian pension scheme, which would redistribute income differences after retirement by means of tax-financed supplementary benefits. Opponents of targeting (closer to two), in contrast, claimed that pension benefits should be strictly proportional to contributions, preserving the equivalence principle and – consequently – status differences. On this conflict dimension, one would expect increasingly pronounced insider-outsider conflicts, because the traditional earnings- and contribution-related pension insurance scheme benefits mainly standard insider employees, whereas targeted reforms improve the pension rights of low-income and atypical workers. Contrary to capitalization, targeting over time raised the heterogeneity not only within the left but also within the right. On the left, most trade unions have, over time, become more skeptical about targeting, whereas on the right, the CDU/CSU and some employer organizations opened up to these new claims. I have again highlighted the movements of the major actors across the four time periods with dotted lines.

As with insurance, the 1970s were a special period for targeting, allowing for consensus among all major political parties. Together with the trade unions, all parties advocated expansive reforms for particular risk groups, such as the self-employed, outsiders, or low-income earners. In this time of prosperity and expansion, only the employers' organizations opposed targeting. In the 1980s, the trade unions maintained solidarity with the SPD – the major opposition

[11]   Interview, IG Metall, Berlin, September 16, 2004.
[12]   Interview, ver.di, Berlin September 20, 2004.
[13]   Interview, DGB, Berlin April 8, 2005; interview, IG Metall, Berlin, September 16, 2004.

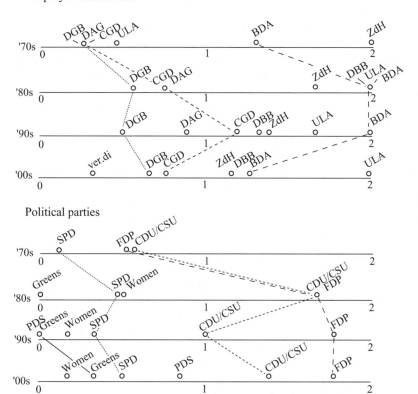

Trade unions and
employer associations

Political parties

FIGURE 7.3. Germany: Average positions of actors on targeting over four time periods, 1971–80, 1981–90, 1991–7, 1998–2004

party – in supporting more targeting reforms. However, the 1980s and 1990s marked the beginning of an important shift on the left of the political spectrum. In the party-parliamentary realm, the Green Party established itself as the main representative of the new, libertarian left. This party soon became the main advocate of targeting, claiming the strengthening of redistributive, tax-financed pension benefits instead of growing insurance benefits. Indeed, the Green Party always supported not only an inclusion of labor market outsiders in the basic insurance but also a more systemic turn to a highly redistributive and more egalitarian universal pension scheme (*soziale Grundsicherung*). This reform strategy was also supported by the SPD in the 1990s, though as a complement to rather than a substitute for the existing insurance scheme. The main (high-skilled) trade unions, by contrast, particularly the DAG, CGD, and DBB, took increasingly skeptical stances on this issue throughout the 1980s and 1990s (see their shift to the right in Figure 7.3). Indeed, the unions represent labor market insiders, who benefit from the equivalence principle and are not necessarily interested in more redistribution. Hence, although to some extent the unions supported the granting of rights to the atypically employed, they always insisted on the primacy of insurance as the basic principle of the German welfare state. In the 1990s, the high-skilled unions (e.g., DAG, CGD, DBB and Union Leitender Angestellter [ULA]) explicitly defended contribution related benefits against the new left. This split between the unions and the left-wing parties reflects the insider-outsider differences in the profile of their constituencies. Together with the right-wing parties and the employers, the main trade unions defended the privileges that insiders have in a Bismarckian insurance system. In this respect, it is perfectly understandable that the service-sector union ver.di has become an advocate of targeting in more recent years, bringing (parts of) the trade union movement again closer to the left-wing parties. Indeed, more than 50 percent of the members of ver.di are women in the service sector, who have much lower stakes in the contribution-related pension insurance than the constituencies of the industrial unions.[14] With this development in the trade union landscape, the pattern of conflict on targeting again slightly changed in the 2000s. Indeed, the red-green government then started to dismantle existing status privileges in the public-sector pension scheme. The 2001 reform, for example, was transposed identically onto the civil servants' pension scheme. This new orientation toward a more egalitarian benefit structure again divided the left, but this time along a cross-class private- and public-sector line. Indeed, the main private-sector peak unions (i.e., ver.di, DGB, CGD) agree with the left-wing parties in arguing that the civil servants' pensions should be aligned on private-sector pensions, whereas the public-sector union DBB and the communist PDS reject any of these attempts.

On the right, major shifts across the spectrum also occurred. Although in the 1970s, the CDU/CSU agreed to the targeting reforms of the social-liberal government, both CDU/CSU and FDP rejected the claims for a restructuring of the German pension system in the 1980s. Still in the 1990s, the Christian democrats rejected the more profound system change, even though they granted special pension rights to the atypically employed in the 1996 and 1997 reforms. Throughout the 1980s and the 1990s, the FDP and the BDA also rejected any major amendment to the insurance system, arguing that social benefits had to reward differences in employees' performance on the labor market. Similar to what happened within the left, however, the pattern changed somewhat in the 2000s, when the abolition of particular privileges of civil servants' pensions came to the forefront. The main employer organizations BDA and ZdH clearly support the cutbacks in the civil servants' pensions, to impose the same sacrifices on them as on the private-sector employees. Among the political parties, however, the FDP and the CDU/CSU remain more critical of the harmonization of the pension regimes. With this shift among employers and right-wing parties, the heterogeneity within the right has increased. Hence, targeting continues to foster class heterogeneity on both sides of the political spectrum.

[14] Interview, ver.di, Berlin, September 20, 2004.

As with targeting, recalibration created strong potentials for cross-class coalitions throughout the observed period. In this case, however, the issue fostered not only some insider-outsider divide within labor but also the potential for value alliances among left- and right-wing political parties. Recalibration in Germany is mostly about the pension coverage of women, by means of either universal means-tested minimum pension schemes (which provide coverage for the often discontinuous employment biographies of women) or by granting them particular pension rights (e.g., splitting, educational benefits). A position close to zero characterizes actors who advocate generous, gender-egalitarian benefit structures and individualized pension rights that are independent of marriage. Opponents of recalibration, in contrast, insist on strictly contribution-related pension benefits that link pension rights very directly to contribution records. The overall picture in Figure 7.4 makes it clear that recalibration is a more important issue in the parliamentary arena than in the corporatist arena: overall, all political parties tend to be more open to the claims for recalibration than trade unions and employers. This is easily understandable, as recalibration benefits the nonworking population. However, there are important differences within labor unions, and the right-wing parties have shifted considerably with regard to these issues.

Three findings are particularly important with regard to Figure 7.4. First, although there was significant consensus for recalibration among the political parties in the 1970s and the 1980s, the Green Party, women's organizations, and – to a lesser extent – the SPD, became the clearest-cut advocates of recalibration and gender equality in pension insurance in the 1990s and 2000s. They indeed represent more women and labor market outsiders than do the right-wing parties and trade unions (see Chapter 4), and they also understood recalibration as a value issue. It was mostly in the 1990s that the issue of the system change from insurance to universalism and individualization became a crucial topic for the Green Party, who considered the insurance system completely unable to deal with post-industrial social structures. The SPD became increasingly favorable to this position in the 1990s, when both parties selected the need for a complementary-minimum pension scheme as one of the crucial issues in the electoral campaign of 1998. In the parliamentary debate on the 1997 reform, the representative of the Green Party, Andrea Fischer, criticized the right-wing government for preserving an outdated, patriarchal system and for closing its eyes to the changing social realities: "It will not be enough to respond to the insufficient old-age protection of women by means of some special ad hoc measures. If so many people fail to live up to a norm – namely the equivalence principle in pension policy – it is not the people who are wrong, but the norm itself."[15] As a result, the red-green government strengthened the pension minima considerably after coming to power, but it also initiated a new direction of reform – one that was more focused on

---

[15] Minutes of the plenary debate in the lower chamber: Deutscher Bundestag, 13. Wahlperiode, 198. Sitzung, 10.10.1997: 17,870 (own translation).

Trade unions and
employers associations

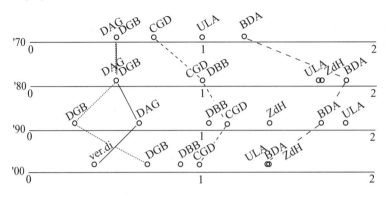

Political parties

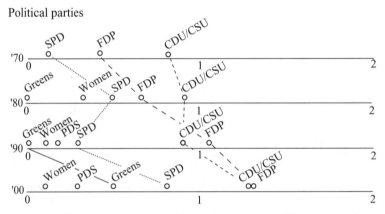

FIGURE 7.4. Germany: Average positions of actors on recalibration over four time periods, 1971–80, 1981–90, 1991–7, 1998–2004

enhancing women's pension rights through increased labor market participation rather than through educational pension credits for the nonemployed.[16]

This debate about the best strategy for improving women's pension rights leads us to the second main finding in Figure 7.4, namely the openness of right-wing parties (CDU/CSU and FDP) to recalibration. Indeed, the FDP shared a left-libertarian view of societal policies in the 1970s and developed into a more traditional right-wing party only slowly over time, especially during the 1980s. In the 1990s and 2000s, the party became far more skeptical of particular privileges

[16] The 2001 reform raised pension benefits and created incentives for mothers of one to work part-time rather than to stop working. In 2004, the speaker of the Social Democrats said in parliament that the best old-age protection is regular employment, covered by social insurance. (Minutes of the plenary debate in the lower chamber: Deutscher Bundestag, 14. Wahlperiode, 147. Sitzung, 26.1.2001: 14,405).

for women, promoting commodification before all else. The CDU/CSU, however, had always defended women's pension rights, though in a quite different manner from that of the libertarian left. Indeed, the conservative government introduced educational benefits for women in 1985 and improved them in 1989 and 1997. The moves toward gender equality were partly a response to sentences of the constitutional court, but they also reflected a strong concern in the party for the valorization of women's educational work. This was a form of conservative recalibration – or more generally, conservative modernization – because it improved women's pension rights without creating any incentive to change existing gender roles (Nullmeier and Rüb 1993). In this sense, the very goal of improving women's pension rights always created room for cross-class agreement between the parties.

Finally, the third insight in Figure 7.4 is that recalibration was never the main concern of the social partners, who represent the (predominantly male) constituencies of labor and capital.[17] Indeed, the peak unions DAG (white-collar, high-skilled workforce) and DGB (blue-collar workforce) mainly agreed to recalibration, but they were never the main advocates of it and did not actively claim it. The more conservative unions (the DBB and the Christian democratic CGD) even took decidedly reluctant stances on this issue, approaching the position of the employers' organizations, which always defended a strictly contribution-related insurance scheme, except for minor educational pension credits.[18] Some trade unions, however, particularly the (predominantly feminized) service-sector union ver.di, have become more sensitive to recalibration in the 2000s.[19] Even the employers' organizations became somewhat more open to a recalibrating strategy that put more emphasis on female labor market participation[20] (though according to the employers, such expansive recalibration should be counterbalanced with heavy cuts in widows' pensions[21]).

In summary, two main trends become apparent from the analysis of actors' positions and movements along the four conflict lines. The first trend is a deepening split between the trade union movement and the left-wing parties on distributional issues in pension politics. Figure 7.5 illustrates the distance between the average position of the Social Democratic Party and the Green Party and the average position of all the peak trade unions.

The relation between the labor movement and the left-wing parties depends on the position of the left in government or in opposition. Therefore, the time points in Figure 7.5 also indicate the governing parties. In the 1970s, there was

[17] Interview, ver.di, Berlin, September 20, 2004; interview, DGB, Berlin, April 7, 2005.
[18] Interview, BDA, Berlin, September 21, 2004; interview, ZdH, Berlin, September 21, 2004.
[19] Interview, ver.di, Berlin, September 20, 2004.
[20] These more favorable stances toward women's pension rights, however, not only are value-driven but also reflect the new problem load that came with the sharp cutbacks on insurance. For women, it has become virtually impossible to accumulate a full contribution record, so that severe old-age poverty can be prevented only by either increased labor market participation or more generous basic pension minima (Anderson and Meyer 2006).
[21] Interview, BDA, Berlin, September 21, 2004.

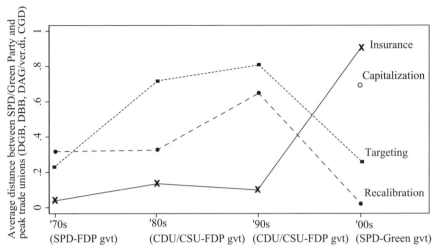

FIGURE 7.5. Divisions within the left in German pension politics: distance between the average positions of SPD/Green Party and trade unions over time

overall little divergence between the left-wing government and the labor movement. It was still a time of expansion and prosperity, and even if the unions were not the main advocates of targeting and recalibration, they largely supported government policy. On these latter two conflict dimensions, the positions of unions and left-wing parties became more differentiated during the years of right-wing government. As shown earlier, the SPD, and – to an even greater degree – the Green Party made the adaptation of the pension insurance system to post-industrial structures a key claim. The unions, by contrast, defended the insurance system, which rather generously protected their insider clientele and remained more skeptical than the left-wing parties of the right-wing strategy of conservative recalibration. This pattern of preferences, however, changed dramatically after 1998, when the SPD and the Green Party took over government. As in the 1970s, the trade unions supported the targeting and recalibrating reforms of the government, all the more so when the left-wing government started to link women's pension rights more closely to incentives for labor market participation. However, the unions and leftist parties increasingly lost common ground, because the left-wing parties started to privilege massive cutbacks with regard to insurance and introduced capitalization. This shift of the SPD and the Green Party created a deep split within the left and dramatically changed the landscape of German pension policy making. The German unions lost their main ally in the parliamentary arena and in government. The SPD was also internally split on the cutbacks, but the unionist wing of the party was less strongly represented in parliament than in the 1970s and 1980s, and the government became increasingly independent of the party base, further reducing the influence of the unions.[22]

---

[22] Interview, DGB, Berlin, April 8, 2005 (see also Trampusch 2004).

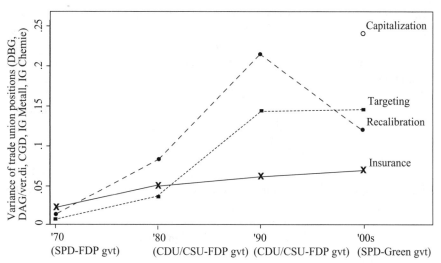

FIGURE 7.6. Heterogeneity within the labor movement in German pension politics: variance in the positions of German trade unions over time

The employers' associations affirm that their demands with regard to insurance cutbacks found even more resonance in the red-green government than in the conservative government of the 1990s.[23] Hence, the new reform strategy of the left, cutting back on insurance while adding basic and supplementary pillars to the pension scheme, created massive divergence within the left (on the fading power of trade unions in German pension politics, see also Häusermann 2010b).

The comparison of the left-wing parties with the average union position, however, somehow obscures the second main trend with regard to actors' positions (i.e., the growing heterogeneity within the labor movement). As in France, the recent reforms have driven the interests of different labor actors apart so that it does not really make sense anymore to speak of labor as a single actor in German pension policy. Figure 7.6 shows the within-labor variance in the preferences of the main private-sector unions.[24]

As in France, trade unions were strongly unified until the 1980s. In a context of prosperity, pension reform was basically a positive-sum game and labor solidarity was easier to achieve. With regard to insurance, the trade unions remained unified throughout the whole period of analysis. They all agreed on claiming generous insurance benefits and rejecting retrenchment. Within-labor divergences started to rise, however, in the 1990s, when some unions, notably CGD and the high-skilled union DAG, were critical of an egalitarian pension scheme (targeting and recalibration), whereas the DGB was more favorable to the claims. Targeting and

[23] Interview, BDA, Berlin, September 21, 2004; interview, ZdH, Berlin, September 21, 2004.
[24] I have excluded the public-sector union DBB from this analysis because it always defended much more conservative positions – notably on recalibration and targeting – and thus it would only inflate the variance.

recalibration remained controversial issues in the labor movement after 1998, with the DGB taking favorable positions on it, and in particular with the creation of ver.di in 2001. It is clearly with regard to capitalization, however, that the labor movement became split most deeply after 1998. As in France, some (high-skilled) unions engaged rather early in an accommodating and pragmatic strategy and focused more on the specific design of individual pension saving schemes than on the rejection of this new principle as such. In Germany, it was notably the IG Chemie that saw in the 2001 reform bill not only a threat to existing pension levels but also an opportunity to develop existing occupational pension schemes with increased governmental support. Hence, with the emergence of this new dimension of pension reform, the coordination of the positions of different sector-specific unions has become more difficult.[25] Overall, the analysis of the conflict lines shows that, as in France, class conflict has become considerably blurred in recent German pension politics. Coalitional dynamics in the 1990s and 2000s have become decidedly multidimensional.

Development of Reform Dimensionality Depending on Time and Austerity

The third hypothesis of the theoretical model developed in this book suggests that politicians tend to tie packages of different conflict dimensions to create majorities for contested reforms. In times of prosperity, this strategy allows for the fostering of ambiguous agreements by catering to different constituencies. The generalized pension consensus that prevailed in Germany until the end of the 1980s seems to be an expression of that. I argue, however, that this practice becomes even more important in times of austerity, when resistance to retrenchment needs to be overcome. The analysis of French pension politics in Chapter 6 demonstrated that a right-wing government skillfully exploited the heterogeneity of the labor movement to weaken left-wing opposition to retrenchment. This situation is directly comparable to pension politics in the 1990s in Germany but somewhat different from the most recent period of German pension politics during which the left-wing parties themselves have become advocates of retrenchment on insurance. However, the red-green government still faced considerable resistance to retrenchment, not only from the unions but also in its own ranks. The reorientation of the party position was highly controversial, and the labor wing of the SPD was very uncomfortable with major decisions by the government. Hence, the incentives for package building were certainly no less powerful in Germany than in France.

I again test the hypotheses on package building and multidimensionality by comparing the number of potential conflict lines included in each reform and the empirical dimensionality of the policy-reform space. The empirical dimensionality is determined by means of factor analyses of the actors' positions on each reform. Table 7.2 presents the evidence.

[25] Interview, DGB, Berlin, April 8, 2005; interview, IG Metall, Berlin, September 16, 2004.

TABLE 7.2. *Dimensionality of Reforms in Germany: results of Factor Analyses*

	The Reform Includes Elements That Belong to...	
	One Conflict Line	More Than One Conflict Line
Purely expansive reform	1976, 1981, 1999 (1 dimensional)	1972, 1974, 1985, 1998 (1 dimensional)
Reform that included retrenchment	1977, 1983 (1 dimensional)	2001 (3 dimensional)
		1989, 1997, 2004 (all 2 dimensional) 1996, 2000, 2001b (all 1 dimensional)

Notes: Factor analysis run on the coded positions of the actors; all results displayed in Tables 7.3 and 7.4, and Appendix 4; Eigenvalue of factors ≥ 1, Varimax rotation; for more details on data, see Appendix 1.

Each year represents the corresponding reform (see Table 7.1 for the reforms). In eleven of sixteen reforms, the governments tied reform packages along different potential conflict lines. Moreover – and in line with our expectations, according to which package building is an important strategy to overcome resistance to retrenchment – when a reform included cuts, package building was indeed the dominant strategy in seven of nine reforms.

All purely expansive reforms resulted in one-dimensional conflict patterns. In 1976, the social-liberal government introduced pension splitting after divorce (recalibration); in 1981, the same government created a particular insurance scheme for artists (targeting); and in 1999, the red-green government extended the coverage of marginally employed workers in the basic public pension scheme (targeting). All of those reforms (upper-left quadrant in Table 7.2) were purely expansive and consisted of only one specific reform element. Because the scope – and thus the financial implications – of the reforms was limited and they responded to rather clear-cut risk profiles in a focused way, they did not give rise to massive contestation. Hence, in the still more prosperous context of the late 1970s and early 1980s, most political parties and the trade unions supported targeting and recalibration, and employers did not mobilize massively against the reforms. In 1999, however, the inclusion in the pension insurance of the marginally employed (*geringfügig Beschäftigte*) with a salary of more than 630 deutsche marks per month was more controversial. Marginal employment had spread quickly over the previous years, and the left-wing government aimed to stop an alleged abuse of the marginal employment status by employers. Indeed, not only are the marginally employed insufficiently protected in the welfare state; they also constitute a flexible and inexpensive workforce for employers, which – in the eyes of the government and the unions – threatened standard employment protection.[26] In addition, by imposing social contribution payments on the

---

[26] Beschlussempfehlung und Bericht des Ausschusses für Arbeit und Sozialordnung zum Entwurf eines Gesetzes zur Neuregelung der geringfügigen Beschäftigungsverhältnisse. Deutscher Bundestag, 14. Wahlperiode, 1.3.1999. Drucksache 14/441.

salaries of the marginally employed, the government tried to seize an opportunity to raise additional revenues for the pension scheme.[27] Although the trade unions demanded more severe restrictions for marginal employment, employers and right-wing parties claimed more flexibility, so that the reform was finally adopted by the new government majority in parliament against criticism from both sides.

The four reforms in the upper-right field all comprised purely expansive reform elements, which belonged to different conflict lines and were therefore able to gather the support of different constituencies. The reforms of the 1970s are particularly interesting, insofar as the government consisted of a social-liberal cross-class coalition. Therefore, it combined the expansion of pension rights (insurance) with targeting and recalibration. Indeed, the social policy of the SPD-FDP government always aimed at societal change (*Gesellschaftspolitik*), which was one of the bases of their – otherwise rather unlikely – coalition (Nullmeier and Rüb 1993). Similarly, the CDU/CSU-FDP government in 1985 combined targeting and recalibrating reform elements in the reform bill and thereby ensured some support from the left for the reform, even though the SPD and the Green Party demanded far more radical steps toward women's pension coverage.[28] The three reforms were adopted in a context of prosperity and did not create trade-offs for any actor. This eased distributional conflicts and facilitated class solidarity, such that all the reforms eventually gave rise to a single dimension of class conflict. The 1998 bill on corrections in social insurance law, finally, was a direct consequence of the victory of the left in the elections, because it invalidated the 1997 cutbacks of the conservative government right after the SPD and Green Party had come to power. The new opposition parties, of course, rejected the reform heavily, together with the employers, creating a clear-cut left-right class conflict on this reform.

More surprising are the two cost-containing reforms of 1977 and 1983, which were purely restrictive but were nevertheless successfully implemented. How can we understand this? Part of the answer lies in the fact that the reforms were adopted in the context of broad household-consolidation measures that implemented cutbacks in a variety of areas. Hence, pensions were only one of the fields in which benefits were constrained. In contrast, the early cutbacks aimed at what

---

[27] Indeed, the initial governmental reform proposal stated that employers have to pay social contributions on the wages of the marginally employed. The latter, however, can choose whether they want to contribute equally in order to earn pension rights. If they chose not to pay social contribution benefits, the employers' payments would go entirely to the basic pension scheme but the employees would have no right to benefits. This break with the insurance principle was heavily criticized by the employers and the trade unions alike (minutes of the public hearings in the parliamentary committee on February 10, 1999), and it was eventually changed in parliament.

[28] A tension between the trade unions and the left-wing parties appeared clearly in this reform, because the SPD and Green Party privileged a more egalitarian benefit structure for women, whereas the trade unions clearly defended the insurance principle and the interests of high-skilled women who had earned their own pension rights (minutes of the parliamentary debates: Deutscher Bundestag, 10. Wahlperiode, 147. Sitzung, 21.6.1985: 10,909 statements of the DGB and DAG in the public hearings of the parliamentary committee, 28.2.1985).

Schludi (2005) calls short-term stabilization; that is, they changed only the level of existing insurance parameters (first-order changes, according to Hall [1993]). Moreover, the reforms counterbalanced the cuts in expenditures by raising additional revenues. Finally, they implemented cutbacks by changing the rules of indexation and financing. Pierson (1996) has argued that these are strategies to implement unpopular pension reforms because they obfuscate the distributional outcome and appear as mere technical changes. However, even though the cutbacks were not as severe as those in the late 1990s, it would be misleading to think of the reforms as consensual or tacit; they were heavily criticized by the opposition parties and trade unions and could be adopted only with the votes of the parliamentary majority as part of a whole consolidation program. The pension consensus among the parties existed only insofar as the opposition parties did not mobilize massively against the cutbacks in pension rights.

The most striking result in Table 7.2, though, is that all the major reforms aimed at retrenchment in the era of austerity from the 1990s onward were indeed packages of several potential conflict lines (lower-right field). In these reforms, the governments tried to split the actors along different conflict lines to divide and weaken the opposition against the highly contested reforms. In 1996 and 2000, however, the minor concessions on targeting that the reforms included were not enough to create a truly multidimensional policy space. The 2001 reform of civil servants pensions remained unidimensional, too, creating a divide between the public and the private sectors. The main opponents of the reform were indeed the civil servants union (DBB), but they also included the union of German cities and local governments (i.e., the public employers), as well as the communist PDS and – more surprisingly – the FDP. The public-sector employers opposed the cutbacks in the civil servants' scheme and remained very skeptical of a harmonization of the public- and private-sector pension regimes, as that would imply that civil servants' pensions would be financed through contributions rather than taxes.

It is no coincidence, however, that the four reforms of the past twenty years, which are named as the most important and most consequential by Schludi (2005), Hinrichs (2000), Schulze and Jochem (2007), and the interviewees, gave rise to multidimensional spaces of policy reform. The cutbacks implemented in all these reforms (1989, 1997, 2001, and 2004) have become increasingly severe, transforming the very structure of the German pension system. Indeed, after the last reform, the first-pillar pension scheme was no longer intended to provide sufficient means for a decent standard of living after retirement. The progressive downsizing of the basic public pension scheme, though, was accompanied by expansive reforms on recalibration, targeting, and – later on – capitalization. The combination of diverse conflict dimensions created multidimensional policy spaces. The factor analysis indeed confirms that the reforms split the actors in new and "unexpected" (Pierson 2001: 427) ways and created opportunities for essentially unpopular reforms. The 1989 reform combined retrenchment with the consolidation of minimum pensions and the expansion of educational pension credits from one to three years (see the case study herein). The policy-reform space was also two dimensional in 1997 (see Table A4.7 in the appendix), because, alongside retrenchment, issues such as the introduction of universal minimum pensions, better pension coverage for women, and higher educational benefits were on the reform agenda, which clearly formed a second, independent dimension of conflict and would have provided far-reaching possibilities for political exchange (for further development, see also Häusermann 2009). In the end, however, the conservative government merely raised educational pension credits, remaining far behind the demands of libertarian actors, such as the Green Party and women's organizations, for a universal minimum protection,[29] and behind the demands of the high-skilled union DAG for improved pension rights for women active on the labor market.[30] Therefore, the 1997 reform was very controversial and contributed eventually to the electoral victory of the left in 1998.

The 2001 reform exemplified the new pension policy strategy of the red-green government: a systemic change from a single-pillar insurance scheme to a multi-pillar pension system, combining universalism and insurance, PAYG, and capitalization (see the case study herein). The 2004 reform continued this strategy (initiated by the expert commission Rürup in 2001) by implementing further cuts, which were highly contested by the trade unions. The latter rejected the reform and demanded compensation, such as a guaranteed-minimum replacement rate. Similarly, the opposition parties raised recalibration as a second conflict dimension, claiming improved benefits for families (see Table A4.11 in the appendix). However, while the red-green government made some concessions to the trade unions, it denied further recalibrating measures for nonworking women. Rather, the government referred to its investments in child-care infrastructure as direct support for women who work and earn their own pension rights.[31] However, even though, in the end, the government introduced a target minimum replacement rate of 46 percent in the law, the major trade unions remained opposed to the reform. This shows that the concessions the government made were actually mainly directed toward the left wings of the government parties to ensure the internal cohesion of the government.

I now show two striking examples of this new pattern of pension policy making in more detail, selecting the reforms most comparable to the French case, namely the pension reforms of 1989 and 2001.

---

[29] Andrea Fischer (Green Party) in the minutes of the parliamentary debate: Deutscher Bundestag, 13. Wahlperiode, 198. Sitzung, 10.10.1997: 17,868.

[30] The DAG, however, rejected the universal minimum pension scheme that was demanded by the Green Party (written statement for the public hearing, 18.7.1997).

[31] "Only an increase in the labor market participation of women will eventually lead to the higher pension rights of parents, mostly women. Therefore the government privileges the improvement of care infrastructure: it invests 4 billion euro in the development of day care schools. Furthermore, day care for children below the age of 3 will be supported with up to an additional 1,5 billion euro per year." (Bericht des Ausschusses für Gesundheit und Soziale Sicherung zum Entwurf eines Gesetzes zur Sicherung der nachhaltigen Finanzierungsgrundlagen der gesetzlichen Rentenversicherung [RV-Nachhaltigkeitsgesetz]. Deutscher Bundestag, 15. Wahlperiode, 10.3.2004. Drucksache 15/2678, p. 12).

TABLE 7.3. *Germany: Results of the Factor Analysis on the Reform of the German Basic Pension System, 1989*

Issues of the Reform Debate	Recalibration and/or Targeting (F1)	Insurance (F2)
Increase of educational pension credits	**0.876**	0.395
Summation of education credits for early retirement rights	**0.926**	0.295
Debate on splitting of contributions and benefits between spouses	**0.871**	0.116
Consolidation of pension minima regulations	**0.673**	**0.707**
Increase of the retirement age	0.355	**0.845**
Indexation of pension to net wages	0.119	**0.937**
Eigenvalue	2.98	2.35
Explained variance	49%	39%

Actors	Factor Scores	Factor Scores
German Women's Council	−1.54	0.55
Green Party Gruene	−0.98	−1.10
Union of Family Organizations	−0.88	0.43
Free Democratic Party FDP	−0.84	1.54
Social Democratic Party SPD	−0.66	−0.32
Union of Trade Unions DGB	−0.30	−1.33
Union of Employees DAG	−0.25	−0.82
Christian Democratic Union CDU/CSU	0.36	0.46
Christian Peak Union CGD	0.37	−0.19
Craft/small-business employers ZdH	0.50	0.95
Public-Sector Union DBB	1.24	−1.71
Union of German Employers BDA	1.29	1.03
Union of Managing Employees ULA	1.70	0.50

Notes: Factor analysis run on the coded positions of the actors; all factors with Eigenvalue ≥ 1; Varimax rotation; data presented in Appendix 1. Bold numbers (factor loadings) indicate the dimensions to which the reform-issue belongs.

Table 7.3 and Figure 7.7 provide the results of the factor analysis of actor positions on the 1989 pension reform. The reform issues belonging to the conflict dimensions of targeting and recalibration (educational pension benefits, splitting) divided the actors in a different way from the cutbacks on insurance (increase of the retirement age, net wage indexation), the issue of pension minima being between the two. They formed two largely independent axes of conflict, which are displayed in Figure 7.7: the horizontal axis shows the alignment of the actors with regard to insurance (F2), and the vertical axis positions the actors with regard to targeting/recalibration (F1).[32]

---

[32] I have turned the vertical axis upside down in Figure 7.7 to place the pro-side of the axis on top.

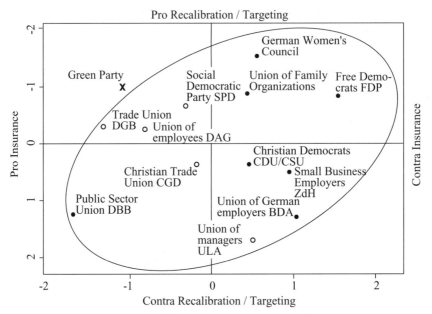

FIGURE 7.7. Germany: Scatterplot of the factor scores of actors in the 1989 reform of the basic public pension scheme

    The actors most in favor of recalibrating reforms were the welfare organizations, the SPD, the Green Party, and the FDP. While the trade unions also supported recalibration, they were more pronouncedly to the left on the insurance axis, which suggests that they rejected the cuts fiercely. As expected, the left-wing parties were more clearly in favor of recalibration and targeting than the trade unions. Hence, with the left-wing parties and the FDP advocating recalibration, one can identify a potential for a social-liberal alliance in favor of the new reform directions, whereas the insurance axis gave rise to a class divide between the trade unions and the left-wing parties on the one hand and the right-wing parties and employers on the other hand. It is particularly striking to note, however, that by 1989, the SPD had taken a rather centrist position on insurance. In this reform, the SPD and CDU were able to find a compromise (Rentenkompromiss 1989; see Nullmeier and Rüb 1993), because the SPD had taken rather moderate positions on insurance and because some of its recalibration-related claims had been taken into account.
    As in Chapter 6, the symbols denoting actor's locations represent their final positions and the ellipse includes all actors who eventually supported the reform. The Green Party (marked by a cross) clearly rejected the reform package, whereas the trade unions and the SPD criticized the reform but eventually did not mobilize against it (marked by a circle). The actors to the right of the insurance axis mainly approved of the reform. Hence, the recalibration axis in Germany did not become the main dividing line, even though concessions on recalibration may

have allowed the SPD and some unions to put up with the reform. However, the class conflict on insurance did not prevail clearly, either, at the end of the reform process. Indeed, most left-wing actors eventually accepted the reform package.[33]

The 1989 reform shows clearly that the potential for a cross-class reform coalition along recalibration and targeting did not fully materialize in Germany; strategic and institutional considerations other than preferences mattered in explaining the final position of the actors. This pattern became increasingly clear in the 2001 reform of the old-age pension system by the SPD-Green government. As Table 7.8 shows, the main issues at hand were insurance cutbacks (the lowering of widows' pensions and general cutbacks on benefit levels), expansive recalibration elements (individualization of benefit rights, educational credits, splitting) and targeting (*Grundsicherung*). Capitalization turned out to be an additional third factor, independent of the other two.

Figure 7.8 displays the positioning of the actors in the two-dimensional space formed by the first two factors. Figure 7.8 clearly illustrates that the Green Party was, once again, the most ferocious advocate of targeting and recalibration and that the SPD took a more favorable position on these issues than the average union. However, the Green Party and the SPD had shifted considerably to the right on insurance and – as seen previously – advocated heavy cuts. This led to a clear rift between the unions and the left-wing parties over insurance. Figure 7.8 also shows that the CDU/CSU, family organizations, and small-business employers advocated conservative reforms on recalibration. Indeed, the red-green government created incentives for mothers to remain active in the labor force. The conservative actors rejected this dimension of the reform, because it would call into question the traditional organization of families. In a similar vein, they criticized splitting and the individualization of means-tested benefits (meaning that children of poor retirees would not have to pay for their parents) on the ground that this would weaken the family as the unit of social insurance. The FDP and the main employers' organization BDA did not advocate very strong preferences on recalibration or targeting. They clearly gave priority to the cutbacks and the introduction of capitalization.

As in the French case, the actors' locations show that the final reform coalition in Germany cannot be predicted accurately merely by the preferences of actors. The Green Party and the employers clearly approved of the reform package (denoted by the dark dots), whereas some trade unions (IG Metall), the welfare organizations of the civil society, and the PDS rejected the whole reform package (cross). In between are the peak trade unions DGB, DAG, and IG Chemie, which criticized retrenchment heavily but eventually did not mobilize against the reform (shown by the circle). Even though the SDP approved of the reform, it appears in this last category, too, because it was internally split. Hence, one could argue

---

[33] Moreover, even the civil servants' trade union DBB accepted the reform. This somewhat implausible position may be explained with reference to the traditionally strong ties between the DBB and the then-governing CDU/CSU, as well as by the fact that the pensions of civil servants basically remained untouched.

TABLE 7.4. *Germany: Results of the Factor Analysis of the Reform of the German Basic Pension System, 2001*

Issues of the Reform Debate	Recalibration and/or Targeting (F1)	Insurance (F2)	Capitalization (F3)
Individualization of poverty relief	**0.865**	0.172	−0.051
Universal minimum pension	**0.744**	0.045	−0.231
Increase of educational pension credits	**0.682**	0.446	0.270
Pension splitting between spouses	**0.872**	−0.164	0.103
Lowering of widows' pension rights	−0.165	**0.926**	−0.161
Cuts in the level of pension benefits	0.305	**0.912**	0.0013
Individual private and occupational pension savings plans	−0.047	−0.970	**0.948**
Eigenvalue	2.649	1.956	1.064
Explained variance	38%	28%	15%
Actors	**Factor Scores**	**Factor Scores**	**Factor Scores**
Green Party Gruene	−1.69	1.30	0.21
German Women's Council	−1.50	0.10	0.94
Union Metal Industry IG Metall	−1.18	−1.06	−0.16
Union of Employees DAG	−0.88	−0.34	−1.30
Democratic Socialists PDS	−0.73	−0.93	−0.13
Social Democratic Party SPD	−0.53	0.95	1.00
Union of Trade Unions DGB	−0.44	−1.20	−1.21
Government SPD/Gruene	−0.41	0.66	0.08
Union Chemical Industry IG Chemie	−0.06	−0.14	0.11
Union of Family Organizations	0.33	−0.55	0.27
Union of German Employers BDA	0.40	1.72	0.06
Free Democratic Party FDP	0.64	1.11	1.13
Small-Business Employers ZdH	0.87	1.49	−1.51
German Family Union	1.18	0.21	0.83
Union of Managing Employees ULA	1.25	−1.10	−1.62
Christian Democratic Union CDU/CSU	1.79	0.00	2.07

Notes: Factor analysis run on the coded positions of the actors; all factors with Eigenvalue ≥1; Varimax rotation; data presented in Appendix 1. Bold numbers (factor loadings) indicate the dimensions to which the reform-issue belongs.

that the government's strategy to divide the unions by introducing targeting and recalibration failed to a large extent, as the latter remained very critical of the reform. However, the package was tied not only to divide the unions but also to ensure sufficient consent within the government parties. Their approval of the reform can be understood only with reference to the combination of conflict lines. The SPD and the Green Party were able to take the responsibility of the heavy

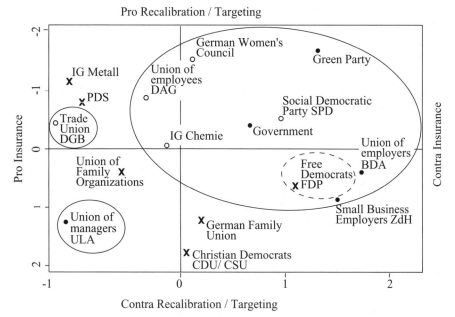

FIGURE 7.8. Germany: Scatterplot of the factor scores (factors 1 and 2) of actors in the 2001 reform of the basic public pension scheme

cuts only, and precisely, because the reform simultaneously expanded benefits with regard to targeting, recalibration, and capitalization.

To put it simply, the reform was designed as a package involving trade-offs. The introduction of a minimum-pension scheme, for instance, was explicitly financed by cutbacks on widows' pensions. The government knew that these issues were not priorities for the unions, but it also knew that they provided answers to the long-standing demands of the SPD and Green Party. In combination, targeting, recalibration, capitalization, and cutbacks on insurance allowed the government to initiate a new pension system, which was less generous (i.e., more viable with regard to long-term demographic and economic pressures) and that simultaneously remained sensitive to the needs and demands of specific social groups, which have been left outside the employment and male-breadwinner-centered organization of the traditional pension system structure.[34] At the same time, the new scheme leaves room for stratification by private and occupational pensions. For the employers such as BDA, the reform was acceptable, because the savings it engendered outweighed the costs implied by recalibration and targeting.

[34] The CDU, however, criticized the reform heavily for the fact that it would not improve significantly the situation of *non-working* mothers with more than 2 children (minutes of the parliamentary debate). Indeed, the red-green government increasingly prioritized the better coverage of *working* women contrarily to the Union. In the parliamentary debates, one representative of the SPD stated: "The best old age insurance is work that is subject to social insurance contribution" (minutes of the parliamentary debate, own translation).

Indeed, the main employers' organization, the BDA, stated that the recalibrating elements were "absolutely plausible" ("durchaus nachvollziehbar"[35]). But for the trade unions, such a reorientation of the reforms was much less acceptable, as their priorities were clearly centered on the defense of the existing levels of insurance benefits (see also Häusermann 2010b).

It is important to note, however, that neither recalibration or targeting nor insurance became the dividing line for the formation of the final reform coalition. Actors vary on their final position, irrespective of where they are positioned on the axes. Among the advocates of recalibration or targeting, the left-wing parties accepted the reform and the trade unions rejected it. Among the advocates of retrenchment, the employers and the government parties accepted the reform, whereas the opposition parties rejected it. This can be explained by the fact that, in Germany, the formation of reform coalitions is determined not only by actors' preferences but also by the dynamics of power fragmentation, coalitional flexibility, and the institutional context of decision making.

Development of Reform Coalitions, Reform Capacity, and Output

The results of the analysis so far show that, in Germany, new conflict dimensions have become increasingly relevant in pension politics. In the major reforms of the recent two decades, they divided the actors along different independent conflict lines. This multidimensionality of the policy-reform space creates potential for actors to overcome the resistance to retrenchment by beneficiaries and trade unions. If actors who are antagonistic in their positions on cutbacks agree on a second dimension of reform (be it targeting, recalibration, or capitalization), there may well be a way to ensure the capacity for reform.

However, the conflict over retrenchment – between trade unions and left-wing parties on the one hand and employers and right-wing parties on the other hand – may be reinforced by a lack of coalitional flexibility. If the labor movement is concentrated and there is a strong party discipline within the government and opposition parties, the danger of reform deadlock may still prevail. In this scenario, new conflict lines might not be able to overcome polarization, preventing the realignment of cross-class coalitions. Chapter 6 showed that, in France's majoritarian government regime, the political parties of the left and the right were indeed unable to agree on the final reform packages, even though they implemented very similar reforms once in government. Conversely, the French trade unions are fragmented; because of this, divergences in the preferences of reformist and industrial unions translated directly into a split on the final reform packages. In the German system, both political parties and labor and capital are concentrated (see Chapter 5). The Proportional Representation (PR) electoral system notwithstanding, government formation in Germany has followed an increasingly bipolar logic over the past thirty years, to 2005, setting

---

[35] Written statement of the BDA in the public hearing before the parliamentary committee, 8.12.2000, Ausschussdrucksache 14/1090: p. 196.

TABLE 7.5. *Relative Importance of Conflict Dimensions: correlations between Factor Scores and Final Actor Positions on German Pension Reforms in 1989, 1997, 2001, and 2004*

	Final Position on 1989 Reform	Final Position on 1997 Reform	Final Position on 2001 Reform	Final Position on the 2004 Reform
Insurance	0.55	0.716	0.336	0.025
Targeting and/or recalibration	0.141	0.536	0.072	0.738
Capitalization			0.369	

Notes: For the results of the factor analysis, see Tables 7.3, 7.4, A4.7, and A4.11; data presented in Appendix 1.

the left (SPD, Green Party) at odds with the right (CDU/CSU, FDP) (Lehmbruch 2000). Trade unions are horizontally and vertically concentrated, as are employer organizations. Hence, as long as the left-wing political parties and the trade unions both reject retrenchment, one should expect the insurance-related class conflict to prevail in pension politics, despite the appearance of new reform dimensions. Because the left-wing parties have shifted to the right on insurance, however, things have become more complicated. If the hypothesis of a lack of coalitional flexibility is true, this would temper the unions' opposition to governmental reforms, and the right-wing parties would oppose cost containment for electoral rather than substantial reasons. Thereby, weak coalitional flexibility is expected to blur the conflict lines, and none of the theoretically identified conflict lines may prevail.

I have tested this hypothesis for all reforms that gave rise to multiple conflict lines. Table 7.5 provides the correlation coefficients between the actor positions on the empirically determined conflict dimensions (factor scores) and their final position on the reform packages.[36] All coefficients greater than 0.5 are highlighted, because they indicate that a conflict dimension is important in explaining coalition formation.

The results in Table 7.5 make it very clear that the red-green government's rise to power in 1998 had deeply transformed the coalitional dynamics in German pension policy making. As long as the right-wing parties (the CDU/CSU and FDP) have been in government, insurance has prevailed as the main conflict line. In 1989, reform was possible, because all the main actors reached a compromise, and the unions and SPD did not mobilize actively against the reform (even though they remained very critical of the cutbacks). Their skepticism explains why the class conflict on insurance remained most closely associated with the final coalitional alignment on the reform. The distributional class conflict, however,

---

[36] Coding scheme for the final positions: 0 = approval, 1 = criticism of the reform without actual mobilization against it, 2 = explicit refusal of the reform package. For more details, see appendix 1.

appeared much more severely in the 1997 reform of the conservative CDU/CSU-FDP government. As expected, the SPD and the trade unions rejected the cost-containing measures, as well as the whole reform package (due, in no small part, to the upcoming electoral campaign in 1998). While the Green Party and the SPD agreed on proposed benefit improvements for families and for educational and care work, they could not give their consent to the reform of the government. Hence, targeting and recalibration emerged on the agenda as major points of contention, but the conflict over insurance eventually clearly prevailed.

This conflict structure changed dramatically when the red-green government implemented its heavy cutbacks after 2000. None of the three conflict lines mobilized in 2001 explains the final positioning of the actors. The red-green government advocated similar positions to those of the trade unions and women's organizations on recalibration, but the actors could not be compensated, as they assigned only secondary importance to these conciliatory measures. Nevertheless, insurance and capitalization did not become determining factors either. Some high-skilled trade unions actually agreed on the introduction of capitalization, but the concentration of the labor movement ensured that the unions still criticized the reform with one voice.[37] In the parliamentary arena, the cutbacks implemented by the left-wing parties strongly resembled similar cutbacks carried out by the conservative parties in the 1997 reform. Hence, according to preferences only, the government should have received the support of the right-wing opposition parties. However, the opposition parties resented the rejection of the 1997 reform. Therefore, they rejected the 2001 reform for reasons of electoral polarization rather than preferences. Interestingly, this institutionally and electorally driven behavior also explains the result on the 2004 reform of the pension scheme. With regard to preferences, this strong cost-cutting reform should have gathered the support of the right- and left-wing parties and the employers. The Christian democrats, however, heavily criticized the reform, despite the fact that they were having a hard time finding arguments against it. In the parliamentary debate, they justified their refusal with procedural reasons and criticized it for lacking improvements for families. This debate on recalibration, however, was clearly a sideline to the reform and served merely to provide the opposition parties with a reason, if not a pretext, to reject a reform that in fact corresponded to many of their own demands.

Hence, left-wing parties' shift to the right on insurance upset the coalitional dynamics in German pension policy making entirely. It should be noted that these coalitional developments illustrate perfectly the claim in hypothesis 4, namely that coalitional dynamics are not exclusively driven by preferences. Indeed, the shift of the SPD and Green Party might have fostered a new cross-class alliance across all major political parties in a country with high coalitional flexibility, such as Switzerland. In Germany, however, the context of electoral party competition did not allow for this coalition. Similarly, the emerging potential for cross-class

---

[37] Interview, ver.di, Berlin September 20th, 2004. The representative of ver.di confirmed that their opposition to the government's reform proposal would have been much stronger if the conservative parties had been in government.

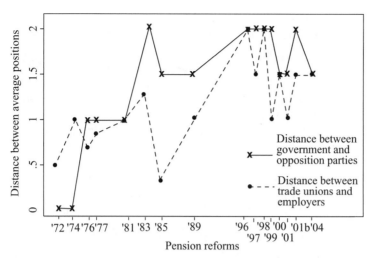

FIGURE 7.9. The effect of coalitional flexibility on class conflict: the development of the average distance between actor positions on German pension reforms over time

coalitions between employers and some trade unions on targeting or on capitalization could not materialize because of the concentration of labor and capital.

Figure 7.9 illustrates this finding. It is based on the final positions of peak trade unions (DGB, DAG, CGD) and employers associations (BDA, ZdH), as well as on the voting behavior of the main political parties (CDU/CSU, FDP, SPD, Green Party) in the lower chamber of parliament. It shows the rise of class conflict with the entry in the era of austerity.

In contrast to France – where the formation of cross-class coalitions between some trade unions and employers on targeting and capitalization has kept class conflict below the average of one in the 1990s – class polarization has always been greater than that level in Germany. This opposition is apparent between labor and capital, and even clearer in the rift between the government and opposition. Until the late 1980s, pension politics was less controversial, because the context of prosperity allowed for a positive-sum reform game. With the beginning of benefit retrenchment in 1989, however, class conflict rose sharply, particularly between 1996 and 1999 (during the right-wing government's changes and the first reform of the left-wing government). The antagonism between labor and capital was somewhat lowered under the red-green government, as the unions initially did not mobilize strongly against the left-wing government. As a leading trade unionist said in an interview, the unions would have fought much more aggressively against the early reforms of the 2000s if the same reform content had been implemented by a right-wing government.[38] This tempered the union's opposition to the red-green reform and even allowed for some compromising in the final output (Schulze and Jochem 2007). Overall, however, the unions unanimously rejected the new orientation of the reforms.

[38] Interview, ver.di, Berlin September 20th, 2004.

The rise of this left-right antagonism is also striking when it comes to the political parties. Until the late 1980s, pension policy remained somewhat absent from the electoral arena and was decided on a more consensual basis. But with retrenchment, the conflict level has risen dramatically and has remained high since, even though the actors' preferences have become more similar. In almost all reforms from the 1990s onward, the opposition parties clearly voted against the government bills. It is only in the most recent reforms the heterogeneity within the SPD has somewhat tempered this antagonism. A striking example of such a purely electorally induced polarization comes in the 2004 reform, when the CDU/CSU turned down a sustainability factor in the pension insurance scheme – lowering pension benefit levels according to demographic criteria. This factor, however, was largely a new version of the same demographic factor that the conservative government had introduced in 1997. Both reforms were so deeply similar, that the completely reversed voting behavior of the parties can be explained only by electoral factors, not by preferences.

This polarization between the political parties and between the social partners does not seriously hinder reform capacity in German pension policy, as long as the government has a sufficient majority to govern. Indeed, aside from the constraints inherent in a coalition government, the numerous veto points that are often referred to in the German case apply only under specific circumstances. The veto power of the Bundesrat is only of relevance if the majorities in both chambers of parliament differ. Hence, multidimensionality has allowed for the circumvention of the veto points within the government coalition, but it was not necessarily needed to split the opposition as long as the government had a stable majority. The costs that veto points impose on the reform capacity increase, however, when the power balance shifts in favor of the opposition parties (Lehmbruch 2000; Manow and Burkhart 2004). This has so far happened twice in the era of austerity. First, the SPD tried to block the conservative pension reforms in the Bundesrat after 1996 for electoral reasons. However, because many reform elements did not affect the Länder directly, the government was nevertheless able to implement severe cutbacks, against which the SPD had protested. The problem grew more pressing, however, during the last few years of the red-green government, when many far-reaching reform proposals needed the approval of the conservative Bundesrat. Because the coalitional flexibility between government and opposition parties was so low, reform stalemate became an even more serious problem in German pension policy making.[39] Eventually, it contributed to the formation of a grand coalition in 2005.

Conclusion

In contrast to Leibfried and Obingers' claim (2003) that German pension reforms have remained minor, my empirical findings on German post-industrial pension

---

[39] The 2001 law proposal has been divided into two parts, one needing the approval by the second chamber and the other one not. This strategy is a way to bypass the approval of the higher chamber.

policy making indicate that the pension regime transformed deeply and paradig-matically between 1989 and 2004 as a result of the shift in actor configurations and coalitional patterns.

As expected, all four post-industrial conflict dimensions – insurance, target-ing, recalibration, and capitalization – have figured prominently on the German pension reform agenda from the 1970s onward. After a set of expansive reforms on insurance, the German economic climate soon turned to austerity and cost containment after 1977. Expansive reforms, however, continued to shape the reform debates, particularly in reference to the strengthening of minimum pen-sion schemes, the coverage of marginally employed workers, the granting of educational pension credits, and the introduction of individual capitalized pen-sion savings plans. This plurality of reform issues present in the reform debates confirms the expectations of our theoretical model; the pension institutions that Germany had inherited from the industrial age were particularly at odds with the challenges of post-industrialism in almost every respect.

The evidence is similarly strong for the second hypothesis, which posits divergent actor configurations with regard to the different reform dimensions. The differentiation of actor positions is most evident in the rising intra-labor divide observed on reforms regarding capitalization, targeting, and recalibration (Figure 7.6). With austerity, trade unions began to advocate more narrow inter-ests: where before, they had been able to speak with a single voice, they gradually came to advocate the interests of their specific core constituencies more selec-tively. High-skilled unions such as the IG Chemie, ULA, and DAG took more favorable positions on capitalization than the low-skilled, blue-collar unions, such as IG Metall. Similarly, targeting and (less acutely) recalibration fostered intra-labor divisions – driving a wedge between trade unions representing a con-stituency that includes a sizable proportion of outsiders (namely ver.di), and insider-unions such as the DBB, the ULA, and (to some extent) the DAG. Like the high-skilled and service-sector unions, the Green Party and the German Social Democrats took increasingly favorable stances on capitalization, targeting, and recalibration. On the one hand, these positions reflect the risk profile of the new left constituencies (high-skilled, feminized, atypical work biographies, outsider status). On the other hand, the positions clearly derive from the libertarian and egalitarian values the new left so clearly stands for.

Until the late 1990s, actor configuration on insurance reforms followed a sim-ilar pattern to the one in France (i.e., increasing class polarization between labor and capital, and between left- and right-wing parties) (see Figure 7.1). With the advent of the red-green government in 1998, however, the two parties shifted dramatically to the right and started to advocate and implement heavy retrench-ment. This move toward cost containment upset the actor configuration across the entire pension policy field and created tremendous levels of conflict between the left-wing parties and the trade union movement (Figure 7.5). So far, the lit-erature has not come to terms with explaining this unexpected reversal of the new left. Kitschelt (2001) gives some theoretical hints as to why the new left-wing government might have been able to impose retrenchment. On the one hand, there were – at the time – "mild electoral trade-offs" (Kitschelt 2001: 275) for the SPD and Green Party (i.e., there was no alternative pro-welfare party for the voters to turn to). On the other hand, the left had the reputation of defending the welfare state. Hence, in a Nixon-goes-to-China logic (Ross 2000), a left-wing party engaging in retrenchment may have been seen as the "lesser evil" by the voters (Kitschelt 2001: 275). While both arguments suggest sensible reasons why the SPD and the Green Party succeeded in implementing cost containment, they do not explain why the parties decided to change their traditional policy goals and focus on retrenchment in the first place. I present two arguments in explanation. First, one must keep in mind the changing electoral basis of these parties. Both – though especially the Green Party – have become increasingly popular among sociocultural professionals, who are highly skilled, often in flexible employment and strongly libertarian. The voters (most often female) are not the core beneficiaries of the male-breadwinner welfare state, and they may be more interested in capitalization or recalibration than in the preservation of existing pension levels. The second argument also relates to this shift in the electoral basis but focuses more squarely on the value aspect of these reforms. Kitschelt (2001) argues that the sociocultural value divide between libertarians and authoritarians is particularly important in countries like Germany, and that this divide impedes welfare retrenchment, because the economic axis is not the locus where parties compete for and/or claim credits. However, in my line of reasoning, I propose an inversion of this argument. Indeed, the importance of the sociocultural value divide in Germany has not been an obstacle to pension reform; quite to the contrary, it has allowed the parties to engage in major reforms because they could compensate cuts with a libertarian reorientation of the pension system by including elements of gender equality, individualization, and outsider protection.

This logic of compensation is evident in the reform packages the governments – both left- and right-wing – have tied. From the 1990s onward, all reform proposals that included retrenchment combined it with expansive elements on recalibration, targeting, and/or capitalization. These packages did split the actors in sufficiently diverse ways, such as to create multidimensional policy spaces; this, in turn, allowed for political exchange. In 1989, the conservative government could thereby ensure some support from the left, and after 1998, it allowed the left-wing government to preserve cohesion among the governing coalition partners and with some high-skilled trade unions. However, because the core constituencies of the major peak unions are largely composed of blue-collar workers (i.e., low-skilled and traditionalist), the new orientation of German pension reforms led to a deep split between the red-green government on the one hand and the trade union movement on the other hand (Figure 7.5). The encompassing reform of the German welfare state comes at a high cost to class-cohesion within the left.

Nevertheless, the capacity for pension policy reform in Germany has remained intact as long as the government had the reforms accepted by its own majority in parliament. As soon as the power balance started to incline toward the opposition, however, reform gridlock became a serious problem. Indeed, the electoral constraints on coalitional flexibility became particularly obvious in the last years of the red-green government, when the conservative opposition rejected any reform proposal by the government, irrespective of its actual policy preferences. This lack of coalitional flexibility eventually led to the formation of a grand coalition of the SPD and the CDU/CSU in 2005, launching a new era in German pension reform.

8

Switzerland

*Recalibration as an Enabling Mechanism
of Pension Compromises*

This chapter shows that targeting and recalibration, in addition to cost containment, became important conflict lines in Swiss pension policy making from the 1980s onward. In addition, the empirical analysis demonstrates how targeting and recalibration have given rise to considerable intra-class heterogeneity and even to the formation of social-liberal value alliances – a coalitional pattern that differs sharply from the increasing class polarization that can be observed with regard to cost containment. Finally, this chapter shows that the Swiss institutional framework – characterized by multiple veto points, power fragmentation, and therefore strong requirements for consensus – was highly important for Swiss pension politics from the creation of these schemes all the way to the present: before the 1970s, these institutions impeded the rapid growth of pension expenditures. But more recently, they enabled reforms by facilitating coalitional flexibility and coalitional engineering. Hence, modernizing compromises (Bonoli 2005; Levy 1999) became a necessary condition for successful reforms.

Let me start the analysis of post-industrial Swiss pension politics with a brief account of the reform trajectory since the early 1970s. The concept of a multi-tiered (as opposed to universal) pension scheme was adopted in a constitutional amendment in 1971, after several years of intense political conflict. The far left and the trade unions had wanted to strengthen the first pay-as-you-go (PAYG) tier, whereas the right favored an expansion of coverage through occupational pensions. The right eventually imposed its policy following a popular vote in 1971, but as a concession to the left, the constitution stated that first-tier pensions should allow a decent standard of living, setting the agenda for strong benefit increases in the eighth reform of the basic pension scheme (Alters – und Hinterlassenenversicherung [AHV]) in 1972. In this reform, the level of public pensions in the first tier was increased by 25 percent, benefits were indexed to a mix of wages and prices, and the financial revenues of the first tier were strengthened (through higher contributions and federal subsidies). While this very generous eighth reform reflected the still-prosperous context of economic growth (Kriesi 1980), the financial conditions of reform worsened shortly afterward. The ninth pension reform in 1976 already contained some elements aimed at retrenchment, in response to the economic crisis of the mid-1970s: the minimum contribution for eligibility to the pension insurance was raised, and pensions for spouses were lowered. Simultaneously, the reform reduced specific privileges of the self-employed and active retirees. The financial leeway for pension benefit increases in the first tier became very limited thereafter. The next big shift in Swiss pension policy occurred in 1982, when the second tier (occupational pensions, *berufliche Vorsorge* [BVG]) was strongly reinforced. Many private occupational pension plans had existed before, but coverage was expanded and, most important, affiliation became mandatory for all workers in stable employment with a yearly income of more than about 25,000 Swiss francs.[1] This reform represented an expansion of occupational pensions to lower-income earners (whereas occupational pensions had previously been a privilege of the high-skilled).[2] However, because first-tier pension benefit levels remained far below the constitutionally mandated level, means-tested complementary pension benefits (*Ergänzungsleistungen* [EL]) had to be increased for retirees living in old-age homes in 1985 and in 1996 (as a substitute for long-term-care insurance). The 1985 reform also contained some measures directed at cost containment, because it stated that the pensioner's own assets (e.g., in real estate) should be taken into account more when establishing his or her rights to complementary benefits.

The occupational pensions of the second tier developed further in 1994, as a result of a reform that guaranteed the transferability of occupational pension savings. Before this reform, mostly lower-income earners tended to lose large parts of their occupational pension savings when changing employers (the so-called golden chains of occupational pensions). In addition, the splitting of second-tier savings in the case of divorce was introduced and the payout of savings to women in case of marriage was abolished, two measures that responded to claims for recalibration. A large step toward gender equality in old-age insurance (Luchsinger 1995; Lepperhoff, Meyer, and Riedmüller 2001) also came in the 1995 reform of the first-tier public pension scheme. Contributions and pension rights were now to be split between both spouses, and women were to be granted educational pension credits for periods of labor market absence. This increase of benefits for women was, however, counterbalanced by retrenchment in the form of a rise in the age of retirement for women from sixty-two to sixty-four years.

In the mid-1990s, the demographic challenge to the pension system received increasing attention, notably after the publication of two governmental reports

---

[1] This amount (about 16,000 euros) corresponds exactly to a yearly maximum first-tier pension. Only income above this level is insured in the second tier, as the tiers are meant to be complementary.

[2] Despite the broadening of access to the second tier in 1982, the latter remained highly exclusionary to women and the atypically employed (Branger 2000; Leuzinger-Naef 1998; Rechsteiner 2002). In the early 1990s, about 18 percent of male labor market participants but about 50 percent of female labor market participants did not qualify for coverage in the second tier (Bundesamt für Sozialversicherungen 1995). Until 2002, the coverage of active women had improved to about 35 percent. Nevertheless, they still received only about 22 percent of the benefits paid by all occupational schemes (CONSOC Recherche 2003).

on the financial challenges to social insurance in Switzerland (IDA FiSo 1 1996; and IDA FiSo 2 1997). The 2003 reform of the occupational pension tier (BVG) consequently lowered pension rights and increased women's retirement age to sixty-five. However, it also included targeted expansion for new risk groups, opening the occupational pension tier to broader groups of atypically employed and part-time employees. Finally, the most recent, eleventh reform of the basic public pension scheme (AHV) was meant to implement drastic cutbacks in pension levels (e.g., increase the age of retirement, lower widows' pensions). However, this reform – exclusively focused on cost containment – was defeated by the left in a popular referendum vote.

As in France and Germany, reforms dealing with the basic parameters of the pension system (i.e., insurance conflicts) became almost exclusively focused on cost containment and retrenchment from the 1990s onward. Thereby, insurance reforms have become a synonym for retrenchment and became very salient on the reform agenda. Nevertheless, it is clear that insurance was not the only conflict line at stake in the reforming of the Swiss pension system. Targeting and recalibration became increasingly important as well. Table 8.1 summarizes the reforms and reform issues that are analyzed in this chapter.

Development of Conflict Lines

Table 8.1 confirms the theoretical expectation that alternative conflict lines become increasingly important in the post-industrial pension politics of the conservative welfare states. More specifically, hypothesis 1 (developed in Chapter 3) suggested that, depending on the misfit among national pension institutions, post-industrial risk profiles, and austerity, new conflicts would become more frequent. Both the absence of capitalization and the emergence of targeting and recalibration on the Swiss pension policy agenda confirm this expectation.

Contrary to pension politics in France and Germany, capitalization is not a separate category for Switzerland, which may seem somewhat paradoxical in a country where capitalized pension funds are so strongly developed. However, as explained in Chapter 3, this reform dimension denotes the political debate surrounding the introduction of capitalized pension funds versus PAYG financed insurance. Certainly, this debate generated significant conflict in France and Germany, as has been shown in Chapters 6 and 7. In Switzerland, however, this conflict was largely resolved by 1972, and the very principle of PAYG versus capitalized financing has not figured prominently in subsequent policy debates.[3] The success of the multitiered design – and the resolution of the conflict over

---

[3] The 1971 vote for the creation of Switzerland's multitiered pension system indeed gave rise to strong polarization between defenders of capitalization and advocates of PAYG. The constitutional article was actually a response by the government to a communist popular initiative claiming the development of the first-tier AHV into a universal, only weakly earnings-related pension system. This initiative, however, received only limited support, mostly from the radical left. It was defeated by a large coalition of right-wing parties and social democrats that pleaded for multiple tiers and financing through both PAYG in the AHV and capitalization in the second tier.

TABLE 8.1. *Development of Conflict Lines in Swiss Pension Reforms*

Reform	Insurance	Targeting	Recalibration
Constitutional amendment 1971	1. Introduction of target benefit levels in the constitution		
8th reform of the basic pension scheme (AHV), 1972	1. Benefit level increase of 25% 2. Increase in pension indexation 3. Granting of a 13th pension benefit per year 4. Reduction of the tax-financed public subsidy to the insurance scheme 5. Increase of contributions to pension insurance		
9th reform of the basic pension scheme (AHV), 1976	1. Indexation of pensions to wages and prices 2. Increase of the required minimum contribution for eligibility 3. Lowering of derived benefits for spouses 4. Increase of tax-financed public subsidies to pension insurance	1. Increase of contribution levels for employed pensioners 2. Increase of contribution levels for the self-employed	
Law on the occupational pension scheme (BVG), 1982	1. Expansion of occupational pension savings plans 2. Introduction of a combined target benefit level for first- and second-tier pensions	1. Mandatory coverage for standard employees	
2nd reform of the complementary pension scheme (EL), 1985		1. Increase of means-tested complementary benefit levels 2. Increased complementary benefits for long-term-care patients	

(continued)

TABLE 8.1 *(continued)*

Reform	Insurance	Targeting	Recalibration
		3. Increase of benefits for homeowners	
		4. Lowering of complementary benefits for wealthy pensioners	
		5. Increase of self-payment in case of sickness	
		6. Measures to fight misuse of benefits	
Reform of transferability of savings in the occupational pension scheme (Freizügigkeitsgesetz FZG), 1994		1. Guarantee of transferability of occupational pension savings in case of labor market mobility	1. Occupational pension savings of women are no longer dissolved in the case of marriage
		2. Harmonization of second-tier pension schemes	2. Splitting of second-tier savings between spouses in case of divorce
10th reform of the basic pension scheme (AHV), 1995	1. Increase of the retirement age for women from 62 to 64		1. Splitting of contributions and pensions between spouses and educational pension credits
	2. Flexible retirement age (with linear cuts in case of early retirement)		
3rd reform of the complementary pension scheme (EL), 1996		1. Increase of rent deductions for eligibility	
		2. Lowering of waiting periods for complementary pensions for foreigners	

TABLE 8.1 *(continued)*

Reform	Insurance	Targeting	Recalibration
		3. Higher complementary pensions for homeowners 4. Improved information for pensioners about benefit eligibility	
1st reform of the occupational pension scheme (BVG), 2003	1. Cutbacks in occupational pension benefit levels 2. Increase of the retirement age for women from 64 to 65	1. Improved occupational pension coverage for low-income earners 2. Improved occupational pension coverage for part-time employees 3. Ceiling of insurable income	1. Introduction of occupational pension benefits for widowers
11th reform of the basic pension scheme (AHV), 2003	1. Increase of the retirement age for women from 64 to 65 2. Cutbacks in widows' pension benefit levels 3. Flexible retirement age (with linear cuts in the case of early retirement) 4. Retrenchment in pension indexation	1. Increase of contribution levels for the self-employed	

the very principle of capitalized pension financing – can be explained by the pre-existing institutional structure of Swiss pension policies. Indeed, capitalization in the form of occupational, often firm-specific, pensions had existed for a long time, and many people already benefited from it. Thus, in contrast to France and Germany, capitalization was not framed as an entirely new attack against solidarity in pension policy. Rather, it was understood as a pragmatic development of preexisting pension institutions. By defining target benefit levels across multiple tiers (in 1982, it was stated that 60 percent of the previous income should be covered by the first and second tiers together), the government managed to turn the systemic debate into a debate over the level of protection, making it clear that the multitiered design of pension policy was compatible with more generous overall pension levels. Therefore, the reforms of the second tier (BVG) listed in Table 8.1 were focused on the specific design of these occupational pensions (i.e., insurance, targeting, and recalibration) rather than on their financing principle as such. As was the case with recalibration in France, the absence of capitalization as a genuinely separate conflict in Switzerland provides evidence for the sequencing argument, according to which preexisting institutions shape the nature of conflicts that emerge subsequently on the policy agenda.

Contrary to capitalization, *targeting* became an important component in Swiss reforms from the 1980s onward, because the preexisting pension scheme was highly stratifying and tended to exclude outsiders. Targeting includes diverse measures, which, despite their differences, all move the highly stratifying pension insurance system toward a more egalitarian, flat-rate, or even means-tested scheme by focusing on the specific needs of particular occupational groups. Targeting in Swiss pension politics has included three types of measure: first, the reduction of status privileges (e.g., the rise in contribution levels for self-employed and working retirees). More frequently, however, targeting measures were expansive, introducing and strengthening the minimum pension or granting insurance rights to specific risk groups to whom they were denied before. The continuous bolstering of the means-tested complementary pension scheme (EL) is a typical example of targeting. These complementary benefits were initially thought to have merely a temporary role in the Swiss pension architecture and were to be abolished once the first-tier pensions were fully developed. In the context of austerity, however, significant first-tier increases have become more and more unmanageable; hence, complementary pensions soon acquired a permanent role as a rather efficient instrument to prevent old-age poverty (Leu, Burri, and Priester 1997; Bundesamt für Statistik 2003; Bundesamt für Sozialversicherungen 2003). Finally, targeting was also prominently used as a reform strategy in the occupational pension scheme (BVG), to temper the exclusionary effects for labor market outsiders. It was mostly the 1994 and 2003 occupational pension reforms that modernized second-tier pensions by making them more accessible to lower-income earners, the atypically employed, and women.

The most striking new conflict line in Switzerland, however, is *recalibration*. Gender segregation in the Swiss labor market is very strong, and most women either are absent from the labor market or work part-time (Wanner and Ferrari 2001). Therefore, eligibility based on labor market participation and earnings-related benefits leads to strongly gendered benefit structures. This pattern is not necessarily dysfunctional in a male-breadwinner society, where most women enjoy sufficient social insurance coverage through their husbands' rights. However, with the rise of family instability and demands for gender equality, the Bismarckian structure of social insurance has become incompatible with pressing social realities. The recalibrating reforms of the 1990s therefore tended to individualize social insurance coverage and to detach it from civil status. In the second-tier reform of 1994, for example, it was decided that marriage would no longer automatically lead to the payoff of funded savings and that accumulated savings should be split between spouses in case of divorce. Similarly, the 1995 reform introduced the splitting of contributions and benefits between spouses in the first tier, thereby individualizing pension rights.

Aside from targeting and recalibration, *insurance* reforms remained important on the pension policy agenda throughout the whole period. While most of the reforms expanded benefit levels for the standard insured in the 1970s and 1980s, the direction of reforms changed dramatically in the 1990s, when insurance reforms aimed almost exclusively for cost containment or even retrenchment. Women's retirement age was raised in the first and second tiers, and benefit levels were cut back in the occupational pension scheme. The (failed) reform of the public pension scheme (AHV) in 2003 aimed to reduce the frequency of pension indexation to every third year (as opposed to the preexisting annual frequency).

Development of Actor Configurations

What are the politics behind the pension reforms? How did the political actors align on the three conflict lines? As the following discussion shows, while insurance-related issues constantly gave rise to class conflict, targeting and especially recalibration tended to blur this conflict. Two contrasting trends clearly emerge from the data. On the one hand, targeting and recalibration generated intra-class heterogeneity of interests, because they were mainly advocated by defenders of labor market outsiders, and received more muted support from trade unions and parties representing insiders. On the other hand, interests alone cannot explain the position of all actors, notably of the market-liberal Freisinnig-Demokratische Partei der Schweiz (FDP), which had become rather favorable to targeting and – even more so – to recalibration. Rather, the increasing social-liberal support for these individualizing and egalitarian reforms must be understood as reflecting a divide between libertarian and traditionalist values. The following figures show the alignment of actors on each of the three conflict lines separately, to identify the prevailing pattern of political conflict.

As expected, reforms on insurance put the left-wing parties and trade unions in opposition to the right-wing parties and the employer associations throughout the whole period. Figure 8.1 shows the positions and movements of the main actors on the insurance conflict line according to their average position on all insurance issues in the 1970s, 1980s, and the 1990s and 2000s. For practical reasons, only the most important (peak) actors are displayed. A value of 0 represents a position in favor of generous pension insurance, such as a low age of retirement, high benefit levels, indexation on wages, high derived benefits for spouses, and an encompassing insurance pool. A value of 2 indicates the opposite, and for cost containment and retrenchment. The peak trade union Schweizerischer Gewerkschaftsbund (SGB), the Christian democratic trade union Christlichnationaler Gewerkschaftsbund (CNG), and the social-democratic Sozialdemokratische

Trade unions and
employer associations

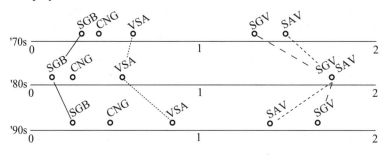

Political parties

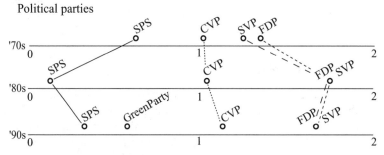

FIGURE 8.1. Switzerland: Average positions of actors on insurance over three time periods, 1971–80, 1981–90, 1991–2003

Partei Schweiz (SPS) all strongly advocated generous pension coverage throughout the whole period, whereas the white-collar union Vereinigung Schweizerischer Angestelltenverbände (VSA) and the Green Party took more moderate positions. On the right, the Swiss Employers' Association Schweizerischer Arbeitgeberverband [SAV]) (large firms) and the Association of Small Businesses and Crafts (Schweizerischer Gewerbeverband [SGV]) rejected a generous pension scheme, together with the market-liberal party FDP and the right-wing conservative party Schweizerische Volkspartei (SVP), with the Christian democratic Christlichdemokratische Volkspartei (CVP) taking an intermediary position. The positions of these actors follow rather straightforwardly from the interests of their constituencies: left-wing parties and unions represent low-skilled or outsider classes of the workforce (e.g., blue-collar workers, low-skilled service sector workers, sociocultural professionals; see Chapter 4 for details). They opposed the interests of capitalists and a highly skilled insider workforce (capital accumulators), who are the main electorate of the FDP. Only the position of the conservative SVP seems at odds with the interests of its most important electorate: the low-skilled, blue-collar workers. However, one should note that the SVP also represents large parts of small businesses, whose economic interests the party defends; its appeal to blue-collar workers, by contrast, rests largely in

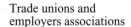

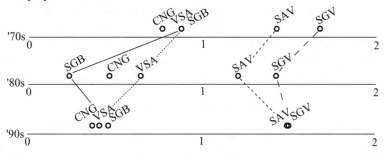

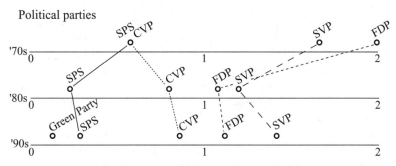

FIGURE 8.2. Switzerland: Average positions of actors on targeting over three time periods, 1971–80, 1981–90, 1991–2003

cultural issues (Kitschelt 1997; Bornschier 2010). Interestingly, the class conflict over insurance sharpened over time; the positions – mainly among political parties – were more polarized in the 1980s and 1990s than they were in the 1970s. This polarization is a direct reflection of the shift toward retrenchment. Indeed, in the 1970s, whereas there was an overall agreement on some expansion, the views of left and right on the adequate reforms in a context of austerity have become antagonistic.

One should expect a different conflict structure in Figure 8.2 with regard to targeting, namely an insider-outsider conflict, as these policies tend to benefit outsiders more directly than insiders. A position close to the value of 0 means that an actor supports generous targeted benefits, whereas a value of 2 indicates that the actor rejects those policies. Somewhat contrary to our expectations, the general pattern resembles class conflict at first glance: the unions, the left-wing parties, and to an extent, the CVP advocate the reduction of status privileges, generous means-tested benefits, and the inclusion of outsiders in the insurance schemes – in opposition to the right-wing parties and employers. This result challenges the hypothesis on insider-outsider conflicts; one would expect insider trade unions to reject the principle of means testing and to favor the equivalence principle of insurance. There is an explanation for this puzzle, however.

The debate over the level of means-tested supplementary pension benefits (EL) has, to an extent, developed into a distributional class struggle, similar to that of insurance. There is still certain opposition of the unions against means testing: in 1985, for instance, SGB and SPS explicitly rejected the "creeping transition" from insurance to assistance.[4] But in the analyzed reform debates, these actors pragmatically tried to achieve benefit levels as generous as possible – viewing the complementary benefits as a functional equivalent to deficient insurance rights.

This left-right opposition represents but one side of the story, however; it is crucial to note two important trends in the actor configurations on targeting, which differ from a distributional class conflict. First, the peak trade unions (SGB and CNG) have not acted as the main advocates of targeting, particularly since the 1990s, when the debate became focused on the adaptation of second-tier pensions to post-industrial labor markets. For example, the transferability of savings in the second tier was a major claim of the high-skilled union VSA (which launched a popular initiative for this reform), of sectoral organizations (e.g., the nurses' union Schweizer Berufsverband des Pflegepersonals [SBK]), and of the Greens and the social-democratic SPS. The trade unions did support the expansion of benefits to outsiders and the atypically employed, but they were not the driving forces for the development of these outsider policies. In a written statement on the eligibility threshold for occupational pensions, the SGB writes that a lowering of the threshold does not correspond to the general strategy of the SGB and that the SGB would prefer to implement expansive reforms in the first tier.[5] Hence, the Greens, the SPS, and the high-skilled union VSA were at the expansive end of the targeting axis in the 1990s, because they represented a large share of women and outsiders (e.g., sociocultural professionals, low-skilled employees; see Chapter 4). In contrast, the peak trade unions SGB and CNG advocate the interests of low-skilled insiders (blue-collar workers), who care more about insurance than about targeting.

The second important trend in Figure 8.2 is the division of the right. The CVP took a favorable stance on targeting, and the market-liberal FDP gravitated toward a centrist position; the employers and the right-wing SVP, by contrast, remained largely opposed to targeting. This new intra-class division is discussed in depth in a position paper by the small-business employers' union SGV with regard to the lowering of the access threshold to occupational pensions in 2003. The paper points to the problem that the "right-wing camp pursues different interests in this reform and therefore does not speak with one voice."[6] The employers' associations SGV and SAV were against lowering of the coordination

---

[4] Written statement of the Swiss Union of Trade Unions (SGB) and the Social Democratic Party in the consultation procedure for the second reform of the complementary pension scheme (25.4.1984).

[5] Written statement of the Swiss Union of Trade Unions (SGB) in the consultation procedure for the 2003 reform of the occupational pension scheme (17.12.1998).

[6] Page 4 of a position paper from the Small Employers Union (SGV) to its member associations (January 2002).

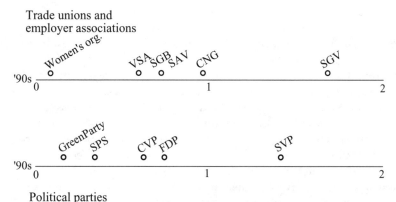

FIGURE 8.3. Switzerland: Average positions of actors on recalibration in the 1990s

deduction, whereas insurance companies were willing to accept broader inclusion of beneficiaries; the FDP was internally divided but amenable to the expansion of occupational pensions to outsiders. Therefore, the SGV warned that "unholy alliances" might appear in this reform, notably a large coalition of left-wing and liberal actors together with the banking sector.[7] This example typifies the shift of the FDP toward a more open stance on targeting and the protection of labor market outsiders. But how can this shift be explained, given that the FDP is mainly the party of capital accumulators (i.e., high-skilled inside labor; see Chapter 4), a group that has a strong interest in the existing earnings-related schemes? A purely interest-based analysis falls short of explaining this pattern. Rather, the answer lies in the fact that targeting involves a conflict between libertarian and traditionalist values, with libertarians favoring gender equality and individualization. This value-based explanation can account for the new position of the FDP, as capital accumulators in Switzerland have a libertarian value profile (see Chapter 4.2). Therefore, part of the FDP supported targeting reforms for societal reasons, creating an opportunity for the formation of a social-liberal value alliance.

This potential for a progressive social-liberal alliance in Swiss welfare state reforms appears even more clearly in the debates on recalibration, which affects women's pension rights entitlements most directly. Recalibration reforms are supposed to generate insider-outsider conflicts, as women are much more likely to be outsiders than men. It is also thought that it will cause a rift between labor market participants and the nonworking population, as well as create value conflicts over the possibility of a progressive versus a male-breadwinner society.

Figure 8.3 shows that the coalitional alignments found with regard to targeting are even clearer when it comes to recalibration. Four reform issues referred to recalibration in the 1990s. The 1994 occupational pension reforms introduced the practice of dividing pension savings after divorce and stated that

[7] Page 4 of a position paper from the Small Employers Union (SGV) to its member associations (January 2002).

women's occupational pension accounts should no longer be dissolved on marriage. The 1995 reform of the public pension scheme (AHV) introduced the splitting of contributions and benefits between spouses and instituted educational pension credits for women who withdraw from the labor market after having children. The 2003 reform of the occupational pension scheme, finally, established gender equality by introducing a widower's pension. As with targeting, the Green Party, the SPS, and the high-skilled employees' association VSA were the main advocates of these reforms, not the low-skilled peak trade unions. This pattern is perfectly plausible given that these parties mobilize a large percentage of (both high- and low-skilled) outsiders and women (compared to the SGB and CNG, who defend the insider interests of mainly lower-skilled, male, blue-collar workers). In the 1994 occupational pension reforms, for instance, the CNG proposed postponing a reform of the savings distribution in case of divorce, whereas the SPS and the Green Party insisted on immediately finding a solution to this new social risk.[8] Again, as with targeting, the unions are not actually opposed to recalibration, but their moderate position indicates that they are less concerned with recalibration than they are with insurance.

Further evidence for the relevance of values in explaining actor configurations on recalibration can be found when looking at the initiations of the reforms. Pension splitting between spouses first became a focus in 1979, at the insistence of a liberal party FDP member of parliament, Cornelia Füeg. As with targeting, the favorable position of the FDP on recalibration can be explained only with reference to sociocultural values, not by interests alone. While the social-democratic electorate includes many outsiders and libertarians, the FDP is clearly a party of insiders, though with libertarian values. Consequently, some – mostly female – members of this party have become very sensitive to the downsides of a male-breadwinner welfare state for gender equality and have built an alliance with left-wing parliamentarians to deal with these problems. Hence, it was an FDP representative – Liliane Nabholz – who, in 1994, tried to forge a compromise on occupational pension splitting in the case of divorce. Similarly, a strong alliance of female members of parliament from the SPS and FDP pushed for improved pension protection for women and pension splitting in the 1995 basic public pensions reform. They did so despite considerable opposition from within their own parties.[9] Senti (1994: 333, own translation) comes to a similar conclusion, noting that "the question of this systemic change in pension policy raised a conflict of values rather than a distributional struggle." Opponents of splitting and educational pension credits based their objection not on the additional expenditures that such changes would require but on a supposed undermining of marriage

[8] Written statement of the Christian peak trade union CNG in the consultation procedure for the 1994 reform of the occupational pension scheme (28.3.1991).
[9] Interview, SPS (member of the parliamentary committee in charge of the tenth reform of the basic pension scheme), Bern, June 28, 2001; Interview, FDP (member of the parliamentary committee in charge of the tenth reform of the basic pension scheme and former president of the federal commission for women's affairs), Bern, June 21, 2001.

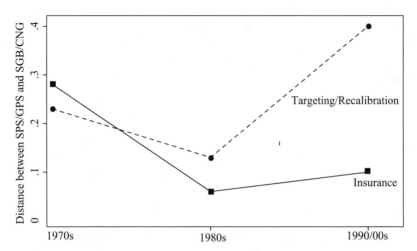

FIGURE 8.4. An increasingly divided left in Swiss pension policy: distance between the average positions of SPS/Greens and SGB/CNG over time

and family structure that would come about with the individualization of pension rights (Senti 1994).

Insider interests and values can also account for the opposition to recalibration, coming mainly from the small businesses association SGV and the right-wing, conservative SVP. Both represent capitalists and inside labor (small firms in the case of the SGV, and small shop owners and blue-collar workers in the case of the SVP), as well as constituencies with a decidedly traditionalist value profile (see Chapter 4). I also hypothesized that recalibration would generate cross-class conflict between labor market participants and the nonworking population. This assumption is difficult to test, admittedly, as women outside the labor market are very weakly organized. As a proxy, one can look at the position of women's organizations in Switzerland (see the Figure 8.3). As expected, those organizations defended recalibration more strongly and vigorously than any other actor, especially the unions.

In summary, two main trends have appeared in Swiss pension policy making over the period at hand. First, there is a growing divide over targeting and – more pointedly – recalibration between the left-wing parties and the trade unions. This divide is most obvious in the positions of the Green Party, the SPS, and the peak trade unions SGB and CNG. Figure 8.4 plots the distance between the average positions of Greens/SPS and CNG/SGB over time with respect to targeting and recalibration. A low value indicates a similar policy position, whereas a high value indicates a divide between parties and unions. It appears that insurance was highly controversial within the left in the 1970s, when the trade unions called for much stronger pension benefit increases than did the SPS. Since then, however, the left has achieved a remarkably cohesive position on insurance, reflecting the growing class polarization that appeared with the rise

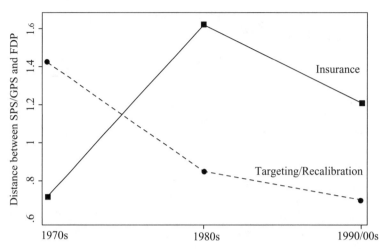

FIGURE 8.5. The formation of a social-liberal value alliance in Swiss pension policy: distance between the average positions of SPS/Greens and FDP over time

of retrenchment. The positions regarding targeting and recalibration have always been more diverse within the left, however, and they became only stronger in the 1990s, when recalibration became an important issue of outsider-oriented reforms.

But this pattern of conflict and consensus within the left reflects only one side of the realignment of Swiss pension policy. The second trend, of course, regards the formation of a potential for social-liberal value alliances on targeting and recalibration. Figure 8.5 shows that, while insurance tends to oppose the right-wing liberals and left-wing actors, targeting and recalibration have become a *terrain d'entente*. Again, a high value indicates strong division between left-wing parties and the FDP, and low values reflect an alliance potential. Insurance was not very divisive in the 1970s, when the left- and right-wing parties largely agreed on the expansion of benefit levels. When financial means became scarcer, however, conflict over retrenchment became the main dividing line among actors. Conversely, targeting split the left- and right-wing parties in the 1970s. At the time, the debates focused squarely on the equalization of contribution levels for the self-employed and workers. While the left-wing parties claimed equal contribution levels for all insured, the FDP wanted to preserve the privileges of the self-employed, one of their core constituencies. Things have changed since then, however. When recalibration and targeting for labor market outsiders appeared more prominently on the agenda, they drove left-wing and liberal actors closer together.

The development of these conflict dimensions has created opportunities for modernizing reforms, particularly in the recent context of retrenchment. The subsequent section develops the analysis of coalitional dynamics in a multidimensional policy space.

Development of Reform Dimensionality Depending on Time and Austerity

The analysis of French and German pension policy making has shown how governments and party elites have skillfully exploited the realignments of actors along the different conflict lines. When retrenchment was at stake, this became particularly apparent: the combination of cutbacks with expansive reforms on other conflict lines has become a winning strategy, giving rise to a multidimensional policy reform space and ambiguous agreements. These findings confirm the theoretical model developed in this book, which holds that elites tend to tie packages of different conflict lines to increase support for reforms or to divide the opposition against them. However, if these theoretical expectations hold for France and Germany, they should – a fortiori – be all the more true for Switzerland, where the formation of supermajorities is particularly important. With the presence of multiple veto points and, in particular, the threat of a popular referendum, it is quite difficult to change the existing benefits structure. Previous research on Swiss policy making (Sciarini 1999; Trechsel and Sciarini 1998) makes this all too clear, showing that for a bill to have a better than 50 percent chance of passing a popular referendum, the bill proposal must first receive a qualified two-thirds majority vote in parliament. Thus, incentives for consensus, or at least for compromise seeking, by political entrepreneurs are very strong in Switzerland.

TABLE 8.2. *Dimensionality of Reforms in Switzerland: Results of Factor Analysis*

	The Reform Includes Elements That Belong to...	
	One Conflict Line	**More Than One Conflict Line**
Purely expansive reform	1971, 1972 (both 1 dimensional) 1996 (2 dimensional)	1982, 1994 (both 1 dimensional)
Reform that included retrenchment	1985 (2 dimensional)	1976, 1995, 2003 (BVG) (all 2 dimensional) 2003 (AHV) (1 dimensional)

Notes: Factor analysis run on the coded positions of the actors; all results displayed in Tables 8.3 and 8.4 and Appendix 5; Eigenvalue of factors ≥ 1, Varimax rotation; for more details on data, see Appendix 1.

For this reason, one would expect that pension reforms in Switzerland combine several different conflict lines, particularly in the context of austerity, and that these combinations of conflict lines would create multidimensional policy spaces. As in the previous two chapters, I test these hypotheses by identifying the number of potential conflict lines in each reform according to Table 8.1 and by computing factor analyses of each reform to identify the actual dimensionality. Table 8.2 summarizes the empirical evidence.[10]

---

[10] These factor analyses are run on the positions of all actors that have taken part in the public consultation on the reforms (see Appendix 1).

My hypothesis suggests that elites combine different conflict lines. The four reforms in the left-hand column, however, defy this expectation. The two early reforms of the 1970s (the constitutional article on the multitiered pension system and the eighth reform of the basic public pension scheme) exclusively included elements dealing with insurance. Empirically speaking, they remained one dimensional, which means that they gave rise to a clear left-right conflict. This is understandable, as in the 1970s, the actors were in a position to easily reach a wide consensus on a certain expansion of benefit levels in the still-prosperous context of welfare state growth (Kriesi 1980). As in France and Germany, elites started to combine different conflict lines only with the transition to a context of austerity. More surprising, and in need of an explanation, are the two reforms of the means-tested complementary pension scheme in 1985 and 1996 (upper- and lower-left quadrants). Both consisted exclusively of targeting elements. Nevertheless, both reforms divided the actors according to two independent logics, as evidenced by the two-dimensional factor analysis results. At first glance, this result seems to challenge the coherence of the theoretically determined conflict line of targeting. However, the second conflict line can be explained straightforwardly because, in both cases, some actors opportunistically protected very small and specific clienteles: both reforms divided the right with regard to the reduction of specific privileges of wealthy pensioners. The 1985 reform proposed to take fully into account the pensioner's fortune – instead of only income – when calculating his or her right to complementary benefits. Conversely, the 1996 reform proposed that homeowners should be privileged when calculating their rights to benefits, to not force elderly people to leave their own homes. In both cases, some right-wing parties, notably the liberal party Liberale Partei der Schweiz (LPS) but also the small businesses association SGV, took a radically different stance on these specific questions than on the overall reforms of complementary pension benefits. On the whole, they advocated only modest benefit increases, but they clearly defended the interests of wealthy pensioners, especially homeowners, in a cross-class coalition with left-wing actors. Because only some of the right-wing actors joined in this logic of specific-interest rent seeking, the solution of the factor analysis became two dimensional.

The six reforms in the right-hand column, by contrast, provide evidence of coalitional engineering (i.e., the strategy of tying reform packages of different conflict lines). Although I expected this type of strategy only in reforms involving retrenchment, the two major revisions of the second tier (the occupational pension scheme in 1982 and 1994) show that package building was also used in purely expansive reforms (upper-right field). In these cases, the packages were tied to foster ambiguous agreements on the reforms (Palier 2005), that is, to cater to different interests in different ways to build majorities. Indeed, the extension of occupational pension coverage in both reforms was highly controversial both in the right and in the left. In 1982, the high-skilled union VSA agreed on the overall strengthening of benefit levels in occupational pension schemes, whereas the peak unions SGB and CNG remained skeptical. However, because the reform also extended coverage to lower-income employees, all the unions eventually supported the reform. As a result, the conflict remained one dimensional. In 1994, the combination of recalibrating and targeting elements created a large social-liberal alliance for the reform, and only a few employer organizations remained opposed. In both cases, the combination of different conflict lines allowed policy makers to buy support for ambiguous agreements.

The lower-right field of Table 8.2, by contrast, typifies the logic of coalitional engineering as theoretically expected. The four reforms combined retrenchment on insurance with expansive elements on targeting and recalibration. Contrary to the logic of the previous strategy – which focused on amassing the support of many actors – the strategy here was to divide the opposition. It became particularly important in the context of retrenchment: the 1976 bill proposal was the first to propose cost containment, signaling the end of the growth euphoria of the 1960s and early 1970s. It was highly controversial at the time and the first bill ever to give rise to a popular referendum on pension policy. The left rejected retrenchment, and the right opposed the increase in the levels of contributions and state subsidies. To achieve a so-called symmetry of sacrifices, the bill included a range of measures of financial consolidation, spreading the sacrifice among beneficiaries, contribution payers, and taxpayers. More specifically, the bill both reduced the level of benefits in the general pension scheme (insurance) and abolished the privileges of the self-employed (targeting). While the right advocated the former set of measures, the left supported the latter. In a similar vein, the 1995 and 2003 reforms combined retrenchment on insurance with expansive reforms on recalibration and targeting, as demanded by the Greens and the SPS (more details on these two reforms follow in the case studies herein).

Attempts to construct a multidimensional policy space failed, however, in the most recent reform of the basic pension scheme in 2003, which was defeated in a popular vote. This reform bill proposed severe retrenchment on insurance and only a minor reduction of privileges for the self-employed. Hence, it remained one dimensional (i.e., the class conflict it generated remained starkly dominant). The reform bill was not balanced enough to create a two-dimensional reform space: in addition to reducing overall pension levels, it also scaled back widows' pensions to a great extent and raised women's retirement age. Unlike former reforms, retrenchment was not balanced by expansive recalibrating measures. Moreover, the government proposed cutbacks on pension rights for dependent spouses and widows (to implement formal gender equality) and at the same time refused to cover part-time work, performed mostly by women, in the occupational pension scheme. For these reasons, some women of the liberal FDP tried to rebalance the bill proposal in parliament. They were aware that recalibration had the potential to bring about the necessary support of the left and, therefore, criticized the one-sided thrust of the bill proposal and the absence of a coherent modernization strategy: "By cutting back on widow's pensions in the first tier, the government takes labor market participation of women for granted, while at the

TABLE 8.3. *Switzerland: Results of the Factor Analysis on the Tenth Reform of the Basic Swiss Pension Scheme, 1995*

Issues of the Reform Debate	Recalibration (F1)	Insurance (F2)
Splitting of contributions and benefits	**0.95**	−0.08
Flexibility of retirement age	**0.77**	0.51
Increase of the retirement age	0.05	**0.97**
Eigenvalues	1.50	1.21
Explained variance	50%	40%

Actors	Factor Scores	Factor Scores
Green Party GPS	−1.34	−1.22
Alliance of Independents LdU	−1.12	1.14
Federal Women's Commission EKFF	−0.98	0.49
Social Democratic Party SPS	−0.85	−1.41
Radical Democratic Party FDP	−0.63	0.95
Union of Swiss Employers SAV	−0.39	0.86
Women's Federation Alliance F	−0.19	0.50
Large Firm Employers Economiesuisse	−0.08	1.05
Swiss People's Party SVP	0.41	0.24
Union of Swiss Trade Unions SGB	0.59	−1.01
Christian Democratic Party CVP	1.03	−0.60
Association of Small Businesses and Crafts SGV	2.31	1.08

Notes: Factor analysis run on the coded positions of the actors; all factors with Eigenvalue ≥1, Varimax rotation; data presented in Appendix 1. Bold numbers (factor loadings) indicate the dimensions to which the reform-issue belongs.

same time refusing to include low-income earners and part-timers in the second tier."[11] This statement by a liberal member of parliament provides additional evidence for the value divide identified above, as it shows that political actors on the right were aware of the potential for a social-liberal value coalition and coalitional engineering.

As in the previous chapters, two examples of this new coalitional dynamic are now presented in more detail. The 1995 and 2003 Swiss pension reforms illustrate the rather stable class-conflict on insurance and the new social-liberal alliance potentials on targeting and recalibration.

Table 8.3 and Figure 8.6 provide the results of the factor analysis and the positioning of the actors in the two-dimensional policy space in the 1995 reform of the first tier AHV (for a detailed account of this reform, see also Bonoli 1999; Häusermann, Mach, and Papadopoulos 2004). In Figure 8.6, the horizontal axis represents actors' positions on insurance (F2; increase in the age of retirement), and the vertical axis is linked to recalibration (F1; splitting and the

[11] Statement by Ch. Egerszegi, FDP, in minutes of the parliamentary debates on the eleventh reform of the basic pension scheme, lower house of parliament, May 7, 2001 (own translation).

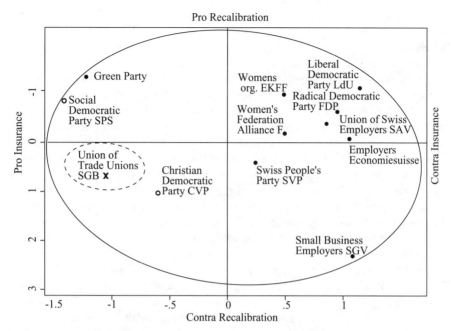

FIGURE 8.6. Switzerland: Scatterplot of the factor scores of actors in the tenth reform of the Swiss pension system, 1995

flexibilization of the retirement age). Several findings are key: first, as was the case in Germany, the Green Party is the main advocate of recalibration, promoting modernization in pension policy. Second, a social-liberal alliance formed with regard to recalibration (the actors at the top of Figure 8.6), including the SPS and the Greens but also the liberal parties FDP and Landesring der Unabhängigen (LdU), the main employers' association SAV and the women's associations. Opposition to recalibration came from the conservative CVP and the small businesses association SGV. Third, the restrictive position of the peak trade union SGB on recalibration is striking. The SGB did not explicitly reject recalibration but took a moderate stance and made it clear that it prioritized the question of the retirement age instead.[12] Hence, the SPS was clearly at odds with the SGB on this dimension. On the issue of insurance, however, the SPS took a clear pro-distributive position, in concert with the SGB. Consequently, a clear left-right conflict can be observed on this second dimension, with the left-wing actors and the CVP opposing right-wing parties and employers. The concentration of employers and liberal parties in the upper-right quadrant – for

---

[12] It seems probable that the positions of the SGB and the modernizing stance of the SAV implied some strategic thinking. It would seem that the SAV signaled that it was ready to accept splitting if, in return, the rise in the age of retirement would be accepted. And the SGB probably wanted to show that it would not accept this increase in the retirement age only for some modernizing concessions.

societal recalibration but also for retrenchment – is specific to Switzerland and indicates that the new-politics dimension (Kitschelt 1994; Pierson 2001) is particularly strong in Switzerland. It is precisely this group of actors who are potential partners of the left in a social-liberal value alliance.

As in the previous chapters, the symbols indicate the final positions of the actors with regard to the whole, strategically tied reform package, and the ellipse includes the final reform coalition.[13] The peak union SGB rejected the reform and launched a referendum campaign against it. By contrast, all actors with a preference for retrenchment agreed on the overall reform (denoted by black dots). Even the SGV, which had a very conservative stance on recalibration, prioritized its preference for retrenchment. Surprisingly, however, even the Christian democratic CVP did not mobilize against the reform once it had a majority in parliament, even though they had advocated a similar stance as the SGB in the beginning of the decision-making process. However, these actors did not want to side with the SGB in the referendum campaign and promoted support for the compromise found in parliament. Most important, however, are the positions of the Greens and the SPS. The Green Party's preference for recalibration was about as strong as its refusal of retrenchment. But the party clearly privileged splitting in the end, making the value conflict the key conflict dimension in the reform. The elites of the social-democratic SPS, for their part, were deeply divided over their voting recommendation on the referendum. Although they had a strong preference against retrenchment, several highly influential (female) members of parliament in the party had contributed to the agreement on splitting and defended it.[14] After an internal vote within the party, the SPS decided to support the entire package, in effect going against the SGB, its traditional ally in social policy making. For the SGB, new benefits for nonworking women were less important than the rise in the age of retirement of working women. By contrast, social recalibration for divorced women had been on the agenda of the SPS for a long time (Häusermann et al. 2004; Häusermann 2010b).[15] Recalibration had become a conflict line with a potential to split the old unionist left from the new value libertarian left in social policy making.

Eight years later, the occupational pension scheme (BVG) reform of 2003 provided another striking example of this divide within the left. The first factor

[13] The combination of the insurance- and recalibration-related elements was employed mainly by some liberal parliamentarians to split opposition from the left against retrenchment (interview, federal office for social insurances, June 21, 2006; interview, FDP (member of the parliamentary committee in charge of the tenth reform of the old-age pension system and former director of SAV), Zurich, July 4).

[14] Interview, SPS (member of the parliamentary committee in charge of the tenth reform of the basic pension scheme), Bern, June 28, 2001; interview, SPS (member of the parliamentary committee in charge of the tenth reform of the basic pension scheme and president of SGB), July 11, 2001.

[15] As a concession to the labor left wing of the party, to whom the retrenchment part of the package was unacceptable, the SPS launched a popular initiative soon after this decision, asking for the "10th reform of the basic pension scheme without an increase of the retirement age." This popular initiative was, however, defeated in the popular vote, as could be foreseen. It was a mere concession to the left wing of the party that had been defeated in the internal vote.

TABLE 8.4. *Switzerland: Results of the Factor Analysis on the First Reform of the Occupational Pension Scheme BVG, 2003*

Issues of the Reform Debate	Targeting and Recalibration (F1)	Insurance (F2)
Lowering of access threshold for occupational pensions	0.82	0.33
Special eligibility conditions for part-time workers	0.92	0.15
Introduction of widowers' pension	0.83	0.14
Ceiling of insurable income	0.79	0.38
Cuts in the level of benefits	0.24	0.83
Increase of the retirement age	0.19	0.85
Eigenvalues	2.91	1.70
Explained variance	49%	28%
Actors	**Factor Score**	**Factor Score**
Green Party GPS	−1.69	0.32
Protestant Women's Organization	−1.57	−0.75
Christian Peak Trade Union CNG	−1.28	0.43
Social Democratic Party SPS	−1.06	−1.20
Women Christian Democrats	−0.84	0.10
Trade Union of Employees VSA	−0.71	0.24
Employers in Construction SBV	−0.33	0.81
Christian-Democratic Party CVP	−0.22	0.18
Swiss Bankers' Association SBV	−0.14	1.77
Radical Democratic Party FDP	0.05	0.50
Public-Sector Union VPOD	0.12	−1.48
Liberal Party LPS	0.50	0.72
Union of Swiss Trade Unions SGB	0.54	−2.32
Union of Swiss Employers SAV	0.79	0.66
Farmers' Union SBV	0.89	−0.38
Employers in Gastronomy Gastrosuisse	0.90	0.83
Swiss People's Party SVP	1.06	0.30
Association of Small Businesses and Crafts SGV	1.68	0.60

Notes: Factor analysis run on the coded positions of the actors; all factors with Eigenvalue ≥ 1; Varimax rotation; data presented in Appendix 1. Bold numbers (factor loadings) indicate the dimensions to which the reform-issue belongs.

in Table 8.4 (F1; the vertical axis in Figure 8.7) represents the conflict over targeting (extension of coverage to low-income and part-time employees, ceiling of insurable income) and recalibration (the introduction of widowers' pensions). The second factor (F2; the horizontal axis in Figure 8.7) opposed supporters and opponents of insurance (lowering of pension levels, indexation and cutbacks in widows' pensions).

Again, the Green Party, women's organizations, the SPS, and some moderate trade unions (the CNG and the white-collar union VSA, representing a

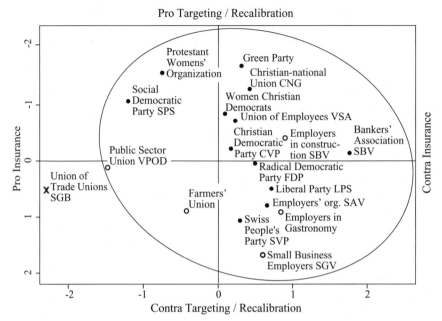

FIGURE 8.7. Switzerland: Scatterplot of the factor scores of actors in the first reform of the occupational pension scheme BVG, 2003

particularly large female workforce) formed the recalibrating pole of the conflict. For these actors, the inclusion of outsiders and women in the second tier became a battle to recognize female work biographies and to create incentives for female labor market participation.[16] These parties confronted a coalition of the conservative SVP, farmers, and the small businesses association SGV. The latter opposed the targeted extension of occupational pension coverage mostly because it employs a large proportion of low-paid, part-time workers who were now to be covered. The SGV argued that it would be highly inefficient to cover these low-income workers by means of occupational pensions rather than in the first tier or with supplementary pensions.[17] By contrast, large-firm and high-skilled employers (e.g., the Swiss Bankers' Association or the SAV) had more favorable positions on these measures, because they had the administrative resources to manage an extension of occupational pensions to their part-time (female) workforce. In addition, it should be noted that the banking sector (e.g., banks, insurance companies) was also in a position to benefit as a stakeholder in the occupational pension business. However, both the employers and the trade unions were split over the extension of the second tier to atypical workers. While CNG and VSA had always claimed this extension, the SGB was rather skeptical at first; it would

[16] Interviews, FDP and SPS (members of the parliamentary committee in charge of the 2003 reform of the second-tier pension scheme), Bern, June 6, 2002.
[17] Interview, SGV, Bern, June 6, 2002.

have preferred better protection for new risk groups in the (more redistributive) basic pension scheme instead of occupational pensions.

As Figure 8.7 shows, intra-union conflicts were even stronger on the distributional divide (insurance) than on targeting and recalibration. The SGB refused the pension cuts categorically, whereas other unions (e.g., CNG, VSA) adopted a much more moderate position, signaling that their primary concern was the extension of coverage to new risk groups. Again, as in the 1995 reform, the potential for a social-liberal alliance for targeting and recalibration had appeared. When looking at the final positions of the actors on this particular reform package, the split in the left appears again very clearly: the SGB remained most critical of the reform, whereas the SPS agreed to it. Overall, all actors with a preference for targeting and recalibration (motivated either by libertarian values or by the interests of their outsider constituency) agreed on the reform, thereby privileging this aspect of the bill over their preferences with regard to insurance. Both reforms in 1995 and 2003 point out strikingly that new conflict dimensions tended to split the left and to blur the class conflict, which prevails on insurance. The institutional context of decision making in Switzerland has clearly played a major role here, as this new pattern of preference alignments in the policy space translated directly to the output and orientation of recent Swiss pension policy development.

Development of Reform Coalitions, Reform Capacity, and Output

For many actors, a multidimensional policy space inevitably involves trade-offs – not only among different preferences (ensuring gains on one conflict line by trading in concessions on a second dimension) but also among different political loyalties. Indeed, the trade unions and left-wing parties, as much as the right-wing parties and the employers' associations, have long-standing historical traditions of class cohesion and organizational proximity. This may make it difficult for the actors to confront their traditional allies in referendum campaigns and in the electoral arena. In France, the majoritarian electoral system makes cross-class agreements between the right- and the left-wing parties impossible, the actual proximity of their preferences notwithstanding. A similar tendency toward polarization can be observed in Germany, where – despite similar preferences – trade unions and employers have also been unable to compromise. This is largely because of the strong vertical and horizontal concentration of such actors. Consequently, coalitional flexibility co-determines the extent to which the multidimensionality of pension policy preferences actually leads to new, cross-class reform coalitions.

The Swiss actor configuration and institutional framework of decision making, however, allows for high coalitional flexibility (see Chapter 5) but also requires large, oversized majorities to successfully defend a reform in a direct democratic referendum (Immergut 1992; Bonoli 2000, 2001). Trade unions and – to a lesser extent – employers are fragmented, and the logic of government formation is highly consensual because of the oversized government coalition. Thus, actors can choose coalitions on specific reforms rather flexibly, and the chances for

TABLE 8.5. *Relative Importance of Conflict Dimensions: correlations between Factor Scores and Final Actor Positions on Swiss Pension Reforms in 1976, 1995, and 2003*

	Final Position on 1976 Reform	Final Position on 1995 Reform	Final Position on 2003 Reform
Insurance (F2)	0.372	0.516	0.474
Targeting (F1)	0.724		0.482
Recalibration (F1)		0.521	

Notes: For the results of the factor analysis, see Tables 8.3, 8.4, and A5.2; data are presented in Appendix 1.

cross-class coalitions to materialize are high. With this in mind, one would expect that, in the reforms combining different conflict lines, class conflict would not necessarily prevail. As earlier, I have tested this hypothesis by looking at the correlations between the actors' positions on the different conflict lines (factor scores) and their final position on the whole reform package.[18] The conflict line (factor) that is the most closely correlated with the final alignment of actors is the prevailing dimension of conflict.

The evidence suggests that class conflict (on insurance) prevailed in none of the three reforms. In 1976, targeting even became the decisive conflict line, because it made some left-wing actors accept the reform, despite the fact that they were opposed to the cutbacks on insurance. In the two more recent reforms, insurance and targeting and/or recalibration have achieved largely equal importance. In the 1995 reform, all actors approving of retrenchment supported the reform, whereas the left remained more skeptical. This pattern was blurred, however, because the Greens and the social-democratic SPS finally lent their support to the reform, putting up with the cutbacks on insurance (Häusermann 2006). Finally, in the 2003 reform of the occupational pension scheme, the opposition was eventually split across both dimensions: the SPS and some women's organizations put up with retrenchment to ensure the targeted expansion of the second tier, thereby privileging outsiders and libertarian values. At the same time, the proposed retrenchment of benefits made some employers' associations and conservative right-wing parties support the reform, despite their reluctance to broaden access to occupational pensions for labor market outsiders. The fact that none of the conflict dimensions emerges as decisive provides evidence for the relevance of coalitional flexibility. Compared to France, where a clear reversal of the reformist trade unions created a new, rather stable structure of political conflict, the Swiss pattern of reform alignments remains variable and flexible. Reform coalitions form anew in every specific reform.

In Switzerland, as in France, the emergence of targeting and recalibration has blurred class-conflict as the decisive conflict in pension politics. This is particularly notable, as it occurred despite economic austerity, which exacerbates class

---

[18] Coding scheme: 0 = approval, 1 = criticism of the reform without actual mobilization against it, and 2 = explicit refusal.

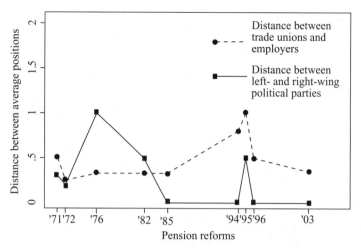

FIGURE 8.8. The effect of coalitional flexibility on class conflict: development of the average distance between actors' positions on Swiss pension reforms over time

antagonisms. With this in mind, we now take a closer look at both the parliamentary and the corporatist arenas. Because the Swiss grand coalition government literally expels party-political opposition in parliament, a distinction between government and opposition gives little information with which to measure class conflict in the Swiss party system. For this reason, I compare the left-wing parties (SPS, Green Party, Partei der Arbeit [PdA]) to the right-wing parties (FDP, LPS, SVP), leaving the Christian democratic parties aside because of their centrist position. With regard to the class conflict between the organizations of labor and capital, I compare the average position of the unions (SGB, CNG, VSA, VPOD, and sectoral unions if they took a position) to the average position of employer organizations (SAV, SGV, and sectoral associations if they took a position). If hypothesis 4 on coalitional flexibility is correct, class conflict should be moderate in both arenas over the entire period. There are two sequentially separated reasons for this: in the 1970s, class polarization was generally lower because of the prosperous context of economic growth, whereas in the context of retrenchment, targeting and recalibration blur class polarization and provide the basis for class compromise.

Figure 8.8 confirms the hypothesis and provides striking results for the role of insider-outsider conflicts and value divides in pension politics. A value of 2 indicates maximum class conflict, whereas a value of 0 represents identical positions. Three main results appear in Figure 8.8. First, the overall low level of class conflict confirms the presence of both strong coalitional flexibility and institutional incentives for class compromise and consensus seeking. Class conflict does not appear to elicit notable polarization in any of these reforms.[19] A comparison

---

[19] With the exception of the 2003 reform of the basic pension system, which is not displayed in this graph, as it was rejected in the popular vote. In this reform process, the polarization was at the maximum level, which is precisely why it was rejected.

with France is telling, given that the conflict between French left- and right-wing parties has never fallen below the value of 1 since 1975, whereas in Switzerland it has never exceeded the value of 1. Second, class conflict between the parties of the left and the right generally exceeded the level of conflict in the corporatist realm until 1982. Polarization between labor and capital was indeed rather low in times of economic prosperity, and the restrictive reform of 1976 generated heterogeneous positions on both sides, which lowered class conflict overall. Among the parties of the left, however, the communist PdA took a critical stance on every reform in the 1970s, refusing to support any kind of class compromise. The early polarization between the parties of the left and the right can be attributed almost exclusively to the role of the PdA. This pattern changed radically after 1985, when the Green Party emerged. This brings us to the third main result displayed in Figure 8.8: from the 1980s onward, class conflict in the parliamentary arena remained constantly lower than in the corporatist arena. The rising level of class conflict on insurance because of austerity became far less manifest among parties than among labor and capital unions. This result carries evidence for the hypothesis that favorable stances on targeting and recalibration of the political parties result from the representation of outsider interests and libertarian values. Indeed, the left-wing parties represent large parts of (high- and low-skilled) outsiders, and more generally women, and are receptive to libertarian values, whereas the trade unions tend to represent insider interests and a more conservative blue-collar constituency. Hence, the left-wing parties, particularly the Greens, were more willing to make concessions on insurance (if they could in exchange ensure compensations with regard to targeting and recalibration) than the unions were, for whom targeting and recalibration never had the same strong priority (on this division in labor, see also Häusermann 2010b).

This differential sensibility to new social needs and demands explains the more generally increasing role of parliament as a locus of decision making, which has been observed in several recent studies on Swiss social policy making (see, e.g., Häusermann et al. 2004; Sciarini, Nicolet, and Fischer 2002; Ballestri and Bonoli 2003; Jegher 1999). Indeed, parliament was traditionally the least important stage of the decision-making process, because the major decision had usually already been made in preceding negotiations in the corporatist and administrative realms. Studies on Swiss decision making in the 1960s and 1970s have unanimously provided striking evidence that the parliament merely enacted bills that the administration, trade unions, and employers had already agreed on (Kriesi 1980; Zehnder 1988; Poitry 1989; Sciarini 1999).[20] In the field of social policy, however, this pattern has changed significantly since the 1990s, be it in the field of pensions, unemployment insurance, labor market policy or disability insurance (for an overview, see Bonoli 2006). In all the major recent reforms, parliament has considerably redesigned the reform bills, and it is striking that the reform

---

[20] "Generally speaking, it is accurate to say that the Swiss Parliament – i.e. the party system represented in the parliamentary arena – at best works as a 'corrective' of previous corporatist decisions" Kriesi (1980: 589, own translation).

elements directed toward new social needs and demands were all agreed on only in parliament.[21] In this respect, the parliamentary committee on social policy of the lower house took the leadership on many reforms in the 1990s and became the main locus of the negotiations of social-liberal value compromises. This change is also linked to a certain organizational emancipation of the parties from labor and capital. Whereas in the industrial era, both the constituencies and the elites of parties and unions were highly interwoven, the electorate of the SPS is today fairly distinct from the trade union constituencies, notably with regard to the representation of women and outsiders (Armingeon and Beyeler 2000). Similarly, the tensions between employers' organizations and right-wing parties have grown. With the increasing pressure for economic competitiveness, individual firms and employers' associations were less willing to pursue an accommodating strategy toward labor (Mach 2006). Therefore, polarization and class conflict among the social partners grew during the 1990s, whereas the political parties proved far more able to respond to new social needs and demands (targeting and recalibration) and to seize opportunities for class compromise.

The Swiss institutional context requires consensus seeking, especially among political parties, as a necessary condition for successful reforms. The 2003 reform of the basic pension system is instructive in this respect. Similar to the 1995 Juppé pension reform in France, this reform bill focused exclusively on retrenchment (insurance) and included no notable concessions to the left, in terms of either targeting or recalibration. Negotiations in parliament had produced a tentative compromise, which was, however, shattered by the right-wing parties, which overestimated their political power. By breaking the compromise, the right-wing parties alienated potential social-liberal allies within the Green Party and the SPS and provoked a unified opposition of parties and labor unions on the left, which successfully fought the reform in a direct democratic referendum.

Conclusion

The analysis of Switzerland's post-industrial pension politics provides ample evidence for the importance of multidimensionality as a condition for successful pension reform. As expected, the misfit between the increasingly expensive and highly stratifying institutional regime of Swiss pension insurance on the one hand and the challenges of austerity and post-industrialism on the other hand have led to the emergence of retrenchment, targeting, and recalibrating reform proposals on the policy agenda. Capitalization, by contrast, did not become much of an issue, because funded (occupational) pensions became a regular part of the Swiss pension architecture in the early 1970s. Most strikingly, recalibration became a salient conflict line in the 1990s. This resulted largely from the blatant

---

[21] Examples include splitting and educational benefits in the tenth reform of the basic pension scheme, active labor market policy in the 1995 reform of the unemployment insurance, occupational pensions for atypical workers in the 2003 reform of the second-tier pension scheme, activation measures in the current reform of disability insurance, and federal subsidies for child-care infrastructure in 2003.

misfit between the previously strongly gendered pension institutions (Leitner and Obinger 1996; Leitner, Ostner, and Schratzenstaller 2004) and post-industrial employment and family patterns.

The evidence for a shifting alignment of actors on these new conflict lines is more nuanced but still readily discernable; it appears quite clearly with regard to insurance reforms, over which class conflict has become even more polarized since the 1980s and 1990s. The only actor that is not in line with the profile of its socio-structural class constituency is the conservative SVP. The SVP – despite its blue-collar electorate – advocated retrenchment and cost containment throughout the entire period. On the whole, however, insurance gave rise to the expected labor-capital conflict in the policy-making processes. The insider-outsider conflict on targeting, by contrast, is less obvious at first glance, as Swiss trade unions tend to support supplementary means-tested pension benefits, even though the main beneficiaries of those benefits are not their own constituency. On further scrutiny, however, the positions of the actors in the single reforms provide evidence for the expected actor configuration. The initiative for targeting reforms never stemmed from the peak trade unions but from the Green Party, the SPS, and the high-skilled union VSA. These latter actors are more sensitive to outsider interests, as they more strongly mobilize the socio-structural classes in which new social risks concentrate. Finally, the most striking finding in the reconfiguration of Swiss alliance patterns is the emergence of a social-liberal value alliance on targeting and recalibration. In the realm of political parties, the alliance included the new left (Greens, SPS) and representatives of the liberal FDP. It became decisive in several reforms during the 1990s, and it accounts for the increasing divide between the old and the new left (left-wing parties versus peak trade unions), a pattern that closely resembles the split between the red-green government and the trade unions in Germany in the late 1990s. What is specific to Switzerland, however, is that the left finds a new ally with capital accumulators, who have a libertarian value profile in this country. In this sense, the Swiss case certainly provides the starkest evidence for the importance of values in post-industrial pension politics.

The Swiss structure of interest associations and political parties allows for strong coalitional flexibility, and the institutional framework of decision making requires the formation of encompassing majorities to lower the risk of a referendum. Therefore, it is hardly surprising that Swiss policy makers so clearly tied packages of diverse conflict lines to foster compromises. The Swiss case shows most strikingly that this strategy of coalitional engineering not only serves to divide the opposition against retrenchment but also has already been important for amassing the support for early expansionary reforms. Nevertheless, in line with the third hypothesis explored in this book, it is only in the context of austerity – when pension politics become a zero-sum game – that these packages actually foster enough intra-class heterogeneity to create a genuinely multidimensional reform space (in 1976, 1995, and 2003). And given the institutional framework, this multidimensionality indeed translated into large cross-class compromises and broad reform coalitions. Thereby, targeting and recalibration (i.e.,

insider-outsider and value conflicts) have become equally or even more important than class in explaining the alignment of actors on the final reform packages.
Therefore, class conflict remained low – especially among political parties – and
the 1990s brought about a series of system-changing reforms to the pension
scheme. However, the Swiss case also demonstrates clearly that reform capacity
depends directly on agency (i.e., the coalitional strategies of policy makers). In
2003, for example, policy makers designed a reform package that combined heavy
retrenchment with only slight recalibration. In this case, retrenchment prevailed
and fostered a strong class polarization that eventually led to the failure of the
bill in a popular referendum vote.

In conclusion, my analysis yields two main insights with regard to reform
capacity and policy outputs in post-industrial Swiss pension politics. First, reforms
are possible, even in times of austerity and despite institutional path dependency,
if and only if policy makers learn from previous experiences and manage to tie
balanced packages catering to diverse interests and different logics of reform.
Second, and consequently, in the context of austerity, Swiss pension policy is
likely to develop not only in the direction of cost containment and retrenchment
but also along the dimensions of targeting and recalibration.

9

Conclusion

Reform Outputs and Political Implications

Over the past thirty years, the pension regimes of France, Germany, and Switzer-land have undergone major transformations. What makes these ongoing transformations paradigmatic is not only a dramatic change in the benefit levels, though one may certainly call the changes transformative if measured by the scope of the cutbacks (Organisation for Economic Co-operation and Development 2007). Moreover, however, these reforms are transformative because they have changed the very structure of these continental pension schemes in two ways. First, there is increasing differentiation of the instruments of old-age income protection, with different policies focusing on different income and risk groups. France and Germany have started to complement or replace part of their basic insurance schemes with tax-financed minimum-income security for the least privileged and with new capitalized pension savings opportunities for the more privileged. In this fashion, their pension regimes have become more redistributive at the lower end of income distribution and increasingly Bismarckian (i.e., earnings-related and inegalitarian) at the upper end. A similar multitiered system has developed in Switzerland since the 1970s. It combines basic public income insurance with means-tested supplementary benefits, on the one hand, and private and occupational pension privileges for high-skilled and high-income earners on the other hand. The second transformative change is that all three countries' reforms have started to shift the regimes away from a male-breadwinner model, reducing the dependency of – mostly female – outsiders on the pension rights of insiders. Minimum pension rights are one of the instruments that benefit people with discontinuous employment biographies. Other reforms, however, have focused even more clearly on gender equality: in all three countries, educational pension credits were introduced, and the pension coverage of atypical and part-time work was improved. The most striking departure from a male-breadwinner model occurred in Switzerland in the mid-1990s, when the insurance regime was refocused on the individual instead of the couple; through pension splitting, both the contributions and the benefits of married spouses were henceforth divided equally and paid into separate pension accounts.

France, Germany, and Switzerland share four similar trends in institutional change: (1) the strengthening of minimum old-age income protection, (2) an increasing emphasis on private or occupational capitalized pension funds, (3) enhanced gender equality in pension policy, and (4) retrenchment (i.e., the scaling back of insurance rights in the basic pension schemes). In combination, the four reform trends are changing the face of continental pension policy in the three countries. To be clear, I do not argue here that fully developed multitiered regimes have emerged in all three countries or that the distributional effects of the pension regimes are no longer gendered. Such an assertion would strongly be overreaching. What this book does show, however, is that there has been a series of systemic reforms that have clearly departed from the logic of continental insurance regimes as they had developed in the industrial era. These reforms may be the beginning of an even farther-reaching transformation, or somewhat less likely, they may stop. However, there is little doubt that, in the long run – and pension politics is always about the long run – the systemic reforms of the past twenty to thirty years set the course for a pension landscape that will differ significantly from the one we have considered typical of continental welfare states.

In this book, I have striven to show that this transformative institutional change in continental welfare states is a result of structural change. The post-industrial welfare state that emerges from the reforms of the past decades will differ from the industrial welfare state not primarily because of agency and leadership, ideology, or functionalist problem pressure, but because post-industrial society is different from industrial society. Socio-structural change affects political parties and interest organizations, and thereby, in combination with strategy and institutions, it affects policy making and policy outputs.

Comparative Summary of Findings

First Set of Findings: Diversified Reform Agendas
Structural change – such as the post-industrialization of labor markets, new patterns of family organization, and cultural value change – does not automatically reshape pension reform agendas. When structural changes stand in stark contrast to the assumptions on which existing institutions are built, however, there arises a misfit: a mismatch that has the potential to create conflict among those actors adhering to the existing institutions and those actors interested in modernization. The misfit argument turned out to be quite powerful in explaining the direction of the pension policy debates in France, Germany, and Switzerland over the past three or four decades. German pension institutions have been significantly challenged in every respect by structural developments. Demographic and economic changes threaten the pension systems' financial viability, post-industrial labor markets create new social risks, and male-breadwinner institutions systematically penalize female work biographies. This plurality of challenges has translated into a very diverse pension reform agenda since the 1970s: high benefit levels, pay-as-you-go (PAYG) financing, and exclusionary eligibility criteria have all been

subject to serious questioning. Hence, insurance, capitalization, recalibration, and targeting have all become relevant reform issues. A similar trend can be observed in France, even though recalibration remained less important because of France's strong female labor market participation rates. Consequently, insurance, capitalization, and targeting dominated French pension policy debates over the observed period. In marked contrast, recalibration became a prominent issue in Switzerland, where female labor market participation is low and where the pension regime had developed in a strongly gender-segregating fashion. Thus, both recalibration and targeting became important issues of modernization. Retrenchment pressure, by contrast, has remained somewhat lower in Switzerland than in Germany and France because of the very late development of generous pension insurance and the early spread of capitalized pension funds.

Hence, insurance, capitalization, targeting, and recalibration have proved theoretically and empirically useful categories for systemizing post-industrial pension reform agendas. Theoretically, all the empirically observed reform issues in each of the countries can be clearly attributed to one of the four categories. And empirically, the coherence of each of the four dimensions has been confirmed by the one-dimensional result of a factor analysis of all actors' positions. However, while insurance and capitalization are empirically separate dimensions, targeting and recalibration are linked, because both deal more generally with the egalitarian coverage of outsiders.

Hence, a first important result of this book is that post-industrial pension politics deal with very different reform dimensions, not just retrenchment. One may ask whether targeting and recalibrating reforms are mere side payments to retrenchment, raising the question of whether these reform dimensions have any relevance in and of themselves. This book provides strong evidence that they do: calls for gender equality and targeted improvements for precarious risk groups emerged as early as in the 1970s in France and Germany, at a time when all signs were still on the expansion of general insurance rights and retrenchment was not yet an issue. Similar claims also arose – to a somewhat lesser extent – in Switzerland from the 1970s onward. The early appearance of these issues on the reform agendas indicates that the alternative reform dimensions have their own structural foundation and are not merely sweeteners of retrenchment.

Second Set of Findings: Crosscutting Conflict Lines

The differentiation of the reform agendas has occurred along with differentiation of the configuration of actors and alliances over time. In the early period of post-industrial pension reform (until the 1980s) the emergence of the four conflict lines did not give rise to a genuinely multidimensional reform space in the reform debates. Rather, all reform dimensions fostered similar actor configurations in the policy-making processes, and intra-labor heterogeneity remained low. This is easily understandable: it was still the era of welfare state growth, which facilitated solidarity and cohesion within the left in favor of any kind of expansive reforms. However – in contrast to the expectations formulated in Chapter 2 – this strong cohesion of the left in the early periods did not make the industrial class conflict the dominant conflict pattern. Rather, there was an agreement – all across the left-right spectrum, and particularly among the major political parties – on the manifold expansions of the pension regimes in the 1970s. Employer organizations were somewhat more skeptical, but even they did not explicitly oppose the trend toward expansion.

It was only the advent of a context of austerity that transformed the positive-sum game of pension policy making into a zero-sum game, thereby sharpening the actors' preference profiles. Moreover, with the transformation of the social class structure, the constituencies of the parties and unions changed, adding further to the differentiation of their positions. Consequently, from the 1980s, the different, independent reform dimensions have fostered different configurations of advocates and opponents in the policy-making processes. Because of this, multiple crosscutting conflict lines have emerged ever more clearly in all three countries.

As expected, the increasingly salient debates on retrenchment opposed labor to capital, and left-wing to right-wing parties. This polarization has become somewhat weaker recently, as the political parties of the new left have shifted toward more accommodating positions on retrenchment. The most radical example of this shift is the German Social Democratic Party's (SPD) and the Green Party's changes in stance after their coming to power in 1998. Once in government, they began to advocate even more radical cutbacks in pension benefit levels than those of their right-wing predecessors. This shift of the left – the traditional allies of the trade unions in the industrial era – is a result of both the increasingly high-skilled profile of their constituencies and of the parties' growing preference for targeting, recalibration, and capitalization.

Capitalization divides the actors along skill rather than industrial class lines, driving a wedge between the parties of the new left and trade unions, and between low- and high-skilled labor unions. In Germany, capitalization radically increased intra-labor heterogeneity, notably between low-skilled sector unions (e.g., IG Metall) and the unions of higher-skilled constituences (e.g., IG Chemie). In France, a similar capitalization-related rift can be observed in the antagonism between the high-skilled union Confédération Générale des Cadres (CGC) and the blue-collar union Confédération Générale du Travail (CGT). Even in Switzerland, the white-collar trade union Vereinigung Schweizerischer Angestelltenverbände (VSA) has always been more favorable to capitalized occupational pension schemes than the blue-collar peak union Schweizerischer Gewerkschaftsbund (SGB). Hence, capitalization fostered considerable intra-labor conflict in all three countries. Moreover, the introduction of capitalized pension funds has also blurred class conflict with regard to capital, opposing the interests of small and large firms.

Capitalization, however, is just one of the dimensions of post-industrial modernization that disrupts the cohesion of labor. Further heterogeneity stems from the divergent interests of insiders and outsiders on targeting and recalibration. In France, the Confédération Française Démocratique du Travail (CFDT) has been taking an increasingly reformist stance for the minimum coverage of precarious work, whereas the CGT wants to preserve a pure equivalence principle in the insurance regime. A similar divide emerged between the German service-sector union ver.di and its counterparts in the industrial (low-skilled) sector, notably IG Metall. In Switzerland, the labor movement has remained somewhat more cohesive, as outsiders have no particular advocate in this realm. However, the insider-outsider divide becomes manifest in a growing rift among the trade unions, who defend insider interests, and the left-wing political parties, who have become increasingly attentive to the needs of outsiders. A similar divide between insider unions and the new-left parties is evident in Germany, whereas the French socialists have remained closer to the unions (not least because of their old-left competitor, the French Communist Party). In summary, targeting and recalibration have clearly upset the actor configuration on the left of the political spectrum. By contrast, insider-outsider divides remain much weaker among capital. There is some evidence that the German Bundesvereinigung der Deutschen Arbeitgeberverbände (BDA) and the Swiss Schweizerischer Arbeitgeberverband (SAV) (which both represent large firms) have become more sensitive to the specific needs and interests of their female outsider workforce. But overall, employers remain highly skeptical of the expansion of specific outsider rights. Things look different, however, when it comes to the moderate right-wing parties. In Switzerland, capital accumulators – the core constituency of the moderate right – have a libertarian value profile. Therefore, the market liberal party, the Free Democratic Party (FDP), has on several occasions become an ally of the parties of the new left to implement policies enforcing outsider interests and gender equality. This social-liberal alliance represents another reconfiguration of pension politics (in addition to skill-level conflicts on capitalization and intra-labor heterogeneity on targeting and recalibration) that considerably blurs the traditional lines of class conflict. It remained, however, specific to Switzerland until the end of the period of analysis of this book (i.e., 2004). In Germany, libertarian values became increasingly crucial for the outsider orientation of the red-green pension strategy between 1998 and 2005, but these values have not fostered cross-class coalitions across the party system during the leftist government. Since then, under the grand coalition, the electoral preconditions have been more favorable for encompassing value coalitions. Finally, social-liberal party alliances have not materialized in France, where the voters of the right generally hold more traditionalist values.

In summary, post-industrial pension politics in France, Germany, and Switzerland have been marked by three distinct actor configurations. Retrenchment is debated along the lines of labor versus capital; the interests of high- versus low-skilled labor and of large versus small firms become manifest in debates on capitalization; and when it comes to targeting and recalibration, insider-outsider divides threaten the cohesion of the left, and opposition between libertarians and authoritarians drives a wedge between the old and the new left.

Third Set of Findings: The Ubiquity of Coalitional Engineering

Given the diverse actor configurations with regard to each individual conflict dimension, it is clear that the continental pension policy space has become multidimensional in the post-industrial era. In the context of growing pressure for austerity, policy makers have increasingly striven to find ways to draw strategically on this multidimensionality: this coalitional engineering involves combining several dimensions in the very same reform packages; indeed, all successful major reforms since the 1990s in France, Germany, and Switzerland combined cuts in insurance rights with expansive reforms on capitalization, targeting, and/or recalibration. And all of the reform packages divided the actors along several independent dimensions, a finding that emerges from factor analyses of the policy preferences of the involved actors. Hence, the striking concurrence of cost-containment policies and multidimensional policy reform spaces is the result of both structure and strategy. On the one hand, the structural condition of austerity has caused actors to confine their interests – catering more narrowly to specific constituencies – and has set the stage for the kind of maneuvering that may occur in a multidimensional policy space. On the other hand, however, the multidimensionality of the reform spaces is also the result of strategy. Until the mid-1980s, policy makers counterbalanced slight cuts in benefit rights with rising contribution levels. The growing economic difficulties, however, subsequently closed off this possibility. Because of this, policy makers started to reorient reforms toward an overall redesign of the pension regime, compensating retrenchment with the expansion of alternative benefit schemes.

The temporal concurrence of this multidimensional pattern in all three countries, and the fact that all major cutbacks from the 1990s onward occurred within such reform packages, constitutes striking evidence to support the argument that the packages reflect deliberate strategies of coalitional engineering.[1] In this fashion, governments have worked to build encompassing cross-class coalitions in support of the reforms. The chances of success of this strategy, however, depend on the coalitional flexibility of political parties, trade unions, and employer organizations. In France and Germany, the strong electoral polarization between government and opposition parties made it impossible for the governments of the countries to create large coalitions including the opposition parties, even in cases where the actual policy preferences of government and opposition were close. Therefore, the conflict between left- and right-wing parties has remained significant in both countries. This stands in marked contrast to consensual Switzerland, where such conflict remains relatively low, as a consequence of the strong coalitional flexibility in the party system. Both major reforms in Switzerland in 1995 and 2003 were supported by all major parties. Coalitional flexibility clearly enhanced the Swiss reform capacity. Reforms also remained viable in France, as the French government do not depend on the approval of the opposition parties to implement changes. In both France and Switzerland, reform capacity was also supported by trade union fragmentation. Because of fragmentation, the heterogeneous policy preferences of different unions were directly

[1] The exclusion of capitalization from such packages in France serves as only further evidence for this finding: indeed, the introduction of individual pension funds in France was highly controversial. The government could pursue this reform strategy only by framing it as an economic policy aimed to increase investment and savings.

reflected in the positions they took on the final reform packages. This enabled the governments to enact reforms with the consent of a part of the trade union movement. Things are more complex in Germany, however, where trade unions are more vertically and horizontally concentrated. German trade unions spoke with more or less one voice until the late 1990s – something that made it difficult for governments to enact reforms against the opposition of the labor movement. In the most recent reforms, however, trade unions have become increasingly fragmented. The different service-sector unions merged into a single organization (Vereinte Dienstleistungsgewerkschaft ver.di) in 2001, to counterbalance the predominance of industrial unions within the Deutscher Gewerkschaftsbund (DGB). Given the increasingly diverging risk profiles of their core constituencies, this institutional reorganization is weakening the cohesion of the trade unions. This trend provided German governments with better chances to have their reforms accepted because it weakened the veto power of the labor movement. As long as the government held a firm majority in parliament, the lacking coalitional flexibility between government and opposition did not hamper the German reform capacity, as long as the government was able to find a compromise within the government coalition. But the negative effect on coalitional flexibility of electoral polarization between political parties became a problem under the divided majorities in the lower and upper chambers of parliament. This friction finally contributed to the breakdown of the red-green government and the formation of the grand coalition in Germany in 2005.

Let me briefly stress here the implications of these findings on coalitional flexibility and coalitional engineering for the literature on veto points and reform capacity. I expected that governments in countries with many veto players would have to engage in coalitional engineering. Depending on the coalitional flexibility of the veto players, coalitional engineering should be more or less successful. Conversely, governments in regimes with centralized power could rely on unilateral strategies to have their reforms implemented. The evidence we find in German, French, and Swiss pension politics not only confirms the relevance of coalitional engineering in power fragmented regimes but goes even further: *all* governments engaged in multidimensional reform politics and package building. Even when not confronted with diverging majorities in parliament or formal veto powers of corporatist actors, the German and French governments combined retrenchment with compensations to have their reforms accepted. This can be understood with reference to Pierson's (2001) theorization of austerity politics: mature welfare states create their own constituencies. Hence, in hard times, and when it comes to retrenchment policies, all governments have to engage in coalitional engineering. This is a key insight for the politics of post-industrial welfare modernization. It bears a forceful and counterintuitive implication for the veto points literature, which assumes that reform capacity should be greater the fewer the number of veto points there are. In the era of austerity, this relationship may be inverted: in a context where any government has to foster encompassing coalitions (with formal or de facto veto players, in parliament, or in the ranks of their own party) as a precondition for successful policy change, countries with a tradition of consensus politics and negotiation may have a comparative advantage. Thereby, a high number of veto points (i.e., a high number of power-sharing institutions) may turn from an obstacle to an asset for a country's reform capacity. The experiences observed in Swiss, French, and German pension policy reform do point in this direction.

This overview of this book's findings on the development of post-industrial pension-reform dynamics may seem to imply that policy makers perfectly understand the nature of multidimensional policy spaces and rationally calculate the compromises they need to make to build successful reform coalitions. Such an interpretation, however, is not correct, as it overestimates the capacity of policy makers to calculate the exchange rates across different dimensions. Two prominent examples suffice to illustrate that policy makers may not be aware of the structural actor configurations they confront. The Juppé reform of the civil servants' pension regime in France in 1995 and the 2003 reform of the Swiss basic pension scheme both provoked tremendous opposition; the proposals have been buried in the polls of Switzerland and in the streets of Paris, respectively. In light of the theoretical model this book proposes, these failures are unsurprising; the dismantling of existing pension rights that both reforms would have entailed was not counterbalanced by any expansive modernization of the pension regime. Hence, policy makers did not necessarily act rationally and underestimated the opportunities and constraints of coalitional engineering. However, the French case also demonstrates that policy makers can learn from mistakes. In reaction to the failure of Juppé's reform bill, the socialist government worked to create institutions that aimed to facilitate negotiation and exchange: Jospin created the Conseil d'orientation des retraites (COR) a permanent consultative body that includes representatives from the government, trade unions, employer organizations, and other social interests. Balladur benefited from this preparatory work in 2003, when he managed to tie a reform package that implemented the very pension cuts that Juppé had proposed in 1995, together with targeting modernization and, consequently, the support of part of the trade unions.

The Bottom Line: A New Landscape of Continental Pension Politics

In conclusion to this summary of the findings, let me highlight the main features of the new politics of post-industrial pension modernization in France, Germany, and Switzerland. In France, the trade union movement has become split between a reformist wing of the CFDT and the CGC, and a blue-collar wing represented most clearly by the CGT. Whereas the former agrees to some extent to a restructuring of the pension regime in the direction of a dual welfare state (Palier 2002), the CGT insists on the preservation of the Bismarckian principles of insider insurance. The right-wing governments have harnessed this actor configuration for the implementation of far-reaching reforms along the lines of cost containment, targeting, and capitalization. In reform processes that involve retrenchment, targeting has become the decisive conflict line for the formation of cross-class reform coalitions among the government, employers, and reformist trade unions.

Pension politics in Switzerland have been characterized by two related trends over the past two decades: (1) an increasing insider-outsider divide between the parties of the new left (the Social Democrats and the Green Party) and the main trade unions and (2) the emergence of a libertarian value alliance of the new left parties and liberal parties. Because of these changes, a broad cross-class alliance of left- and right-wing parties, as well as employers, became the driving force of pension modernization in the 1990s. These parties have worked to reform the pension scheme in the direction of cost containment, recalibration, and targeting. However, this pattern of preferences has not become a stable new actor configuration in Swiss pension politics: coalitional flexibility remains very high, and broad agreements must and can be found anew in each reform process.

Germany has experienced the most sweeping reconfiguration of actor alliances. Although the conservative government had already succeeded in fostering modernizing packages in the early 1990s, it was the Social Democratic Party and the Green Party's shift toward retrenchment after 1998 that overthrew the cohesion within the ranks of the left. Since then, the divide between a libertarian new left (favoring cost containment, recalibration, and capitalization) and the main blue-collar unions (defending the industrial insurance scheme) has manifested. The new orientation of government policy has also stirred growing insider-outsider tensions in the labor movement, further weakening its veto power. Consequently, the German pension scheme moved in the direction of a diversified multitiered regime as long as the government held a firm majority in parliament. When the opposition became too strong, however, German reform capacity collapsed and with it the red-green government.

What This Book Tells Us about Pension Modernization in Other Continental Countries

This book analyzed French, German, and Swiss pension reforms to test and prove the validity of a theoretical framework that conceptualizes welfare state reform in continental Europe more generally. While the analyses cannot be extended in detail for more countries or policy fields in the confined space of a single research monograph, I would like to show briefly that the argument indeed travels to other continental pension reform trajectories. On the basis of the literature,[2] the following paragraphs therefore give a succinct account of the reform agendas, coalitional dynamics, and reform outputs in the Netherlands, Sweden, Italy, Spain, and Austria, five countries that share a continental, Bismarckian structure in their pension regimes with France, Germany, and Switzerland. The Dutch, Swedish, and Italian experiences illustrate almost paradigmatically the dynamics

---

[2] The discussion of the pension trajectories in these five countries is based on the following studies: the Netherlands, Anderson (2007) and Hemerijck and Marx (2010); Sweden, Anderson and Immergut (2007) and Schludi (2005); Italy, Natali and Rhodes (2008), Ferrera and Jessoula (2007), Natali (2003), and Baccaro (2002); Spain, Chuliá (2007), Guillén (2010), and Natali and Rhodes (2008); and Austria, Schludi (2005), Busemeyer (2005), and Schulze and Schludi (2007).

analyzed in this book: governments that – by coalitional engineering – manage to divide opponents in a way that opens up unexpected reform opportunities. Spain and Austria are particularly interesting with regard to the lack of coalitional flexibility they confronted in the electoral and corporatist arenas, respectively. Spanish governments escaped deadlock through institutional and strategic innovation, whereas the Austrian reform trajectory illustrates the breaks that electoral competition and trade union concentration put on pension modernization.

The Dutch pension system most clearly resembles the Swiss regime, because it has long been organized in two separate pillars: the first pillar, Algemene Ouderdomswet (AOW) is a universal flat-rate public pension scheme that is mostly regulated by the law, and the second pillar is a quasi-mandatory funded occupational pension scheme covering about 90 percent of all wage earners and regulated by the social partners under supervision of the government. As in Switzerland, the tradition of funded occupational pensions explains why capitalization as such did not become an issue on the agenda. Rather, the pension-reform debate revolved around insurance, recalibration, and targeting. Several modernizing reforms had already been implemented in the 1980s, such as the improvement of portability in the second tier in 1987 and the individualization of benefits for spouses in AOW in 1985 (Anderson 2007). The reforms gathered enough support without being part of package deals, as they were expansive and did not lower existing pension rights. Reforms became more controversial and more difficult by the mid-1990s, when the social-liberal (purple) government started to put a stronger emphasis on the need for financial consolidation and cost containment. The Dutch party system allows for coalitional flexibility, and therefore the government was able to find a multidimensional compromise on the reform of the first pillar in 1996 by raising contribution rates (insurance) while at the same time introducing a reserve fund invested in government bonds. The combination of higher contribution rates (as advocated by the social-democratic Dutch Labour Party [Partij van de Arbeid PvdA]) and capitalization (as advocated by the liberal People's Party for Freedom and Democracy [Volkspartij voor Vrijheid en Democratie VVD] and the Christian-democratic Christian Democratic Appeal [Christen Democratisch Appèl CDA]) fostered a large reform coalition in parliament. The most important and telling reform of the 1990s, however, concerned the second pillar of capitalized occupational pensions. In several green papers published since 1991, the social-liberal government affirmed a double objective for this reform: cost containment and modernization. It pressed for a switch from final earnings to average earnings for the calculation of benefits, for equal rights for unmarried couples in terms of survivor pensions, and for improved coverage for part-time workers. The social partners did not strongly oppose the latter proposals but clearly rejected the switch to average earnings. During the heated conflict between government and the social partners, in 1996, Prime Minister Wim Kok defended the calculation change not for its cost containing effects but on the grounds of recalibration and targeting, saying that "the final salary formula represented the wrong kind of solidarity, because mainly white-collar workers with above average incomes benefited from the rule" (qtd. in Anderson 2007: 745). He argued that savings resulting from a change to this rule could be used for the expansion of coverage to outsiders and the atypically employed. After long and hard negotiations with the different unions, the social partners and the government reached a covenant in 1997, implementing cost controls, mobility-enhancing measures, a reduction of the breadwinner bias, and increased coverage in the second pillar. Coalitional engineering had succeeded because of multidimensionality, high coalitional flexibility, and the existence of a strong and institutionalized tradition of negotiation and compromising.

The Swedish pension regime overhaul of 1994 presents an equally exemplary and telling instance of multidimensional politics and coalitional engineering. Before 1994, the Swedish system consisted of a first-tier, flat-rate social insurance (Folkspension) and a second-tier, earnings-related, defined-benefit, PAYG scheme (the Allmän Tilläggspension [ATP]). The 1994 reform added a universal tax-financed minimum pension, cut back the combined first and second tier to a (notional) defined-contribution PAYG scheme, and created an additional private mandatory pillar on a fully funded basis (the premium reserve system). Hence, all four reform dimensions – insurance, capitalization, targeting, and recalibration – were on the agenda of Swedish pension reform in the 1990s, both in proposals initiated by the left-wing government before 1991 and in the reform proposal of the right-wing Bildt government in 1992. Because the reform was a clear continuation of a process that had already begun, the new right-wing government of liberal, conservative, and center parties appointed a parliamentary working group, including the Social Democrats, with the task of consolidating the pension system's financial sustainability, strengthening the link between contributions and benefits, and encouraging the increase in long-term savings. Both the contents of the reform and the reasons for which it received the support of almost all parties, unions, and employer organizations illustrate perfectly the dynamics of coalitional engineering and the effects of the strong coalitional flexibility in Sweden. On the side of retrenchment, the reform replaced the 15–30 rule (i.e., pensions were calculated on the best fifteen of thirty years) by a defined-contribution lifetime-earnings benefit formula and stated that pensions would henceforth be indexed on wages. The abolition of the 15–30 rule implied the biggest losses for high-skilled, white-collar employees, whereas it had less stark implications for low-skilled workers with long employment biographies. This retrenchment was compensated for by elements of recalibration (the splitting of pension rights between spouses, pension credits for care work and higher education), targeting (tax-financed guaranteed-minimum pension) and capitalization (2.5 percent of earnings were to be mandatorily placed in individual investment accounts). This compromise managed to meet the demands of the Social Democrats for the preservation of a strong public insurance scheme, the claims of the liberal right for a strengthening of the equivalence principle, and conservative demands for the recognition of care work. The major challenge, of course, was the opposition by the trade unions to the cuts. Swedish trade unions are concentrated, which should weaken their coalitional flexibility, but in this reform, they became increasingly divided. While the white-collar union Tjänstemännens Centralorganisation (TCU) rejected the passage to the lifetime-earnings formula (high-skilled employees were the hardest hit), the main peak union Landsorganisationen i Sverige (LO) was divided and remained silent. Within the LO, metal workers (blue-collar insiders) rejected the cuts, but the union of municipal workers supported it. Municipal workers are mostly women who work in lower-income jobs, many of whom either stood to gain from improved minimum protection or had long working careers (more then thirty years of contribution), which were not valued at all before the reform (Anderson and Immergut 2007). Anderson and Meyer (2003) even point out that the biggest winners of the reform are the lowest-income earners and people with very fragmented employment careers, who receive the higher guaranteed-minimum pension. Hence, through skillful coalitional engineering, a large party-political coalition managed to profoundly transform the Swedish pension regime with the support of the most relevant actors even among trade unions.

If trade union fragmentation became the key to successful reforms in Sweden, this is even more true for Italy, a country that experienced its most significant pension reform in 1995, under the technocratic Dini government. Economic downturn and the accession process to the Economic and Monetary Union had put severe austerity pressures on the agenda of the very generous Italian pension scheme. In this context, the government proposed introducing a new benefit calculation formula that would strengthen the equivalence principle, punish early and flexible retirement with linear cuts, and gradually phase out seniority pensions. The propositions for heavy retrenchment were obviously received with vigorous opposition by the trade unions, which were keen to defend the acquired rights of their core constituency (i.e., mature cohorts of insider workers). The key to reform was once more found in capitalization and targeting. The two issues appeared almost naturally on the agenda of the Italian pension system, in which private pension savings were hardly existent before and that was characterized by very fragmented and unequal insurance conditions for dependent workers, public-sector employees, and the self-employed. Hence, the technocratic government proposed strengthening capitalized supplementary pension schemes (offering the unions an important role in the management of these schemes [Natali 2003]), to increase contribution rates for the self-employed, to harmonize insurance conditions between the public and the private sector, to open up social insurance to atypical workers, and to introduce pension credits for periods of child rearing. According to Natali and Rhodes (2008: 36), the goal of the government was to "distribute the financial burden in a way as to defend the underprotected categories of the population, thus meeting the objective of both equity and effectiveness." Given the fragmentation of the Italian party system in the mid-1990s and the relative independence and credibility of the technocratic government, coalitional flexibility in parliament allowed for a compromise on the reform. The employers' organization, Confindustria, by contrast, refused to sign the agreement on the reform, because it considered the retrenchment insufficient, but it did not mobilize against it and the main resistance to overcome clearly came from the trade unions. The unions were open to raising contribution levels for the self-employed, and they negotiated long transition periods to shelter part of their mature constituencies from the effects of cutbacks, but the retrenchment still had effects on part of their clientele. In this difficult context, the structural weakness of the three Italian union confederations in terms of fragmentation, organizational structures, and coordination became an asset for reform capacity, because the unions did not have strong coordinated leadership and did not speak with one voice. Rather, they organized a secret ballot referendum on the reform, in which 64 percent of the 4.5 million voters approved of the changes. Heterogeneity within labor shows in the votes of various worker categories (Baccaro 2002): voting patterns were influenced by the way the reform affected different categories of workers, and the results reflected the different traditions of trade union militancy. In the end, the reform was adopted because it fostered a heterogeneous coalition of winners among the mature insiders in the private sector who were largely exempted from the cutbacks, atypical workers, and middle- and higher-income classes, whereas the losers were the self-employed and younger cohorts of workers in the private sector.

The Netherlands, Sweden, and Italy are cases characterized by strong coalitional flexibility among both parties and trade unions. Spain is somewhat different in its majoritarian electoral system, which has resulted in a concentrated party system. Nevertheless, the country managed to profoundly reform its pension system by means of the 1997 Toledo Pact (Chuliá 2007). The Spanish reform does not, however, confound expectations on the importance of coalitional flexibility – quite the contrary. It illustrates that in a context of austerity, even majoritarian governments have to negotiate and compromise to achieve reform. Indeed, the Toledo Pact was enacted with the support of both the right-wing government and the social-democratic opposition, as well as the employers' Confederación Española de Organizaciones Empresariales (CEOE) and the main trade unions Unión General de Trabajadores (UGT) and Comisiones Obreras (CC.OO). How was this possible? Economic and Monetary Union pressure, austerity, and the lack of social assistance had, by the 1990s, created a consensus in Spain that there was a need for both consolidation and expansion of the social security system (Guillén 2010). The right-wing government installed a parliamentary committee with representatives from all parties in 1996, to outline the contours of a rationalization of the Spanish social security system. The resulting Toledo Pact was a concerted agreement that included a new pension formula based on longer contribution periods and lower final pensions (retrenchment); harmonization of contributions among different insurance schemes (targeting); increased minimum pensions for outsiders, widows, and orphans (recalibration); and the introduction of a new, tax-financed reserve fund to finance noncontributory benefits (targeting). According to Guillén (forthcoming), the reform brought a reduction of core workers' rights and modest amelioration of the conditions for noncore workers. The Spanish reform package has a very striking resemblance to the 1993 French Balladur reform, which also introduced cutbacks and a special fund for the financing of noncontributory benefits. This strategy of dualization (Palier and Martin 2007), however, divided the trade unions in France, and it was strongly rejected by the left-wing opposition parties. How can we explain that a similar reform was so consensually adopted by the Spanish left and trade unions? The coalitional flexibility of trade unions was certainly enhanced by the fact that the agreement stated only the fundamental objectives, not the concrete means of implementation. More important, however – and this distinguishes the Spanish from the French case – the Toledo Pact stated explicitly that the Spanish pension system could not be radically transformed, either in a capitalized scheme or in a mere minimum-protection scheme (Chuliá 2007). Thereby, the unions were guaranteed that public social insurance would remain the centerpiece of Spanish pension policy. Indeed, the French CGT rejected the special reserve fund in 1993 precisely on the ground that it was only a first step toward the dismantling of the insurance principle (see Chapter 6). Even more surprising, however, is the agreement of the left-wing opposition party, the Social Democrats, to the reform. Chuliá (2007) explains this "grand coalition" by pointing out that both parties put a very high estimate on the electoral risk of pension cutbacks (equally high for both sides) and that they informally agreed to exclude the question from electoral competition. This is striking evidence for a point I elaborated previously: in times of austerity, even majoritarian governments cannot act unilaterally, and power sharing transforms them from an obstacle to an asset for reform capacity. Similarly, Chuliá (2007: 545) notes that "the [Toledo] pact had transformed this policy area into a sort of multiple partisan veto player system," meaning that a majoritarian, centralized government voluntarily introduced more veto power into the system to achieve reform.

The consequences of a lack of coalitional flexibility on pension reform can be observed in the case of Austria, the last example discussed here. Austria has a prototypical continental pension regime with very high levels of benefits and expenditures. However, during the 1990s, Austria also experienced increasing competition between the major parties – the Christian democrats, Österreichische Volkspartei (ÖVP), and the social democrats, Sozialdemokratische Partei Österreichs (SPÖ) (government coalition partners until 2000) – and, most important, a highly concentrated and organized labor movement in the Austrian Federation of Trade Unions, Österreichischer Gewerkschaftsbund (ÖGB). Hence, throughout the 1990s, the Austrian pension trajectory was marked by a series of attempts at retrenchment, which fostered strong polarization and opposition by a unified trade union movement (Schludi 2005; Schulze and Schludi 2007). Two attempts at cutbacks in 1994 and 1995 were almost completely withdrawn by the government because they came under strong attack by both the ÖGB and the Freiheitliche Partei Österreichs (FPÖ), the then-rising right-wing populist party of Jörg Haider, who was keen to gain the support of blue-collar workers. In 1996, a further attempt at retrenchment and limiting early retirement was again heavily watered down because both government parties (ÖVP and SPÖ) tried to exempt their constituencies from the effects of cutbacks. In light of reform stalemate, the government reached for external input in 1997 and asked the German pension expert Professor Bert Rürup for advice. Not surprisingly, he recommended a multidimensional package consisting of retrenchment measures (e.g., extending the reference salary period from fifteen to twenty years, limiting early retirement, making cutbacks in civil servants' pensions) and an increase in coverage for outsiders (i.e., targeting, recalibration). However, in contrast to the other countries we have looked at, a strategy of coalitional engineering including compensation for outsiders failed to divide trade unions in Austria, where labor was highly concentrated and spoke with one voice against the reform plans. Again, the reform was watered down with exemptions for core insiders. The right-wing government in place after 2000 eventually understood that pension modernization for outsiders did not have the potential to create sufficient support for successful reform. Rather, compensations had do be directed at the narrow clienteles of the powerful actors. Hence, the 2003 reform by the ÖVP-FPÖ government included benefits cuts on the one hand and several concessions on the other hand: the conservative electorate of the ÖVP was compensated with incentives for mothers of young children to exit the labor market, and the blue-collar constituencies of the FPÖ and the trade unions were compensated with special pension provisions and a hardship fund for workers in physically demanding jobs. Although this certainly was an instance of multidimensional coalitional engineering, the 2003 reform did not implement any systemic changes but reinforced the existing distributive arrangements. The result of this pattern of narrow reforms and insider compensation is that Austria experienced much less actual modernization and policy innovation than the other continental countries, and this can be directly attributed to the effects of weak coalitional flexibility.

What This Book Tells Us about Welfare State Modernization in Other Policy Fields

In this book, I applied the theoretical framework of multidimensional reform politics to pension reform, arguing that old-age income security, as the "cornerstone of the industrial welfare state" (Bonoli 2006: 21), is a good case for the hard testing of these arguments on the post-industrial determinants of alliance formation. However, I contend that the logic of the argument – a fortiori – also applies to other policy fields. The specific reform dimensions and actor configurations will, of course, differ from one field to another, but basically, post-industrialism implies multidimensional policy spaces in all major areas of the welfare state. Thus, we cannot understand the overall modernization of the continental welfare regimes unless we understand the coalitional dynamics that drive this process.

I would like to briefly illustrate how the analytical model in this book can be generalized by applying it to continental family policy, a field that has become radically challenged by post-industrialism and today is at the center of heated debates in most countries. France, Germany, and Switzerland differ more strongly with regard to family policy than with regard to pensions, but the underlying post-industrial reform dynamics are clearly comparable (for further elaboration, see also Häusermann 2006b). A conservative family policy is one of the hallmarks of the industrial continental welfare regimes (van Kersbergen 1994). The main instruments of continental family policy are financial transfers in the form of family allowances. These allowances are mostly contribution financed by

Conclusion*

211

employers and employees, or by employers only, because they have traditionally been granted to the male breadwinner as a part of his income. Family allowances – especially if they depend on the full-time employment of the male breadwinner – can be considered a conservative policy instrument because they consolidate the dependency of children and women on the male breadwinner. They are also typically universal (i.e., not means tested) because they serve as an instrument of familialism rather than social policy: the main goal of family allowances is not poverty prevention but strengthening the core family as the basic unit of society. In addition, financial transfers discourage female labor market participation because they compensate unpaid care work rather than facilitate the conciliation of work and care.[3]

A focus on the misfit between traditional policies and post-industrial structural developments makes it clear that continental family policy has become challenged both with regard to the generosity of transfer levels and with regard to the eligibility criteria they rely on. These two challenges account for the two dimensions, along which the debates on post-industrial family policy modernization are structured. First, the generosity of financial transfers to families determines the extent to which parents are decommodified (i.e., freed from the constraints of labor market participation). This classic left-right conflict line divides the traditional advocates of state support for families (notably political parties of the old left, Christian democrats, and trade unions) and the supporters of market liberalism (market liberal right-wing parties and capital). Second, debates on eligibility criteria deal with the question of whether policies should focus on the core family or on the individual. It opposes supporters of a conservative orientation on the core family to advocates of an individualized scheme. Consequently, it deals with societal modernization and therefore splits libertarians and traditionalists. The two conflict lines are analytically independent. When combined, they result in four possible directions of family policy modernization. First, low benefits that are allocated to the main income earner make caregivers depend on the labor market income of the head of the family. This is the classical male breadwinner model. Second, if the state allocates generous financial transfers to caregivers directly, it recognizes the value of unpaid (female) care work while preserving differential gender roles. Such a strategy may be seen as a kind of conservative modernization. Third, a liberal but progressive policy orientation invests in work-care conciliation policies to create incentives for female "commodification." By trying to align female employment biographies on the traditional male patterns of continuous labor market participation, such policies also foster more similar gender roles. Fourth, interventionist and progressive policies aim to enable both parents to participate equally in work and care. The four possible orientations of reform account for the multidimensional space of continental family policy modernization. According to the arguments developed in this book, policy makers should exploit this multidimensionality in the policy space and design reform packages

[3] In the 1950s and 1960s, this model was indeed modern: the right of mothers not to work was a symbol of social and economic progress and wealth in the middle classes (Naumann 2005).

in a way that will enable political exchange. They may either combine different modernizing policies to amass the necessary political support in ambiguous agreements or compensate cuts on one dimension with expansion on another dimension. The following succinct account of some of the major family policy reforms in France, Germany, and Switzerland over the past two decades indeed confirms this model.

France developed a strong natalist family policy during the interwar period that was based on very generous child allowances for large families. From the 1970s onward, both socialist and conservative governments have, in addition, started to invest heavily in the expansion of external child-care infrastructure. Therefore, family policy expenditure had reached very high levels by the end of the 1990s, when financial austerity increasingly started to constrain policy choices. At the same time, high unemployment rates reinforced the arguments of conservative actors who had always questioned high female labor market participation (Jenson and Sineau 2001). These conservative claims, however, contrasted with the demands for work-care policies coming from feminists, the left-wing parties, and employers of high-skilled women. Therefore, the conservative government in 1994 designed a reform package that drove family policy in the direction of a highly differentiated regime, providing specific incentives and benefits for different groups of beneficiaries (*Loi relative à la famille*): it increasingly transformed universal family allowances into means-tested benefits (what Commaille, Strobel, and Villac [2002] call the socialization of family policy). Yet at the same time, the government simultaneously compensated the cutbacks on two fronts. First, it extended generous educational benefits (*Allocation parentale d'éducation [APE]*) for low-skilled mothers of two and more, allowing these women to withdraw from the labor market for three years. This strategy met the demands of conservatives and allowed for the unburdening of unemployment insurance. Second, the conservative government expanded tax benefits and subsidies for nannies and childminders, allowing high-skilled women to remain active on the labor market (*Allocation pour la garde de l'enfant à domicile [AGED]* and *Allocation pour l'emploi familial d'une assistante maternelle agrégée [AFEAMA]*). With this strategy of political exchange, the government was able to ensure the agreement of conservatives, employers, and parts of the trade unions with the reform (Vallat 2002). The subsequent socialist government did not fundamentally alter this architecture of the family policy regime in the reform of 2000 (*Loi de financement de la sécurité sociale 2000*), but it put more emphasis on work-care conciliation (crèches) and on interventionist progressive modernization (e.g., paternity leave and benefit rights for part-time working parents). This combination of reform goals fostered a broad reform coalition of the new left, trade unions, and employers. Hence, although many observers characterize the architecture of French family policy as contradictory or incoherent (Commaille et al. 2002; Fagnani and Letablier 2005), I would argue that the diversity of policy orientations makes perfect sense when we look at politics (i.e., at the underlying coalitional dynamics that drive family policy development). Political exchange (i.e., the combination of different policies for different constituencies) was indeed the *conditio sine qua non* of policy change.

German family policy has always been less diverse than its French counterpart and traditionally has been more clearly focused on the male breadwinner orientation (i.e., on financial transfers to families) (Gerlach 2005). But this traditionalist focus has become both ineffective in terms of low birth rates and politically challenged by libertarian claims for gender equality and by market-liberal demands for increased female labor market participation. The reform of the federal law on educational benefits in 2000 (*Bundeserziehungsgeldgesetz*) provides a telling example of the coalitional strategy the red-green government adopted in this context. The government advocated the legal right to part-time employment for all parents of children under the age of three, and incentives for both parents to share parental leave more equally. This socially progressive focus of the new left government policy collided both with the interests of employers for increased (female) full-time labor market participation and with more conservative ideas from the Christlich Demokratische Union (CDU), the Christlich Soziale Union (CSU) and family organizations. Therefore, the government combined its bill proposal with incentives to shorten parental leave from two to one years (to accommodate employers) and with a means-tested, flat-rate educational benefit for low-income families (accommodating part of the conservative actors). Thereby, the government exploited the multidimensionality of the policy space and mobilized support both among the employers and conservative parties for a reform that reoriented German family policy toward gender equality and work-care conciliation.[4] Since 2005, the grand coalition has continued this multidimensional path of family policy modernization, by combining elements of societal modernization, work-care conciliation, and the recognition of care work in a model that is supposed to enable the free choice for parents regarding the division of work and care in the family.

In Switzerland, family policy remained very weakly developed until the 1990s in most cantons and at the national level (Dafflon 2003). Lacking an actual state family policy, Switzerland was a pronounced example of a male-breadwinner model, and it came into conflict with both the claims for support of (female) care work and the claims for gender equality and work-care conciliation from the early 1990s. Quite paradoxically, however, the scant provision in terms of family policy benefits and services has turned out to be a problematic starting configuration for the modernization of Swiss family policy. Indeed, the government could not compensate expansion on one dimension of reform with cutbacks on a different dimension, because there is little that could actually be cut back. On the contrary, Swiss policy makers needed to find a difficult balance when faced with a choir of simultaneous and diverging claims for increasing family allowances, parental leave schemes, child-care infrastructure, and maternity insurance. In France, the government could deal with a similar range of divergent claims by limiting the spending on general family allowances and reinvesting more heavily in modernization and targeted benefits. But the situation is

---

[4] The approval of family policy reforms by the opposition parties is always a necessary condition, as the Länder are strongly involved in family policy making.

different in Switzerland: every expansive reform just adds to existing costs. There is no opportunity for reallocation. Therefore, the government tried to combine several expansive reforms in packages. In 1999, the government engaged in coalitional engineering by combining maternity insurance for working mothers with birth allowances for all mothers, irrespective of labor market participation— two (contradictory) measures that were supposed to ensure support from both left-wing and conservative actors (*Mutterschaftsversicherungsgesetz*). Instead of fostering an ambiguous agreement in favor of the reform, however, this strategy produced a coalition of employers, market-liberal and conservative parties *against* the bill, which eventually failed in a direct democratic referendum. In 2004, the government thus put forward a more limited proposal for maternity insurance for working mothers only (*Erwerbsersatzordnung*), which indeed received the necessary support of a social-liberal coalition in parliament and at the polls. In 2003, a similar coalition of employers, market-liberal, and left-wing parties also adopted a new law supporting external child-care infrastructure (*Anstossfinanzierung für familienergänzende Betreuungsplätze*; see Ballestri and Bonoli 2003). However, the social-liberal reform coalitions remain precarious because every reform of Swiss family policy raises expenditure levels, and all political actors insist on concentrating the scarce resources on their preferred dimension of family policy modernization.

This very cursory evidence from French, German, and Swiss family policy developments makes it clear that in the field of family policy, as with pensions, the conceptualization of policy dynamics in a multidimensional reform space allows us to make sense of recent policy performance and to explain coalition patterns that may seem surprising or unlikely at first glance. Levy (1999: 244) is probably among the first to see more than fortuitous policy-making dynamics in these packages, as he described the "features of a particular kind of reform strategy, the vice-into-virtue strategy." According to Levy (1999: 240), such a strategy consists in reducing the "vices" of continental welfare states (notably inegalitarian status privileges) and redirecting the saved funds into more "virtuous" directions, such as poverty prevention or activation. In line with Levy's claim, it comes out very clearly from the analyses in this book that modernizing expansion of the welfare state is a very strong currency for governments to buy agreement for otherwise unpopular changes. In pensions, probably the most inert policy of all, it even allowed governments to enact retrenchment with the support of large cross-class coalitions. However, modernization, especially in the field of pension policy, is to some extent a nonrenewable resource. Once gender equality is formally introduced in a pension regime, for instance, there is not much more recalibration to offer in a subsequent reform. This does not mean that there is no more leeway for politics. However, in the future, policy makers might have to build on the interdependency of policy fields to exploit multidimensional policy spaces: by linking reforms in pension rights with modernization in other fields such as activation or work-care conciliation policies, post-industrial modernization may remain on the agenda of continental welfare states. Germany has provided a first telling example of such a cross-policy strategy in 2004: savings expected from cuts in unemployment benefits (in the context of the Hartz IV reforms) were imperatively allocated to the creation of external child-care infrastructure for young parents (*Tagesbetreuungsausbaugesetz*).

Theoretical Implications of This Book

The first contribution this book makes is to the literature on institutional change. I have suggested an analytical and empirical approach to analyze the politics of gradual transformative change – proposing that, by looking at the interaction of structure and institutions, we can identify a limited set of conflict lines or reform dimensions that are available for political mobilization in the policy-making arenas. These reform dimensions divide individuals in different sets of winners and losers according to their specific risk profile. If we establish the link among the risk profiles, the socio-structural classes to which they correspond and the collective actors who represent these classes, we are able to explain the reform dynamics in a policy field over a certain period. This insight bears two implications: first, we should not look at single reforms but at the reform dynamics in a policy field over a longer time span. Indeed, single reform processes are manifestations of an underlying pattern of conflict lines and actor configurations. The latter develop slowly, however, because they depend on gradual structural developments. If we focus solely on single case studies of reforms, we might fail to grasp that underlying pattern. One telling example of this risk can be found in the analyses of the shift of the German SPD and Green Party toward retrenchment in pension policy. If one looks at the 2001 reform only, one might be misled by the scope and abruptness of this shift and refer to ad hoc arguments to explain it, such as Chancellor Gerhard Schröder's personal preferences, a sudden ideational change (Hering 2004), or a deeper insight of the SPD in an "indispensable" necessity for financial consolidation (Schludi 2005: 141; Kitschelt and Streeck 2003: 29–30). It is only if we see this shift in the light of the changing risk profile of the new-left constituencies and of the government's encompassing reform strategy that the larger picture of this reform emerges. The second implication deals with the importance of socio-structural micro-foundation. A process analysis of single reforms may reveal the coalition of collective actors who finally succeeded in implementing a reform. But if we want to explain why this coalition emerged, and why it defended the policy preferences we observe, it is worthwhile and necessary to focus on the socio-structural basis of the collective actors, in addition to variables such as strategy and institutional constraints.

This leads me to the second theoretical contribution of this book. I have shown that cross-class alliances and intra-class heterogeneity are not surprising or fortuitous anomalies in welfare policy making; rather, they are inherent in the post-industrial class structure itself. Labor markets have become highly differentiated both in terms of vertical stratification and in terms of horizontal segmentation along the lines of sectors and work logics (Oesch 2006; see Chapter 3). This differentiation leads to new divides in the left and the right: in the industrial era, the social-democratic parties and trade unions mobilized similar electoral constituencies, namely blue-collar workers. But in the wake of post-industrialization, sociocultural professionals have become a second, if not the main constituency, of the new left (i.e., green parties and the social democrats). Because of this shift, the power of the former left now relies on two constituencies with diametrically opposed profiles in terms of skill levels, labor market status, and values (Kitschelt and Rehm 2005; Häusermann 2008). Blue-collar workers are low-skilled, traditionalist-leaning insiders, whereas sociocultural professionals tend to be high-skilled libertarians with a high proportion of outsiders and women. It is hardly surprising that their interests in a particular welfare state design diverge widely in almost every respect. This development also explains the growing split between political parties of the (new) left and trade unions, which still mainly represent blue-collar workers (Häusermann 2010b). At the right end of the political spectrum, similar difficulties arise among employers, (new) conservative political parties, and market-liberal political parties. Blue-collar workers have become the core constituency of the new populist right-wing parties, which defend decidedly traditionalist values but also have a vague economic preference profile (Kitschelt 1997; Bornschier 2010). Market-liberal and moderate conservative parties, by contrast, rely on a core constituency of capital accumulators. This socio-structural class is highly skilled and has a more libertarian value profile. This growing heterogeneity of the right-wing electorate becomes particularly relevant in post-industrial welfare state politics, as social policy preferences are increasingly structured by skill levels and values. Given the heterogeneous constituencies of what was known as the labor movement and as the bourgeois camp in the industrial era, it is not so surprising that configurations of actors and alliances in social policy making increasingly cut across this old class cleavage.

My third and final theoretical contribution suggests that the same socio-structural developments also explain why values have become an important determinant for coalition formation in post-industrial welfare politics. The electorate of the new left is strongly libertarian, yet holds diffuse preferences with regard to state interventionism. The decidedly libertarian value profile of the new-left constituencies may become a major motivation for welfare reforms along the lines of outsider protection and gender equality. Both the Swiss and the German social democrats and green parties formulated pension reforms along these lines. In Switzerland, the parties even formed a social-liberal value coalition with the market-liberal Freisinnig-Demokratische Partei der Schweiz (FDP) in several major pension reforms. This value dimension of post-industrial welfare reform is not merely an ancillary dimension in the reconfiguration of pension politics. In Switzerland, the Social Democrats and the Green Party were caught in a dilemma in 1995, when they had to choose whether to support the gender egalitarian pension reform and accept cutbacks or to refute the whole reform package on the grounds of their opposition to retrenchment. Against the expectations of many observers, they put up with retrenchment and privileged gender equality, thereby confronting the trade union movement in a popular referendum campaign. Similarly, the red-green government in Germany fought painful struggles in both parties to reorient the pension scheme from insider insurance toward recalibration for women and outsiders with discontinuous employment biographies. Distributional preferences alone cannot explain these shifts, because neither low-skilled outsiders nor nonemployed women (the main beneficiaries of such measures) are the electoral strongholds of these parties. Rather, the sociocultural dimension of libertarian versus traditionalist values has become a relevant determinant of actor configurations and reform outputs in post-industrial continental welfare politics.

Political Implications of This Book

In conclusion, this book bears several insights – and raises several questions – that are relevant for policy makers and for a normative appreciation of the recent changes. For policy makers, it is crucial to understand the conditions under which modernization is possible in the hard times of growing needs and scarce resources. To this end, the first insight of my study suggests that welfare state reform is actually possible in a context of austerity under two conditions. First, policy makers must be willing and able to understand and exploit the multidimensionality of the policy space. Second, the institutional framework of decision making must allow for some coalitional flexibility of the potential veto players.

A second insight that arises from the analysis in this book suggests that the industrial trade unions have lost much of their power in post-industrial pension politics, because the labor movement has become very heterogeneous (see also Häusermann 2010b). The new driving forces of pension policy modernization are parties of the libertarian new left, the market-liberal (and in some countries, value libertarian) right-wing parties, employers in large firms, and trade unions that either mobilize high-skilled labor or have opened up to the needs and preferences of outsiders. All these actors form a broad, cross-class coalition that has managed to implement major changes in conditions that are highly hostile to reform.

However, reform capacity as such is not the relevant issue. The truly relevant question here is whether continental welfare states can remain financially viable and meet new social needs and demands. This question relates, of course, to the distributive effects of the modernized continental welfare states. As I outlined at the beginning of this chapter, the reforms of the past thirty years have transformed the pension regimes of Germany, France, and Switzerland into two seemingly contradictory directions. These regimes have been redesigned so as to become both more egalitarian at the bottom of the income distribution and more inegalitarian for the middle and higher income levels. For the least privileged income classes, namely labor market outsiders, there have been expansive reforms to cover atypical forms of employment and to create a rather universalistic minimum pension security. Therefore, the pension rights of labor market outsiders, nonemployed, and women with discontinuous employment biographies have improved somewhat, despite the context of austerity. This may certainly be interpreted as a successful modernization of the continental regimes. In contrast, however, pension rights in the general insurance schemes have been cut back drastically. These cuts will be offset only partially by benefits from capitalized pension funds, because middle- and low-income earners are unable to accumulate substantial pension savings. The actual losers of these reforms thus appear to be middle-class labor market insiders, who had been among the main beneficiaries of the industrial male-breadwinner welfare state. In the light of these trends, it seems quite clear that continental welfare regimes are not converging to a different regime type, neither the Anglo-Saxon one nor the Scandinavian one. Rather, they seem to be becoming less continental at the bottom and more continental at the top of the income distribution. There will be more outsider coverage, less insider security, and still a very high level of (institutionally reinforced) vertical stratification, given the rising importance of private and occupational capitalized pension funds.

A normative assessment of these trends depends on the criteria of evaluation, of course. As far as income inequality is concerned, the bottom line of these reforms may look rather poor, because private and occupational pension schemes reproduce and even amplify inequalities. However, equality has never been a key objective of the continental welfare regimes. Hence, it may be misleading to judge them by a goal they were never meant to pursue. Poverty alleviation may be a more universally valid indicator of welfare state success. Post-industrialism has created a range of new poverty risks, such as being a single mother, atypically employed, a divorced woman, or (more generally) a low-skilled outsider. For these risk groups, the orientation toward more minimum outsider coverage (targeting and recalibration) tends to improve their social rights. These improvements matter even if we balance them against the simultaneous cutbacks in the basic pension schemes, especially because these post-industrial risk groups never had very high stakes in the industrial insurance schemes. In this sense, this policy development can be viewed as a success in terms of modernization. But in a welfare state that relies on targeted (often tax-financed) minimum protection for particularly underprivileged social groups, the key questions are, of course, whether the level of the minimum is high enough to prevent poverty, and whether the least privileged social groups have opportunities to improve their social status in the long run. The answer to this second question certainly depends not on pension modernization alone but on labor market activation policies, education rights, and child-care infrastructure. Therefore, the modernization of the continental welfare state in all areas of social policy is a necessary condition not only for the financial viability of these regimes but also for their social viability in the post-industrial era.

Appendix 1: Mapping the Policy Space: A New Approach to the Analysis of Policy Change

This appendix presents the methodological approach of this book, including the selection of the reforms and actors included, the coding procedure, sources, and methods of analysis.

A1.1. Selection of Reforms and Actors Included in the Analysis

The study includes all thirty-six pension reforms that took place in Germany, France, and Switzerland between 1970 and 2005. Tables A1.1–A1.3 provide an overview and the references to the official documentation (call number).

The choice of actors is an important issue. If the goal is to understand policy dynamics, it is best to include all actors who actually participated in the reforms and who have a say in the specific country. The analyses in this book include all political parties that made a statement on the reform in the plenary parliamentary debates (France, Germany) or in the official consultation procedure that preceded parliamentary debates (Switzerland).[1] A similar approach guided the selection of trade unions and employer organizations for the cases of Germany and Switzerland. The major peak trade unions and employer organizations participate in all reforms, which is why they are included in all the analyses. In addition, sectoral trade unions and employer organizations were included, if they delivered their own separate statements in the consultation procedures, because the separate statements are indications of intralabor or intracapital conflict. In France, such an inductive approach to the selection of corporatist actors is impossible, as there is no official consultation procedure. Therefore, the three major trade unions (Confédération Générale du

---

[1] In majoritarian systems such as France, this criterion excludes minor parties (e.g., the radical right-wing National Front), whereas the same criterion includes even small parties in consensual and multiparty Switzerland. This difference is meaningful, however, as the actual actor networks differ between countries, and the difference is relevant for explaining national dynamics of coalition formation and reform outputs.

TABLE A1.1. *France*

Reform	Reform Issues
1 **Pension law 1971** (Loi du 31.12.1971 dite Boulin portant amélioration des pensions de vieilles du régime général de sécurité sociale et du régime des travailleurs salarés agricoles; loi 71–1132)	1.1. Pension increase 1.2. Early retirement for disabled workers 1.3. Introduction of a one-year educational pension credit
2 **Law on complementary pensions 1972** (Loi du 29.12.1072 portant généralisation de la retraite complémentaire au profit des salariés et anciens salariés; loi 72–1223)	2.1. Complementary pension insurance becomes mandatory for all employees 2.2. Pension coverage for unemployed 2.3. Debate on the harmonization of complementary pensions for managers and employees
3 **Law on pension increase 1975** (Loi du 3.1.1975 portant diverses améliorations et simplifications en matière de pensions ou allocation des conjoints survivants, des mères de famille et des personnes agées; loi 75–3)	3.1. Increase in widows' pensions 3.2. Support for the reentry of widows in the labor market 3.3. Extension of basic insurance coverage to lower incomes 3.4. Extension of educational pension credits to three years
4 **Law on pension eligibility 1975** (Loi du 30 décembre 1975 relative aux conditions d'accès à la retraite de certains travailleurs manuels; loi 1279)	4.1. Early retirement for workers with particularly long careers 4.2. Early retirement for mothers of three and more
5 **Pension law 1983** (Loi du 31.5.1983 portant diverses mesures relatives aux prestations de vieillesse; loi 83–430)	5.1. Lowering of the retirement age to 60 5.2. Minimum pension
6 **Pension law 1993** (Loi du 22.7.1993 relative aux pensions de retraite et à la sauvegarde de la protection sociale; loi 93–936)	6.1. Increase in the retirement ages 6.2. Lower benefit levels (extention of the calculation period) 6.3. Indexation of pensions on prices 6.4. Increase of the Contribution de Solidarité Généralisée (1% for pension insurance) 6.5. Fund (Fonds de Solidarité Vieillesse) for the financing of noncontributory benefits
7 **Law on pension savings 1997** (Loi Thomas du 26.3.1997 créant les plans d'épargne retraite; loi 97–277)	7.1. Capitalized pension savings plans
8 **Law on financing social security 1999** (Loi du 23.12.1998 de financement de la sécurité sociale pour 1999; loi 98–1194)	8.1. Creation of a reserve fund within the FSV 8.2. Indexation of pensions on prices

TABLE AI.I *(continued)*

Reform	Reform Issues
9 **Law on income savings 2001** (Loi du 19.2.2001 sur l'épargne salariale; loi 2001–152)	9.1. Individual long-term savings plans 9.2. Small-business savings plans
10 **Pension law 2003** (Loi du 21.8.2003 portant réforme des retraites; loi 2003–775)	10.1 Lowering of benefit levels 10.2. Lowering of widows' pensions 10.3. Individual pension savings plans 10.4. Harmonization of public and private pension programs 10.5. Increase in the minimum pension 10.6. Early retirement for workers with particularly long careers 10.7. Educational pension credits for civil servants

Notes: The reform chronology for France is mainly based on Palier 2002, Schludi 2005, Bonoli 2000, Vail 2004, and http://www.ladocfrancaise.gouv.fr.

Travail [CGT], Confédération Française Démocratique du Travail [CFDT], Confédération Générale des Cadres [CGC]) and the two major employer organizations (Mouvement des Entreprises de France [MEDEF] and Confédération Générale des Petites et Moyennes Entreprises [CGPME]) are included. Finally, on the matter of social interests, I included those societal organizations that made a statement in the consultation procedures and public hearings in Switzerland and Germany.[2]

A1.2. Mapping the Policy Space: Coding

In political science, the mapping of actor configurations is widely used in research on party systems and coalition formation (see, e.g., Kitschelt 1994; Laver and Hunt 1992; Budge et al. 2001; Kriesi et al. 2008). Political parties can be located on the basis of the preferences and values of their constituencies (Kitschelt 1994), or with regard to expert judgments (Laver and Hunt 1992). However, the coding of actor positions on the basis of actors' own statements comes closest to a representation of the policy space in the way the actors construct and perceive it themselves. Budge and colleagues (2001), for instance, code party manifestos. Kriesi and colleagues (2008), by contrast, focus on the statements political parties issue through the press. In this book, I adapt a similar strategy to the study of policy change.

When analyzing actual policy reforms, the relevant information lies in the positions actors defend in the very decision-making processes, as they represent

[2] Consequently, no societal interest organizations are included in the French case. Again, the lack of such actors in the analysis of French pension reforms has a substantial rationale: generally, societal interests have little possibility of intervention in the French reform processes.

TABLE A1.2. *Germany*

Reform	Reform Issues
1 **Pension reform law 1972** (Rentenreformgesetz 1972; VI/0323)	1.1. Lowering of the retirement age (flexible retirement at 63)
	1.2. Acceleration of pension indexation
	1.3. Introduction of a minimum pension for low-income earners with long careers
	1.4. Voluntary access to the basic public pension scheme for self-employed
	1.5. Voluntary access to the basic public pension scheme for nonemployed
	1.6. Educational pension credit (one year)
2 **Law on the improvement of occupational pensions 1974** (Gesetz zur Verbesserung der betrieblichen Altersversorgung 1974; VII/0213)	2.1. Increase of occupational pension levels
	2.2. Guarantee of individual pension savings in case of labor market mobility
3 **First reform of the marital law 1976** (Erstes Ehereformgesetz 1976; VII/0415)	3.1. Splitting of pension rights after divorce
4 **Law on pension adaptations 1977** (Gesetz zur zwanzigsten Rentenanpassung und zur Verbesserung der Finanzgrundlagen der gesetzlichen Rentenversicherung (20. RAG) 1977; VIII/0008)	4.1. Postponing of pension indexation
	4.2. Increase of pension contribution levels
	4.3. Increase of contributions to the basic pension by insurance and sickness insurance
	4.4. Lowering of reserve funds for the basic pension
5 **Law on social insurance for artists 1981** (Künstlersozialversicherungsgesetz 1981; IX/0016)	5.1. Introduction of pension insurance for artists
6 **Law on the public budget 1983** (Gesetz zur Wiederbelebung der Wirtschaft und Beschäftigung und zur Entlastung des Bundeshaushaltes (Haushaltbegleitgesetz) 1983; IX/0106)	6.1. Postponing of pension indexation
	6.2. Increase of contribution rates to basic pension scheme
	6.3. Increase of sickness insurance contributions to be paid by pensioners
7 **Reform of widows' pensions and educational benefits 1985** (Hinterbliebenenrenten – und Erziehungszeitengesetz 1985; X/155)	7.1. Expansion of minimum pension regulation
	7.2 Harmonization of widows' and widowers' pensions
	7.3. One-year educational pension credit

TABLE AI.2 *(continued)*

Reform	Reform Issues
8 **Pension reform law 1989** (Rentenreformgesetz 1989; XI/186)	8.1. Increase of the retirement age
	8.2. Indexing of pensions on net instead of gross wages
	8.3. Consolidation of minimum pension regulations
	8.4. Expansion of educational pension credits
	8.5. Summation of educational pension credits for early retirement
	8.6. Debate on the splitting of pension rights between spouses
9 **Pension reform law 1996** (Rentenreformgesetz 1996 (Wachstums – und Beschäftigungsförderungsgesetz); XIII/152)	9.1. Increase of the retirement age
	9.2. Lowering of coverage in case of career interruptions for training
	9.3. Cuts in disability payments by the basic pension scheme
	9.4. Coverage of marginally employed workers by the pension insurance
10 **Pension reform law 1997** (Rentenreformgesetz 1997; XIII/320)	10.1. Lowering of pension levels (demographic factor)
	10.2. Cuts in early retirement options
	10.3. Lowering of disability pensions
	10.4. Increase of financial stability of the basic pension scheme (through 1% of VAT)
	10.5. Debate on the introduction of a means-tested universal pension coverage
	10.6. Increase of educational pension credits
	10.7. Debate on an individualized pension insurance for women
11 **Bill on corrections in social insurance law 1998** (Gesetz zu Korrekturen in der Sozialversicherung und zur Sicherung der Arbeitnehmerrechte 1998; XIV/6)	11.1. Abolition of the 1997 demographic factor
	11.2. Abolition of the 1997 cuts in disability pensions
	11.3. Improved coverage of part-time employees in the basic pension program
12 **Law on marginal employment 1999** (Gesetz zur Neuregelung der geringfügigen Beschäftigungsverhältnisse 1999; XIV/13)	12.1. Coverage of marginally employed workers in pension insurance

(continued)

TABLE AI.2 *(continued)*

Reform	Reform Issues
13 **Reform of disability pensions 2000** (Gesetz zur Reform der Renten wegen verminderter Erwerbsfähigkeit 2000; XIV/182)	13.1. Cuts in disability pension levels 13.2. Introduction of a new disability pension scheme with lower benefits 13.3. Direct payments of the unemployment insurance to the basic pension scheme for coverage of unemployed
14 **Pension reform law 2001** (Rentenreform 2001: Altersvermögensgesetz 2001; XIV/248 / Altersvermögensergänzungsgesetz 2001; XIV/215 Gesetz zur Verbesserung des Hinterbliebenenrentenrechts 2001; XIV/255)	14.1. Lowering of widows' pension benefits 14.2. Lowering of general pension benefit levels 14.3. Introduction of individual pension savings plans 14.4. Introduction of a universal, means-tested minimum pension insurance 14.5. Improved pension coverage for parents 14.6. Debate on the splitting of contributions and benefits between spouses 14.7. Individualization of poverty relief (children do not have to pay for parents)
15 **Reform of civil servants' pensions 2001** (Versorgungsänderungsgesetz 2001; XIV/344)	15.1. Introduction of individual pension savings plans for civil servants 15.2. Lowering of benefit levels for civil servants 15.3. Lowering of the level of widows' pensions for civil servants 15.4. Increase of educational pension credits for civil servants
16 **Law on pension sustainability 2004** (RV-Nachhaltigkeitsgesetz 2004; XV/174)	16.1. Lowering of general pension benefit levels (*Nachhaltigkeitsfaktor*) 16.2. Cuts in early retirement options 16.3. Lowering of pension coverage in case of employment interruption for training 16.4. Introduction of a target minimum replacement rate (46%) and a maximum contribution rate (22%) 16.5. Increase in pension coverage for families

Notes: The reform chronology for Germany is based on Alber 1987, Schmidt 1998, Schludi 2005, and http://dip.bundestag.de.

TABLE AI.3. *Switzerland*

Reform	Reform Issues
1 **Constitutional amendment on the multipillar pension regime 1972** (3-Säulenartikel; BV 34ter)	1.1. Introduction of replacement rate target levels in the constitution
2 **8th reform of the basic pension scheme 1972** (8. Revision der Alters – und Hinterbliebenenversicherung AHV; BBl 1971 II: 1057ff)	2.1. Pension level increase of 25%
	2.2. Indexation of pensions on prices and wages
	2.3. Introduction of a 13th pension benefit per year
	2.4. Reduction of the tax-financed public contribution to the insurance program
	2.5. Increase of earnings-related contributions to pension insurance
3 **9th reform of the basic pension scheme 1976** (9. Revision der Alters – und Hinterbliebenenversicherung AHV; BBl 1976 III: 1ff)	3.1. Indexation of pensions on wages and prices
	3.2. Increase of the minimum contribution to pension insurance
	3.3. Lowering of derived benefits for spouses
	3.4. Increase of tax-financed public contribution to pension insurance
	3.5. Increase of contribution levels for employed pensioners
	3.6. Increase of contribution levels for self-employed
4 **Introduction of the law on the occupational pension scheme 1982** (Bundesgesetz über die berufliche Vorsorge BVG; BBl 1976 I: 149ff)	4.1. Expansion of occupational pension savings plans
	4.2. Introduction of a combined replacement rate target level for public and occupational pensions
	4.3. Mandatory occupational second pillar pension insurance for standard employees
5 **2nd reform of the means-tested supplementary pension scheme 1985** (Zweite Revision des Bundesgesetzes über Ergänzungsleistungen zur AHV/IV; BBl 1985 I: 98ff)	5.1. Increase of means-tested complementary pension benefits
	5.2. Increased complementary benefits for long-term-care patients
	5.3. Increase of benefits for homeowners
	5.4. Lowering of complementary benefits for pensioners with own savings
	5.5. Increase of individual financial responsibility in case of sickness
	5.6. Measures to fight abuses

(*continued*)

TABLE A1.3 *(continued)*

Reform	Reform Issues
6 **Reform of labor market mobility in the occupational pension scheme 1994** (Bundesgesetz über die Freizügigkeit in der beruflichen Vorsorge; BBl 1992 III: 533ff)	6.1. Guarantee of individual pension savings in case of labor market mobility 6.2. Harmonization of occupational second-pillar pension programs 6.3. No dissolution of pension savings for women in case of marriage 6.4. Splitting of second-pillar savings between spouses in case of divorce
7 **10th reform of the basic pension scheme 1995** (10. Revision der Alters – und Hinterbliebenenversicherung AHV; BBl 1990 II: 1ff)	7.1. Increase of the retirement age for women from 62 to 64 7.2. Flexible retirement age (without public subsidies for lower-income pensioners) 7.3. Splitting of contributions and pensions between spouses and educational pension credits
8 **3rd reform of the means-tested supplementary pension scheme 1996** (Dritte Revision des Bundesgesetzes über Ergänzungsleistungen zur AHV/IV; BBl 1997 I: 1197ff)	8.1. Increase of rent deductions for poor pensioners 8.2. Lowering of waiting periods for supplementary pensions for foreigners 8.3. Higher supplementary pensions for homeowners 8.4. Improved information for pensioners about benefit eligibility
9 **1st reform of the occupational pension scheme 2003** (1. Revision des Bundesgesetzes über die berufliche Vorsorge BVG; BBl 2000 III: 2675ff)	9.1. Cutbacks in occupational pension levels 9.2. Increase of the retirement age for women to 65 9.3. Improved occupational pension coverage for low-income earners 9.4. Improved occupational pension coverage for part-time employees 9.5. Ceiling of insurable income 9.6. Introduction of occupational pension benefits for widowers
10 **11th reform of the basic pension scheme 2003** (11. Revision der Alters – und Hinterbliebenenversicherung AHV; BBl 2000 II: 1865ff)	10.1. Increase of the retirement age for women to 65 10.2. Cutbacks in widows' pension levels 10.3. Flexible retirement age (without public subsidies for lower-income pensioners) 10.4. Cutbacks in pension indexation 10.5. Increase in contribution levels for self-employed

Notes: The reform chronology for Switzerland is based on the Année Politique Suisse reform data books (Institut für Politikwissenschaft der Universität Bern 1970-2003), Kriesi 1980, Bonoli 2000, Binswanger 1987 and http://www.admin.ch.

genuine policy preferences of the political actors who make the reforms. The added value of coding the positions instead of just observing them qualitatively consists in the possibilities for empirical analysis that come with the quantification: actor locations and their shifts can be represented graphically in the policy space and the data allow for the calculation of indicators of distance and proximity, as well as conflict and consensus. For the empirical analyses in this book, I have coded detailed actor positions at two points of the decision-making process and complemented this quantitative data with more qualitative information from primary documents and interviews.

The initial positions were coded on a scale ranging from 0 to 2, and codes are attributed relative to the reform proposal that is presented by the government. The value 0 indicates that the actor in question favors more generous social rights than what the government proposal contains; the value 1 means that the actor supports the content of the governmental bill proposal; and the value 2 means that the actor claims a less generous coverage of the risk or need at stake than what is proposed by the government. This code scheme was applied to four aspects of every reform issue:

1. *Intervention:* whether any state intervention is required on the social problem at stake, 0 meaning that the actor wants stronger or faster action on the issue and 2 meaning that the actor argues for less, later, or no intervention.
2. *Scope:* to whom the reform should apply (i.e. the circle of people who should be affected by it). Here, 2 means that improvements should be granted to fewer people and retrenchment implemented on a greater scope of recipients. The reverse applies to a position coded 0.
3. *Level:* how high the benefit levels should be, 2 meaning that the actor claims lower benefit levels and service standards than what is proposed by the government, and 0 meaning that the actor claims more generous benefit or services.
4. *Competence:* at what level of decision making the policy should be regulated (e.g., national, substate, sectoral, firm). Here, 2 indicates that the actor supports a more liberal position (i.e., more discretion for firms, substate levels). By contrast, a score of 0 means that the actor claims a uniform solution for the whole country and far-reaching competences for the central government.

The foregoing coding scheme reflects only the general framing of the positions. Debates on each reform issue deal with very specific questions and alternatives, so that the specific meaning of the codes must be defined and identified for each and every one of the 135 reform issues at stake. A specific code scheme is important to grasp the precise meaning of an actor's statement. An example may be helpful for illustrating these issue-specific codes: I present an issue from the Swiss occupational pension reform of 2003, namely the extension of mandatory occupational pension coverage to part-time workers (reform-issue number 9.4. in the list of selected Swiss reforms in Table A1.3). The following is the code scheme used to identify the position of the actors on this specific reform proposal:

1. *Intervention:* Should the social insurance coverage of part-time employees in the Swiss occupational pension tier be improved? o = yes, immediately; 1 = yes, but in a series of steps; 2 = no intervention is necessary.

2. *Scope:* To what extent should part-time employees be included in the mandatory occupational pension tier? o = even part-time employees who earn less than the proposed threshold should be included; 1 = part-timers who earn at least 16,000 Swiss francs per year (i.e., the threshold proposed in the governmental reform proposal) should be covered; 2 = only part-time employees whose income lies above a higher threshold than the one proposed should be included.

3. *Level:* How much of their income should be covered in the mandatory occupational pension insurance (i.e., what is the appropriate level of the coordination deduction for part-timers)? o = the coordination deduction should be lower than what the government proposes; 1 = the coordination deduction for part-time employees should be proportional to their labor market participation (as specified in the government proposal); 2 = the coordination deduction should be greater than what the government proposes.

4. *Competence:* At what level should the specific regulations of part-time work coverage in the occupational pension tier be decided? o = all of them should be stated in the national law; 1 = the national level should decide only about minimum regulations; 2 = the regulation should be left to the individual employers or pension funds.

I have spelled out such a specific code scheme for all 135 reform issues and coded the statements of the relevant actors for each of them in a FileMaker entry mask. For the empirical analysis, I then used a single position value per reform issue by averaging the codes on the four aspects. The positions of the actors on the four aspects tend to be highly correlated (they result in a single dimension in a factor analysis). Therefore, one can average the four observations to create a single value for the position of each actor with regard to each reform issue.[3] On the whole, the database contains about 8000 single observations of preferences, for a total of about 2000 actor positions.

The coding of the final actor positions on the thirty-six reform packages is straightforward: o = the actor approved of the reform; 1 = the actor criticized the reform, but did not mobilize opposition against it, and 2 = the actor

---

[3] Of course, actor positions exist only with regard to those issues that were relevant for the reform debate. The competence issue, for instance, was uncontroversial (i.e., not relevant) for most reforms, as most pension regulations are made at the federal level anyway. Where this issue was lacking, the position of the actor corresponds to the average of the three observations on intervention, scope, and level. When an actor did not mention his or her position on a specific issue, I assumed that he or she agreed with the government proposal.

explicitly refused the reform. This second step of coding contains about 540 actor positions.

A1.3. Sources and List of Interviews

The choice of the adequate sources for coding is, of course, crucial. I relied mostly on written statements by political parties, trade unions, employer organizations, and societal organizations in consultation procedures or hearings at the beginning of the reform processes. In both Germany and Switzerland, consultation of the relevant interests is strongly institutionalized and well documented.[4] In France, however, there are no official consultations or hearings in the reform processes. Trade unions and employers intervene in more informal ways, which – most of the time – cannot be traced back in official documents. Hence, data collection in France was based on the official publications of trade unions and employer organizations and on interviews for the more recent cases.[5] For political parties, early debates in the lower chambers of the French, German, and Swiss parliaments served as an additional source for coding or cross-checking of the preferences of political parties.[6] The data on the final positions of the actors on reform packages is based on the parties' voting behavior in the final votes in parliament, as well as on secondary literature, media reports, and information from the following interviews:

France
- Secretary general of the governmental council for pension policy Conseil d'Orientation des Retraites (COR), July 12, 2005, Paris.
- Director of social policy at the French employers' association Mouvement des Entreprises de France (MEDEF), July 13, 2005, Paris.
- Trade union secretary of Confédération Générale du Travail (CGT), July 20, 2005, Paris.

[4] In Germany, official hearings take place in the respective parliamentary committee (here, Anhörung im Parlamentarischen Ausschuss für Arbeit und Soziales). The coding relies on the written statements of actors and on the minutes of the hearings. These documents are available at the German parliamentary archives. In Switzerland, the early positions of all actors can be observed by means of their written contributions to the official consultation procedure (*Vernehmlassungsverfahren*), which precedes every major reform. These statements and all related documents (government bill proposals and explanatory reports) are publicly available in ministries and the federal archives. For the few reforms for which no such consultation procedure took place, I relied on the minutes of the extraparliamentary committees and secondary case-study literature.

[5] The coding was based on a systematic research in the publications of the Confédération Générale des Cadres (*Cadres et maîtrise*), the Confédération Générale du Travail (*Le Peuple/Force ouvrière*), and the Confédération Française des Travailleurs (*Syndicalisme*) over the 1970s and 1980s. For the more recent reforms of the 1990s and 2000s, I relied on interviews with the representatives of these trade unions and of employer organizations.

[6] For France, the reports of the parliamentary committees and the plenary debates occur in the lower chamber (Assemblée Nationale), where each faction discusses the elements of each reform; for Germany, the Plenarprotokoll, 2. Lesung, of the lower chamber (Bundestag); and for Switzerland, the Eintretens- und Detaildebatte of the lower chamber (Nationalrat) and minutes of the parliamentary committees.

- Representative of the employers' association of small businesses Confédération Générale des Petites et Moyennes Entreprises (CGPME), July 19, 2005, Paris.
- National secretary of social security of the trade union Confédération Générale des Cadres (CGC), July 19, 2005, Paris.
- Trade union secretary of Confédération Française Démocratique du Travail (CFDT), July 13, 2005, Paris.
- Representative of the national union of French families Union Nationale des Associations Familiales, July 20, 2005, Paris.

Germany
- Vice director of the German trade union of civil servants Deutscher Beamten-Bund (DBB), September 21, 2004, Berlin.
- Representative for gender-equality policy at the German union of trade unions Deutscher Gewerkschaftsbund (DGB), April 6, 2005, Berlin.
- Director of social policy of the union Vereinte Dienstleistungsgewerkschaft (ver.di), September 20, 2004, Berlin.
- Director of social policy of the German employers' association Bundesvereinigung der Deutschen Arbeitgeberverbände (BDA), September 23, 2004, Berlin.
- Head of division for pension policy of the German union of trade unions Deutscher Gewerkschaftsbund (DGB), April 7, 2005, Berlin.
- Dr. Frank Nullmeier, University of Bremen, member of the Rürup Committee, April 6, 2005, Berlin.
- Head of division social policy of the German employers' association of small businesses Zentralverbandes des Deutschen Handwerks (ZdH), September 21, 2004, Berlin.
- Director of social policy at the German union of metal workers IG Metall, September 16, 2004, Berlin.
- Director of social policy of the union of executives Union Leitender Angestellter (ULA), September 23, 2004, Berlin.

Switzerland
- Former director of the Swiss employers' association Schweizerischer Arbeitgeberverband (SAV), former member of the liberal party Freisinnig-Demokratische Partei (FDP) in the parliamentary committee for social policy, July 4, 2001, Zurich.
- Former vice director of the federal office for social insurance Bundesamt für Sozialversicherungen (BSV), June 21, 2001, Bern.
- Former secretary general of the Swiss union of trade unions Schweizerischer Gewerkschaftsbund (SGB), former member of the social-democratic Sozialdemokratische Partei (SPS) in the parliamentary committee for social policy, July 7, 2001, Geneva.
- Former member of the Christian-democratic Christlichdemokratische Volkspartei (CVP) in the parliamentary committee for social policy, July 2, 2001, Sion.

- Former secretary-general of the Swiss union of trade unions Schweizerischer Gewerkschaftsbund (SGB), June 18, 2001, Lausanne.
- Vice director of the Swiss employers' association of small businesses Schweizerischer Gewerbeverband (SGV), June 6, 2002, Bern.
- Member of the liberal party Freisinnig-Demokratische Partei (FDP) in the parliamentary committee for social policy, June 6, 2002, Bern.
- Former member of the social-democratic Sozialdemokratische Partei (SPS) in the parliamentary committee for social policy, June 28, 2001, Bern.
- Former director social policy of the Swiss employers' association Schweizerischer Arbeitgeberverband (SAV), August 10, 2001, Zurich.
- Former member of the liberal party Freiheitlich-Demokratische Partei (FDP) in the parliamentary committee for social policy, June 21, 2001, Bern.
- Member of the social-democratic Sozialdemokratische Partei (SPS) in the parliamentary committee for social policy, June 6, 2002, Bern.
- Director and head of the division of social policy of the Swiss employers' association Schweizerischer Arbeitgeberverband (SAV), October 20, 2004, Zurich.

A1.4. Methods

To identify the different dimensions of conflict in the reforms, I analyzed the positions of the actors by means of principal component factor analysis and multidimensional scaling. Only the results of the factor analyses are shown.[7] Some remarks are important with regard to the applicability and robustness of factor analysis for the study of small data matrices. First, the number of observations (actors) in relation to the number of items (reform issues) is naturally rather small (the ratio is between 2 and 5) in comparison with what the specialized literature recommends.[8] I argue that factor analysis is nevertheless useful and applicable, because the dimensionality is cross-checked with multidimensional scaling (MDS) analysis and because I use the results of factor analysis in an illustrative way that is constantly complemented with more qualitative analyses. Second, one must be cautious because the small number of actors may make the results less robust.[9] I have rerun all factor analyses without the major organizations of labor and capital (DGB and BDA in Germany; SGB and SAV/Economiesuisse

---

[7] One may ask whether factor analysis is the appropriate technique, given that the underlying (coded) variables are ordinal scale. I argue that it is, because, first, the actor position used in the analysis is the average of four codes (i.e., a quasi-metric variable). Second, I cross-checked the dimensionality of the reform by means of multidimensional scaling to verify that it was identical. The reason I present the results of the factor analyses in this book is that factor analysis allows for a dimensional analysis and provides more easily interpretable information on the content of the extracted factors.

[8] Cattell (1978) argues that the minimum ratio should be between 3 and 6, and Gorsuch (1983) maintains that the results are reliable beyond a ratio of 5.

[9] A small observations-to-items ratio may lead to misclassification problems (i.e., some items being attributed to the wrong factors). Indeed, the estimates (factor loadings) are less reliable with small samples, and this must be kept in mind when interpreting factor loadings that are not clear cut.

in Switzerland). Finally, the dimensionality (i.e., the result of the factor analysis) depends to some extent on the number of issues included. This means that the selection of reform issues is crucial. As outlined previously, I relied on documents and interviews to ensure a complete list of all relevant issues at stake.

The quantitative analyses and their interpretation were embedded in a more qualitative tracing of the processes, the issues at stake, and actor's motivations and strategies. I used reports of the parliamentary committees and the plenary debates in parliaments, as they contain the arguments that actors advance for or against a policy. The coded data on actor positions was also complemented by information from the interviews with the representatives of the main trade unions and employer organizations (the positions and arguments of political parties being much better documented in written form). These interviews (see lists of interviews herein) provided expert judgments on the saliency of particular reform issues and reputational data on the relative importance and strategies of different actors.

Appendix 2: Appendix to Chapter 3

TABLE A2.1. *Classification of Occupations in Postindustrial Class Groups (based on Kitschelt and Rehm 2005 and Oesch 2006)*

Independent Work Logic	Technical Work Logic	Organizational Work Logic	Interpersonal Work Logic	
Large employers, self-employed professionals, and petty bourgeoisie with employees (CA) Self-employed ≤24	Technical experts (CA) 21 Physical, mathematical and engineering science professionals	Higher-grade managers (CA) 11 legislators and senior officials; 12 corporate managers	Sociocultural (semi)professionals (SCP) 22 life science and health professionals; 23 teaching professionals; 24 other professionals'	Professional/ managerial employees
	Technicians (MSF) 31 physical and engineering science associate professionals	Associate managers (CA) 13 general managers	32 life science and health associate professionals; 33 teaching associate professionals; 34 other associate professionals	Associate professional and managerial employees
Petty bourgeoisie without employees (MSF) Self-employed >24	Skilled crafts (BC) 71 extraction and building trades workers; 72 metal, machinery, and related trades workers; 73 precision, handicraft, printing, and related trades workers; 74 other craft and related trades workers	Skilled office workers and routine office workers (MSF) 41 office clerks; 42 customer service clerks	Skilled service and routine service (LSF) 51 personal and protective services workers; 52 models, salespersons and demonstrators; 91 sales and services elementary occupations	Generally and vocationally skilled workers
	Routine operatives and routine agriculture (BC) 61 market-oriented skilled agricultural and fishery workers; 92 agricultural, fishery, and related laborers; 81 stationary-plant and related operators; 82 machine operators and assemblers; 83 drivers and mobile-plant operators; 93 laborers in mining, construction, manufacturing, and transport			Low- and unskilled workers

Note: Two-digit numbers in front of job descriptions are ISCO88–2d codes.

Appendix 3: Appendix to Chapter 6

Results of the Factor Analysis on French Pension Reforms, 1971–2003

TABLE A3.1. *France: Results of the Factor Analysis on the Pension Law (Loi Boulin), 1971*

	Basic Analysis	Robustness Analysis
Issues of the Reform Debate	Factor 1	Factor 1
Pension increase	0.915	945
One-year educational pension credit	0.795	0.51
Early retirement for disabled workers	0.897	0.895
Eigenvalue	2.14	1.96
Explained variance	71%	65%
N	11	9

Notes: Factor analysis run on the coded positions of the actors; all factors with Eigenvalue ≥ 1; data presented in Appendix 1; basic analysis run with all actors included, and robustness analysis run without Confédération Générale du Travail (CGT) and Conseil National du Patronat Français (CNPF).

TABLE A3.2. *France: Law on Complementary Pensions, 1972*

	Basic Analysis	Robustness Analysis
Issues of the Reform Debate	Factor 1	Factor 1
Mandatory character of the complementary pension programs	0.924	0.966
Pension coverage for unemployed	0.902	0.876
Debate on the harmonization of complementary pensions for managers and employees	0.792	0.925
Eigenvalue	2.3	2.56
Explained variance	76%	85%
N	10	8

Notes: Factor analysis run on the coded positions of the actors; all factors with Eigenvalue ≥ 1; data presented in Appendix 1; basic analysis run with all actors included, and robustness analysis run without Confédération Générale du Travail (CGT) and Conseil National du Patronat Français (CNPF).

TABLE A3.3. *France: Law on Pension Increase, 1975a*

Issues of the Reform Debate	Basic Analysis Factor 1	Robustness Analysis Factor 1	Factor 2
Increase of widows' pensions	0.796	−0.128	0.89
Labor market participation incentives for widows	0.756	0.554	0.652
Three-year educational pension credit	0.811	0.774	0.21
Wider access to insurance	0.763	−0.786	0.345
Eigenvalue	2.45	1.62	1.3
Explained variance	61%	40%	33%
N	11	9	9

Notes: Factor analysis run on the coded positions of the actors; all factors with Eigenvalue ≥ 1; data presented in Appendix 1; basic analysis run with all actors included, and robustness analysis run without Confédération Générale du Travail (CGT) and Conseil National du Patronat Français (CNPF). Without the latter two actors, the solution becomes two-dimensional because most actors – except for the CNPF – are rather favorable to the improvements for widows (factor 2), whereas a class conflict prevails on the educational credit and access to insurance.

TABLE A3.4. *France: Law on Pension Eligibility, 1975b*

Issues of the Reform Debate	Basic Analysis Factor 1	Robustness Analysis Factor 1
Early retirement for workers with particularly long careers	0.974	0.965
Early retirement for mothers of three or more	0.974	0.965
Eigenvalue	1.9	1.864
Explained variance	95%	93%
N	11	9

Notes: Factor analysis run on the coded positions of the actors; all factors with Eigenvalue ≥ 1; data presented in Appendix 1; basic analysis run with all actors included, and robustness analysis run without Confédération Générale du Travail (CGT) and Conseil National du Patronat Français (CNPF).

TABLE A3.5. *France: Pension Law, 1983*

Issues of the Reform Debate	Basic Analysis Factor 1	Robustness Analysis Factor 1
Lowering of the retirement age to 60	0.914	0.891
Introduction of a minimum pension	0.914	0.891
Eigenvalue	1.652	1.589
Explained variance	83%	79%
N	10	8

Notes: Factor analysis run on the coded positions of the actors; all factors with Eigenvalue ≥ 1; data presented in Appendix 1; basic analysis run with all actors included, and robustness analysis run without Confédération Générale du Travail (CGT) and Conseil National du Patronat Français (CNPF).

TABLE A3.6. *France: Law on the Financing of Social Security, 1999*

	Basic Analysis	Robustness Analysis
Issues of the Reform Debate	**Factor 1**	**Factor 1**
Reserve fund (FdR) in the Fonds de Solidarité Vieillesse	0.909	0.958
Indexation of pensions on prices	0.909	0.958
Eigenvalue	1.65	1.83
Explained variance	83%	92%
N	9	7

Notes: Factor analysis run on the coded positions of the actors; all factors with Eigenvalue ≥ 1; data presented in Appendix 1; basic analysis run with all actors included, and robustness analysis run without Confédération Générale du Travail (CGT) and Conseil National du Patronat Français (CNPF).

TABLE A3.7. *France: Law on Income Savings, 2001*

	Basic Analysis	Robustness Analysis
Issues of the Reform Debate	**Factor 1**	**Factor 1**
Individual long-term savings plans	0.934	0.895
Small-business savings plans	0.934	0.895
Eigenvalue	1.75	1.6
Explained variance	87%	80%
N	11	9

Notes: Factor analysis run on the coded positions of the actors; all factors with Eigenvalue ≥ 1; data presented in Appendix 1; basic analysis run with all actors included, and robustness analysis run without Confédération Générale du Travail (CGT) and Conseil National du Patronat Français (CNPF).

Appendix 4: Appendix to Chapter 7

Results of the Factor Analysis on German Pension Reforms, 1972–2004

TABLE A4.1. *Germany: Results of the Factor Analysis on the Pension-Reform Law, 1972*

Issues of the Reform Debate	Basic Analysis Factor 1	Robustness Analysis Factor 1
Lowering of the retirement age (flexible retirement at 63)	0.922	0.909
Introduction of a minimum pension for low-income earners with long careers	0.957	0.967
Voluntary access to the basic public pension scheme for self-employed	0.763	0.834
Voluntary access to the basic public pension scheme for nonemployed	0.643	0.679
Acceleration of pension indexation	0.846	0.813
Educational pension credit (one year)	0.806	0.789
Eigenvalue	4.12	4.2
Explained variance	69%	78%
N	11	9

Notes: Factor analysis was run on the coded positions of the actors; all factors with Eigenvalue ≥ 1; data are presented in Appendix 1; basic analysis run with all actors included, and robustness analysis run without Deutscher Gewerkschaftsbund (DGB) and Bundesvereinigung der Deutschen Arbeitgeberverbände (BDA).

TABLE A4.2. *Germany: Results of the Factor Analysis on the Law on the Improvement of Occupational Pensions, 1974*

Issues of the Reform Debate	Basic Analysis Factor 1	Robustness Analysis Factor 1
Increase of occupational pension levels (lower age of retirement and indexation)	0.987	0.999
Guarantee of individual pension savings in case of labor market mobility	0.987	0.999
Eigenvalue	1.92	1.99
Explained variance	97%	98%
N	8	6

Notes: Factor analysis was run on the coded positions of the actors; all factors with Eigenvalue ≥1; data are presented in Appendix 1; basic analysis run with all actors included, and robustness analysis run without Deutscher Gewerkschaftsbund (DGB) and Bundesvereinigung der Deutschen Arbeitgeberverbände (BDA).

TABLE A4.3. *Germany: Results of the Factor Analysis on the Law on the Pension Adaptation, 1977*

Issues of the Reform Debate	Basic Analysis Factor 1	Robustness Analysis Factor 1	Factor 2
Postponing of pension indexation	0.786	0.51	0.843
Increase of pension contribution levels (*Beitragsbemessungsgrenze*)	0.937	0.906	0.008
Increase of contributions to the pension scheme by unemployment and sickness insurance schemes	0.711	0.806	−0.538
Lowering of reserve funds for the basic pension scheme	0.932	0.964	−0.007
Eigenvalue	2.87	2.65	1
Explained variance	72%	67%	25%
N	10	8	8

Notes: Factor analysis was run on the coded positions of the actors; all factors with Eigenvalue ≥1; data are presented in Appendix 1; basic analysis run with all actors included, and robustness analysis run without Deutscher Gewerkschaftsbund (DGB) and Bundesvereinigung der Deutschen Arbeitgeberverbände (BDA).

TABLE A4.4. *Germany: Results of the Factor Analysis on the Law on the Public Budget,*
1983

	Basic Analysis	Robustness Analysis
Issues of the Reform Debate	Factor 1	Factor 1
Postponing of pension indexation	0.98	0.955
Increase of contribution rates to basic pension scheme	0.958	0.949
Increase of sickness insurance contributions to be paid by pensioners	0.96	0.952
Eigenvalue	2.8	2.71
Explained variance	93%	90%
N	8	6

Notes: Factor analysis was run on the coded positions of the actors; all factors with Eigenvalue ≥ 1; data are presented in Appendix 1; basic analysis run with all actors included, and robustness analysis run without Deutscher Gewerkschaftsbund (DGB) and Bundesvereinigung der Deutschen Arbeitgeberverbände (BDA).

TABLE A4.5. *Germany: Results of the Factor Analysis on the Reform of Widows' Pensions*
and Educational Benefits, 1985

	Basic Analysis	Robustness Analysis
Issues of the Reform Debate	Factor 1	Factor 1
Expansion of minimum pension regulations	0.875	0.863
Harmonization of widows' and widowers' pensions	0.877	0.846
One-year educational pension credit	0.859	0.785
Eigenvalue	2.27	2.07
Explained variance	76%	69%
N	12	10

Notes: Factor analysis was run on the coded positions of the actors; all factors with Eigenvalue ≥ 1; data are presented in Appendix 1; basic analysis run with all actors included, and robustness analysis run without Deutscher Gewerkschaftsbund (DGB) and Bundesvereinigung der Deutschen Arbeitgeberverbände (BDA).

TABLE A4.6. *Germany: Results of the Factor Analysis on the Pension-Reform Law, 1996*

	Basic Analysis	Robustness Analysis
Issues of the Reform Debate	Factor 1	Factor 1
Increase of the retirement age	0.967	0.986
Lowering of coverage in case of career interruptions for training	0.96	0.948
Cuts in disability payments by the basic pension scheme	0.974	0.967
Coverage of marginally employed workers by the pension insurance	0.941	0.941
Eigenvalue	3.69	3.69
Explained variance	92%	92%
N	13	11

Notes: Factor analysis was run on the coded positions of the actors; all factors with Eigenvalue ≥ 1; data are presented in Appendix 1; basic analysis run with all actors included, and robustness analysis run without Deutscher Gewerkschaftsbund (DGB) and Bundesvereinigung der Deutschen Arbeitgeberverbände (BDA).

TABLE A4.7. *Germany: Results of the Factor Analysis on the Pension-Reform Law, 1997*

	Basic Analysis		Robustness Analysis	
Issues of the Reform Debate	Factor 1	Factor 2	Factor 1	Factor 2
Lowering of pension levels (demographic factor)	0.64	0.715	0.512	0.823
Cuts in early retirement options	0.04	0.932	0.05	0.939
Lowering of disability pensions	0.45	0.737	0.305	0.868
Increase of value-added tax for federal pension subsidies	0.87	0.113	0.874	0.261
Debate on the introduction of a means-tested universal pension coverage	0.693	0.292	0.685	0.163
Increase of educational pension credits	0.932	0.175	0.954	0.125
Debate on an individualized pension insurance coverage for women	0.813	0.505	0.785	0.525
Eigenvalue	4.62	1.06	4.53	1.29
Explained variance	66%	15%	65%	18%
N	14	14	12	12

Notes: Factor analysis was run on the coded positions of the actors; all factors with Eigenvalue ≥ 1; data are presented in Appendix 1; basic analysis run with all actors included, and robustness analysis run without Deutscher Gewerkschaftsbund (DGB) and Bundesvereinigung der Deutschen Arbeitgeberverbände (BDA).

TABLE A4.8. *Germany: Results of the Factor Analysis on the Bill on Corrections in Social Insurance Law, 1998*

Issues of the Reform Debate	Basic Analysis Factor 1	Robustness Analysis Factor 1
Abolition of the 1997 demographic factor	0.974	0.975
Abolition of the 1997 cuts in disability pensions	0.981	0.981
Improved coverage of part-time employees in the basic pension scheme	0.916	0.925
Eigenvalue	2.75	2.77
Explained variance	92%	92%
N	10	8

Notes: Factor analysis was run on the coded positions of the actors; all factors with Eigenvalue ≥ 1; data are presented in Appendix 1; basic analysis run with all actors included, and robustness analysis run without Deutscher Gewerkschaftsbund (DGB) and Bundesvereinigung der Deutschen Arbeitgeberverbände (BDA).

TABLE A4.9. *Germany: Results of the Factor Analysis on the Reform of Disability Pensions, 2000*

Issues of the Reform Debate	Basic Analysis Factor 1	Robustness Analysis Factor 1
Direct payments of the unemployment insurance to the basic pension scheme for coverage of unemployed	0.829	0.809
Cuts in disability pension levels	0.938	0.917
Introduction of a new disability pension scheme with lower benefits	0.945	0.928
Eigenvalue	2.46	2.36
Explained variance	82%	79%
N	9	7

Notes: Factor analysis was run on the coded positions of the actors; all factors with Eigenvalue ≥ 1; data are presented in Appendix 1; basic analysis run with all actors included, and robustness analysis run without Deutscher Gewerkschaftsbund (DGB) and Bundesvereinigung der Deutschen Arbeitgeberverbände (BDA).

TABLE A4.10. *Germany: Results of the Factor Analysis on the Reform of Civil Servants Pensions, 2001*

	Basic Analysis	Robustness Analysis
Issues of the Reform Debate	Factor 1	Factor 1
Introduction of individual pension savings plans for civil servants	0.783	0.588
Lowering of benefit levels for civil servants	0.825	0.828
Lowering of the level of widow's pensions for civil servants	0.882	0.884
Increase of educational pension credits for civil servants	0.856	0.783
Eigenvalue	2.8	2.45
Explained variance	70%	60%
N	12	10

Notes: Factor analysis was run on the coded positions of the actors; all factors with Eigenvalue ≥ 1; data are presented in Appendix 1; basic analysis run with all actors included, and robustness analysis run without Deutscher Gewerkschaftsbund (DGB) and Bundesvereinigung der Deutschen Arbeitgeberverbände (BDA).

TABLE A4.11. *Germany: Results of the Factor Analysis on the Law on Pension Sustainability 2004*

	Basic Analysis		Robustness Analysis	
Issues of the Reform Debate	Factor 1	Factor 2	Factor 1	Factor 2
Lowering of general pension benefit levels (Nachhaltigkeitsfaktor)	0.641	0.631	0.882	−0.259
Cuts in early retirement options	0.935	0.218	0.884	0.427
Lowering of pension coverage in case of employment interruption for training	0.444	0.81	−0.159	0.96
Introduction of a target minimum replacement rate (46%) and a maximum contribution rate (22%)	0.962	0.164	0.851	0.152
Increase in pension coverage for families	0.045	0.928	0.342	0.687
Eigenvalue:	3.39	1.01	2.57	1.52
explained variance	68%	20%	51%	30%
N	10	10	8	8

Notes: Factor analysis run on the coded positions of the actors; all factors with Eigenvalue ≥ 1; data are presented in Appendix A; basic analysis run with all actors included, and robustness analysis run without Deutscher Gewerkschaftsbund (DGB) and Bundesvereinigung der Deutschen Arbeitgeberverbände (BDA).

Appendix 5: Appendix to Chapter 8

Results of the Factor Analysis on Swiss Pension Reforms, 1971–2003

TABLE A5.1. *Switzerland: Results of the Factor Analysis on Eighth Reform of the Basic Pension Scheme (AHV), 1972*

Issues of the Reform Debate	Basic Analysis Factor 1	Robustness Analysis Factor 1
Pension level increase of 25%	0.951	0.926
Indexation of pensions on prices and wages	0.925	0.911
Introduction of a 13th pension benefit per year	0.882	0.798
Reduction of the tax-financed public subsidies to the insurance scheme	0.856	0.754
Increase of earnings-related contributions to pension insurance	0.530	0.495
Eigenvalue	3.55	3.14
Explained variance	98%	97%
N	10	8

Notes: Factor analysis run on the coded positions of the actors; all factors with Eigenvalue ≥ 1; data presented in Appendix 1; basic analysis run with all actors included, and robustness analysis run without Partei der Arbeit (PdA) and Schweizerischer Arbeitgeberverband (SAV).

TABLE A5.2. *Switzerland: Results of the Factor Analysis on the Ninth Reform of the Basic Pension Scheme (AHV), 1976*

Issues of the Reform Debate	Basic Analysis		Robustness Analysis	
	Factor 1	Factor 2	Factor 1	Factor 2
Indexation of pensions on wages and prices	0.473	0.611	−0.077	0.962
Increase of tax-financed public subsidies to pension insurance	−0.215	0.754	−0.334	−0.609
Increase of contribution levels for employed pensioners	0.983	0.004	0.825	0.47
Increase of the minimum contribution to pension insurance	0.474	0.808	0.501	0.668
Increase of contribution levels for self-employed	0.976	−0.108	0.86	0.404
Lowering of derived benefits for spouses	−0.224	0.833	0.919	0.09
Eigenvalue	2.57	2.15	3.52	1.24
Explained variance	43%	36%	59%	21%
N	9	9	7	7

Notes: Factor analysis run on the coded positions of the actors; all factors with Eigenvalue ≥ 1; data presented in Appendix 1; basic analysis run with all actors included, and robustness analysis run without. Schweizerischer Gewerkschaftsbund (SGB) and Schweizerischer Arbeitgeberverband (SAV).

TABLE A5.3. *Switzerland: Results of the Factor Analysis on the Law on the Occupational Pension Scheme (BVG), 1982*

Issues of the Reform Debate	Basic Analysis	Robustness Analysis
	Factor 1	Factor 1
Expansion of occupational pension savings plans	0.85	0.822
Introduction of combined replacement-rate target level for public and occupational pensions	0.876	0.854
Mandatory occupational second-pillar pension insurance for standard employees	0.904	0.9
Eigenvalue	2.307	2.21
Explained variance	77%	74%
N	20	18

Notes: Factor analysis run on the coded positions of the actors; all factors with Eigenvalue ≥ 1; data presented in Appendix 1; basic analysis run with all actors included, and robustness analysis run without Schweizerischer Gewerkschaftsbund (SGB) and Schweizerischer Arbeitgeberverband (SAV).

TABLE A5.4. *Switzerland: Results of the Factor Analysis on the Second Reform of the Complementary Pension Scheme (EL), 1985*

Issues of the Reform Debate	Basic Analysis		Robustness Analysis	
	Factor 1	Factor 2	Factor 1	Factor 2
Increase of means-tested complementary pension benefits	0.903	0.191	0.922	0.057
Increased complementary benefits for long-term-care patients	0.873	0.108	0.91	0.033
Increase of benefits for homeowners	0.753	0.187	0.804	0.222
Lowering of complementary benefits for pensioners with own savings	0.001	0.912	−0.068	0.958
Increase of individual financial responsibility in case of sickness	0.487	0.552	0.711	0.495
Measures to fight abuses	0.264	0.732	0.362	0.554
Eigenvalue	3.04	1.17	3.28	1.2
Explained variance	51%	19%	55%	20%
N	21	21	19	19

Notes: Factor analysis run on the coded positions of the actors; all factors with Eigenvalue ≥1; data presented in Appendix 1; basic analysis run with all actors included, and robustness analysis run without Schweizerischer Gewerkschaftsbund (SGB) and Schweizerischer Arbeitgeberverband (SAV).

TABLE A5.5. *Switzerland: Results of the Factor Analysis on the Reform of the Labor Market Mobility in the Occupational Pension Scheme (FZG-BVG), 1994*

Issues of the Reform Debate	Basic Analysis	Robustness Analysis
	Factor 1	Factor 1
Guarantee of individual pension savings in case of labor market mobility	0.876	0.926
Harmonization of occupational second-pillar pension schemes	0.901	0.935
No dissolution of pension savings for women in case of marriage	0.909	0.937
Splitting of second-pillar savings between spouses in case of divorce	0.886	3.413
Eigenvalue	3.189	3.413
Explained variance	80%	85%
N	25	23

Notes: Factor analysis run on the coded positions of the actors; all factors with Eigenvalue ≥1; data presented in Appendix 1; basic analysis run with all actors included, and robustness analysis run without Schweizerischer Gewerkschaftsbund (SGB) and Schweizerischer Arbeitgeberverband (SAV).

TABLE A5.6. *Switzerland: Results of the Factor Analysis on the Third Reform of the Complementary Pension Scheme (EL), 1996*

Issues of the Reform Debate	Basic Analysis		Robustness Analysis	
	Factor 1	Factor 2	Factor 1	Factor 2
Increase of rent deductions for poor pensioners	0.68	−0.276	0.814	0.29
Lowering of waiting periods for complementary pensions for foreigners	0.943	0.05	0.872	−0.072
Increase of complementary pensions for homeowners	0.051	0.951	0.053	0.86
Improved information for pensioners about benefit eligibility	0.406	−0.693	0.83	0.023
Eigenvalue	1.87	1.12	2.17	1.01
Explained variance	47%	28%	54%	25%
N	19	19	17	17

Notes: Factor analysis run on the coded positions of the actors; all factors with Eigenvalue ≥1; data presented in Appendix 1; basic analysis run with all actors included, and robustness analysis run without Schweizerischer Gewerkschaftsbund (SGB) and Schweizerischer Arbeitgeberverband (SAV).

TABLE A5.7. *Switzerland: Results of the Factor Analysis on the Eleventh Reform of the Basic Pension Scheme (AHV), 2003*

Issues of the Reform Debate	Basic Analysis	Robustness Analysis
	Factor 1	Factor 1
Increase of the retirement age	0.914	0.882
Cutbacks in widows' pension levels	0.746	0.64
Flexible retirement age (without public subsidies for lower income earners)	0.91	0.907
Cutbacks in pension indexation	0.932	0.907
Increase in contribution levels for self-employed	−0.788	−0.774
Eigenvalue	3.71	3.42
Explained variance	74%	69%
N	19	17

Notes: Factor analysis run on the coded positions of the actors; all factors with Eigenvalue ≥1; data presented in Appendix 1; basic analysis run with all actors included, and robustness analysis run without Schweizerischer Gewerkschaftsbund (SGB) and Schweizerischer Arbeitgeberverband (SAV).

References

Abrahamsen, Yngve, Jochen Hartwig and Bernd Schips (2003). Volkswirtschaftliche Auswirkungen verschiedener Demographieszenarien und Varianten zur langfristigen Finanzierung der Alterssicherung in der Schweiz. *Forschungsbericht Nr. 12/03. Bundesamt für Sozialversicherungen*. Bern: Beiträge zur Sozialen, Sicherheit.

Abramovici, Gérard (2002). "Der Sozialschutz: Rentenausgaben", *Statistik kurz gefasst. Thema 3–6/2002*. Luxembourg: Eurostat: 1–8.

Alber, Jens (1987). *Der Sozialstaat in der Bundesrepublik 1950–1983*. Frankfurt: Campus.

Alber, Jens (2001). "Recent Developments of the German Welfare State: Basic Continuity or Paradigm Shift," ZeS Working Paper 6/2001. Bremen: Centre for Social Policy Research, University of Bremen.

Allmendinger, Jutta (2000). "Wandel von Erwerbs – und Lebensverläufen und die Ungleichheit zwischen den Geschlechtern im Alterseinkommen," in Winfried Schmähl und Klaus Michaelis (eds.), *Alterssicherung von Frauen. Leitbilder, gesellschaftlicher Wandel und Reformen*. Wiesbaden: Westdeutscher, Verlag, 61–80.

Amenta, Edwin (2003). "What We Know about the Development of Social Policy: Comparative and Historical Research in Comparative and Historical Perspective," in James Mahoney and Dietrich Rueschemeyer (eds.), *Comparative Historical Analysis in the Social Sciences*. Cambridge: Cambridge University Press, 91–130.

Anderson Karen (2007). "The Netherlands: Political competition in a proportional system," in Ellen M. Immergut, Karen M. Anderson, and Isabelle Schulze (eds.), *The Handbook of West European Pension Politics*. Oxford: Oxford University Press, 713–57.

Anderson Karen and Ellen M. Immergut (2007). "Sweden: After Social Democratic Hegemony," in Ellen M. Immergut, Karen M. Anderson and Isabelle Schulze (eds.), *The Handbook of West European Pension Politics*. Oxford: Oxford University Press, 349–95.

Anderson, Karen and Julia Lynch (2007). "Reconsidering Seniority Bias: Ageing, Internal Institutions, and Union Support for Pension Reform," *Comparative Politics* 39(2): 189–208.

Anderson, Karen M. and Traute Meyer (2003). "Social Democracy, Unions and Pension Politics in Germany and Sweden," *Journal of Public Policy* 23(1): 23–54.

Anderson, Karen and Traute Meyer (2004). "The Third Way in Welfare State Reform? Social Democratic Pension Politics in Germany and Sweden," in Giuliano Bonoli and Martin Powell (eds.), *Social Democratic Party Policies in Contemporary Europe*. London: Routledge, 141–60.

Anderson, Karen M. and Traute Meyer (2006). "New Social Risks and Pension Reform in Germany and Sweden: The Politics of Pension Rights for Childcare," in Klaus Armingeon and Giuliano Bonoli (eds.), *The Politics of Post-Industrial Welfare States*. London: Routledge, 171–91.

Anderson, Robert and Jocelyn A. J. Evans (2003). "Values, Cleavages and Party Choice in France 1988–1995," *French Politics* 1: 83–114.

Armingeon, Klaus (1988). *Die Entwicklung der westdeutschen Gewerkschaften 1950–1985*. Frankfurt: Campus, Verlag.

Armingeon, Klaus (2001). "Institutionalising the Swiss Welfare State," *West European Politics* 24(2), 145–68.

Armingeon, Klaus (2004). "Institutional Change in OECD Democracies, 1970–2000," *Comparative European Politics* 2(2): 212–38.

Armingeon, Klaus (2006). "Reconciling Competing Claims of the Welfare State Clientele," in Klaus Armingeon and Giuliano Bonoli (eds.), *The Politics of Post-Industrial Welfare States*. London: Routledge, 100–122.

Armingeon, Klaus, Fabio Bertozzi, and Giuliano Bonoli (2004). "Swiss Worlds of Welfare," *West European Politics* 27(1): 20–44.

Armingeon, Klaus and Michelle Beyeler (2000). "Gewerkschaftsmitgliedschaft: Beitrittsmotive und Fragmentierungen," in Klaus Armingeon and Simon Geissbühler (eds.), *Gewerkschaften in der Schweiz. Herausforderungen und Optionen*. Zurich: Seismo, 39–69.

Armingeon, Klaus and Giuliano Bonoli (2006). *The Politics of Post-Industrial Welfare States*. London: Routledge.

Baccaro, Lucio (2002). "Negotiating the Italian Pension Reform with the Unions: Lessons for Corporatist Theory," *Industrial and Labor Relations Review* 55(3): 413–31.

Baldwin, Peter (1990). *The Politics of Social Solidarity: Class Bases of the European Welfare States 1875–1975*. Cambridge: Cambridge University Press.

Ballestri, Yuri and Giuliano Bonoli (2003). "L'état social suisse face aux nouveaux risques sociaux : Genèse et déterminants de l'adoption du programme de subventions pour les crèches," *Swiss Political Science Review* 9(3): 35–58.

Balthasar, Andreas, Oliver Bieri, Peter Grau, Kilian Küenzi, and Jürg Guggisberg (2003). *Der Übergang in den Ruhestand – Wege, Einflussfaktoren und Konsequenzen. Bericht im Rahmen des Forschungsprogrammes zur längerfristigen Zukunft der Alterssicherung*. Forschungsbericht, Nr. 2/03. Bundesamt für Sozialversicherungen. Bern: Beiträge zur Sozialen, Sicherheit.

Bartolini, Stefano (2000). *The Political Mobilization of the European Left, 1860-1980: The Class Cleavage*. Cambridge: Cambridge University Press.

Baumgartner, Frank and Bryan D. Jones (1993). *Agendas and Instability in American Politics*. Chicago: University of Chicago Press.

Baumgartner, Frank and Bryan D. Jones (2002). *Policy Dynamics*. Chicago: University of Chicago Press.

Bertozzi, Fabio, Giuliano Bonoli, and Benoît Gay-des-Combes (2005). *La réforme de l'état social en Suisse. Vieillissement, Employ, Conflict Travail-Famille*. Lausanne: Presses Polytechniques et Universitaires, Romandes.

Binswanger, Peter (1987). *Histoire de l'AVS*. Bern: Pro, Senectute.

Birchfield, Vicki and Markus M. L. Crepaz (1998). "The Impact of Constitutional Structures and Collective and Competitive Veto Points on Income Inequality in Industrialized Democracies," *European Journal of Political Research* 34: 175–200.

Bleses, Peter and Martin Seeleib-Kaiser (2004). *The Dual Transformation of the German Welfare State*. Basingstoke, U.K.: Palgrave Macmillan.

Bonoli, Giuliano (1997). "Pension Politics in France: Patterns of Co-operation and Conflict in Two Recent Reforms," *West European Politics* 20(4): 160–81.

Bonoli, Giuliano (1999). "La 10e révision de l'AVS : une politique consensuelle de retranchement?" in André Mach (ed.), *Globalisation, néo-libéralisme et politiques publiques dans la Suisse des années 1990*. Zurich, Seismo, 191–216.

Bonoli, Giuliano (2000). *The Politics of Pension Reform: Institutions and Policy Change in Western Europe*. Cambridge: Cambridge University Press.

Bonoli, Giuliano (2001a). "The Institutionalization of the Swiss Multipillar System," paper presented at the conference Political Economy of Pension Reform, Institute for Advanced Studies, Delmenhorst (Germany), May 3–5.

Bonoli, Giuliano (2001b). "Political Institutions, Veto Points, and the Process of Welfare State Adaptation," in Paul Pierson (ed.), *The New Politics of the Welfare State*. Oxford: Oxford University Press, 238–264.

Bonoli, Giuliano (2004). "The Institutionalisation of the Swiss Multipillar Pension System," in Martin Rein and Winfried Schmähl (eds.), *The Political Economy of Pension Reform*. London: Edward Elgar- 102–22.

Bonoli, Giuliano (2005a). "The Politics of the New Social Policies: Providing Coverage against New Social Risks in Mature Welfare States," *Policy and Politics* 33(3): 431–49.

Bonoli, Giuliano (2005b). "Switzerland: Negotiating a New Welfare State in a Fragmented Political System," in Peter Taylor-Gooby (ed.), *New Risks, New Welfare: The Transformation of the European Welfare State*. Oxford: Oxford University Press, 157–180.

Bonoli, Giuliano (2006a) "Les politiques sociales," in Ulrich Klöti, Peter Knoepfel, Hanspeter Kriesi, Wolf Linder, Yannis Papadopoulos, and Pascal Sciarini (eds.), *Handbuch der Schweizer Politik*, 4th ed. Zurich: NZZ, Verlag.

Bonoli, Giuliano (2006b). "New Social Risks and the Politics of Post-Industrial Social Policies," in Klaus Armingeon and Giuliano Bonoli (eds.), *The Politics of Post-Industrial Welfare States: Adapting Post-War Social Policies to New Social Risks*. London: Routledge.

Bonoli, Giuliano (2007). "Time Matters: Postindustrialization, New Social Risks and Welfare State Adaptation in Advanced Industrial Democracies," *Comparative Political Studies* 40(5): 495–520.

Bonoli, Giuliano, Vic George, and Peter Taylor-Gooby (2000). *European Welfare Futures: Towards a Theory of Retrenchment*. Cambridge: Polity Press.

Bonoli, Giuliano and Benoît Gay-des-Combes (2003). "Prospektive Simulation der Altersvorsorge vor dem Zeithorizont 2040," *Soziale Sicherheit CHSS* 3: 125–7.

Bonoli, Giuliano and André Mach (2000). "Switzerland: Adjustment Politics within Institutional Constraints," in Fritz W. Scharpf and Vivien A. Schmidt (eds.), *Welfare and Work in the Open Economy, vol. 2, Diverse Responses to Common Challenges*. Oxford: Oxford University Press, 131–174.

Bonoli, Giuliano and Bruno Palier (1998). "Changing the Politics of Social Programmes: Innovative Change in British and French Welfare Reforms," *Journal of European Social Policy* 8(4): 317–30.

Bonoli, Giuliano and Bruno Palier (2000). "How Do Welfare States Change? Institutions and Their Impact on the Politics of Welfare State Reform," *European Review* 8(2): 333–52.

Bonoli, Giuliano and Bruno Palier (2007). "When Past Reforms Open New Opportunities: Comparing Old Age Insurance Reforms in Bismarckian Welfare Systems," *Social Policy and Administration* 41(6): 555–73.

Bornschier, Simon (2005). "Unis dans l'opposition à la mondialisation? Une analyse de la convergence programmatique des partis populistes de droite en Europe," *Revue Internationale de Politique Comparée* 12(4): 415–32.

Bornschier, Simon (2010). *Cleavage Politics and the Populist Right: The New Cultural Conflict in Western Europe.* Philadelphia: Temple University Press.

Boyer, Robert (1990). *The Regulation School: A Critical Introduction.* New York: Columbia University Press.

Branger, Katja (2000). *Lebensbedingungen älterer Menschen in der Schweiz unter besonderer Berücksichtigung der Dimension Geschlecht.* Discussion Document for the United Nations Economic Commission for Europe (UNECE) Working Session on Gender Statistics, Orvieto, Italy, October 11–13.

Bridgen, Paul and Traute Meyer (2008). "Politically Dominant but Socially Flawed: Projected Pension Levels for Citizens at Risk in Six European Multi-Pillar Pension Systems," in Martin Seeleib-Kaiser (ed.), *Welfare State Transformations: Comparative Perspectives.* Basingstoke, U.K.: Palgrave Macmillan, 111–131.

Bruhnes, Bernard (1992). *Rapport sur les retraites.* Paris: La Documentation française.

Budge, Ian, Hans-Dieter Klingemann, Andrea Volkens, Judith Bara, Eric Tanenbaum, Richard C. Fording, Derek J. Hearl, Hee Min Kim, Michael McDonals, and Silvia Mendez (2001). *Mapping Policy Preferences: Estimates for Parties, Electors and Governments 1945–1998.* Oxford: Oxford University Press.

Bundesamt für Sozialversicherungen (1995). *Bericht des eidgenössischen Departementes des Innern zur heutigen Ausgestaltung und Weiterentwicklung der schweizerischen 3-Säulen-Konzeption der Alters-, Hinterlassenen – und Invalidenvorsorge.* Bern: Beiträge zur Sozialen, Sicherheit.

Bundesamt für Sozialversicherungen (2003). *Statistik der Ergänzungsleistungen zur AHV und IV 2002.* Bern: Beiträge zur Sozialen, Sicherheit.

Bundesamt für Statistik (2001). *Szenarien zur Bevölkerungsentwicklung der Schweiz 2000–2060.* Neuchâtel: Bundesamt für Statistik.

Bundesamt für Statistik (2003). *Die schweizerische Altersvorsorge im Spiegel der Einkommens – und Verbrauchserhebung 1998.* Neuchâtel: Bundesamt für Statistik.

Bundesamt für Statistik (2004). *Die berufliche Vorsorge in der Schweiz. Pensionskassenstatistik 2002.* Neuchâtel: Bundesamt für Statistik.

Bunel, Jean (1995) *La transformation de la representation patronale en France, CNPF et CGPME.* Paris: Commissariat General du Plan.

Busemeyer, Marius R. (2005). "Pension Reform in Germany and Austria: System Change vs. Quantitative Retrenchment," *West European Politics* 28(3): 569–91.

Campbell, Andrea L. and Julia Lynch (2000). "Whose 'Gray Power'? Elderly Voters, Elderly Lobbies, and Welfare Reform in Italy and the United States," *Italian Politics and Society* 53: 11–39.

Castles, Francis G. (2004). *The Future of the Welfare State: Crisis Myths and Crisis Realities.* Oxford: Oxford University Press.

Cattacin, Sandro, Matteo Gianni, Marcus Mänz, and Véronique Tattini (2002). *Retour au Travail! Le Workfare comme Instrument de Réforme.* Fribourg: Presses Universitaires de Fribourg.

Cattell, Raymond B. (1978). *The Scientific Use of Factor Analysis in Behavioral Sciences*. NewYork: Plenum.

Charpin, Jean-Michel, Catherine Zaidman and Jean-Marc Aubert (1999). *L'avenir de nos retraites. Rapport au Premier ministre*. Paris: La Documentation française.

Chulià, Elisa (2007). "Spain: Between Majority Rule and Incrementalism," in Ellen M. Immergut, Karen M. Anderson, and Isabelle Schulze (eds.), *The Handbook of West European Pension Politics*. Oxford: Oxford University Press, 499–554.

Clasen, Jochen and Daniel Clegg (2006). "Beyond Activation: Reforming European Unemployment Protection Systems in Post-Industrial Labour Markets," *European Societies* 8 (4): 527–53.

Clayton, Richard and Jonas Pontusson (1998). "Welfare-State Retrenchment Revisited: Entitlement Cuts, Public Sector Restructuring and Inegalitarian Trends in Advanced Capitalist Societies," *World Politics* 51 (October): 67–98.

Clegg, Daniel (2007). "Continental Drift: On Unemployment Policy Change in Bismarckian Welfare States," *Social Policy and Administration* 41(6): 597–617.

Commaille, Jacques, Pierre Strobel, and Michel Villac (2002). *La politique de la famille*. Paris: Editions la Découverte.

Commissariat général du Plan (1991). *Rapport de la mission Retraites, Mission Cottave*. Paris: La Documentation française.

CONSOC Recherche (2003). *Situation économique des rentiers. Analyse introductive et générale dans la perspective d'une 13ème rente AVS*. Report by Valérie Legrand-Germanier and Stéphane Rossini for the Swiss Union of Trade Unions. Bern: CONSOC Recherche.

Cooke, Lynn Prince (2001). "Impact of Dual Careers on Average Family Size: Comparison of 11 Countries," Luxembourg Income Study Working Paper No. 267. Luxembourg: Luxembourg Income Study.

Da Conceiçao-Heldt, Eugénia (2006). "France: The Importance of the Electoral Cycle," in Ellen M. Immergut, Karen M. Anderson, and Isabelle Schulze (eds.), *The Handbook of West European Pension Politics*. Oxford: Oxford University Press, 150–201.

Dafflon, Bernard (2003). *La politique familiale en Suisse: enjeux et défis*. Lausanne: Réalités Sociales.

Deitch, C. (2004). "Gender and Popular Support for the Welfare State: Cross-National Trends in a Period of Restructuring," paper prepared at the International Sociological Association Research Committee 19 conference Welfare State Restructuring: Processes and Social Outcomes, Paris, September 2–4.

Dienel, Christiane (2002). *Familienpolitik. Eine praxisorientierte Gesamtdarstellung der Handlungsfelder und Probleme*. Weinheim: Juventa.

Ebbinghaus, Bernhard and Jelle Visser (2000). *The Societies of Europe: Trade Unions in Western Europe since 1945*. New York: Palgrave, Macmillan.

Ebbinghaus, Bernhard (2001). "When Labour and Capital Collude: The Political Economy of Early Retirement in Europe, Japan and the USA," in Bernhard Ebbinghaus and Philip Manow (eds.), *Comparing Welfare Capitalism. Social Policy and Political Economy in Europe, Japan and the USA*. London: Routledge, 76–101.

Ebbinghaus, Bernhard (2006a). "From Path Dependence to Path Departure in Welfare Reform Analysis," *European Politics and Society Newsletter* 5(2): 1–4.

Ebbinghaus, Bernhard (2006b). "Trade Union Movements in Post-Industrial Welfare States: Opening Up to New Social Interests?" in Klaus Armingeon and Giuliano Bonoli (eds.), *The Politics of Post-Industrial Welfare States: Adapting Post-War Policies To New Social Risks*. London: Routledge, 123–142.

Ebbinghaus, Bernhard and Philip Manow (2001). *Comparing Welfare Capitalism. Social Policy and Political Economy in Europe, Japan and the USA*. London: Routledge.

Eidgenössische Finanzkontrolle (2004). *Berufliche Vorsorge. Evaluation der Besteuerung und Vorsorgewirkung von Kapitalzahlungen aus den Säulen 2 und 3a*. Bern: Eidgenössische Finanzkontrolle.

Engeli, Isabelle and Silja Häusermann (2009). "Government Strategies for Successful Reforms in Controversial Policy Fields," EUI Working Paper SPS No. 2009/1. European University Institute, Florence.

Erikson, R. and J. H. Goldthorpe (1993). *The Constant Flux*. Oxford: Oxford University Press.

Esping-Andersen, Gösta (1990). *The Three Worlds of Welfare Capitalism*. Princeton, NJ: Princeton University Press.

Esping-Andersen, Gösta (1996a). "After the Golden Age? Welfare State Dilemmas in a Global Economy," in Gösta Esping-Andersen (ed.), *Welfare States in Transition: National Adaptations in Global Economies*. London: Sage, 1–32.

Esping-Andersen, Gösta (1996b). "Welfare States without Work: The Impasse of Labour Shedding and Familialism in Continental European Social Policy," in Gösta Esping-Andersen (ed.), *Welfare States in Transition: National Adaptations in Global Economies*. London: Sage: 66–87.

Esping-Andersen, Gösta (1999a). "Politics without Class? Post-Industrial Cleavages in Europe and America," in Herbert Kitschelt, Peter Lange, Gary Marks, and John D. Stephens (eds.), *Continuity and Change in Contemporary Capitalism*. Cambridge: Cambridge University Press, 293–316.

Esping-Andersen, Gösta (1999b). *Social Foundations of Postindustrial Economies*. Oxford: Oxford University Press.

Esping-Andersen, Gösta and Marino Regini (2000). *Why Deregulate Labor Markets?* Oxford: Oxford University Press.

Estevez-Abe, Margarita (2006). "Gendering the Varieties of Capitalism: A Study of Occupational Segregation by Sex in Advanced Industrial Societies," *World Politics* 59 (1): 142–75.

Estevez-Abe, Margarita, Torben Iversen, and David Soskice (2001). "Social Protection and the Formation of Skills: A Reinterpretation of the Welfare State," in Peter A. Hall and David Soskice (eds.), *Varieties of Capitalism: The Institutional Foundations of Comparative Advantage*. New York: Oxford University Press, 145–183.

Fagnani, Jeanne and Marie-Thérèse Letablier (2005). "La politique familiale française," in M. Maruani (ed.), *Femmes, genre et société*, 167–75, Collection l'État des Savoirs. Paris: La Découverte.

Ferrera, Maurizio (1996). "The Southern Model of Welfare in Social Europe," *Journal of European Social Policy* 6(1): 17–37.

Ferrera, Maurizio and Elisabetta Gualmini (2000). "Italy. Rescue from Without?" in Fritz W. Scharpf and Vivien A. Schmidt (eds.), *Welfare and Work in the Open Economy*, vol. 2, *Diverse Responses to Common Challenges*. Oxford: Oxford University Press, 351–398.

Ferrera, Maurizio and Elisabetta Gualmini (2004). *Rescued by Europe? Social and Labour Market Reforms in Italy from Maastricht to Berlusconi*. Amsterdam: Amsterdam University Press.

Ferrera, Maurizio, Anton Hemerijck, and Martin Rhodes (2004). *The Future of European Welfare States: Recasting Welfare for a New Century*. Oxford: Oxford University Press.

Ferrera, Maurizio and Matteo Jessoula (2007). "Italy: A Narrow Gate for Path-Shift," in Ellen M. Immergut, Karen M. Anderson, and Isabelle Schulze (eds.), *The Handbook of West European Pension Politics*. Oxford: Oxford University Press, 396–453.

Finlayson, Ann (1988). *Whose Money Is It Anyway? The Showdown on Pensions*. Markham: Penguin.

Flora, Peter and Jens Alber (1981). "Modernization, Democratization and the Development of Welfare States in Western Europe," in Peter Flora and Arnold Heidenheimer (eds.), *The Development of Welfare States in Europe and America*. New Brunswick, NJ: Transaction Books.

Fluder, Robert (1996). *Interessenorganisationen und kollektive Arbeitsbeziehungen im öffentlichen Dienst der Schweiz: Entstehung, Mitgliedschaft, Organisation und Politik seit 1940*. Zurich, Seismo.

Fluder, Robert, H. Ruf, W. Schöni, and M. Wicki (1991). *Gewerkschaften und Angestelltenverbände in der schweizerischen Privatwirtschaft: Entstehung, Mitgliedschaft, Organisation und Politik seit 1940*. Zurich: Seismo.

Frey, Tim (2009). *Die Christdemokratie in Westeuropa – Der schmale Grat zum Erfolg*. Baden-Baden: Nomos.

Fuchs, Johann (2003). "Fachkräftemangel und demographischer Wandel. Möglichkeiten und Grenzen der Aktivierung heimischer Personalreserven," in Seminar für Handwerkswesen an der Universität Göttingen (ed.), *Fachkräftesicherung im Handwerk vor dem Hintergrund struktureller Wandlungen der Arbeitsmärkte*. Dauderstadt: Mecke, 83–117.

Gees, Thomas (2004). "Successful as a 'Go-between': The Conservative People's Party in Switzerland," in Michael Gehler and Wolfram Kaiser (eds.), *Christian Democracy in Europe since 1945*. London: Routledge, 38–53.

Gerlach, Irene (2005). *Familienpolitik*. Wiesbaden: Verlag für Sozialwissenschaften.

Gilliand, Pierre (1993). "Politique sociale," in G. Schmidt (ed.), *Handbuch Politisches System der Schweiz. Band 4. Politikbereiche*. Bern: Haupt.

Gorsuch, Richard L. (1983). *Factor Analysis*, 2nd ed. Hillsdale, NJ: Lawrence Erlbaum.

Gourevitch, Peter (1986). *Politics in Hard Times: Comparative Responses to International Economic Crises*. Ithaca, NY: Cornell University Press.

Grunberg, Gérard (2006). "The French Party System and the Crisis of Representation," in Pepper D. Culpepper, Peter A. Hall, and Bruno Palier (eds.), *Changing France: The Politics That Markets Make*. London: Palgrave Macmillan, 223–43.

Guillén, Ana (2010). "Defrosting the Spanish Welfare State: The Weight of Conservative and Corporatist Traditions," in Bruno Palier (ed.), *A Long Goodbye to Bismarck? The Politics of Welfare Reforms in Continental European Welfare States*. Amsterdam: Amsterdam University Press.

Hacker, Jacob S. (1998). "The Historical Logic of National Health Insurance: Structure and Sequence in the Development of British, Canadian and U.S. Medical Policy," *Studies in American Political Development* 12(1): 57–130.

Hacker, Jacob S. (2002). *The Divided Welfare State: The Battle over Public and Private Social Benefits in the United States*. Cambridge: Cambridge University Press.

Hacker, Jacob S. (2004). "Privatizing Risk without Privatizing the Welfare State: The Hidden Politics of Social Policy Retrenchment in the United States," *American Political Science Review* 98(2): 243–60.

Hacker, Jacob S. (2005). "Policy Drift: The Hidden Politics of US Welfare State Retrenchment," in Wolfgang Streeck and Kathleen Thelen (eds.), *Beyond Continuity: Institutional Change in Advanced Political Economies*. Oxford: Oxford University Press, 40–82.

Hall, Peter A. (1986). *Governing the Economy: The Politics of State Intervention in Britain and France*. Cambridge, U.K.: Polity Press.

Hall, Peter A. (1993). "Policy Paradigms, Social Learning, and the State: The Case of Economic Policymaking in Britain," *Comparative Politics* 25(3): 275–96.

Hall, Peter A. (2006). "Introduction: The Politics of Social Change in France," in Pepper D. Culpepper, Peter A. Hall, and Bruno Palier (eds.), *Changing France: The Politics That Markets Make*. London: Palgrave Macmillan, 1–28.

Hall, Peter A. and David Soskice (2001). *Varieties of Capitalism: The Institutional Foundations of Comparative Advantage*. New York: Oxford University Press.

Hassenteufel, Patrick and Bruno Palier (2007). "Towards Neo-Bismarckian Health Care States? Comparing Health Insurance Reforms in Bismarckian Welfare Systems," *Social Policy and Administration* 41(6): 574–96.

Häusermann, Silja (2002). Flexibilisation des relations d'emploi et sécurité sociale. La réforme de la loi suisse sur la prévoyance professionnelle. Unpublished manuscript. Lausanne: Idheap.

Häusermann, Silja (2006). "Changing Coalitions in Social Policy Reforms: The Politics of New Social Needs and Demands," *Journal of European Social Policy* 16(1): 5–21.

Häusermann, Silja (2006b). "Different Paths of Family Policy Modernization in Continental Welfare States: Changing Dynamics of Reform in German and Swiss family policies since the mid-70s," paper presented at the annual conference of the Swiss Political Science Association, Balsthal, November 2–3.

Häusermann, Silja (2008). "What Explains the "Unfreezing" of Continental European Welfare States?" paper presented at the annual conference of the American Political Science Association, Boston, August 28–31.

Häusermann, Silja (2009). "Policy Flexibility vs. Policy Inertia: Coalitional Dynamics in German Pension Reform," in Giliberto Capano and Michael Howlett (eds.), *European and American Experiences in Policy Change: Policy Drivers and Policy Dynamics*. London: Routledge, 43–67.

Häusermann, Silja (2010a). "Reform Opportunities in a Bismarckian Latecomer: Restructuring the Swiss Welfare State," in Bruno Palier (ed.), *A Long Goodbye to Bismarck? The Politics of Welfare Reforms in Continental European Welfare States*. Amsterdam: Amsterdam University Press.

Häusermann, Silja (2010b). "Solidarity with Whom? Why Organized Labor Is Losing Ground in Continental Pension Politics," *European Journal of Political Research*.

Häusermann, Silja, André Mach, and Yannis Papadopoulos (2004). "From Corporatism to Partisan Politics: Social Policy Making under Strain in Switzerland," *Swiss Political Science Review* 10(2): 33–59.

Häusermann, Silja and Hanna Schwander (2009). "Identifying Outsiders across Countries: Similarities and Differences in Patterns of Dualisation," Recwowe Working Paper No. 09/09.

Heclo, Hugh (1974). *Modern Social Politics in Britain and Sweden: From Relief to Income Maintenance*. New Haven, CT: Yale University Press.

Hemerijck, Anton and Ive Marx (2010). "Redirecting Continental Welfare in Belgium and the Netherlands," in Bruno Palier (ed.), *A Long Goodbye to Bismarck? The Politics of Welfare Reforms in Continental Europe*. Amsterdam: Amsterdam University Press.

Hemerijck, Anton, Brigitte Unger, and Jelle Visser (2000). "How Small Countries Negotiate Change: Twenty-Five Years of Policy Adjustment in Austria, the Netherlands and Belgium," in Fritz W. Scharpf and Vivien A. Schmidt (eds.), *Welfare and Work in the*

Open Economy, vol. 2, *Diverse Responses to Common Challenges*. Oxford: Oxford University Press, 175–263.

Hering, Martin (2004a). *Rough Transition: Institutional Change in Germany's "Frozen" Welfare State*. Ph.D. dissertation, Johns Hopkins University, Baltimore.

Hering, Martin (2004b). "Turning Ideas into Policies: Implementing Modern Social Democratic Thinking in Germany's Pension Policy," in Giuliano Bonoli and Martin Powell (eds.), *Social Democratic Party Policies in Contemporary Europe*. London: Routledge, 102–22.

Hinrichs, Karl (2000). "Auf dem Weg zur Alterssicherungspolitik – Reformperspektiven in der gesetzlichen Rentenversicherung," in Stephan Leibfried and Uwe Wagschal (eds.), *Der deutsche Sozialstaat. Bilanzen – Reformen – Perspektiven*. Schriften des Zentrums für Sozialpolitik, Bd. 10, Bremen, 276–305.

Hinrichs, Karl (2005). "New Century – New Paradigm: Pension Reforms in Germany," in Toshimitsu Shinkawa and Giuliano Bonoli (eds.), *Ageing and Pension Reform around the World: Evidence from Eleven Countries*. Cheltenham: Edward Elgar, 47–73.

Hiscox, Michael J. (2001). "Class versus Industry Cleavages: Inter-Industry Factor Mobility and the Politics of Trade," *International Organization* 55(1): 1–46.

Huber, Evelyne, Charles Ragin, and John D. Stephens (1993). "Social Democracy, Christian Democracy, Constitutional Structure, and the Welfare State," *American Journal of Sociology* 99(3): 711–49.

Huber, Evelyne and John D. Stephens (1998). "Internationalization and the Social Democratic Model: Crisis and Future Prospects," *Comparative Political Studies* 31(3): 353–97.

Huber, Evelyne and John D. Stephens (2001). *Development and Crisis of the Welfare State: Parties and Policies in Global Markets*. Chicago: University of Chicago Press.

Huber, Evelyne and John D. Stephens (2006). "Combating Old and New Social Risks," in Klaus Armingeon and Giuliano Bonoli (eds.), *The Politics of Post-Industrial Welfare States*. London: Routledge, 143–67.

IDA FiSo 1 (1996). Interdepartementale Arbeitsgruppe "Finanzierungsperspektiven der Sozialversicherungen": *Bericht über die Finanzierungsperspektiven der Sozialversicherungen unter besonderer Berücksichtigung der demographischen Entwicklung*. Bern: Bundesamt für Sozialversicherungen.

IDA FiSo 2 (1997). Interdepartementale Arbeitsgruppe "Finanzierungsperspektiven der Sozialversicherungen": *Analyse der Leistungen der Sozialversicherungen; Konkretisierung möglicher Veränderungen für drei Finanzierungsperspektiven*. Bern: Bundesamt für Sozialversicherungen.

Immergut, Ellen M. (1992). *Health Politics: Interests and Institutions in Western Europe*. Cambridge: Cambridge University Press.

Immergut, Ellen M. and Karen M. Anderson (2006). "Editor's Introduction: The Dynamics of Pension Politics," in Ellen M. Immergut, Karen M. Anderson, and Isabelle Schulze (eds.), *The Handbook of West European Pension Politics*. Oxford: Oxford University Press, 1–47.

Inglehart, Ronald (1977). *The Silent Revolution: Changing Values and Political Styles among Western Publics*. Princeton, NJ: Princeton University Press.

Inglehart, Ronald and Pippa Norris (2000). "The Developmental Theory of the Gender Gap: Women's and Men's Voting Behavior in Global Perspective," *International Political Science Review*, 21(4): 441–63.

Institut für Politikwissenschaft der Universität Bern (1970-2003). *Année politique suisse*. Bern: Universität Bern.

International Social Survey Program (1996). *ISSP: Role of Government III, 1996* (ZACAT computer file). Cologne, Germany: Zentralarchiv für Empirische Sozialforschung (producer) and Mannheim, Germany: GESIS Leibniz Institute for the Social Sciences.

Iversen, Torben, Thomas Cusack, and Philipp Rehm (2006). "Risks at Work: The Demand and Supply Sides of Government Redistribution," *Oxford Review of Economic Policy* 22(3): 365–89.

Iversen, Torben and Frances Rosenbluth (2006). "The Political Economy of Gender: Explaining Cross-National Variation in the Gender Division of Labor and the Gender Voting Gap," *American Journal of Political Science* 50: 1–19.

Iversen, Torben and David Soskice (2001). "An Asset Theory of Social Policy Preferences," *American Political Science Review* 95(4): 875–93.

Iversen, Torben and David Soskice (2006). "Electoral Institutions and the Politics of Coalitions: Why Some Democracies Redistribute More Than Others," *American Political Science Review*, 100(2): 165–181.

Iversen, Torben and Anne Wren (1998). "Equality, Employment and Budgetary Restraint: The Trilemma of the Service Economy," *World Politics* 50(July): 507–46.

Jacobs, Alan M. (2004). *Governing for the Long Term: Democratic Politics and Policy Investment*. Cambridge, MA: Department of Government, Harvard University.

Jaumotte, Florence (2003). "Female Labour Force Participation: Past Trends and Main Determinants in OECD Countries," OECD Economics Department Working Papers ECO/WKP(2003)30, No. 376.

Jegher, Annina (1999). *Bundesversammlung und Gesetzgebung*. Bern: Haupt.

Jenson, Jane and Mariette Sineau (1994). "François Mitterrand and French Women: *Un rendez-vous manqué*," *French Politics and Society* 12(4): 35–52.

Jenson, Jane and Mariette Sineau (2001). *Who Cares? Women's Work, Childcare, and Welfare State Redesign*. Toronto: University of Toronto Press.

Katzenstein, Peter J. (1987). *Policy and Politics in West Germany: The Growth of a Semi-sovereign State*. Philadelphia: Temple University Press.

Katzenstein, Peter J. (1985). *Small States in World Markets*. Ithaca, NY: Cornell University Press.

Kirchheimer, Otto (1966). "The Transformation of the Western European Party Systems," in Joseph LaPalombara and Myron Weiner (eds.), *Political Parties and Political Development*. Princeton, NJ: Princeton University Press, 177–200.

Kitschelt, Herbert (1994). *The Transformation of European Social Democracy*. Cambridge: Cambridge University Press.

Kitschelt, Herbert (1997). *The Radical Right in Western Europe: A Comparative Analysis*. Ann Arbor: University of Michigan Press.

Kitschelt, Herbert (2001). "Partisan Competition and Welfare State Retrenchment: When Do Politicians Choose Unpopular Policies?," in Paul Pierson (ed.), *The New Politics of the Welfare State*. Oxford: Oxford University Press, 265–302.

Kitschelt, Herbert (2003). "Political-Economic Context and Partisan Strategies in the German Federal Elections 1990–2002," *West European Politics* 26(4): 125–52.

Kitschelt, Herbert and Philip Rehm (2005). "Work, Family and Politics: Foundations of Electoral Partisan Alignments in Postindustrial Democracies," paper prepared for delivery at the annual meeting of the American Political Science Association, Washington, D.C., September 1–4.

Kitschelt, Herbert and Philip Rehm (2006). "New Social Risk and Political Preferences," in Klaus Armingeon and Giuliano Bonoli (eds.), *The Politics of Post-Industrial Welfare States: Adapting Post-War Policies to New Social Risks*. London: Routledge, 52–82.

Kitschelt, Herbert and Wolfgang Streeck (2003). "From Stability to Stagnation: Germany at the Beginning of the Twenty-First Century," *West European Politics* 26(4): 1–34.

Knight, Jack (1999). *Explaining the Rise of Neo-Liberalism: The Mechanisms of Institutional Change*. Unpublished manuscript, Washington University in St. Louis, St. Louis, MO.

Kolinsky, Eva (1993). "Party Change and Women's Representation in Unified Germany," in Joni Lovendusky and Pippa Norris (eds.), *Gender and Party Politics*. London: Sage, 113–46.

Korpi, Walter (1983). *The Democratic Class Struggle*. London: Routeledge and Kegan.

Korpi, Walter and Joakim Palme (2003). "New Politics and Class Politics in the Context of Austerity and Globalization: Welfare State Regress in 18 Countries. 1975–95," *American Political Science Review* 97(3): 425–46.

Kriesi, Hanspeter (1980). *Entscheidungsstrukturen und Entscheidungsprozesse in der Schweizer Politik*. Frankfurt: Campus, Verlag.

Kriesi, Hanspeter (1986). "Einleitung," in Peter Farago and Hanspeter Kriesi (eds.), *Wirtschaftsverbände in der Schweiz. Organisation und Aktivitäten von Wirtschaftsverbänden in vier Sektoren der Industrie*. Grüsch: Rüegger, 1–18.

Kriesi, Hanspeter (1998a). *Le système politique suisse*. Paris: Economica.

Kriesi, Hanspeter (1998b). "The Transformation of Cleavage Politics: The 1997 Stein Rokkan Lecture," *European Journal of Political Research* 33(2): 165–88.

Kriesi, Hanspeter (1999). "Movements of the Left, Movements of the Right: Putting the Mobilization of Two New Types of Social Movements into Political Context," in Herbert Kitschelt, Peter Lange, Gary Marks, and John D. Stephens (eds.), *Continuity and Change in Contemporary Capitalism*. Cambridge: Cambridge University Press, 398–423.

Kriesi, Hanspeter, Edgar Grande, Romain Lachat, Martin Dolezal, Simon Bornschier, and Timotheos Frey (2006). "Globalization and the Transformation of the National Political Space: Six European Countries Compared," *European Journal of Political Research* 45(6): 1–36.

Kriesi, Hanspeter, Edgar Grande, Romain Lachat, Martin Dolezal, Simon Bornschier, and Timotheus Frey (2008). *West European Politics in the Age of Globalization*. Cambridge: Cambridge University Press.

Kuhnle, Stein (2000). *Survival of the European Welfare State*. London: Routledge.

Künzi, Kilian and Markus Schärrer (2004). *Wer zahlt für die Soziale Sicherheit und wer profitiert davon? Eine Analyse der Sozialtransfers in der Schweiz*. Zurich: Rüegger.

Laver, Michael and W. Ben Hunt (1992). *Policy and Party Competition*. New York: Routledge.

Laver, Michael and Norman Schofield (1990). *Multiparty Government: The Politics of Coalition in Europe*. Oxford: Oxford University Press.

Lehmbruch, Gerhard (2000). *Parteienwettbewerb im Bundesstaat. Regelsysteme und Spannungslagen im politischen System der Bundesrepublik Deutschland*. Wiesbaden: Westdeutscher, Verlag.

Leibfried, Stephan and Herbert Obinger (2003). "The State of the Welfare State: German Social Policy between Macroeconomic Retrenchment and Microeconomic Recalibration", *West European Politics* 26(4): 199–218.

Leimgruber, Matthieu (2008). *Solidarity without the State? Business and the Shaping of the Swiss Welfare State, 1890–2000*. Cambridge: Cambridge University Press.

Leitner, Sigrid and Herbert Obinger (1996). "Feminisierung der Armut im Wohlfahrtsstaat. Eine strukturelle Analyse weiblicher Armut am Beispiel der

Alterssicherung in Österreich und in der Schweiz," *Swiss Political Science Review* 2(4): 1–35.

Leitner, Sigrid, Ilona Ostner, and Margrit Schratzenstaller (2004). *Wohlfahrtsstaat und Geschlechterverhältnis im Umbruch. Was kommt nach dem Ernährermodell?* Wiesbaden: VS Verlag für Sozialwissenschaften.

Lepperhoff, Julia, Traute Meyer, and Barbara Riedmüller (2001). "Zur Alterssicherung der Frau in Deutschland und in der Schweiz," *Leviathan* 29(2): 199–217.

Leu, Robert E., Stefan Burri, and Tom Priester (1997). *Lebensqualität und Armut in der Schweiz*. Bern: Haupt.

Leuzinger-Naef, Susanne (1998). "Flexibilisierte Arbeitsverhältnisse im Sozialversicherungsrecht," *Soziale Sicherheit* 3: 125–43.

Levy, Jonah (1999). "Vice into Virtue? Progressive Politics and Welfare Reform in Continental Europe," *Politics and Society* 27(2): 239–73.

Levy, Jonah (2000). "France: Directing Adjustment?" in Fritz W. Scharpf and Vivien Schmidt (eds.), *Welfare and Work in the Open Economy*, vol. 2. Oxford: Oxford University Press, 308–50.

Lewis, Jane (1992). "Gender and the Development of Welfare Regimes," *Journal of European Social Policy* 2(3): 159–73.

Lewis, Jane (1993). *Women and Social Policies in Europe: Work, Family and the State*. Aldershot: Edward Elgar.

Lijphart, Arend (1999). *Patterns of Democracy: Government Forms and Performance in Thirty-Six Countries*. New Haven, CT: Yale University Press.

Lipset, Seymour M. and Stein Rokkan (1985). "Cleavage Structures, Party Systems, and Voter Alignments," in Seymour M. Lipset (ed.), *Consensus and Conflict. Essays in Political Sociology*, 113–85. New Brunswick, NJ: Transaction Books.

Lister, Ruth (2004). "The Third Way's Social Investment State," in Jane Lewis and Rebecca Surender (eds.), *Welfare State Change: Towards a Third Way?* Oxford: Oxford University Press, 157–82.

Luchsinger, Christine (1995). *Solidarität, Selbständigkeit, Bedürftigkeit. Der schwierige Weg zu einer Gleichberechtigung der Geschlechter in der AHV 1939–1980*. Zurich: Chronos.

Mach, André (2006). *La Suisse entre internationalisation et changements politiques internes. La législation sur les cartels et les relations industrielles dans les années 1990*. Zurich: Rüegger.

Mach, André and Daniel Oesch (2003). "Collective Bargaining between Decentralization and Stability: A Sectoral Model Explaining the Swiss Experience during the 1990s," *Industrielle Beziehungen* 10(4): 160–82.

Mahoney, James and Kathleen Thelen (2010). "A Theory of Gradual Instituitional Change," in James Mahoney and Kathleen Thelen (eds.), *Explaining Institutional Change: Ambiguity, Agency and Power*. Cambridge: Cambridge University Press, 1–37.

Manow, Philip (2001). "Comparative Institutional Advantages of Welfare State Regimes and New Coalitions in Welfare State Reforms," in Paul Pierson (ed.), *The New Politics of the Welfare State*. Oxford: Oxford University Press, 146–64.

Manow, Philip (2002). "The Good, the Bad and the Ugly: Esping-Andersens Sozialstaats-Typologie und die konfessionellen Wurzeln des westlichen Wohlfahrtsstaates," *Kölner Zeitschrift für Soziologie und Sozialpsychologie* 54(2): 203–25.

Manow, Philip (2002). *Social Protection, Capitalist Production. The Bismarckian Welfare State and the German Political Economy from the 1880s to the 1990s*. Habilitationsschrift, Universität Konstanz.

Manow, Philip and Simone Burkhart (2004). " Legislative Autolimitation under Divided Government – Evidence from the German Case 1976–2002," Max Planck Institut für Gesellschaftsforschung (MPIfG) Discussion Paper 04/11. Cologne: Max Planck Institute for the Study of Societies.

Manow, Philip and Eric Seils (2000). "Adjusting Badly: The German Welfare State, Structural Change, and the Open Economy," in Fritz W. Scharpf and Vivien A. Schmidt (eds.), *Welfare and Work in the Open Economy*, vol. 2, *Diverse Responses to Common Challenges*. Oxford: Oxford University Press, 264–307.

Mares, Isabela (2000). "Strategic Alliances and Social Policy Reform: Unemployment Insurance in Comparative Perspective," *Politics and Society* 28(2): 223–44.

Mares, Isabela (2001a). "Enterprise Reorganisation and Social Insurance Reform: The Development of Early Retirement in France and Germany," *Governance* 14(3): 295–317.

Mares, Isabela (2001b). "Firms and the Welfare State: When, Why and How Does Social Policy Matter to Employers?" in Peter A. Hall and David Soskice (eds.), *Varieties of Capitalism: The Institutional Foundations of Comparative Advantage*. New York: Oxford University Press, 184–212.

Mares, Isabela (2003a). *The Politics of Social Risk*. Cambridge: Cambridge University Press.

Mares, Isabela (2003b). "The Sources of Business Interests in Social Insurance: Sectoral versus National Differences," *World Politics* 55(2): 229–58.

Marques-Pereirea, Bérengère and Olivier Paye (2001). "Belgium: The Vices and Virtues of Pragmatism," in Jane Jenson and Mariette Sineau (eds.), *Who Cares? Women's Work, Childcare, and Welfare State Redesign*. Toronto: University of Toronto Press, 56–87.

Martin, Cathie Jo (1995). "Nature or Nurture? Sources of Firm Preferences for National Health Reform," *American Political Science Review* 89: 898–913.

Martin, Cathie Jo (1997). "Mandating Social Change: the Business Struggle over National Health Reform," *Governance* 10(4): 397–428.

Meyer, Traute (1998). "Retrenchment, Reproduction, Modernization: Pension Politics and the Decline of the German Breadwinner Model," *Journal of European Social Policy* 8(3): 212–27.

Morgan, Kimberly (2006). *Working Mothers and the Welfare State: Religion and the Politics of Work-Family Policies in Western Europe and the United States*. Palo Alto, CA: Stanford University Press.

Mühlberger, Ulrike (2000). *Neue Formen der Beschäftigung. Arbeitsflexibilisierung durch atypische Beschäftigung in Österreich*. Vienna: Braumüller.

Müller Hans-Peter and Manfred Wilke (2003). "Gewerkschaftsfusionen: Der Weg zu modernen Multibranchengewerkschaften," in Wolfgang Schroeder and Bernhard Wessels (eds.), *Die Gewerkschaften in Politik und Gesellschaft der Bundesrepublik Deutschland*. Wiesbaden. Westdeutscher Verlag, 122–43.

Myles, John (1984). *Old Age in the Welfare State: The Political Economy of Public Pensions*. Lawrence: University of Kansas Press.

Myles, John and Paul Pierson (1997). "Friedman's Revenge: The Reform of 'Liberal' Welfare States in Canada and the United States," *Politics and Society* 25: 443–72.

Myles, John and Paul Pierson (2001). "The Comparative Political Economy of Pension Reform," in Paul Pierson (ed.), *The New Politics of the Welfare State*. Oxford: Oxford University Press, 305–33.

Natali, David (2003). "The Role of Trade Unions in the Pension Reforms in France and Italy in the 1990s: New Forms of Political Exchange?" European University Institute Working Paper SPS, No. 2003/3. Florence: European University Institute.

Natali, David and Martin Rhodes (2004). "The 'New Politics' of the Bismarckian Welfare State: Pension Reforms in Continental Europe," European University Institute Working Paper SPS, No. 2004/10. Florence: European University Institute.

Natali, David and Martin Rhodes (2008). "The 'New Politics' of Pension Reforms in Continental Europe," in Camila Arza and Martin Kohli (eds.), *Pension Reform in Europe*. London: Routledge, 55–75.

Naumann, Ingela (2005). "Child Care and Feminism in West Germany and Sweden in the 1960s and 1970s," *Journal of European Social Policy* 15(1): 47–63.

Neidhart, Leonhard (1970). *Plebiszit und pluralitäre Demokratie. Eine Analyse der Funktionen des schweizerischen Gesetzesreferendums*. Bern: Francke.

Neuhold, Christine (1999). "Atypische Beschäftigung in Deutschland und Frankreich," in Emmerich Talos (ed.), *Atypische Beschäftigung. Internationale Trends und sozialstaatliche Regelungen*. Vienna: Manz, 36–81.

Nova, Colette and Silja Häusermann (2005). *Endlich existenzsichernde Renten. Erste Säule stärken – 3000 Franken Rente für alle*. Dossier 34, Bern: Schweizerischer Gewerkschaftsbund.

Nullmeier, Frank and Friedbert W. Rüb (1993). *Die Transformation der Sozialpolitik. Vom Sozialstaat zum Sicherungsstaat*. Frankfurt: Campus.

Obinger, Herbert (1998). *Politische Institutionen und Sozialpolitik in der Schweiz*. Frankfurt: Peter Lang.

O'Connor, Julia (1993). "Gender, Class and Citizenship in the Comparative Analysis of Welfare State Regimes: Theoretical and Methodological Issues," *British Journal of Sociology* 44(3): 501–18.

Oesch, Daniel (2005). "Remodelling Class to Make Sense of Party Support: Class Voting in Britain, Germany and Switzerland," paper presented at the European Consortium for Political Research General Conference, September 8-10, Budapest.

Oesch, Daniel (2006). *Redrawing the Class Map: Stratification and Institutions in Germany, Britain, Sweden and Switzerland*. London: Palgrave Macmillan.

Organisation for Economic Co-operation and Development (2005). *Pensions at a Glance: Public Policies across OECD Countries*. Paris: Organisation for Economic Co-operation and Development.

Organisation for Economic Co-operation and Development (2007). *Pensions at a Glance: Public Policies across OECD Countries*. Paris: Organisation for Economic Co-operation and Development.

Orloff, A. S. (2006). "From Maternalism to 'Employment for All': State Policies to Promote Women's Employment across the Affluent Democracies," in Jonah Levy (ed.), *The State after Statism*. Cambridge, MA: Harvard University Press, 230–68.

Orloff, Ann Shola (1993). "Gender and the Social Rights of Citizenship: The Comparative Analysis of Gender Relations and Welfare States," *American Sociological Review* 58(3): 303–28.

Orloff, Ann Shola (1996). "Gender in the Welfare State," *Annual Review of Sociology* 22: 51–78.

Orloff, Ann Shola and Theda Skocpol (1984). "Why Not Equal Protection? Explaining the Politics of Public Social Welfare in Britain and the United States, 1880s–1920s," *American Sociological Review* 49: 726–50.

Palier, Bruno (2002). *Gouverner la sécurité sociale*. Paris: Presses Universitaires de France.

Palier, Bruno (2003a). *La réforme des retraites*. Paris: Presses Universitaires de France.

Palier, Bruno (2003b). "Facing the Pension Crisis in France," in Noel Whiteside and Gordon Clarke (eds.), *Pension Security in the 21st Century: Redrawing the Public-Private Divide*. Oxford: Oxford University Press, 93–114.

Palier, Bruno (2005). "Ambiguous Agreement, Cumulative Change: French Social Policy in the 1990s," in Wolfgang Streeck and Kathleen Thelen (eds.), *Beyond Continuity: Institutional Change in Advanced Political Economies*. Oxford: Oxford University Press, 127–44.

Palier, Bruno (2006). "The Long Good Bye to Bismarck? Changes in the French Welfare State," in Pepper D. Culpepper, Peter A. Hall, and Bruno Palier (eds.), *Changing France: The Politics That Markets Make*. London: Palgrave Macmillan, 107–28.

Palier, Bruno and Christelle Mandin (2004). "France: A New World of Welfare for New Social Risks?" in Peter Taylor-Gooby (ed.), *New Risks, New Welfare: The Transformation of the European Welfare State*. Oxford: Oxford University Press, 111–31.

Palier, Bruno and Claude Martin (2007). "From a 'Frozen Landscape' to Structural Reforms: The Sequential Transformation of Bismarckian Welfare Systems," *Social Policy and Administration* 41(6): 535–54.

Palier, Bruno (2010). *A Long Goodbye to Bismarck? The Politics of Welfare Reforms in Continental Europe*. Amsterdam: Amsterdam University Press.

Peacock, Alan R. and Jack Wiseman (1961). *The Growth of Public Expenditure in the United Kingdom*. Princeton, NJ: Princeton University Press.

Pfenning, Astrid and Thomas Bahle (eds) (2000). *Families and Family Policies in Europe: Comparative Perspectives*. Frankfurt: Peter Lang.

Pierson, Paul (1996). "The New Politics of the Welfare State," *World Politics* 48(2): 143–79.

Pierson, Paul (2000a). "Increasing Returns, Path Dependence, and the Study of Politics," *American Political Science Review* 94(2): 251–67.

Pierson, Paul (2000b). "Not Just What, but When: Timing and Sequence in Political Processes," *Studies in American Political Development* 14(1): 73–93.

Pierson, Paul (2000c). "Three Worlds of Welfare State Research," *Comparative Political Studies* 33 (6/7): 791–821.

Pierson, Paul (2001). "Coping with Permanent Austerity: Welfare State Restructuring in Affluent Democracies," in Paul Pierson (ed.), *The New Politics of the Welfare State*. Oxford: Oxford University Press, 410–56.

Pierson, Paul (2004). *Politics in Time: History, Institutions and Social Analysis*. Princeton, NJ: Princeton University Press.

Poitry, Alain-Valéry (1989). *La fonction d'ordre de l'Etat. Analyse des mécanismes et des déterminants sélectifs dans le processus législatif suisse*. Bern: Lang.

Pontusson, Jonas und Peter Swenson (1996). "Labor Markets, Production Strategies and Wage Bargaining Institutions: The Swedish Employer Offensive in Comparative Perspective," *Comparative Political Studies* 29(2): 223–50.

Powell, Bingham (2000). *Elections as Instruments of Democracy: Majoritarian and Proportional Visions*. New Haven, CT: Yale University Press.

Queisser, Monika und Dimitri Vittas (2000). *The Swiss Multi-Pillar Pension System: Triumph of Common Sense?* Development Research Group, Washington: World Bank.

Rabinowitz, George and Stuart E. Macdonald (1989). "A Directional Theory of Issue Voting," *American Political Science Review* 83(1): 93–121.

Rechsteiner, Rudolf (2002). *Flexibilität und soziale Sicherung in der Schweiz unter besonderer Berücksichtigung der Alterssicherung.* Basel: Selbstverlag.

Reinberg, Alexander and Markus Hummel (2003). "Steuert Deutschland langfristig auf einen Fachkräftemangel zu?" *Institut für Arbeitsmarkt – und Berufsforschung der Bundesanstalt für Arbeit,* Institut für Arbeitsmarkt- und Berufsforschung Kurzbericht, 9, Nürnberg, 1–8.

Rhodes, Martin (2001). "The Political Economy of Social Pacts: 'Competitive Corporatism' and European Welfare Reform," in Paul Pierson (ed.), *The New Politics of the Welfare State.* Oxford: Oxford University Press, 165–94.

Rhodes, Martin and David Natali (2004). "Trade-Offs and Veto Players: Reforming Pensions in France and Italy," *French Politics* 2(1): 1–23.

Riedmüller, Barbara (2000). "Frauen – und familienpolitische Leitbilder im deutschen Alterssicherungssystem," in Winfried Schmähl und Klaus Michaelis (eds.), *Alterssicherung von Frauen – Leitbilder, gesellschaftlicher Wandel und Reformen.* Wiesbaden: Westdeutscher, Verlag, 36–45.

Riker, William H. (1986). *The Art of Political Manipulation.* New Haven, CT: Yale University Press.

Riker, William H. (1987). *The Theory of Political Coalitions.* New Haven, CT: Yale University Press.

Rokeach, Milton (1973). *The Nature of Human Values.* New York: Free Press.

Rueda, David (2005). "Insider-Outsider Politics in Industrialized Democracies: The Challenge to Social Democratic Parties," *American Political Science Review* 99(1): 61–74.

Rueda, David (2006). *Social Democracy Inside Out.* Oxford: Oxford University Press.

Rusciano, Frank Louis (1992). "Rethinking the Gender Gap: The Case of West German Elections, 1949–1987," *Comparative Politics* 24(3): 335–57.

Sabatier, Paul A. and Hank C. Jenkins-Smith (1993). *Policy Change and Learning: An Advocacy Coalition Approach.* Boulder, CO: Westview.

Sainsbury, Diane (1994). "Women's and Men's Social Rights: Gendering Dimensions of Welfare States," in D. Sainbury (ed.), *Gendering Welfare States.* London: Sage, 150–169.

Scharpf, Fritz W. (2000). "The Viability of Advanced Welfare States in the International Economy: Vulnerabilities and Options," *Journal of European Public Policy* 7(2): 190–228.

Scharpf, Fritz W. and Vivien A. Schmidt (2000). *Welfare and Work in the Open Economy: From Vulnerability to Competitiveness.* Oxford: Oxford University Press.

Schickler, Eric (2001). *Disjointed Pluralism: Institutional Innovation and the Development of the U.S. Congress.* Princeton, NJ: Princeton University Press.

Schludi, Martin (2005). *The Reform of Bismarckian Pension Systems: A Comparison of Pension Politics in Austria, France, Germany, Italy and Sweden.* Amsterdam: Amsterdam University Press.

Schludi, Martin (2008). "Between Conflict and Consensus: The Reform of Bismarckian Pension Regimes," in Camila Arza and Martin Kohli (eds.), *Pension Reform in Europe.* London: Routledge, 76–99.

Schluep, Kurt (2003). *Finanzierungsbedarf in der AHV (inkl. EL).* Forschungsbericht, Nr. 10/03. Bundesamt für Sozialversicherungen, Bern: Beiträge zur Sozialen, Sicherheit.

Schmähl, Winfried (1997). "The Public-Private Mix in Pension Provision in Germany," in Martin Rein and Eskil Wadensjö (eds.), *Enterprise and the Welfare State*. Cheltenham: Edward Elgar, 99–148.

Schmähl, Winfried (2000). "Alterssicherung von Frauen im Prozess ökonomischen, gesellschaftlichen und politischen Wandels," in Winfried Schmähl und Klaus Michaelis (eds.), *Alterssicherung von Frauen – Leitbilder, gesellschaftlicher Wandel und Reformen*. Wiesbaden: Westdeutscher, Verlag, 9–35.

Schmähl, Winfried and Klaus Michaelis (2000). *Alterssicherung von Frauen – Leitbilder, gesellschaftlicher Wandel und Reformen*. Wiesbaden: Westdeutscher, Verlag.

Schmidt, Manfred (1998). *Sozialpolitik in Deutschland. Historische Entwicklung und internationaler Vergleich*. Opladen: Leske und Budrich.

Schmidt, Manfred G. (2000). "Immer noch auf dem "mittleren Weg"? Deutschlands Politische Ökonomie am Ende des 20. Jahrhunderts," in Roland Czada und Hellmut Wollmann (eds.), *Von der Bonner zur Berliner Republik. 10 Jahre deutsche Einheit*. Wiesbaden: Westdeutscher, Verlag, 491–514.

Schmidt, Vivien (1999). "The Changing Dynamics of State-Society Relations in the Fifth Republic," *West European Politics* 22(4): 141–65.

Schmitter, Philippe C. (1979). "Still the Century of Corporatism?" in Philippe C. Schmitter und Gerhard Lehmbruch (eds.), *Trends toward Corporatist Intermediation*, 7–48. London: Sage.

Schmitter, Philippe C. and Wolfgang Streeck (1981). "The Organization of Business Interests: A Research Design," rev. discussion paper IIMV/LMP 81–13. Berlin, Wissenschaftszentrum.

Schroeder, Wolfgang and Stephen J. Silvia (2003). "Gewerkschaften und Arbeitgeberverbände," in Wolfgang Schroeder and Bernhard Wessels (eds.), *Die Gewerkschaften in Politik und Gesellschaft der Bundesrepublik Deutschland*. Wiesbaden. Westdeutscher, Verlag, 246–72.

Schroeder, Wolfgang and Bernhard Wessels (2003). "Das deutsche Gewerkschaftsmodell im Transformationsprozess: Die neue deutsche Gewerkschaftslandschaft," in Wolfgang Schroeder and Bernhard Wessels (eds.), *Die Gewerkschaften in Politik und Gesellschaft der Bundesrepublik Deutschland*. Wiesbaden: Westdeutscher, Verlag, 11–40.

Schulze, Isabelle (2007). *Der Einfluss von Wahlsystemen auf Politikinhalte. Electoral Threat in der Rentenpolitik*. Baden-Baden: Nomos.

Schulze, Isabelle and Sven Jochem (2007). "Germany: Beyond Policy Gridlock," in Ellen M. Immergut, Karen M. Anderson, and Isabelle Schulze (eds.), *The Handbook of West European Pension Politics*. Oxford: Oxford University Press, 660–712.

Schulze, Isabelle and Martin Schludi (2007). " Austria: From Electoral Cartels to Competitive Coalition-Building," in Ellen M. Immergut, Karen M. Anderson, and Isabelle Schulze (eds.), *The Handbook of West European Pension Politics*. Oxford: Oxford University Press, 555–604.

Schwartz, Herman (2001). "Round Up the Usual Suspects! Globalization, Domestic Politics, and Welfare State Change," in Paul Pierson (ed.), *The New Politics of the Welfare State*. Oxford: Oxford University Press, 17–44.

Sciarini, Pascal (1999). "La formulation de la décision," in U. Klöti, Peter Knoepfel, Hanspeter Kriesi, Wolf Linder, and Yannis Papadopoulos (eds.), *Handbuch der Schweizer Politik*. Zurich: NZZ, Verlag, 491–528.

Sciarini, Pascal, Sarah Nicolet, and Alex Fischer (2002). "L'impact de l'internationalisation sur les processus de décision en Suisse: Une analyse quantitative des actes législatifs 1995–1999," *Swiss Political Science Review* 8(3/4): 1–34.

Scott, J. (1992). *Social Network Analysis*. Newbury Park, CA: Sage.

Senti, Martin (1994). *Geschlecht als politischer Konflikt. Erfolgsbedingungen einer gleichstellungspolitischen Interessendurchsetzung*. Bern: Haupt.

SGK-N (2002). *Bericht der Kommission für soziale Sicherheit und Gesundheit (SGK-N) über den Vorsorgeschutz für Teilzeitbeschäftigte und Personen mit kleinen Einkommen, über die Anpassung des Umwandlungssatzes und über die paritätische Verwaltung der Vorsorgeeinrichtungen*, March. Bern: Vereinigte Bundesversammlung.

Shepsle, Kenneth A. (1979). "Institutional Arrangements and Equilibrium in Multidimensional Voting Models," *American Journal of Political Science* 23(1): 27–59.

Siegel, Nico and Sven Jochem (2003). *Konzertierung, Verhandlungsdemokratie und Reformpolitik im Wohlfahrtsstaat. Das Modell Deutschland im Vergleich*. Opladen: Leske und Budrich.

Skocpol, Theda (1992). *Protecting Soldiers and Mothers*. Cambridge, MA: Harvard University Press.

Stephens, John D. (1979). *The Transition from Capitalism to Socialism*. London: Macmillan.

Stephens, John D., Evelyne Huber and Leonard Ray (1999). "The Welfare State in Hard Times," in Herbert Kitschelt, Peter Lange, Gary Marks, and John D. Stephens (eds.), *Continuity and Change in Contemporary Capitalism*. Cambridge: Cambridge University Press, 164–193.

Streeck, Wolfgang (1991). "On the Institutional Conditions of Diversified Quality Production", in Egon Matzner and Wolfgang Streeck (eds.), *Beyond Keynesianism: The Socio-Economics of Production and Employment*. London: Edward Elgar, 21–61.

Streeck, Wolfgang and Kathleen Thelen (2005). *Beyond Continuity: Institutional Change in Advanced Political Economies*. Oxford: Oxford University Press.

Suter, Christian and Marie-Claire Mathey (2000). "Wirksamkeit und Umverteilungseffekte staatlicher Sozialleistungen," *info:social* 3, 1–80.

Swank, Duane and Cathie Jo Martin (2001). "Employers and the Welfare State: The Political Economic Organization of Firms and Social Policy in Contemporary Capitalist Democracies," *Comparative Political Studies* 34(8): 889–923.

Swenson, Peter A. (1991a). "Bringing Capital Back In, or Social Democracy Reconsidered: Employer Power, Cross-Class Alliances, and Centralization of Industrial Relations in Denmark and Sweden," *World Politics* 43(4): 513–44.

Swenson, Peter A. (1991b). "Labor and the Limits of the Welfare State: The Politics of Intraclass Conflict and Cross-Class Alliances in Sweden and West Germany," *Comparative Politics* 24(2): 379–99.

Swenson, Peter A. (2002). *Capitalists against Markets: The Making of Labor Markets and Welfare States in the United States and Sweden*. New York: Oxford University Press.

Tabah, Léon (1986). *Vieillir solidaires. Rapport du Commissariat général du Plan*. Paris: La Documentation française.

Taddei, Dominique, Jean-Michel Charpin and Olivier Davanne (1999). *Retraites choisies et progressives*. Paris: Conseil d'analyse économique.

Talos, Emmerich (ed.) (1999). *Atypische Beschäftigung. Internationale Trends und sozialstaatliche Regelungen*. Vienna: Manz, Verlag.

Taylor-Gooby, Peter (2005). *New Risks, New Welfare: The Transformation of the European Welfare State*. Oxford: Oxford University Press.

Teulade, René (1989). *Rapport de la Commission protection sociale*. Paris: La Documentation française.

Teulade, René (1999). *L'avenir de nos systèmes de retraite*. Paris: Conseil économique et social, Direction des journaux officiels.

Thelen, Kathleen (2001). "Varieties of Labor Politics in Developed Democracies," in Peter A. Hall and David Soskice (eds.), *Varieties of Capitalism: The Institutional Foundations of Comparative Advantage*. New York: Oxford University Press, 71–103.

Thelen, Kathleen (2004). *How Institutions Evolve: The Political Economy of Skills in Germany, Britain, the United States, and Japan*. Cambridge: Cambridge University Press.

Titmuss, Richard (1958). *Essays on the Welfare State*. London: Allen and Unwin.

Trampusch, Christine (2004). "Von Verbänden zu Parteien. Der Elitenwechsel in der Sozialpolitik," *Zeitschrift für Parlamentsfragen* 35(4): 646–66.

Trampusch, Christine (2005). "Institutional Resettlement: The Case of Early Retirement in Germany," in Wolfgang Streeck and Kathleen Thelen (eds.), *Beyond Continuity: Institutional Change in Advanced Political Economies*. New York: Oxford University Press, 203–28.

Trechsel, Alexandre H. and Pascal Sciarini (1998). "Direct Democracy in Switzerland: Do Elites Matter?" *European Journal of Political Research* 38(1): 99–124.

Tsebelis, George (2002). *Veto Players: How Political Institutions Work*. Princeton, NJ: Princeton University Press.

Vail, Mark I. (1999). "The Better Part of Valour: The Politics of French Welfare Reform," *Journal of European Social Policy* 9(4): 311–30.

Vail, Mark I. (2004). "The Myth of the Frozen Welfare State and the Dynamics of Contemporary French and German Social-Protection Reform," *French Politics* 2: 151–83.

Vallat, Jean-Philippe (2002). *La politique familiale en France (1945–2001). Construction des intérêts sociaux et transformation de l'Etat-Providence*. Ph.D. dissertation, Institut d'études politiques, Paris.

Van Kersbergen, Kees (1995). *Social Capitalism: A Study of Christian Democracy and the Welfare State*. London: Routledge.

Van Kersbergen, Kees and Philip Manow (2009). *Religion, Class Coalitions and Welfare States*. Cambridge: Cambridge University Press.

Visser, Jelle (1987). *In Search of Inclusive Unionism: A Comparative Analysis*. Ph.D. dissertation, University of Amsterdam.

Visser, Jelle, Patrick Dufour, René Mouriaux, and Françoise Subilieu (2000). "France," in Bernhard Ebbinghaus and Jelle Visser (eds.), *The Societies of Europe: Trade Unions in Western Europe since 1945*. London: Macmillan, 237–78.

Visser, Jelle and Anton Hemerijck (1997). *A Dutch Miracle: Job Growth, Welfare Reform and Corporatism in the Netherlands*. Amsterdam: Amsterdam University Press.

Wanner, Philippe and Antonella Ferrari (2001). *La participation des femmes au marché du travail*. Neuchâtel: Forum Suisse pour l'Étude des Migrations.

Wasserman, S. and K. Faust. (1994) *Social Network Analysis*. Cambridge: Cambridge University Press.

Wendt, Claus and Theresa Thompson (2004). "The Need for Social Austerity versus Structural Reform in European Health Systems: A Four-Country Comparison of Health Reforms," *International Journal of Health Services* 34(3): 415–33.

Wessels, Bernhard (2004). "The German Party System: Developments after Unification," in Werner Reutter (ed.), *Germany on the Road to "Normalcy": Policies and*

Politics of the Red-Green Federal Government (1998–2002). New York: Palgrave Macmillan.

Wilensky, Harold (1975). *The Welfare State and Equality: Structural and Ideological Roots of Public Expenditures*. Berkeley: University of California Press.

Zehnder Ernst (1988). *Die Gesetzesüberprüfung durch die schweizerische Bundesversammlung: Untersuchung der parlamentarischen Veränderung von Vorlagen des Bundesrates in der Legislaturperiode 1971–1975*. Entlebuch: Huber, Druck.

Index